"In *Genesis*, I followed a romantic dream to find and share a pristine world that all too often is beyond our eyes and reach."

Sebastião Salgado

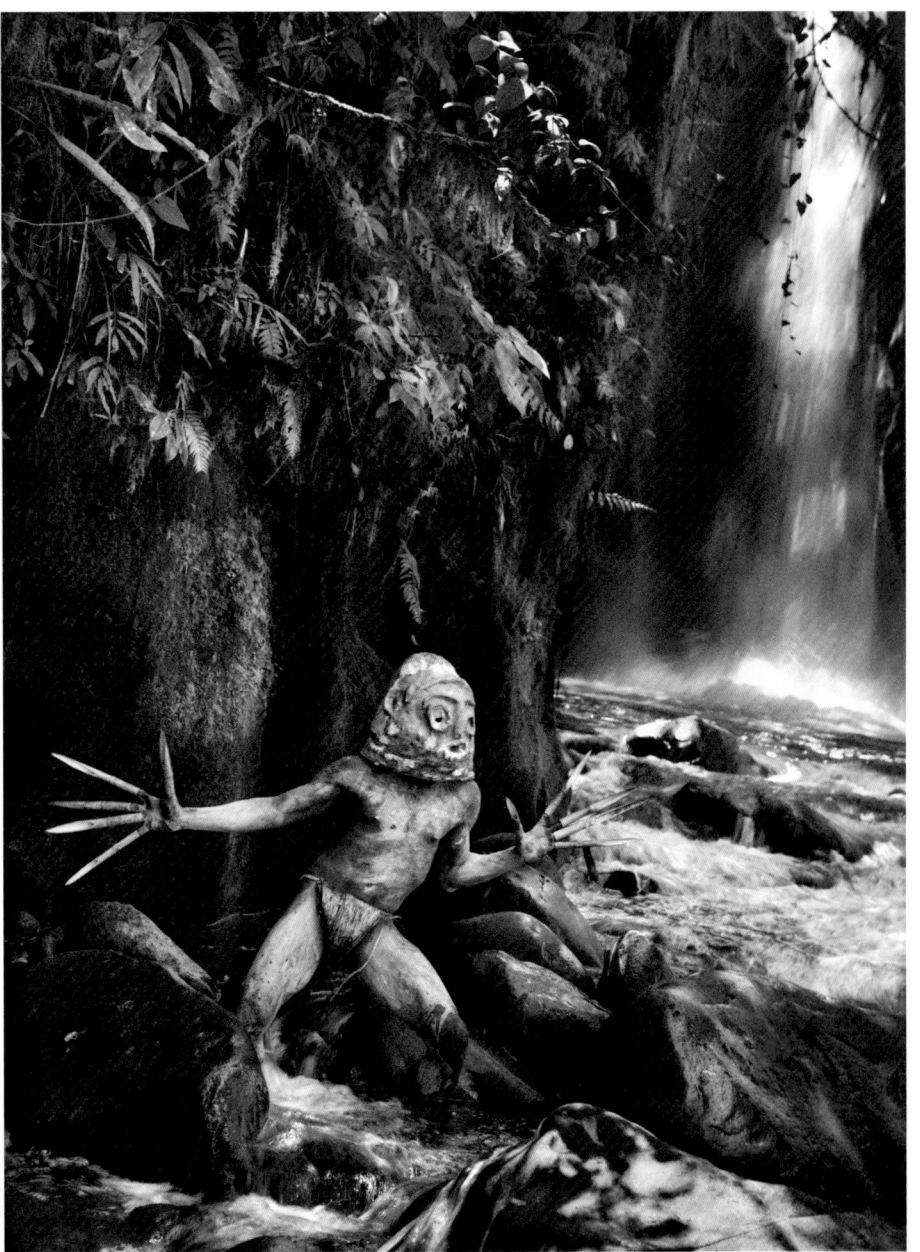

SEBASTIÃO SALGADO

GENESIS

Editing, Concept & Design
LÉLIA WANICK SALGADO

TASCHEN

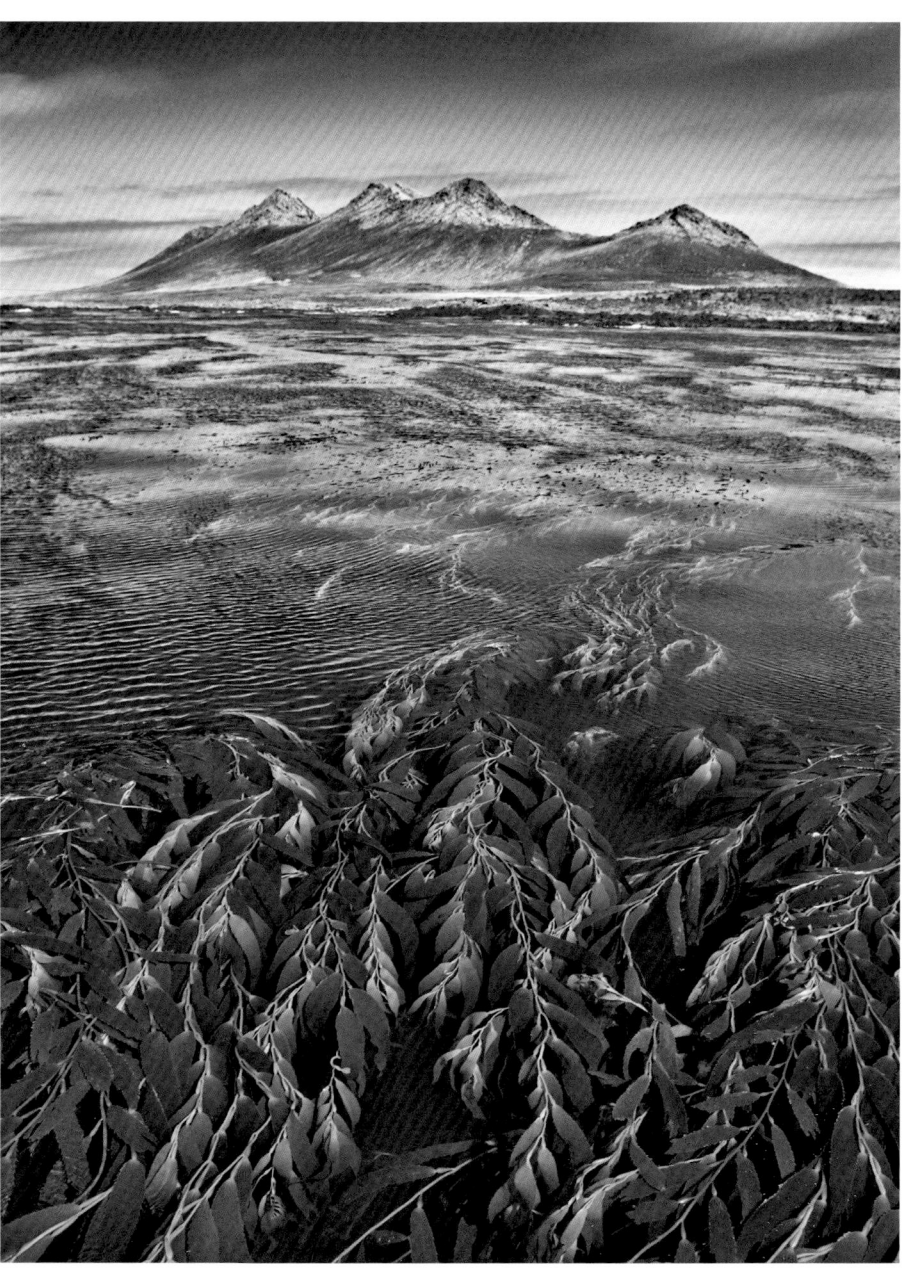

FOREWORD

At the end of the 1990s, I completed a long series of photo essays on the unparalleled movement of peoples across the globe. It involved recording the massive migration of peasants from rural areas to cities on several continents. It led me to follow destitute refugees fleeing armed conflicts and natural disasters, and I accompanied young men willing to risk all in the hope of finding a better life in some far-off land. I witnessed much suffering and great courage, but most of all I saw violence and brutality such as I had never even imagined before. By the time the project was over, I had lost all faith in the future of humanity.

Yet these same years brought a happy coincidence. My father asked me and my wife, Lélia Deluiz Wanick, to take over a property in the Vale do Rio Doce in Brazil's Minas Gerais state that had once been our family's cattle ranch. We accepted reluctantly. It was there that I grew up with my seven sisters, surrounded by tropical vegetation alive with birds and wild animals, by rivers full of fish and by rolling hills that set us imagining the world beyond. But this paradise had vanished. By the mid-1990s, as with so many farms in the region, deforestation and erosion had left the land lifeless.

It was then that Lélia, my partner in every adventure of my life, had the bold idea of recreating a forest with the very same local species that once prospered there. We hoped for nothing less than the rebirth of the small ecosystem that I knew as a child. We planted over 300 different species of trees and, as saplings slowly turned the land green, we watched in wonder as birds, butterflies, beetles, and tropical flowers returned. With reforestation, instead of turning into flash floods, heavy seasonal rain was also absorbed by the soil and, in time, allowed rivers and creeks to flow year-round. And to our delight, fish and even alligators reappeared.

Marveling at nature's ability to restore itself, we grew more anxious about the fate of the planet at large. We understood the absurdity of the idea that nature and humanity can somehow be separated. We also recognized that the breakdown in our links to nature poses a genuine threat to humanity. Through the rapid urbanization of the past 100 years, we have lost touch with the wilderness, animals, and plants that represent the very essence of life on Earth. We may know how to subjugate nature, but we easily forget that we depend on it for our very survival.

These reflections became the seeds for a new long-term photographic project, focused on nature. Initially, we conceived it as a protest against how we are abusing our planet. We planned to show how pollution of our air, water, and land has become the price of development; how global warming is bringing climate change with alarming consequences; how industrial farming, large-scale cattle ranching, and logging are decimating rainforests.

But after we saw life returning to what was once our property and has since become a national park, we changed our minds. With our faith restored by the spectacle of hundreds of thousands of new trees and the fresh life they rekindled, we decided instead to explore the beauty of our planet. So, over the next eight years, I made 32 trips to distant corners of the globe, often joined by Lélia, sometimes by our son, Juliano, and most of the time accompanied by my invaluable colleague Jacques Barthélemy. Our mission was to seek out the land and seascapes, the animals and ancient communities that have escaped the long—and often destructive—arm of modern man.

We called the project *Genesis* because we imagined turning back the clock to the volcanic eruptions and earthquakes that shaped the Earth; to the air, water, and fire that gave birth to life; to the oldest animal species that still resist domestication; to remote tribes whose way of life is largely unchanged; and to extant early forms of human organization. I wanted to examine how humanity and nature have long coexisted in what we now call ecological balance.

This work is the record of my journey, a visual ode to the majesty and fragility of Earth. But it is also a warning, I hope, of all that we risk losing.

My approach was not that of a journalist or scientist or anthropologist. In *Genesis*, I followed a romantic dream to find and share a pristine world that all too often is beyond our eyes and reach. My goal was not to go where man had never before set foot, although untamed nature is usually to be found in pretty inaccessible places. I simply wanted to show nature at its best wherever I found it. And I found it in boundless spaces of immense biodiversity which, amazingly, cover almost half the Earth's surface: in giant, largely untouched deserts; in the frozen lands of the Antarctic and the north of the planet; in vast expanses of tropical and temperate forest; and in mountain ranges of awe-inspiring splendor. Discovering this unspoiled world has been the most rewarding experience of my life.

My earlier projects, *Workers*, *Migrations*, and many others, were voyages through the trials and tribulations of humanity. This one was my homage to the grandeur of nature. Traveling on foot, in boats, small planes, or balloons, all the while photographing volcanoes, icebergs, deserts, or jungles, I beheld a world unchanged over millennia. And with animals in the wild, from the penguins, sea lions, and whales of the Antarctic and South Atlantic to the lions, wildebeest, and elephants of Africa, I felt privileged to watch the endlessly repeated cycles of life.

My search for ancient communities proved more complex. There are still "uncontacted" tribes in the jungles of the Amazon and New Guinea, but of the remote peoples I visited, only the Zo'é Indians in the Amazon and the Stone Korowai in West Papua have barely been touched by the outside world. Many others maintain strong identities and have kept the age-old shapes of their wooden homes, their languages, religious rituals, hunting methods, and diets. But they no longer live in total isolation. Visits by missionaries and even by groups of ecotourists are bringing the frontier of our consumer society ever closer to them.

My aim was to portray these peoples as close as possible to their ancestral way of life. Some might wear secondhand clothes distributed by evangelical groups, but I wanted to show the ceremonial attires and tribal customs of which they are most proud and which in a few decades may survive only in photographs. Sooner or later, the modern world will touch them—or they will go looking for it. I wanted to capture a vanishing world, a part of humanity that is on the verge of disappearing, yet in many ways still lives in harmony with nature.

The subjects of our research—landscapes, animals, and peoples—often overlapped. In designing this book, we have therefore opted for five broad chapters, each representing a large region that may also embrace several major ecosystems. The result is a mosaic, the mosaic presented by nature itself. It is this that *Genesis* celebrates.

Sebastião Salgado

Page 2: The mudmen performers are among the most striking figures of the imaginative world of the Highlands. Paya, Western Highlands Privince, Papua New Guinea. July and August 2008.

Page 4: These marine algae, known as giant bladder kelp (*Macrocystis pyrifera*), spread like garden weeds in the extremely cold waters of the South Atlantic. The mountains of Steeple Jason Island are visible in the background. Falkland Islands. November and December 2009.

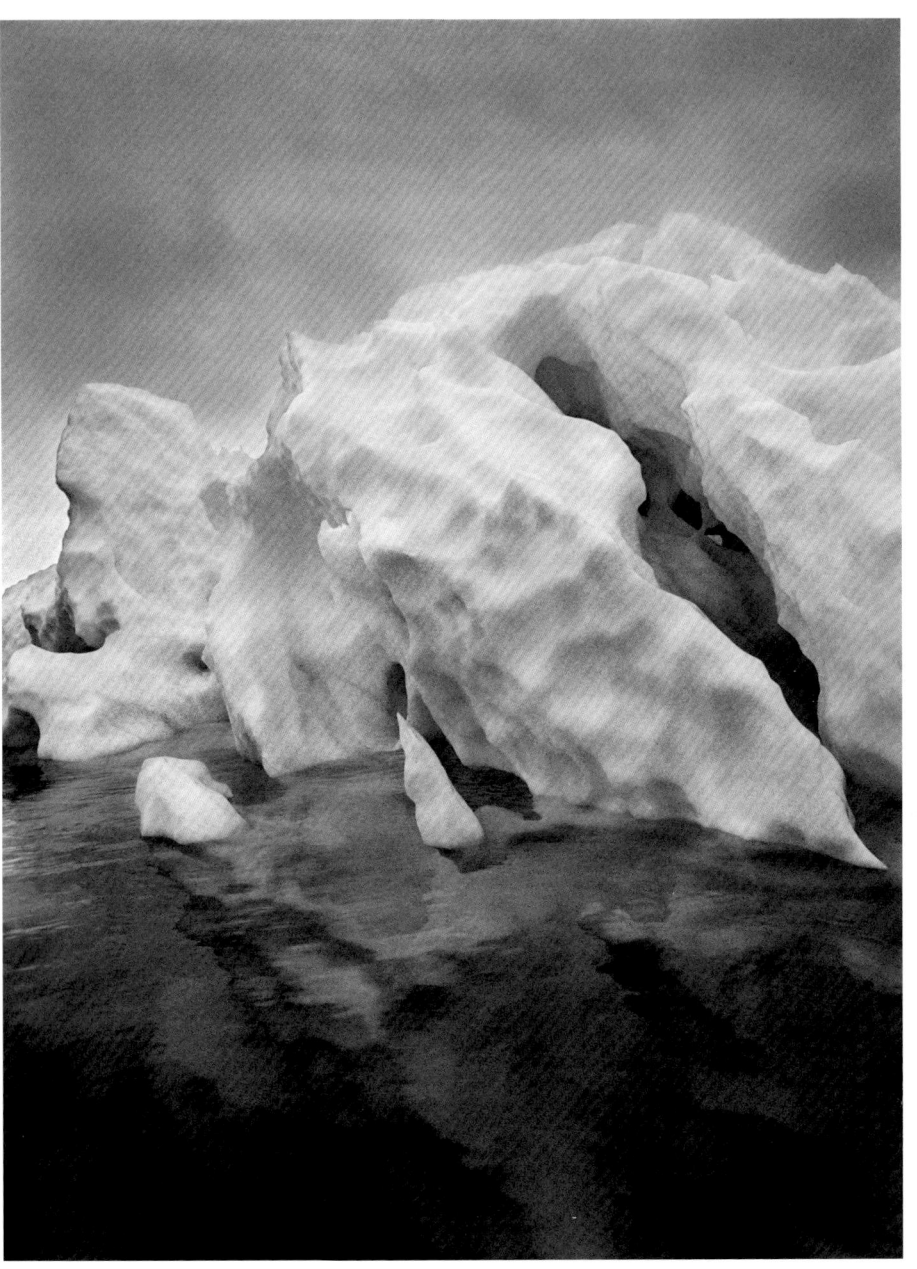

PLANET SOUTH

Twice the size of Australia, Antarctica seems even larger on maps because its landmass lies hidden beneath a vast frozen blanket that stretches hundreds of miles into the southern oceans. The coldest, driest and windiest of the world's five continents, Antarctica's fierce ecosystem reaches as far as the Falkland Islands, South Georgia, and the South Sandwich Islands, and the southern mountains and coasts of Argentina and Chile. And yet in this harsh environment, the cycle of life goes on. How could it not be part of *Genesis*?

The only viable time for nonscientists to visit the region is during the southern hemisphere's summer. Heading by boat south from Cape Horn, we stopped briefly at the Diego Ramírez Archipelago, miniscule islands absolutely crammed with albatross. Some 500 miles (800 kilometers) of wild sea later, as we approached the Antarctic itself, I was stunned by the sheer size of the icebergs, the islands and the mainland beyond. Its mountain range, 2,200 miles (3,500 kilometers) long, with peaks above 14,500 feet (4,500 meters), was beyond our reach. But we landed on Deception Island, an almost perfect ring, which is entered through a narrow passage. And on King George Island, we found a colony of Gentoo and Adélie penguins cohabiting comfortably with herds of elephant seals, the world's largest seals, some weighing five tons.

On some islands, the snow cover melts in the summer, but we were warned of the perils of walking on the ice and glaciers of the mainland because of hidden crevasses. And the weather can change without notice. Our 120-foot (36-meter) boat was designed so that it would rise above rather than be crushed by ice, but we were still trapped for three days before the wind changed and the ice pack moved away. Sailing into the Weddell Sea was particularly hazardous because of the number of icebergs, some barely visible, others almost alarmingly large. Several had flat surfaces as long as an airport runway. One stood out because it was topped by a massive cube of ice, a sight so monumental that we called it "the cathedral."

Another trip to the south took us on a smaller vessel, from the Falkland Islands, home to huge concentrations of giant albatross, to South Georgia. On this lonely island, with its tiny human population, we found royal and macaroni penguins as well as the Antarctic cormorant and the southern giant petrel. Along with native sea lions and sea elephants, the island even has reindeer, introduced by Norwegian whalers a century ago. It then took us four days of rough seas to reach the South Sandwich Islands, nine tiny uninhabited volcanic islands, in the main covered in ice. Since they have no beaches, we approached them in a Zodiac inflatable boat and literally leapt ashore to find huge colonies of penguins. I really felt I was at the end of the world.

On the South American mainland, Antarctica still felt close, with the 48 glaciers of the Southern Patagonian Ice Field filling valleys that span the borders of Chile and Argentina. This area of the southern Andes is so inaccessible that, to this day, it has been only partly explored. We traveled on foot, camping in subzero temperatures and accompanied by the constant growl of the glaciers as they drag along stones and rocks deep under the ice. Across the globe, scientists are monitoring the shrinking of glaciers as global temperatures rise. We saw this happening at the edge of Lake Argentino, where large pieces of the Perito Moreno Glacier near Calafate break off and tumble into the water continuously.

I could not leave the South Atlantic without recording the southern right whale, which migrates to the Antarctic during the summer, then heads north to breed. One of the largest breeding grounds is off the Valdés Peninsula on Argentina's Atlantic coast, a natural sanctuary shaped like a crab with two sheltered gulfs. To spend several weeks in a boat among these whales was one of the most poignant experiences of my life. While we waited for the best light to photograph, 50-foot (15-meter) whales and their young played around us, sometimes coming so close that we could have stroked them. And who would not be moved by one of nature's grandest spectacles: a 40-ton animal leaping into the sky and then crashing back into the water?

Other creatures come to the peninsula to breed, including elephant seals, which become very aggressive during the mating season. The orca, commonly known as the killer whale, also hunts close to shore. It is a majestic and terrifying animal and, here, its chosen prey is the sea lion, which comes to breed on the beaches of the peninsula. Half a century ago, local fishermen stopped hunting sea lions, but these animals still fear humans. So to photograph them, I hid in a sand hole, knowing that the orcas were lying in wait should I frighten any sea lions into the sea. But, sooner or later, they must lead their young to the water and, inevitably, on several occasions, I saw an orca seize a baby in its teeth and swim away. I was saddened, but how could I question nature's ways?

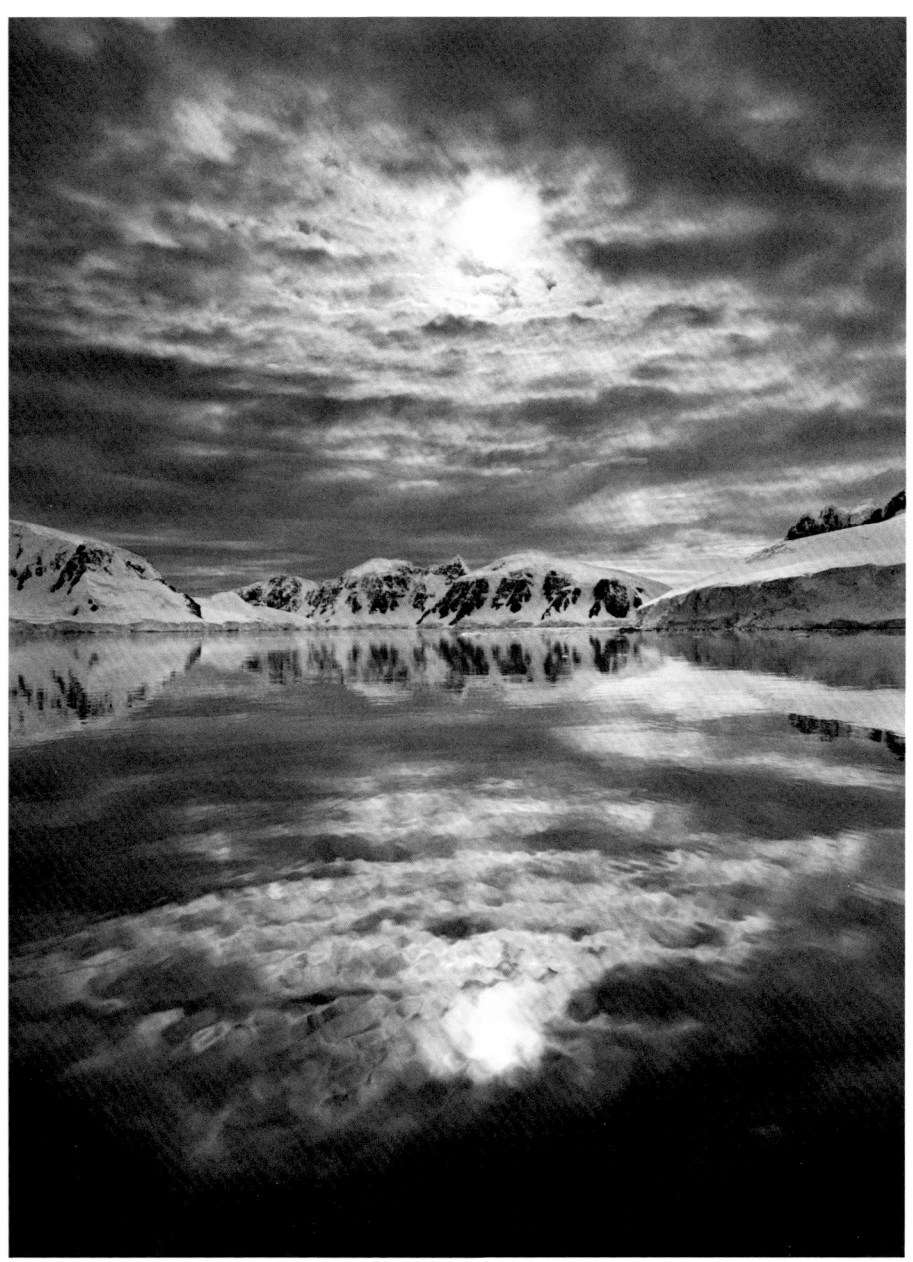

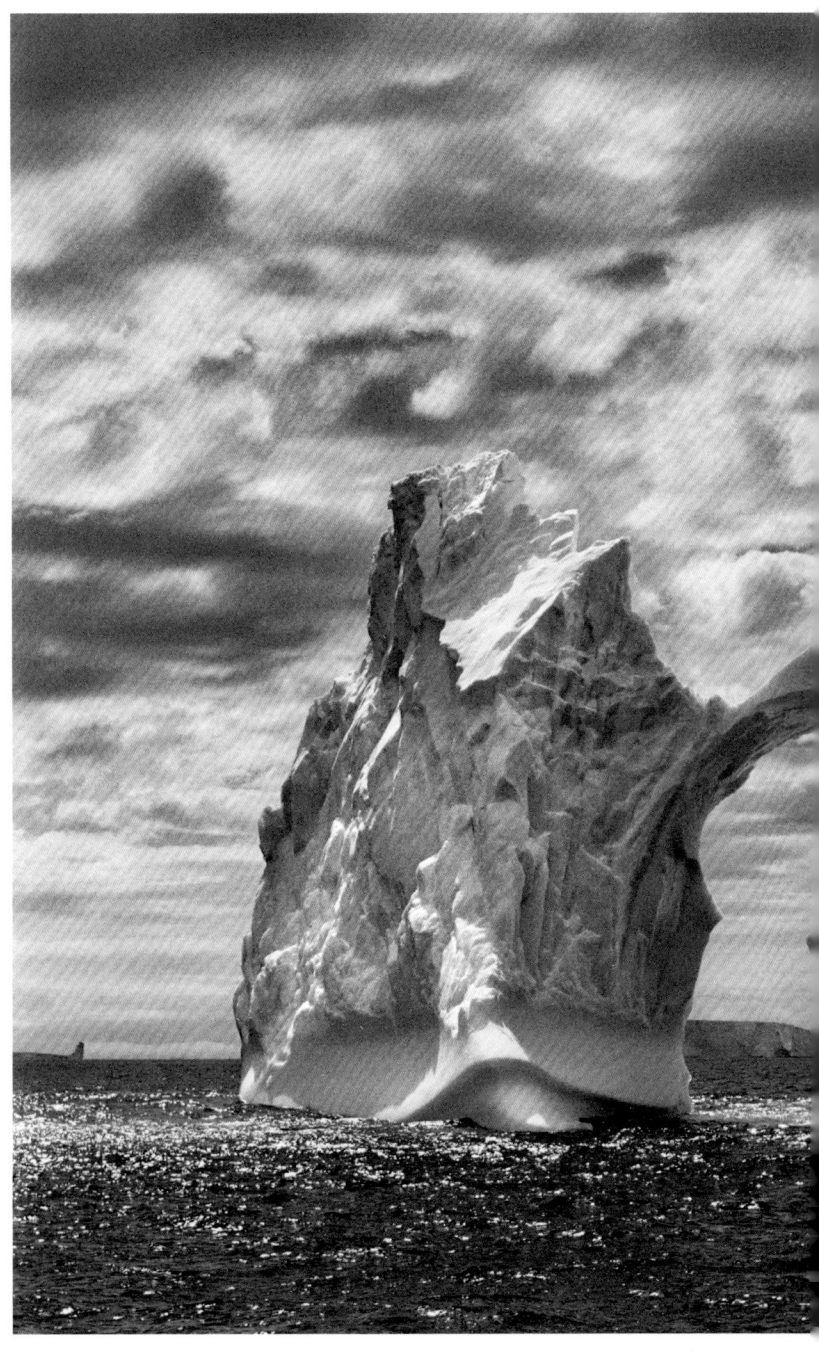

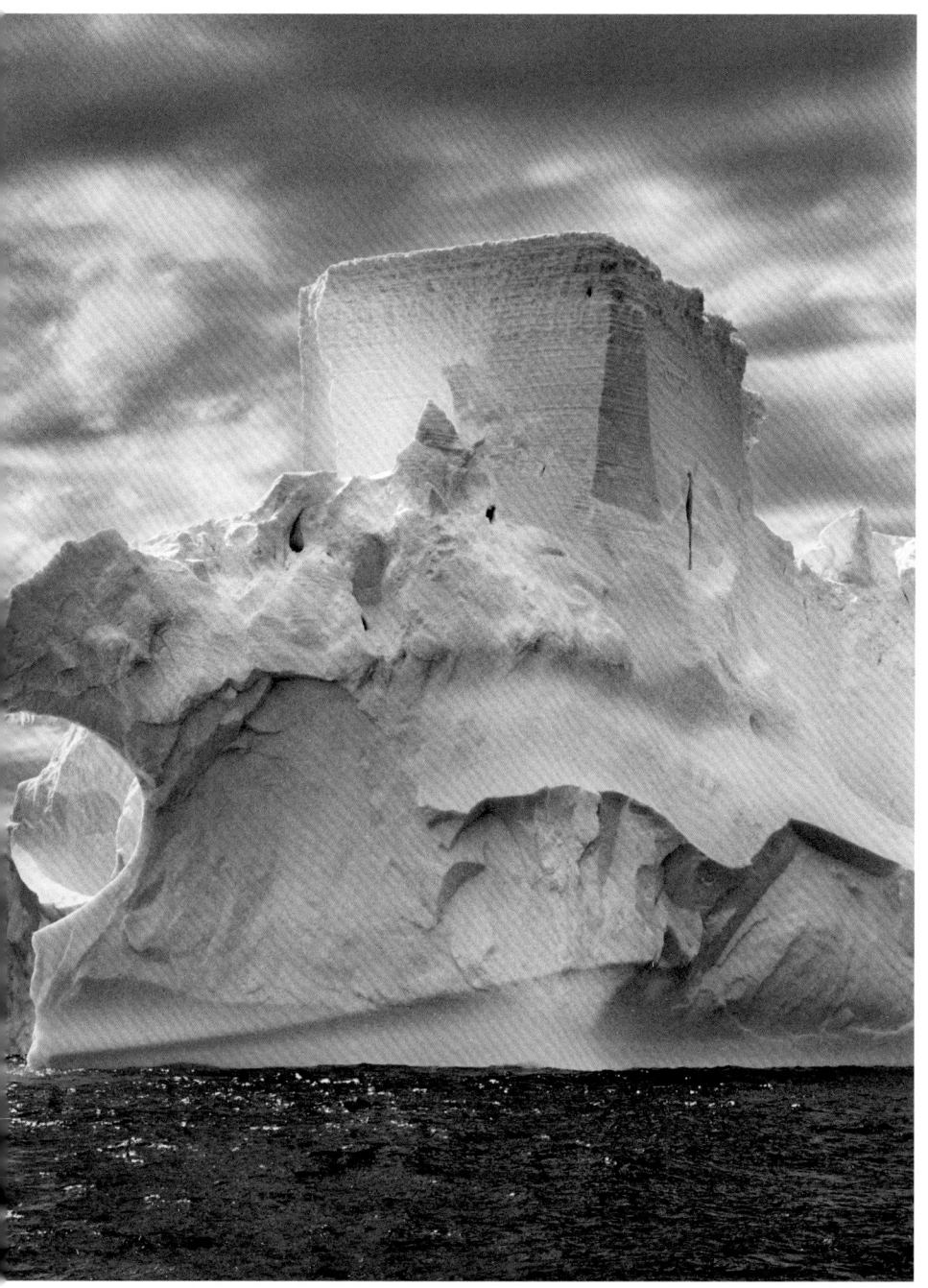

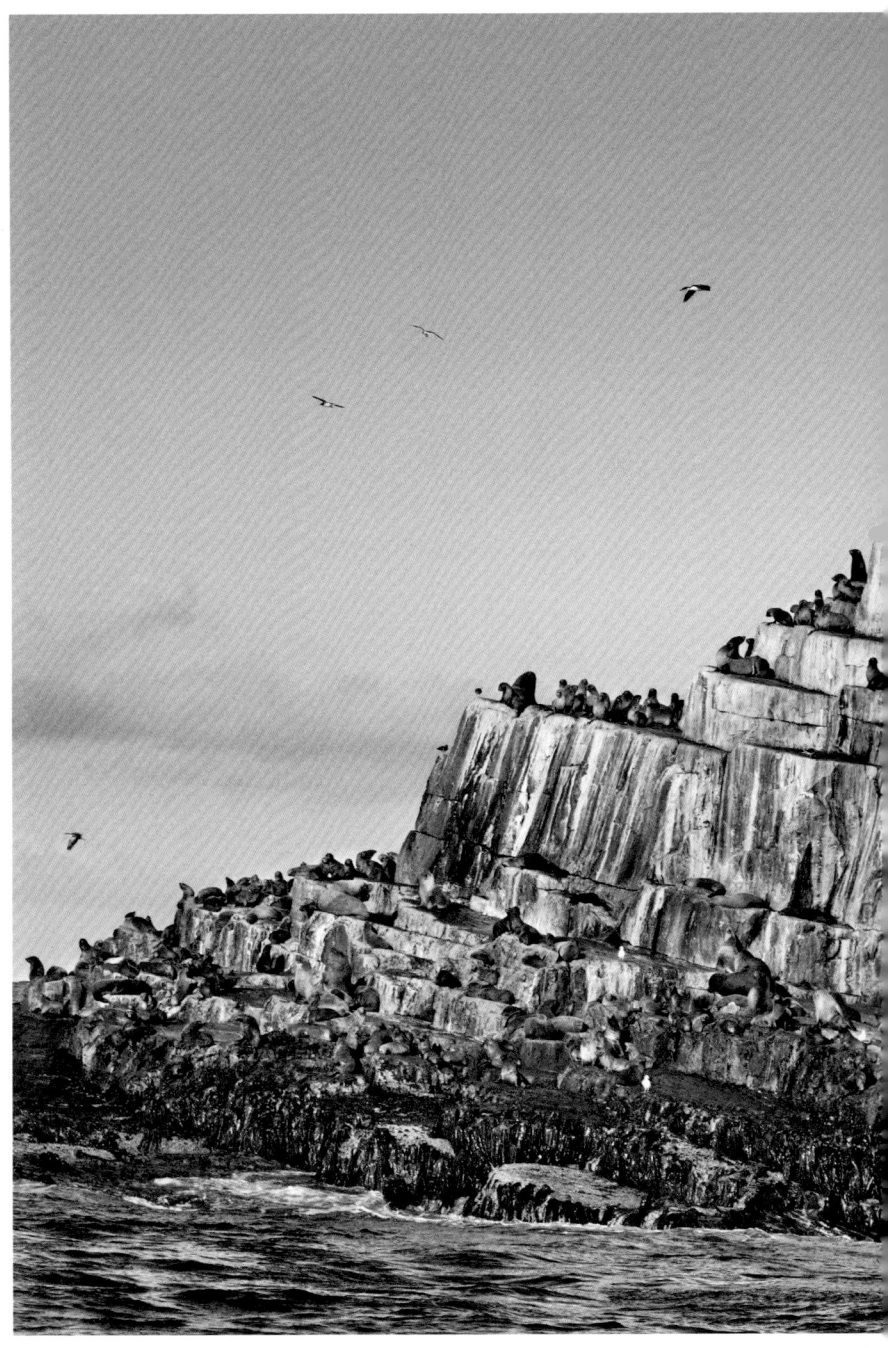

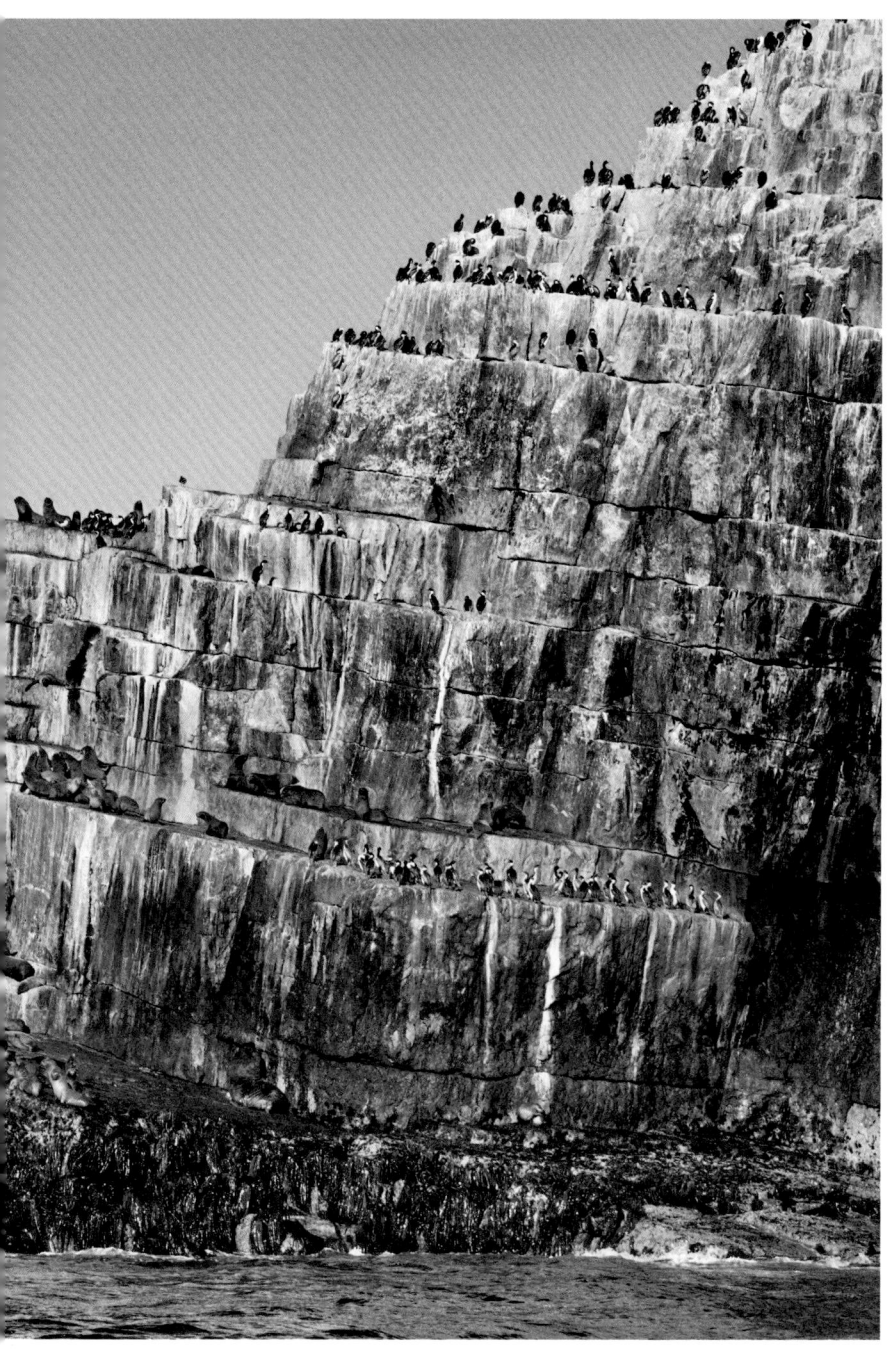

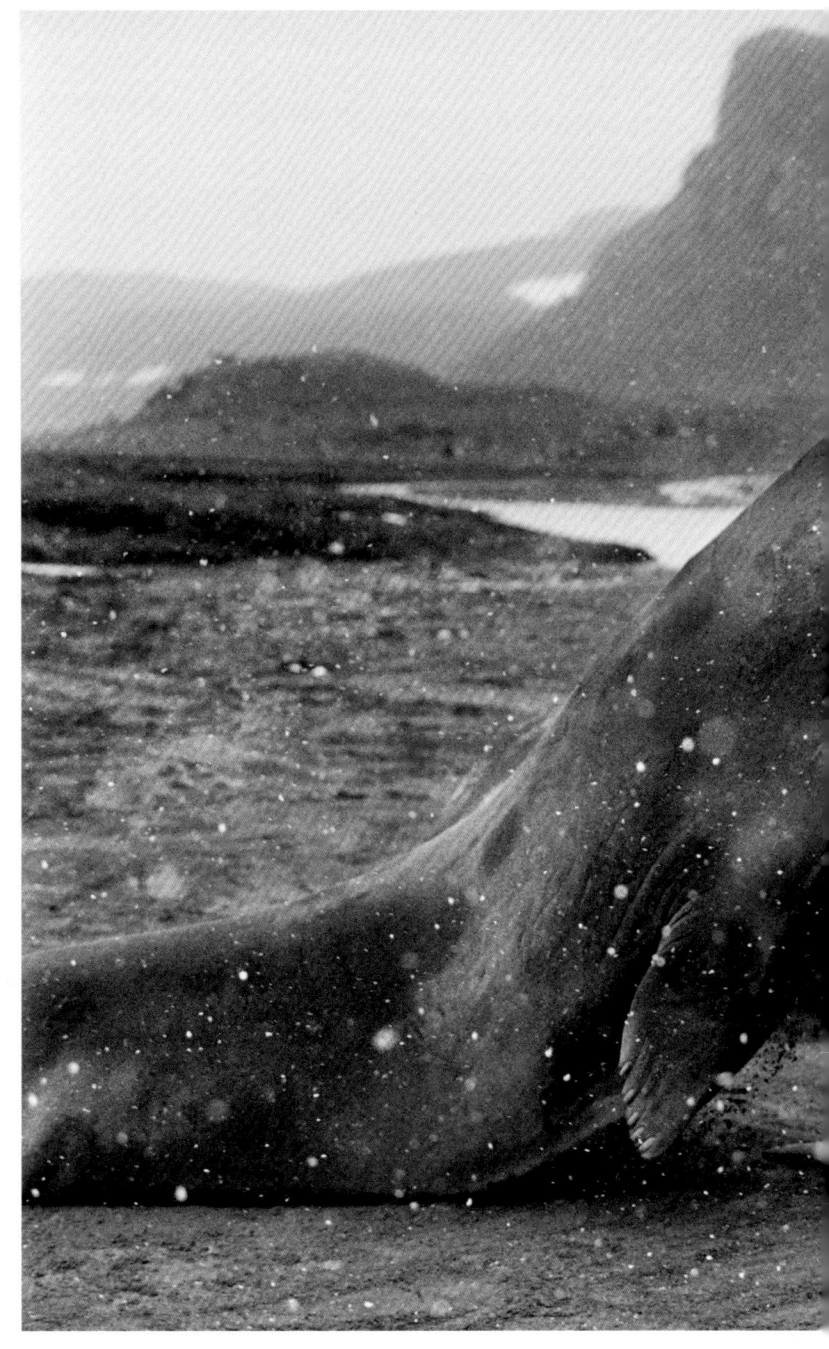

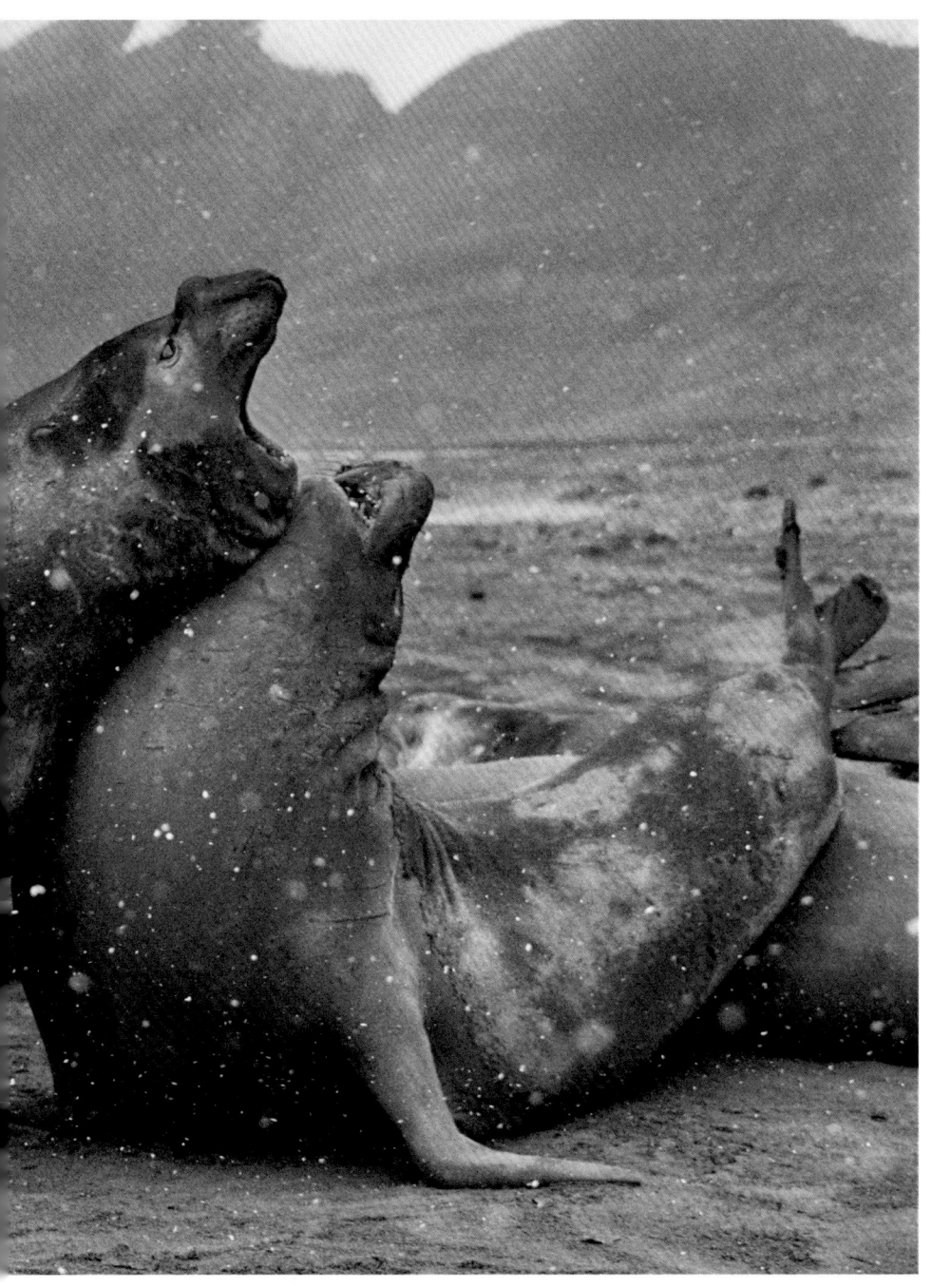

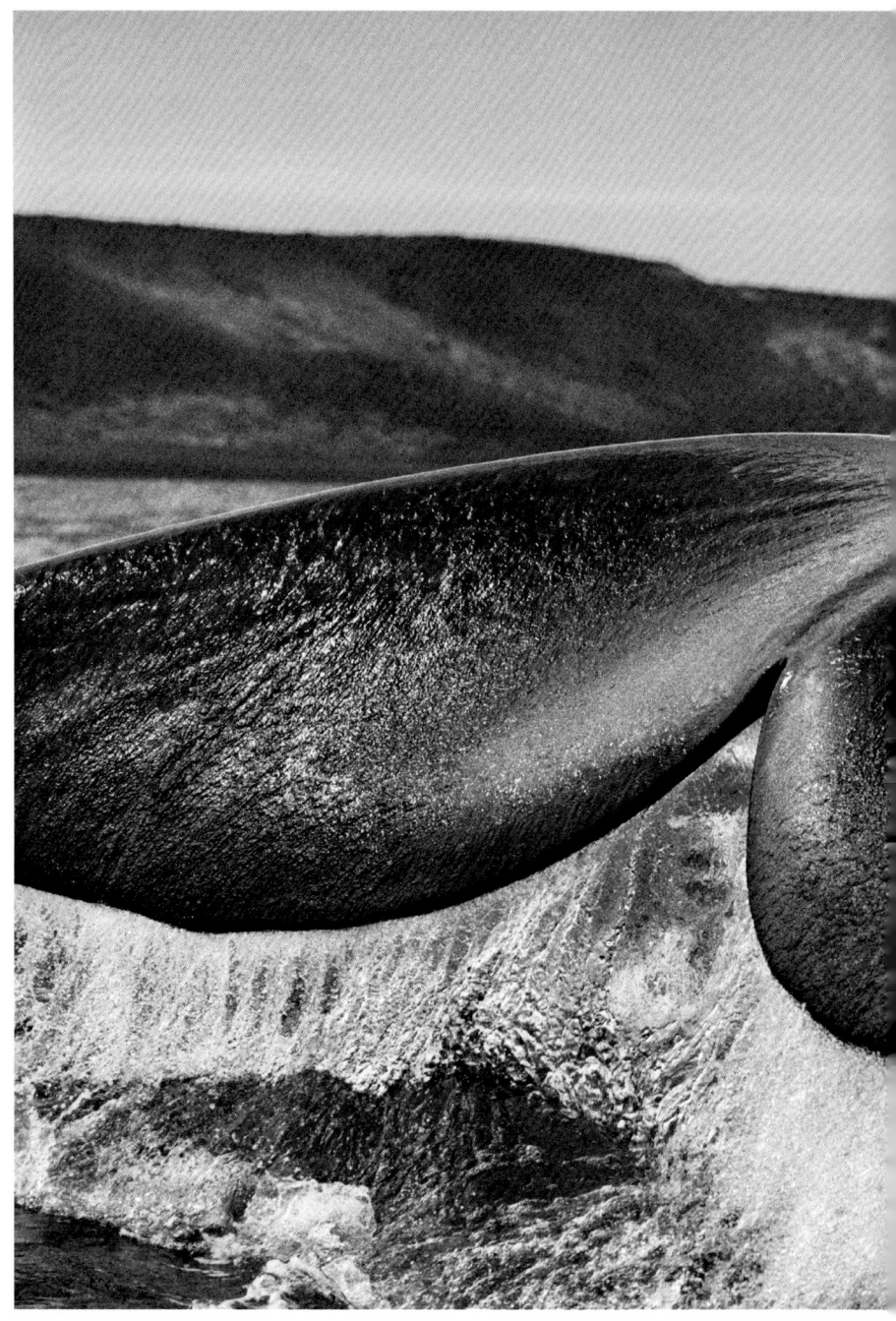

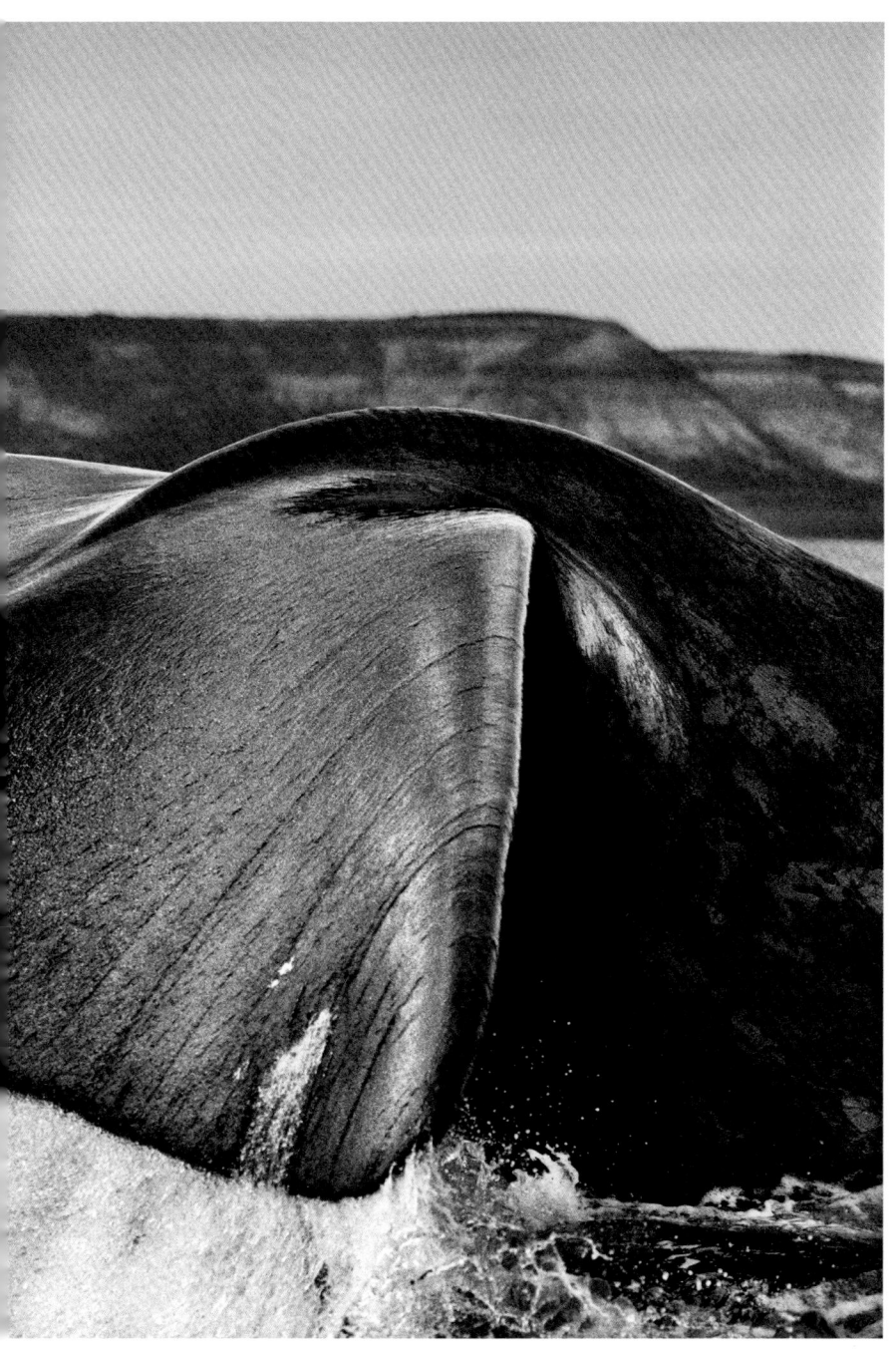

Page 8: Iceberg moving on the Weddell Sea. Antarctic Peninsula. January and February 2005.

Page 11: Mount Français on Anvers Island, beside the Gerlache Strait, offers one of the most spectacular views of the Antarctic Peninsula. January and February 2005.

Pages 12/13: Iceberg between Paulet Island and the South Shetland Islands on the Weddell Sea. At sea level, earlier flotation levels are clearly visible where the ice has been polished by the ocean's constant movement. High above, a shape resembling a castle tower has been carved by wind erosion and detached pieces of ice. Antarctic Peninsula. January and February 2005.

Pages 14/15: Eddystone Rock. Colonies of fur seals (*Arctocephalus gazella*) and rock shags, or Magellanic cormorants (*Phalacrocorax magellanicus*), are grouped on the eroded terraces of the rock, the northernmost point of the Falkland Islands. November and December 2009.

Pages 16/17: On King George Island, off the Antarctic Peninsula, there is a large concentration of elephant seals (*Mirounga leonina*). As adults, these animals, weighing four to five tons, are the largest seals in the world. Young males gather in small groups and practice harmless combat. This training is crucial preparation for the mating season: their aim is to gather a large number of females in a harem, but they must be ready to fight off other males who try to separate a female in order to mate with her. On the Antarctic islands or on the coasts of Patagonia, a male elephant seal may control as many as 100 females. Antarctic Peninsula. January and February 2005.

Pages 18/19 and opposite: Southern right whales (*Eubalaena australis*), drawn to the Valdés Peninsula because of the shelter provided by its two gulfs, the Golfo San José, and the Golfo Nuevo, often navigate with their tails upright in the water. When a tail stands immobile for tens of minutes, it is probable that the whale is completely vertical in the water in a kind of resting position; it has also been claimed that the whales use their tails as a sail, allowing the wind to do the work. After close observation, it is possible to predict when a whale will jump: a sudden and swift movement of the tail provides the burst of energy that enables the whale to project its massive body out of the water. Valdés Peninsula. Argentina. September and October 2004.

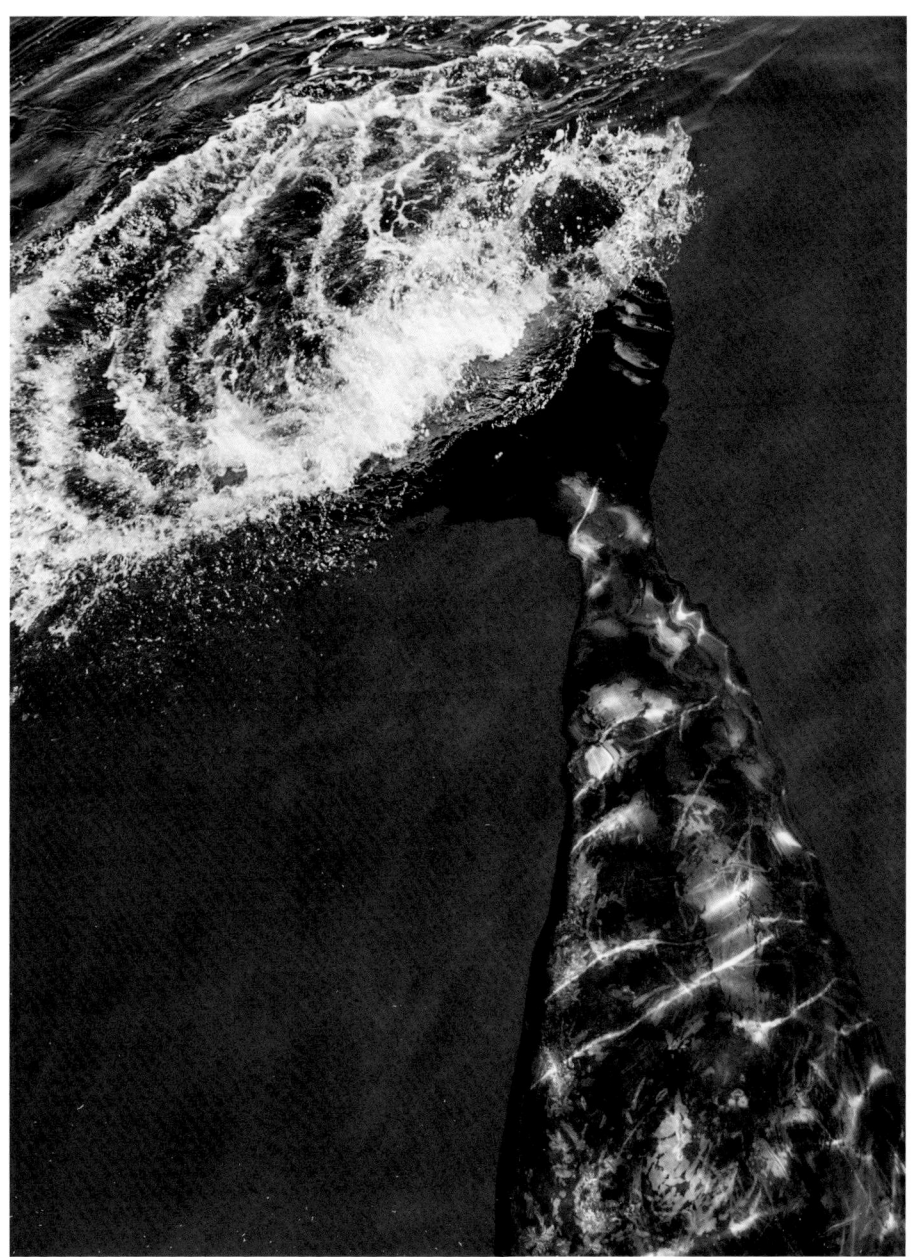

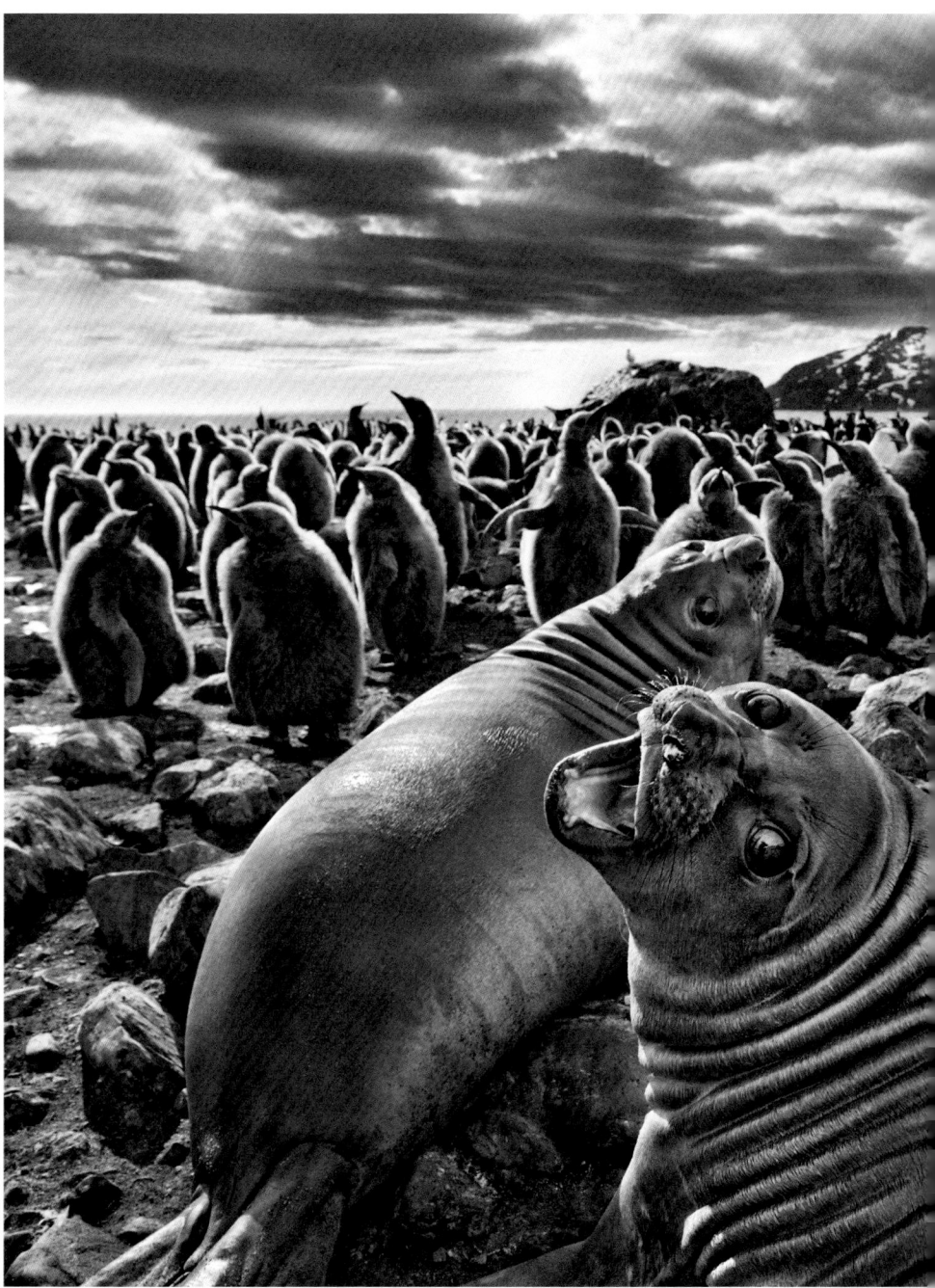

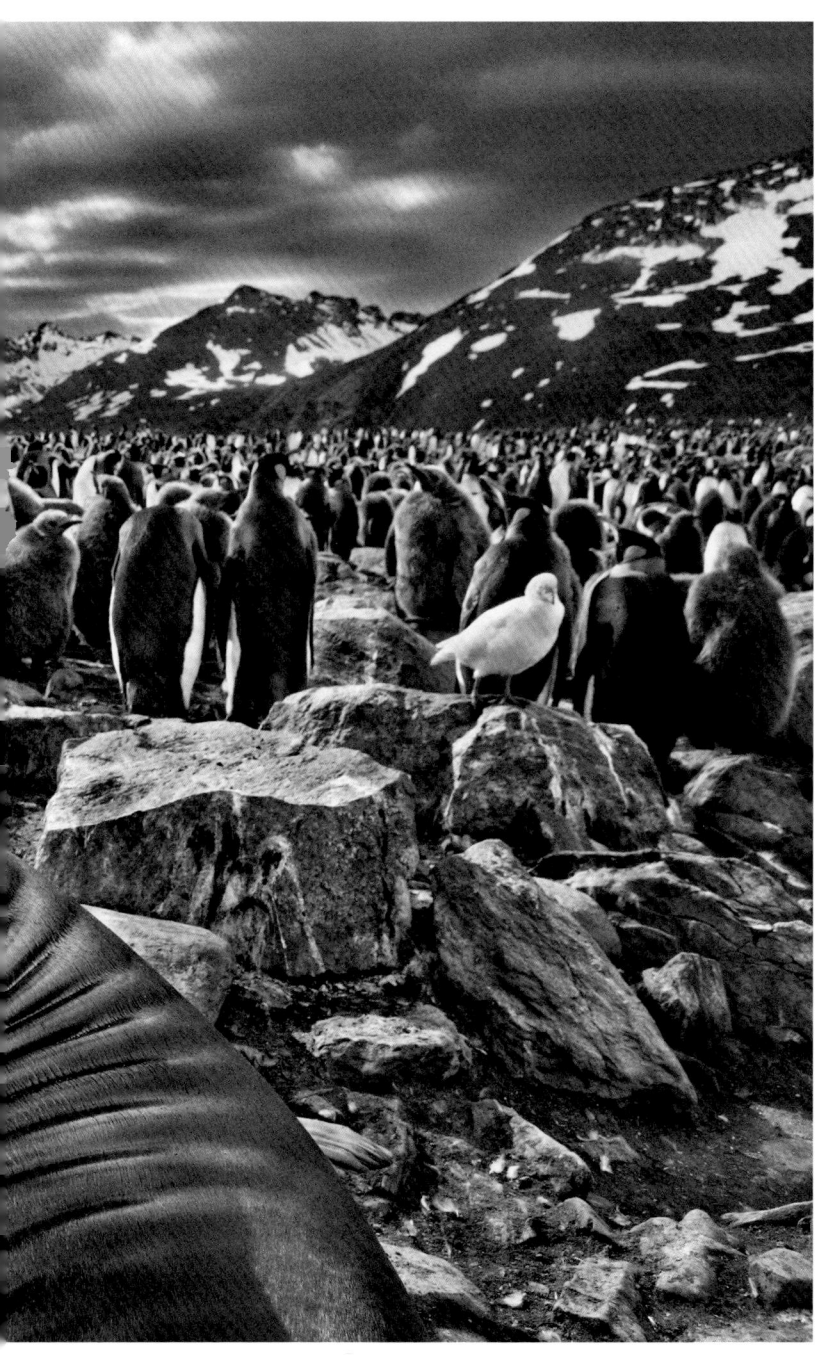

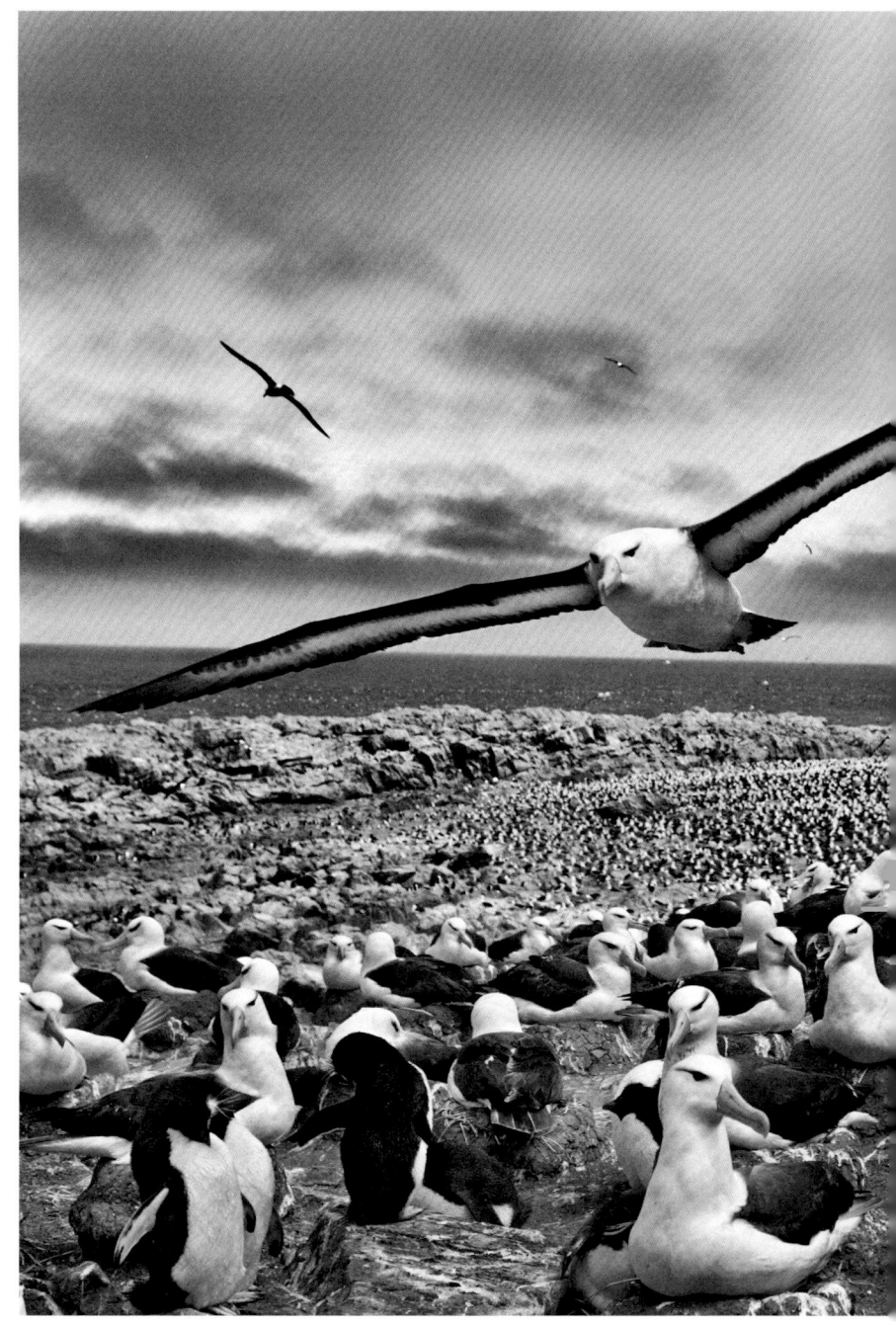

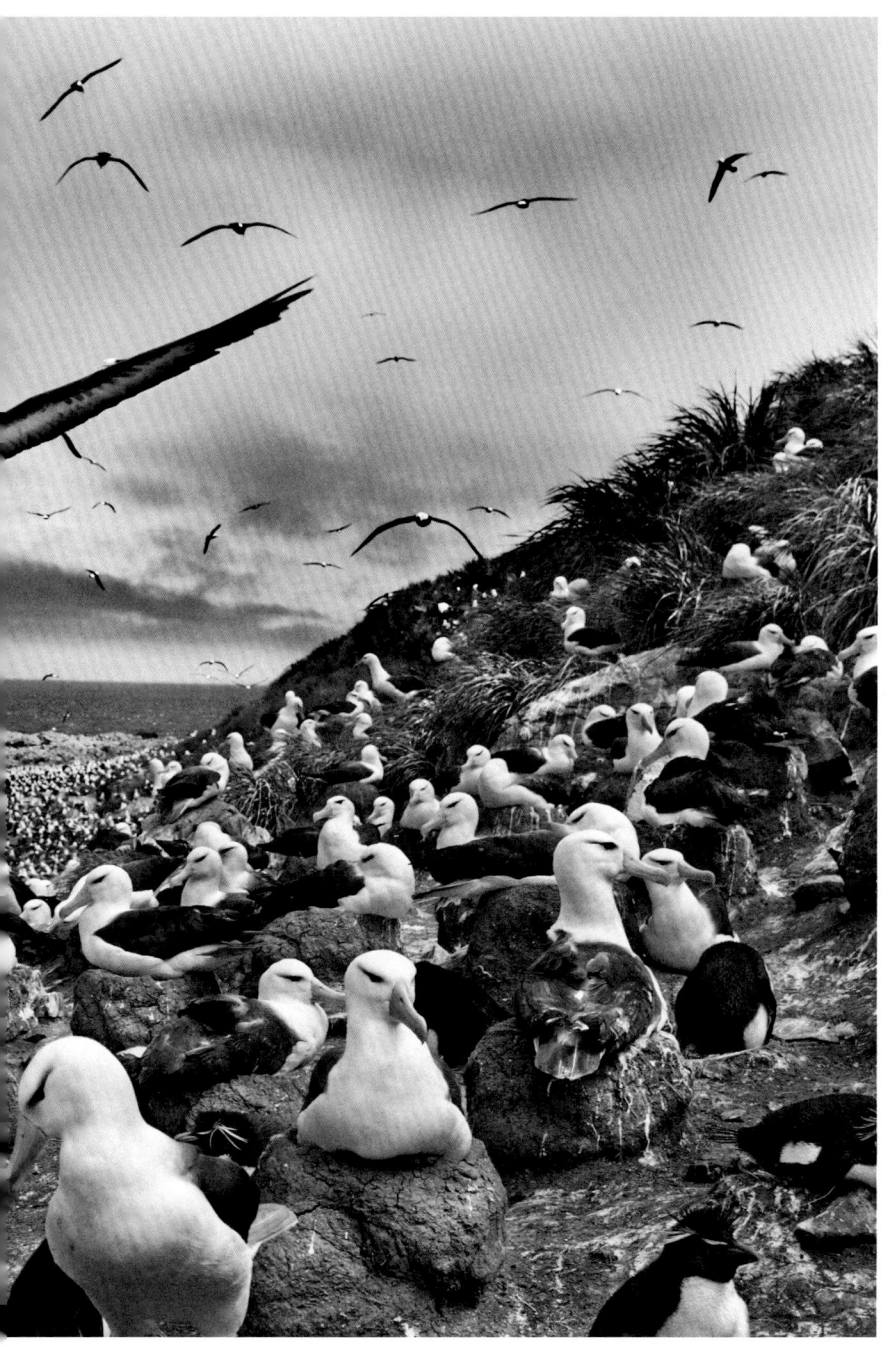

Pages 22/23: Southern elephant seal calves (*Mirounga leonina*) at Saint Andrews Bay. South Georgia. November and December 2009.

Pages 24/25: The Jason Islands are a cluster of 12 islands on the westernmost point of the Falkland Islands. These photographs were taken on Steeple Jason Island, home to more than 500,000 couples of black-browed albatrosses (*Thalassarche melanophris*), the largest colony of albatrosses in the world. Falkland Islands. November and December 2009.

Opposite: A colony of black-browed albatrosses (*Thalassarche melanophris*) on the archipelago of Willis Islands; visible in the background is Bird Island. South Georgia. November and December 2009.

Pages 28/29: King penguins (*Aptenodytes patagonicus*) at Saint Andrews Bay. This immense bay, with spectacular mountains to one side, is home to the largest colony of king penguins in the world (approximately 300,000 couples). South Georgia. November and December 2009.

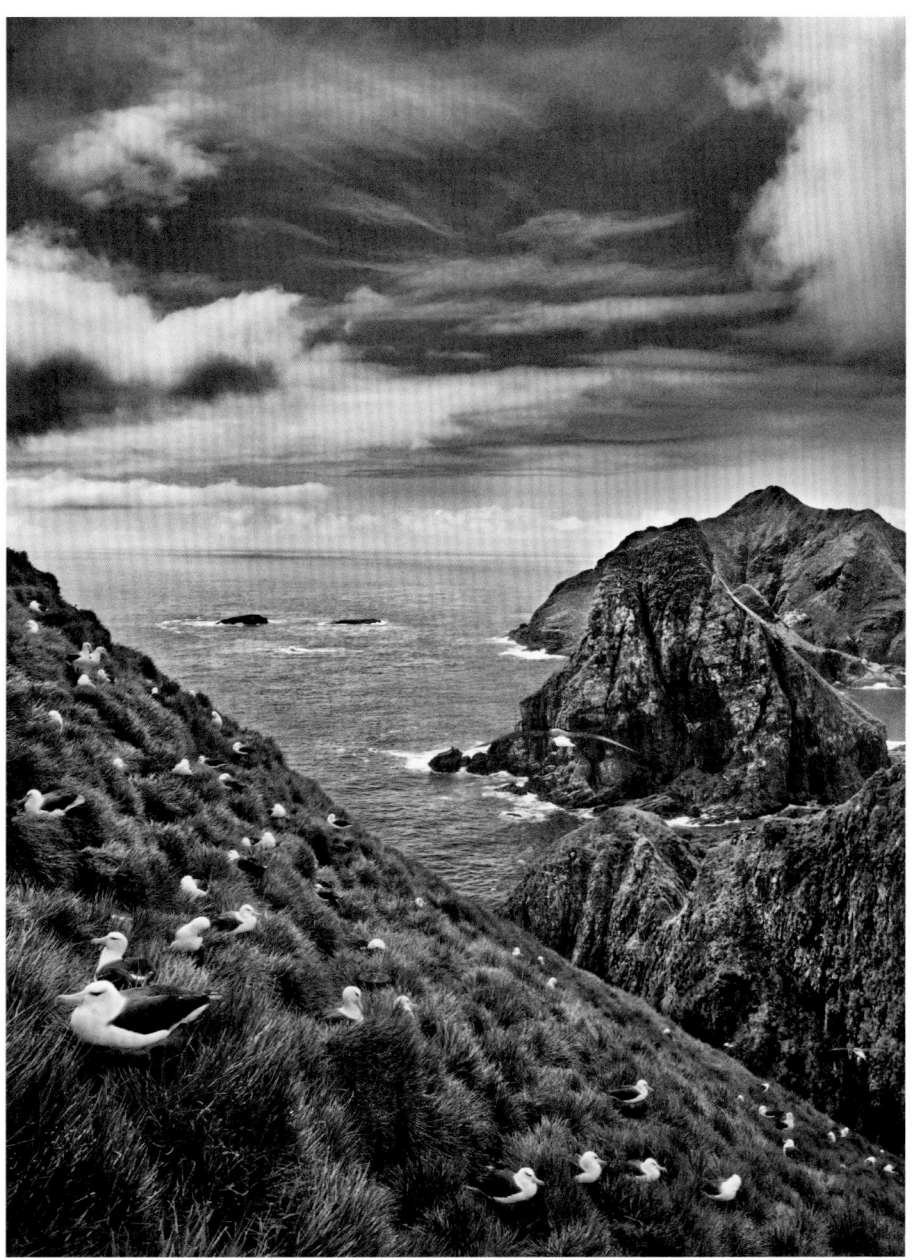

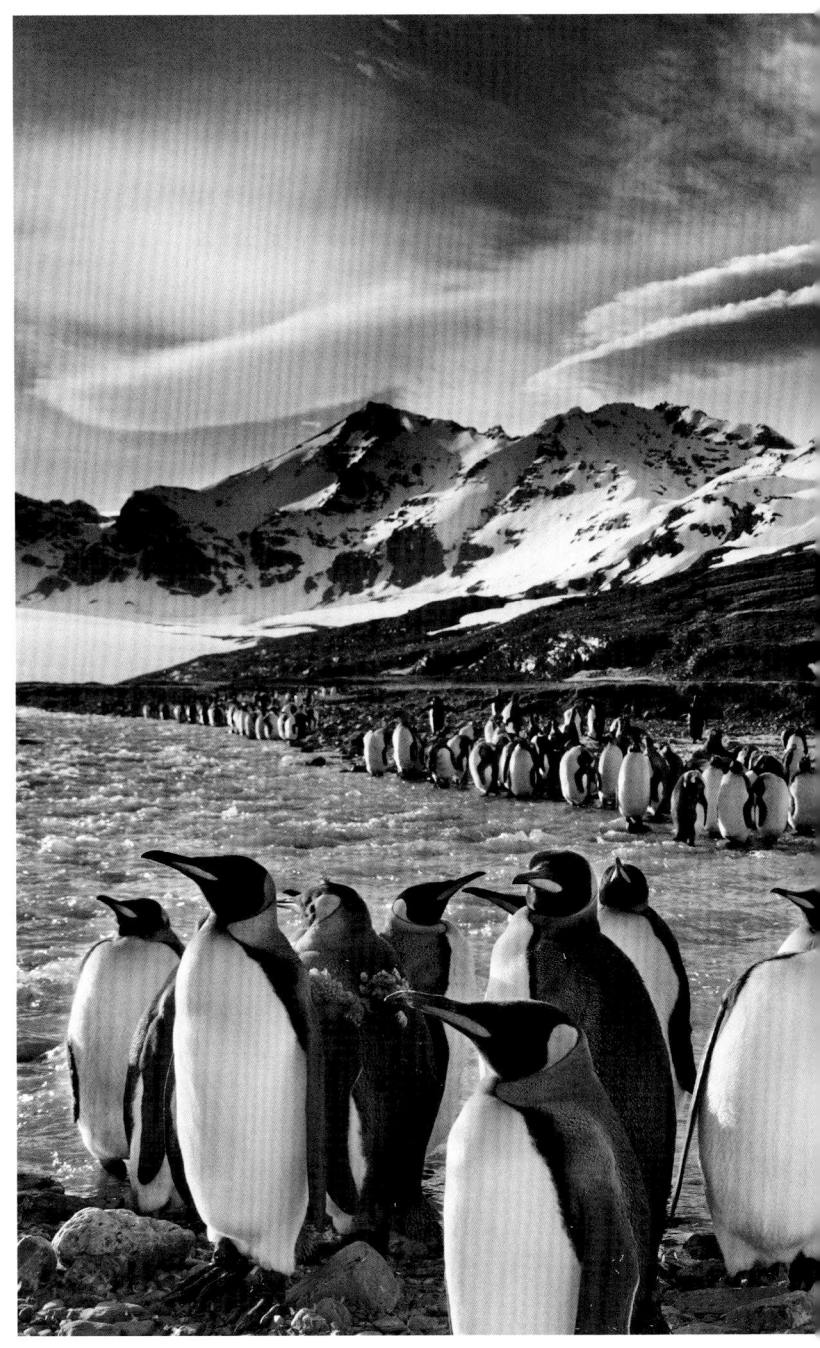

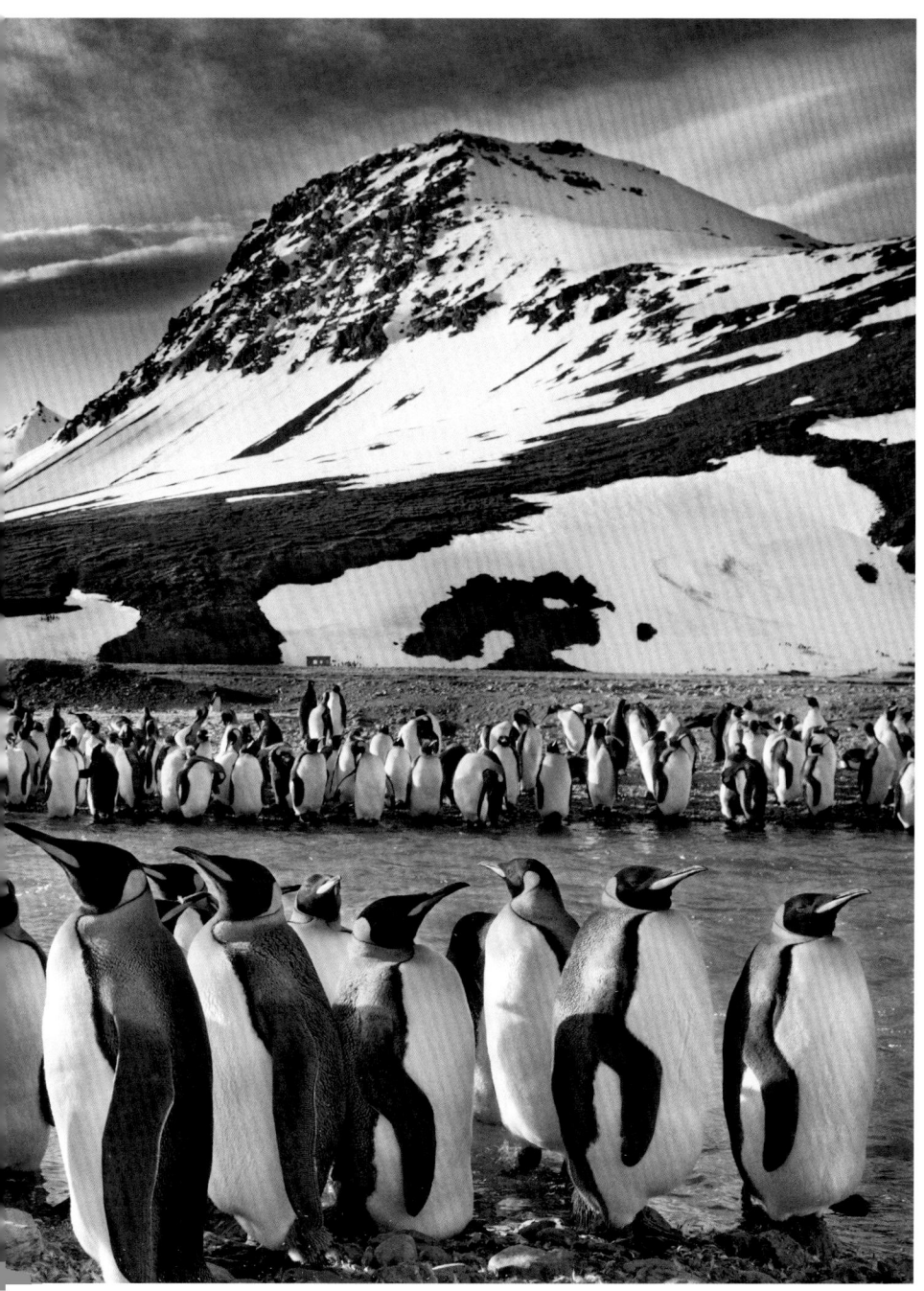

Opposite: Cerro Torre, part of a mountain range in the Southern Patagonian Ice Field, stands out for its elegant and slender peak. The mountain itself is 10,200 feet (3,128 meters) high, but its summit rises like a jagged knife, with vertical drops of between 3,600 and 4,900 feet (1,100 and 1,500 meters) on three sides. Often hidden by swirling clouds, Cerro Torre has proved an immense challenge to mountain climbers, few of whom have ever conquered it. Adding to their difficulties, fierce westerly winds blowing across the icecap have covered its rock face with a thick mantle of ice and a slippery mushroom of rime ice. Argentine Patagonia. March and April 2007.

Pages 32/33: A colony of king penguins (*Aptenodytes patagonicus*) at Gold Harbour Bay. South Georgia. November and December 2009.

Pages 34/35: Chinstrap penguins (*Pygoscelis antarctica*) on an iceberg located between Zavodovski and Visokoi islands. South Sandwich Islands. November and December 2009.

Pages 36/37: A colony of black-browed albatrosses (*Thalassarche melanophris*) on the archipelago of Willis Islands; in the background one can see Trinity and Bird Island. South Georgia. November and December 2009.

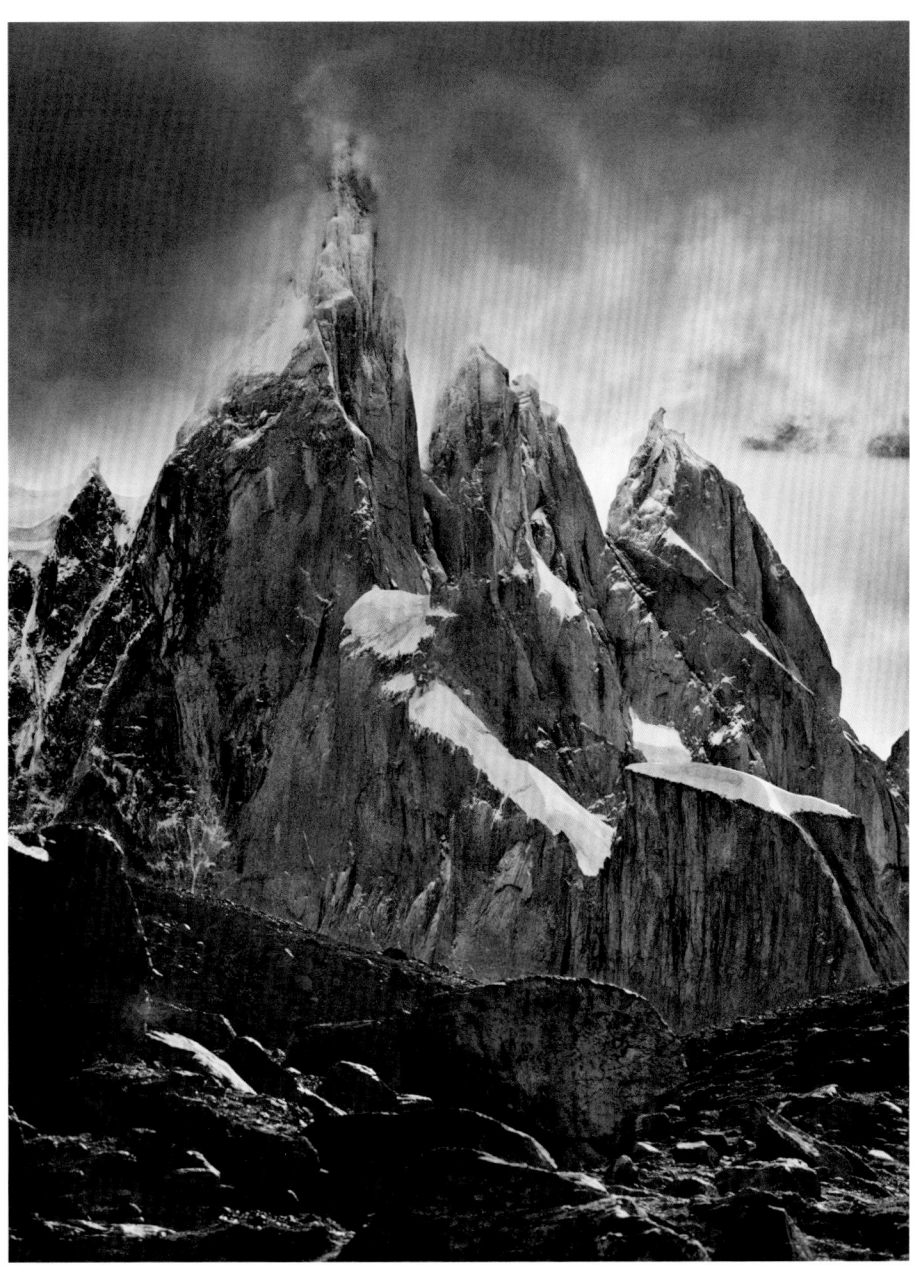

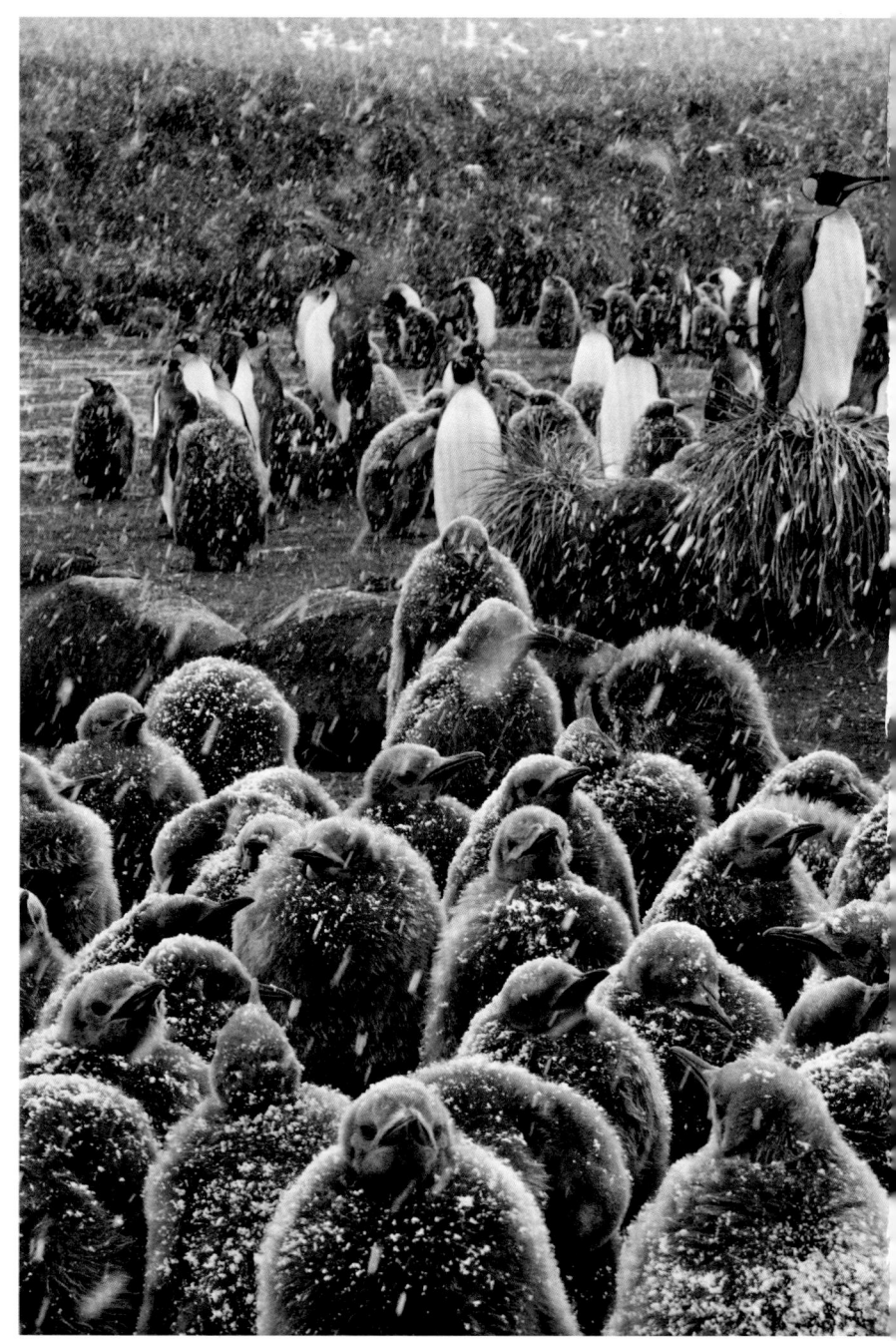

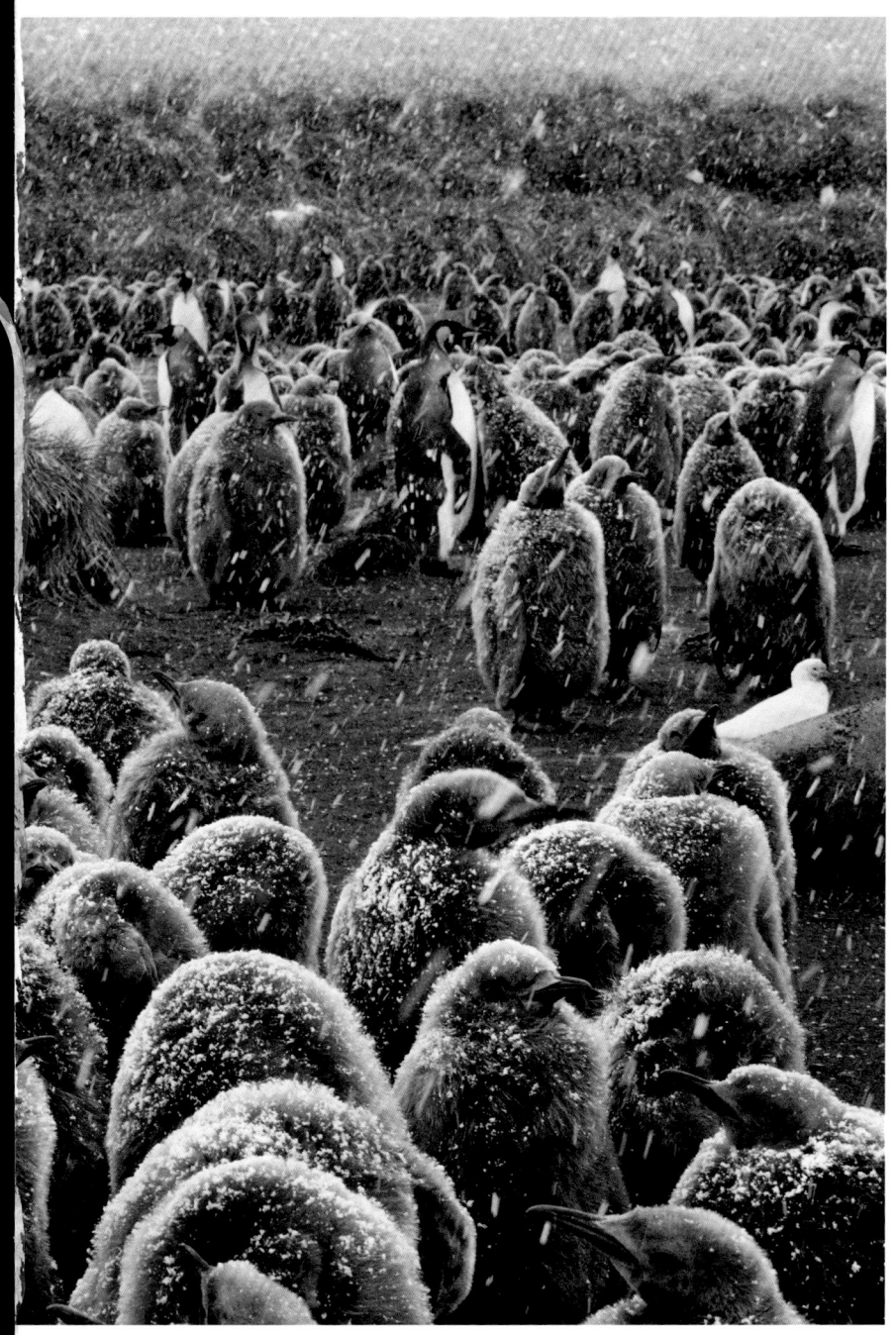

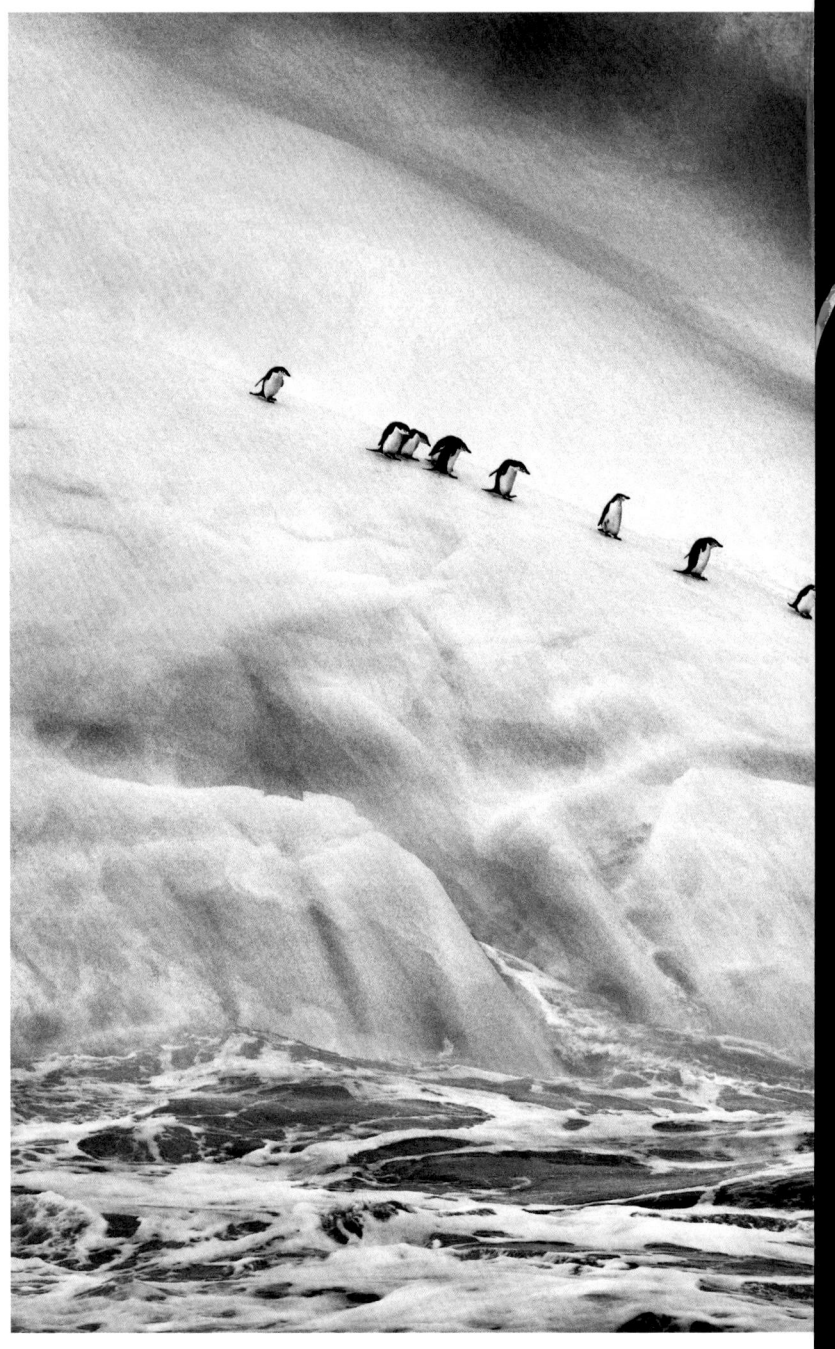

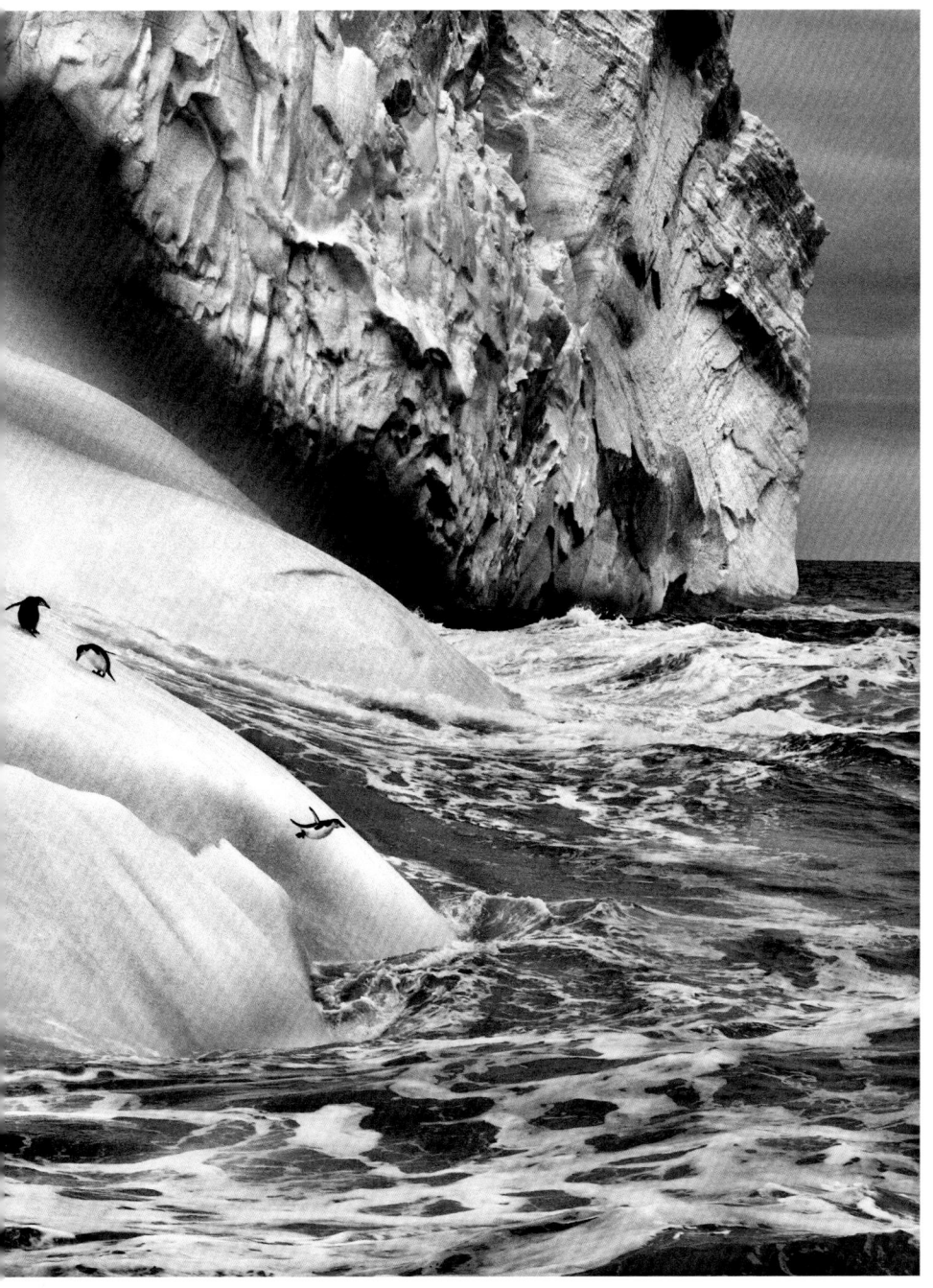

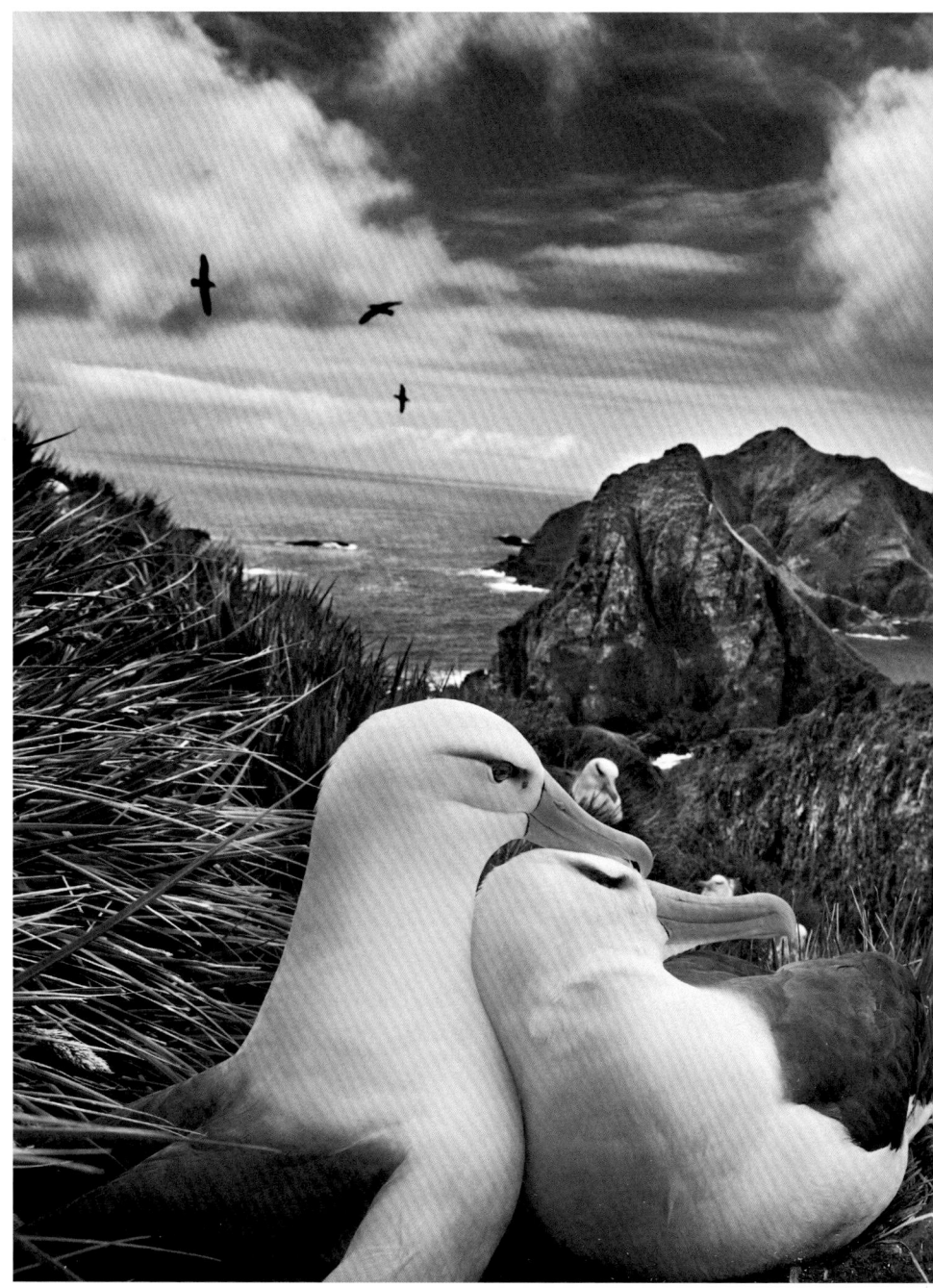

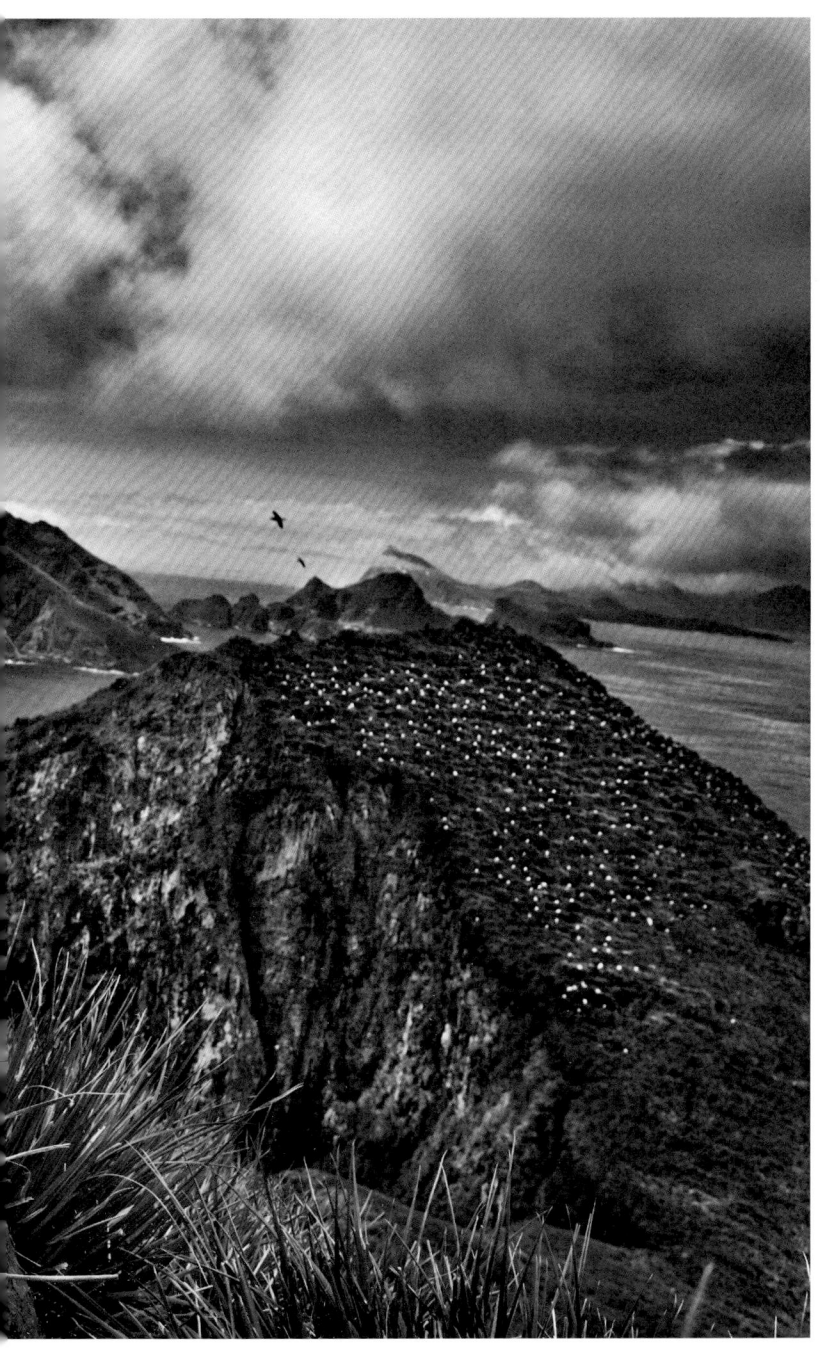

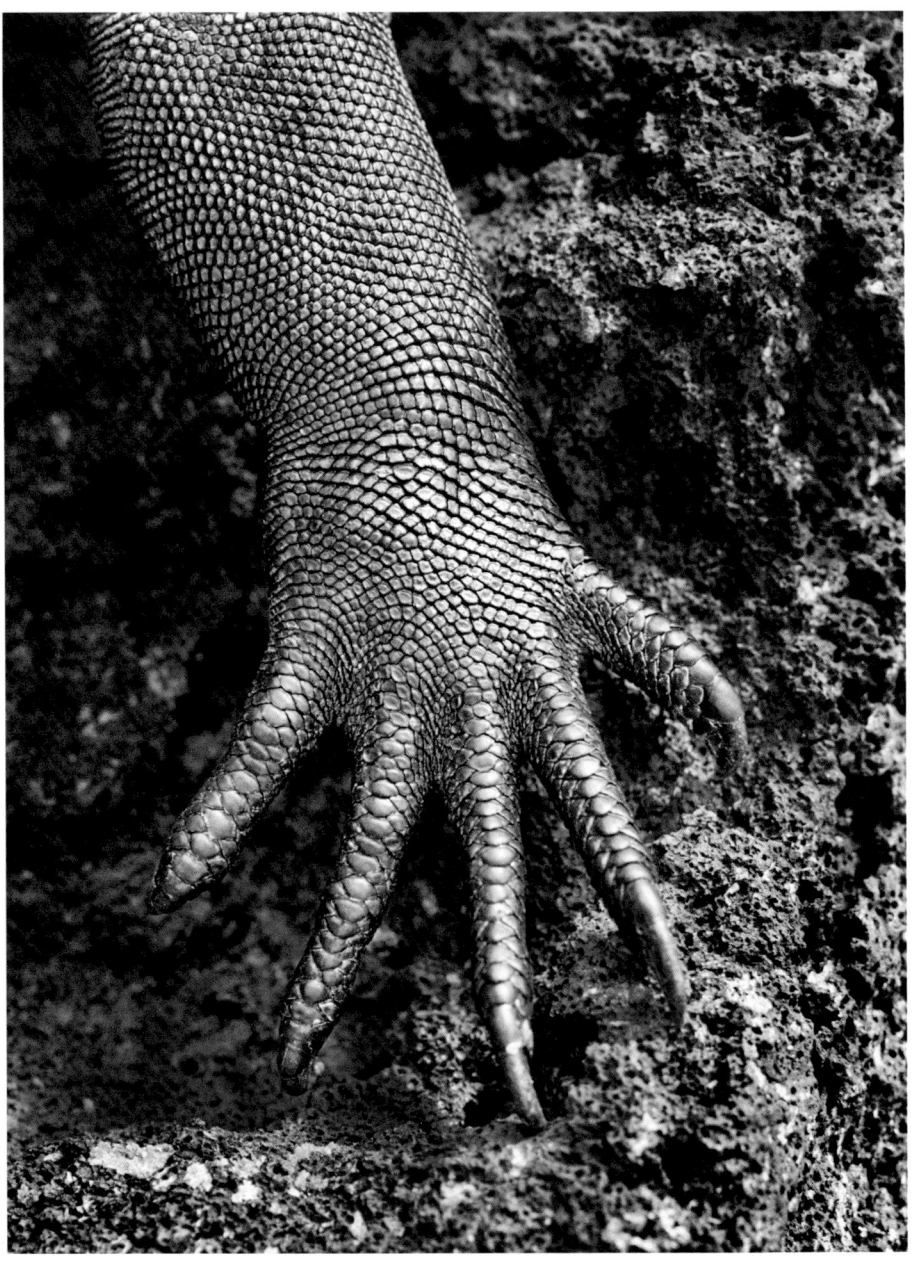

SANCTUARIES

Isolated islands offer ideal conditions for the development and survival of endemic flora and fauna. As a result, unique animal and plant species are often concentrated in small geographical areas. Their principal threat is the encroachment of human settlements. While some ancient tribes still live "inside" nature much as their forebears did, this harmony is also often disturbed by modern man. Thus, in what were once safe refuges, ancestral ways of life, rare animals and unique plants are inescapably threatened with extinction.

I started my voyage on the Galápagos Islands, that extraordinary natural laboratory that inspired Darwin's theory of evolution. Its multiple creatures have survived in good measure because they have had no predators, except during the 18th and 19th centuries, when passing seamen hunted the giant tortoise for food. Today, the tortoises are protected, along with the other animals I was able to photograph, from marine iguanas, fur seals, and sea lions to brown pelicans, great frigate birds, and flightless cormorants. And, astonishingly, all this life flourishes beside fields of lava and at the base of active volcanoes.

Madagascar, the large island off the east coast of southern Africa, is another of the world's biodiversity "hotspots." Close to 90 percent of its tens of thousands of animal and plant species can be found nowhere else on earth. It has no fewer than 860 varieties of orchids and 170 of palm trees. The lemur, a monkey-like primate that is the island's most distinctive animal, appears in over 100 different subspecies.

Traveling up the arid west coast, we drove past stunning sand dunes formed by broad riverbeds which are dry much of the year. The baobab tree, with its distinctive bloated trunk, is quite the strangest of the flora. Madagascar boasts six of the eight species of baobab trees found on earth. Further inland, I came across the tsingy, among the most bizarre geological formations I have ever seen. Formed over millions of years by crushed shells, their surfaces as sharp as broken glass, they rise 160 to 330 feet (50 to 100 meters) out of the undergrowth like huge stalagmites. In the humid northeast of the island, vast stretches of rainforest remain. But I often saw telltale plumes of smoke where jungle is being cleared by fire to make room for cattle farms. As a memory bank of evolution, Madagascar is at risk.

On islands off the west coast of Sumatra, the sanctuaries of several ethnic groups are also being invaded. From the 1960s, the Indonesian government decided to bring these traditional hunter-gatherers into settlements. It required adults to convert to either Islam or Christianity. Many did, but a few clans stayed in the jungles of Siberut Island. Those were the Mentawai people we wanted to meet.

Noted for their spirituality and body art, the Mentawai still build everything out of natural products of the rain forest, including their uma, which serves as dormitory, kitchen, and temple. In the jungle, men usually wear only tree-bark loincloths and some women cover themselves with dresses of woven leaves. They have no need to grow their food since they are surrounded by abundant animal and plant life. Every clan has several shamans, each with a different responsibility, such as dance and song rituals and foretelling the future.

New Guinea, the mountainous island north of Australia, is one of the world's most pristine natural habitats, with over 1,000 known languages and ethnic groups. The island is divided politically, with independent Papua New Guinea to the east and the Indonesian province of West Papua, also known as Irian Jaya, to the west.

In Papua New Guinea, we traveled into the fertile valleys, wild rivers, and untamed sawtoothed mountains of the southern highlands. Several ethnic communities allowed us to record their *singsings*, elaborate ceremonies for which the people decorate their bodies with paint, plants, shells, beads, and animal teeth. The Huli, the region's largest group, now wear Western clothes. But for fiestas, Huli wigmen also paint their faces and wear wigs made with their own hair. In the Asaro region, the mudmen frighten their enemies by covering themselves in mud and donning large white masks made of packed mud.

The island's least assimilated group is Irian Jaya's Stone Korowai, also known as "gentle cannibals" because they hunt down and eat those deemed to be sorcerers. Men are naked except for a penis sheath and women wear only a short grass skirt. Since clan warfare is common, their chief lives in a house built 100 feet (30 meters) above the ground.

The Mek tribe, on the other hand, has had more contact with Western missionaries and, for Christian religious services, tribesmen often wear old Western clothes. Even the local pastor, who wears nothing but a long penis sheath during the week, puts on a donated Western shirt for church on Sunday.

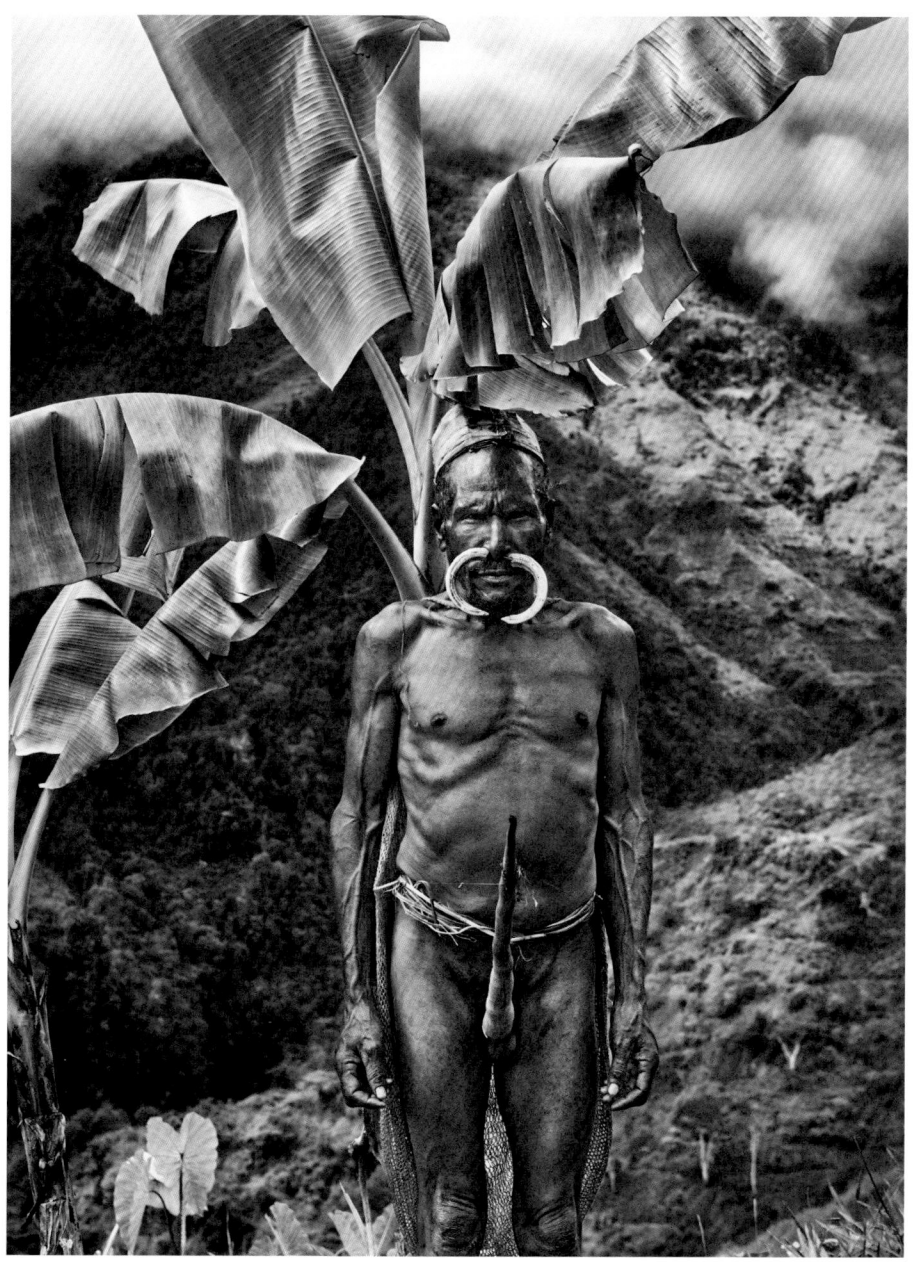

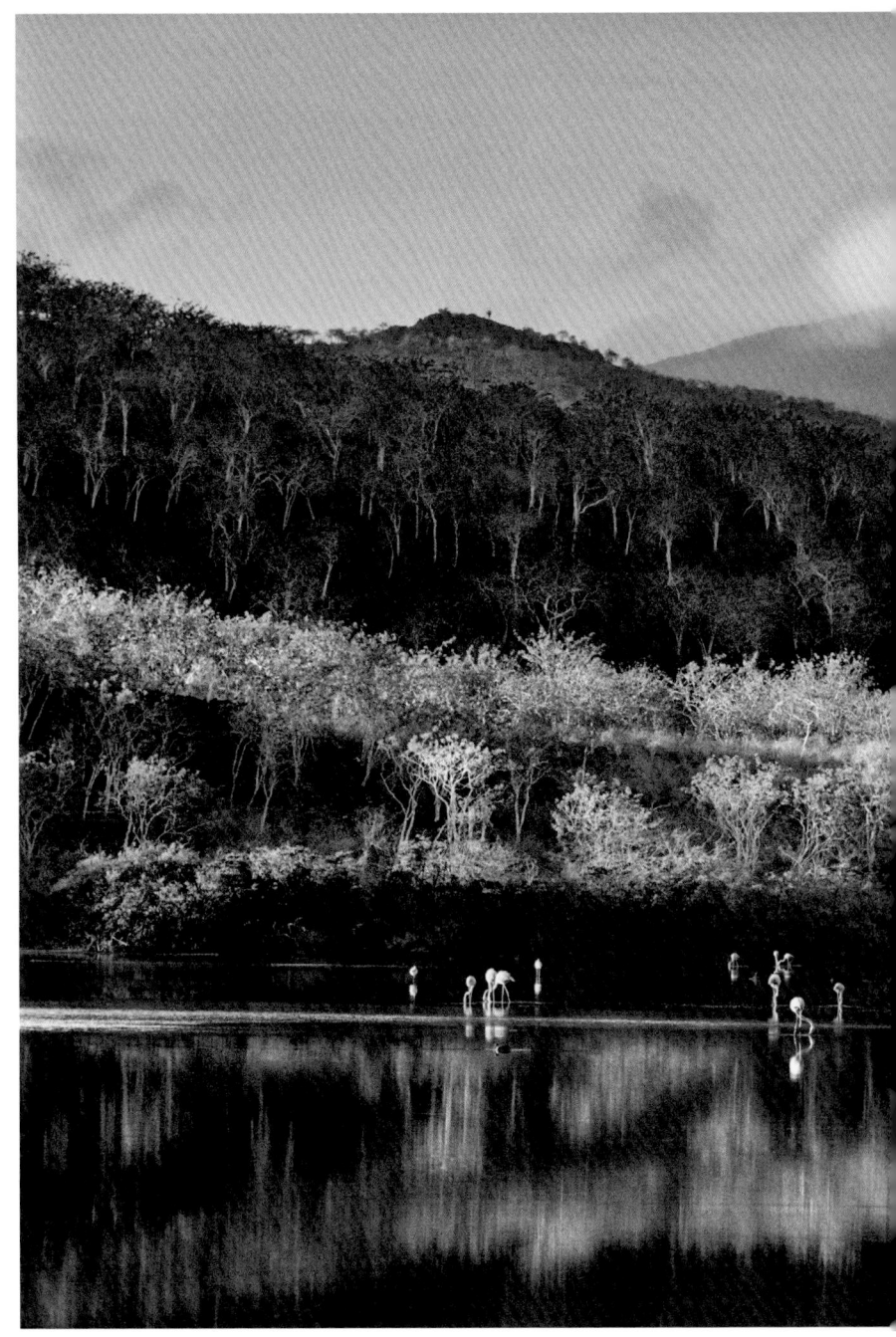

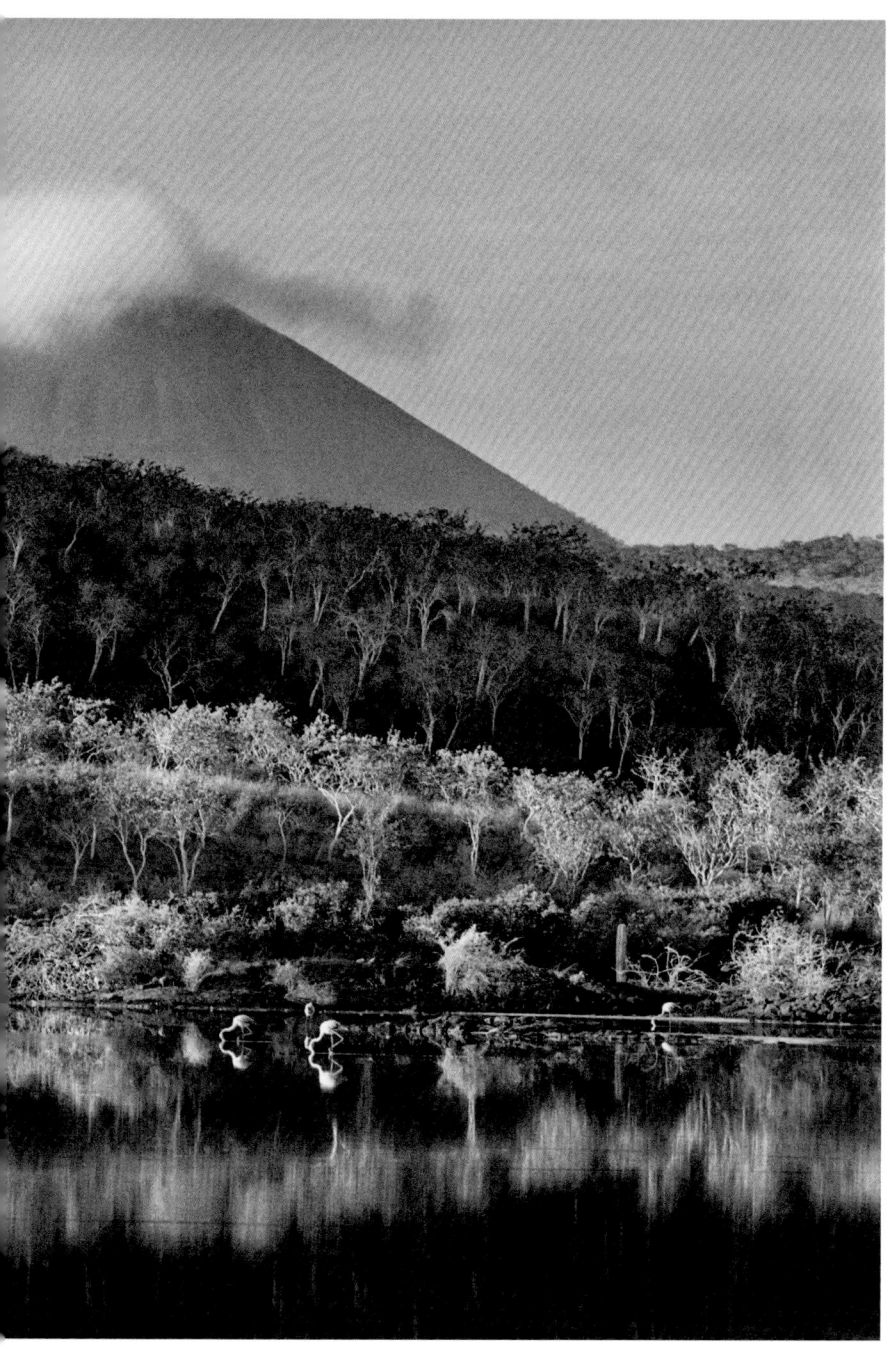

THE GALÁPAGOS

Pages 38, 42 through 49

The Galápagos, celebrated for their extraordinary number of rare endemic species, form an archipelago of volcanic islands in the Pacific some 605 miles (970 kilometers) west of Ecuador. Today, the islands and their surrounding waters form a national park and a biological marine reserve. But their importance was first drawn to the world's attention by the English naturalist Charles Darwin, who visited the Galápagos in 1835 during his round-the-world voyage on the HMS *Beagle*. His observations and the specimens he collected played a fundamental role in shaping his groundbreaking theory of evolution by natural selection.

Geologically speaking, the archipelago is still unstable. It is located on the Nazca Plate, a tectonic plate that is moving very gradually under the South American Plate to the east. It is thought that some islands were formed as far back as 90 million years ago, but they have since disappeared. The 15 main islands and three smaller islands visible today are much newer, dating back between one and five million years. In fact, two of the newest islands, Isabela, the archipelago's largest, and Fernandina, each barely a million years old, are still being formed by volcanic activity, with Fernandina's volcano having erupted as recently as April 2009. The Galápagos are spread over 17,000 square miles (45,000 square kilometers), with the most northern island 137 miles (220 kilometers) from the southernmost. They also vary enormously in size and altitude, some with peaks of up to 9,800 feet (3,000 meters), which has further added to the diversity of species on the different islands. But some generalizations are possible. Vegetation is usually to be found beside shores, saltwater lagoons, and boulder-strewn beaches, while protected coves and lagoons are dominated by mangrove swamps. Inland areas near sea level are arid, but fog banks throughout the night and into the morning provide humidity at higher elevations, even during the dry season. In some places, moisture is retained in temporary pools, allowing a fern-grass-sedge to grow in the upper reaches of some islands. The reptiles, insects, birds, and other animals found on the islands may at first sight appear familiar, but most belong to species endemic to the Galápagos. For instance, all the reptiles, except for two marine tortoises, are endemic. These include the Galápagos giant tortoise, the mon arch of the islands, with 11 subspecies found on different islands, all of which are endangered. Also endemic are terrestrial iguanas, marine iguanas, three racer species, several species of lava lizards and geckos. The variety of birds is no less extraordinary. There are, for example, 13 species of Darwin's finches, including the Floreana tree finch and the mangrove finch. Other noteworthy species include dark-rumped petrels, Galápagos flightless cormorants, Galápagos penguins, lava gulls, Floreana mockingbirds, Galápagos hawks, lava herons, nocturnal swallowtailed gulls, Galápagos rails, thick-billed flycatchers, Galápagos martins, and Galápagos doves. Six species of native mammal are also known: Galápagos fur seal, Galápagos sea lion, two species of rice rat, bat, and hoary bat. Marine fauna include several species of shark, ray, and cetacean, while green turtles and hawksbill turtles are also common, with green turtles nesting on sandy beaches.

Page 38: Marine iguana (*Amblyrhynchus cristatus*). Like other ectothermal reptiles, the marine iguana must regulate its own body temperature: as soon as the sun rises, it lies flat, warming as much body area as possible until the temperature reaches 95.9° Fahrenheit (35.5° Celsius); it then changes position to avoid overheating. The marine iguana needs a high body temperature in order to swim, to move about, and to digest. Galápagos. Ecuador. January, February, and March 2004.

Page 41: The Yali people live in West Papua's Jayawijaya mountain range, a stunningly rugged terrain, with rivers carving narrow gorges and steep-sided valleys. This remote and spectacular landscape shielded the Yali from contact with the modern world until Christian missionaries penetrated the area in the 1970s. But even now, like many isolated peoples, the Yali have what to outsiders seems like a charmingly simple life. Yali men wear traditional "skirts" composed of long strips of rattan, roughly a fifth of an inch (five millimeters) in width, which are wrapped around the midriff and then open out into a rustic skirt. The front is held up by a *koteka*, a penis cover made from a dried-out gourd. Ethnic groups can often be identified by the shape of the men's *koteka*. West Papua. Indonesia. September 2010.

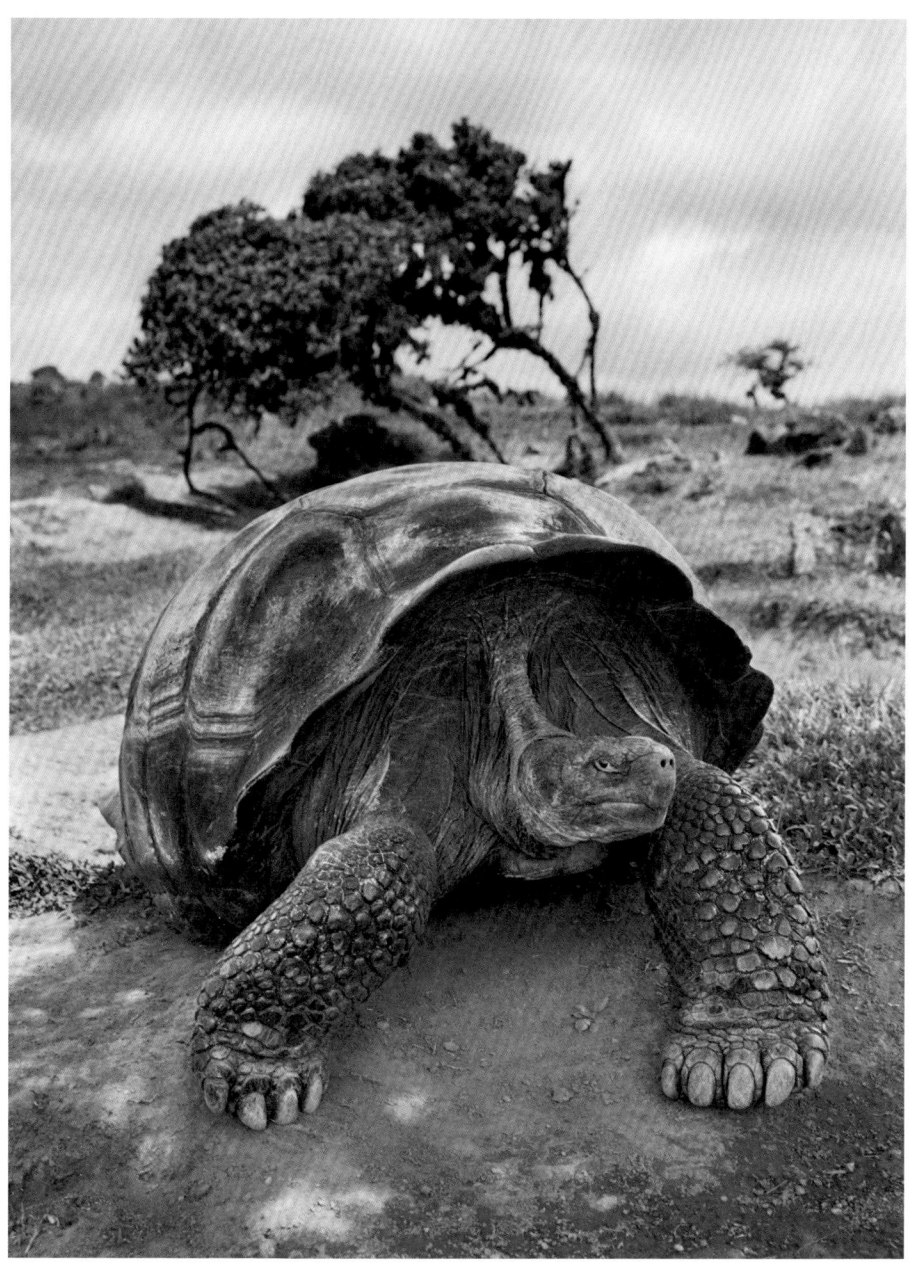

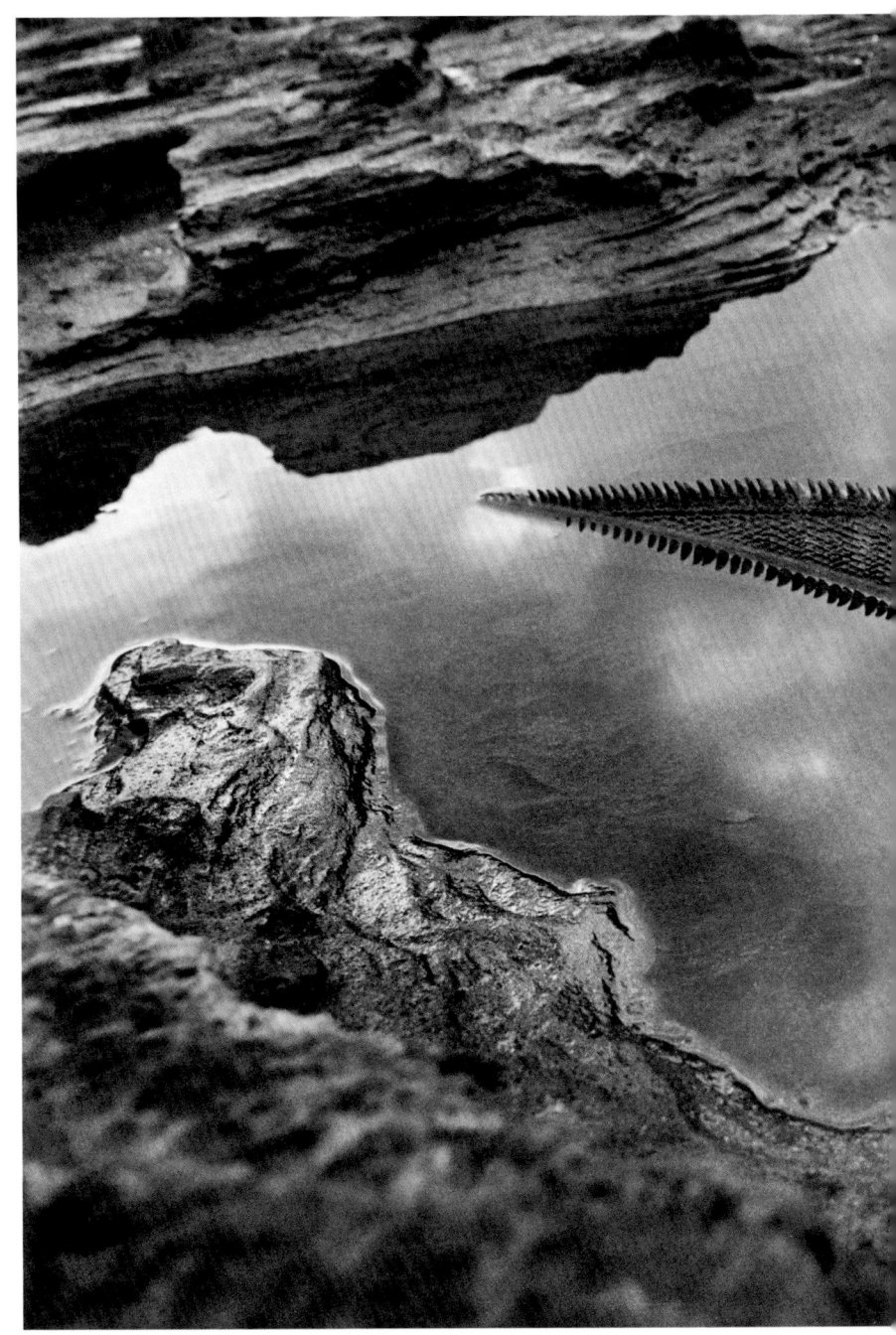

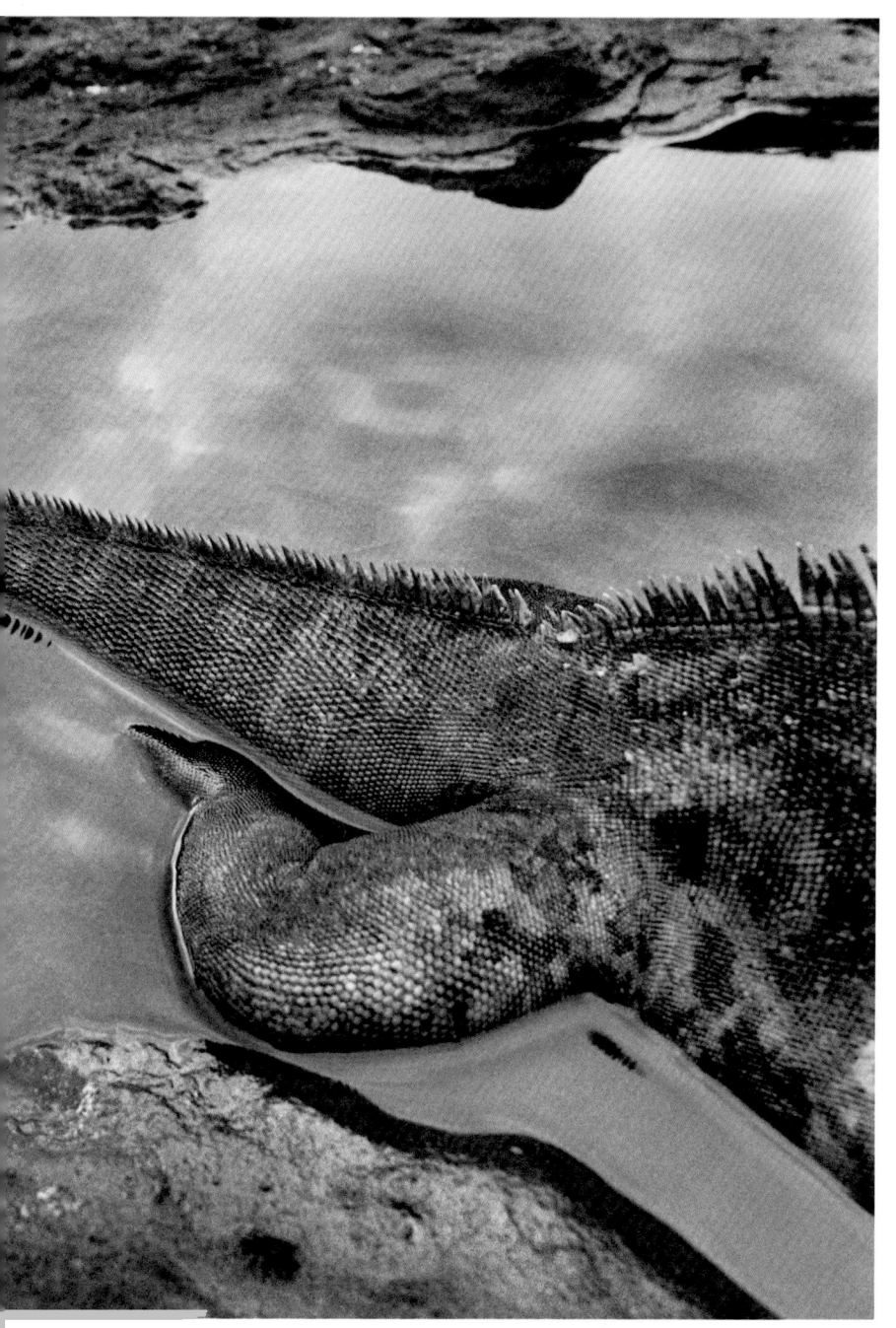

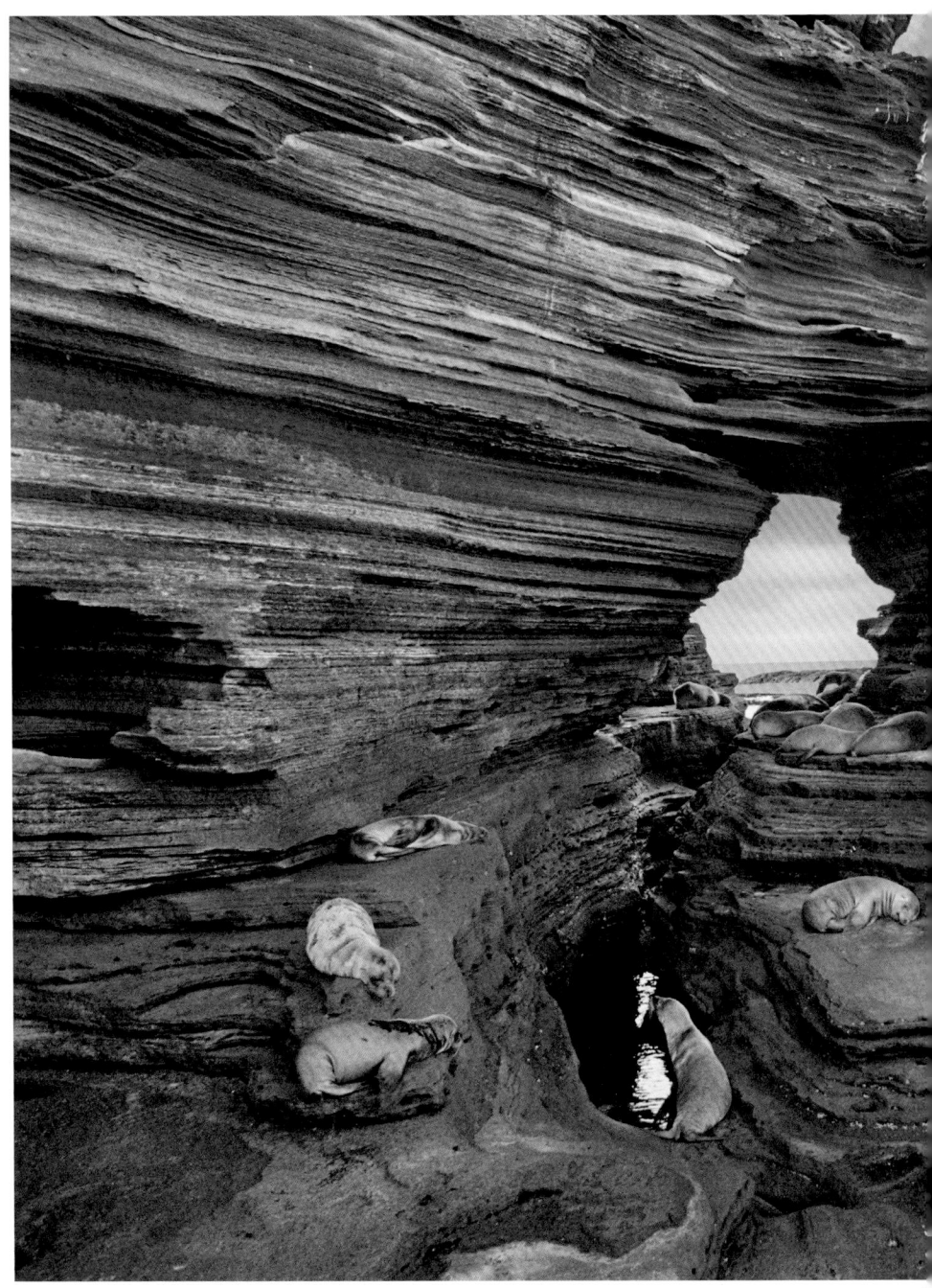

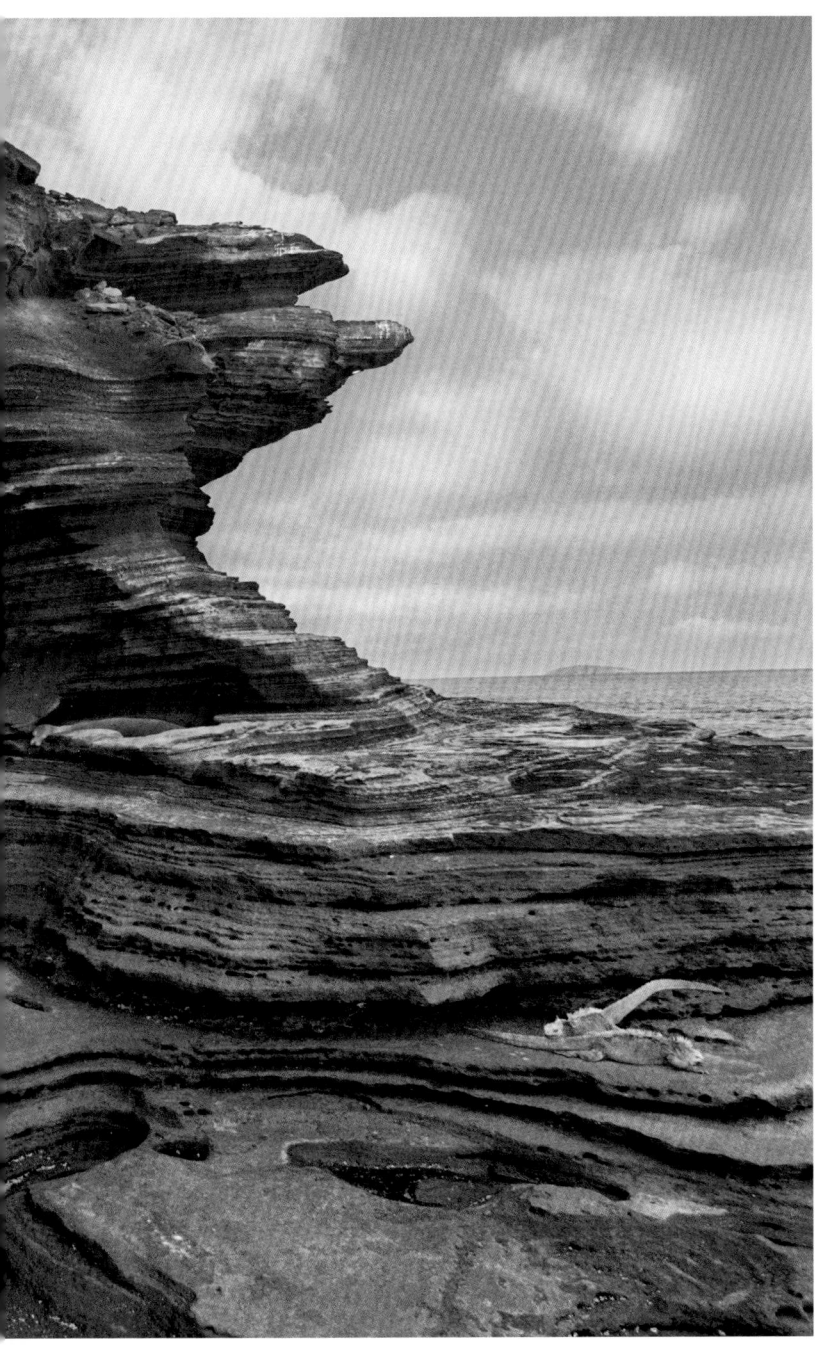

Pages 42/43: Punta Cormorant, Floreana Island. Despite its name, there are no cormorants in this area of the island. But I did find 21 greater flamingos (*Phoenicopterus ruber*) on a salty lagoon behind the beach. The flamingos fly from island to island, seeking out small lagoons where they can find their main food, water boatmen (*Trichocorixa reticulata*), and shrimp (*Artemia salina*). The greater flamingos' population in the Galápagos stands at around 500. Galápagos. Ecuador. January, February, and March 2004.

Page 45: Giant tortoise (*Geochelone elephantopus*) on the rim of the crater of Alcedo Volcano on Isabela Island. These antediluvian animals are in every way impressive: they may measure 5 feet (1.5 meters) and weigh up to 550 pounds (250 kilos); they can live for more than 150 years; and, outside the mating season, they choose to live in solitude. While their tiny young, weighing just 3 ounces, 80 grams, at birth, are easy prey for hawks (*Buteo galapagoensis*), the giant tortoises have no predators today. But in the 18th and 19th centuries, they were hunted mercilessly by pirates, whalers, sealers, and settlers to the point that, on some islands where they were once numerous, they were completely exterminated. Their value aboard ship was that they could survive for a long time without food or water and provided fresh meat when none was available. Galápagos. Ecuador. January, February, and March 2004.

Pages 46/47: Marine iguana (*Amblyrhynchus cristatus*). This animal is a perfect example of adaptation and evolution. The first marine iguanas apparently came to the archipelago from the American mainland, almost 620 miles (1,000 kilometers) to the east. They were probably transported by sea currents atop tree trunks, pieces of land with foliage, and other objects floating on the water and, once here, they were forced to adapt to local conditions. A smaller number of these migrants remained land iguanas and can be found on only a few islands, but the majority evolved into marine animals: they learned to swim, to feed on seaweed, to dive, and to remain submerged for long stretches; they even developed special glands to excrete excess salt from their food intake. It is the only type of iguana in the world able to live in salty waters. Galápagos. Ecuador. January, February, and March 2004.

Pages 48/49: Sea lions (*Zalophus californianus*) at Puerto Egas in James Bay. Santiago Island. The Galápagos sea lion is one of the largest of the archipelago's animals, weighing up to 550 pounds (250 kilos), although it is still smaller than the sea lions of California, where it originated. This group is resting in the shadow of beautiful rocks formed by piled and compacted volcanic ash; these formations, known as tuff, are rather soft and are easily eroded by the wind and sea. Galápagos. Ecuador. January, February, and March 2004.

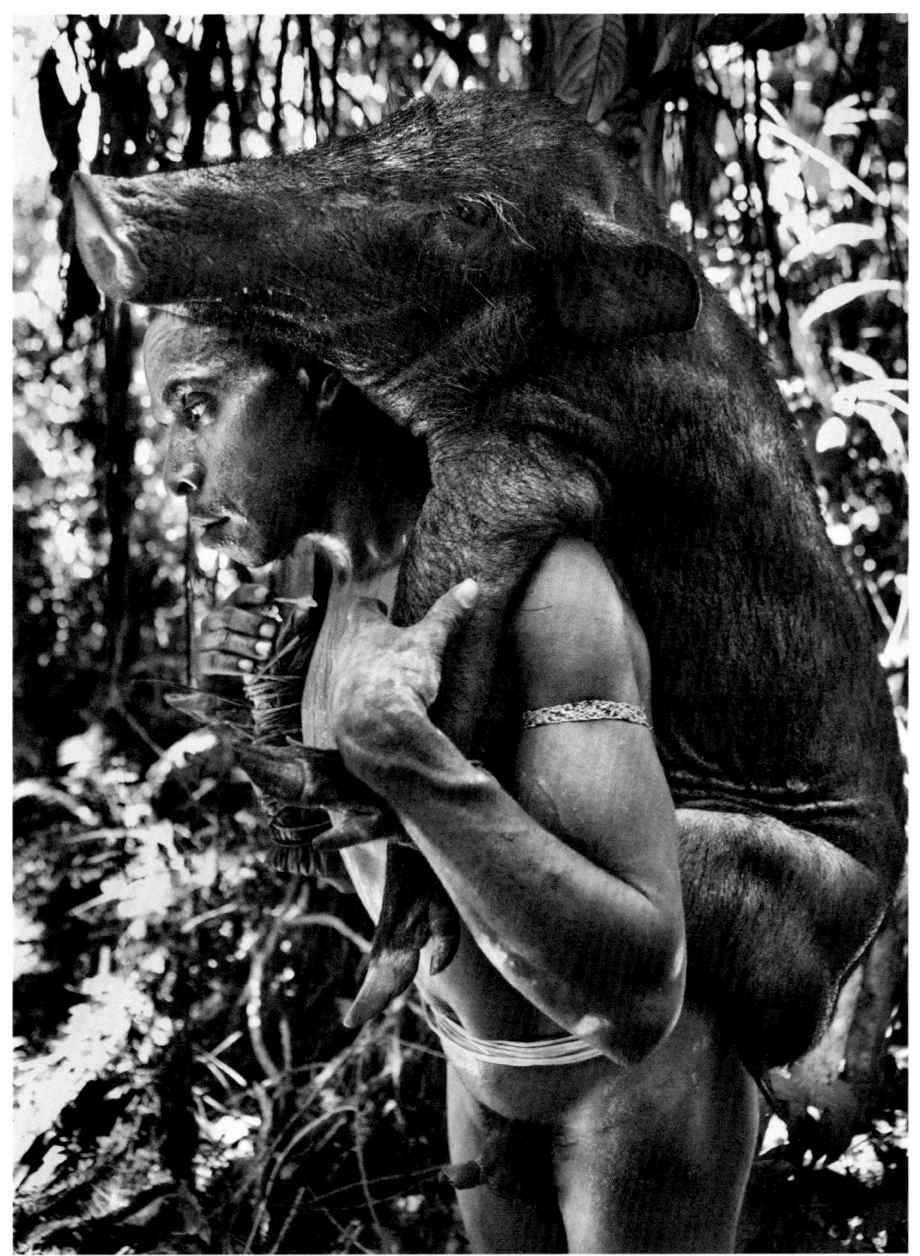

ETHNIC GROUPS OF IRIAN JAYA, INDONESIA

Pages 41, 51 through 62

West Papua, which was known as Irian Jaya until 2000, is the Indonesian-ruled western half of the island of New Guinea, one of the most pristine refuges for ancient human settlements on Earth. The independent state of Papua New Guinea, occupying the eastern half of the island, is also of great ethnographic significance. The western half has a population of some three million, dominated by ethnic Papuans, Melanesians, and Austronesians, but also embracing numerous traditional groups living in dense forests and inaccessible mountains, among these the Korowai, who lived in total isolation until the 1970s. In fact, while Indonesian is the official language, spoken in towns and major cities like Jayapura (renamed Port Numbay), estimates of the number of Indigenous languages still spoken in the region range from 200 to over 700, with Dani, Yali, Ekari and Biak among the most widely used.

The Netherlands granted Indonesia independence in 1949, but held on to the western half of this island as Dutch New Guinea until 1962. This explains why the predominant religion is Christianity (often combined with traditional beliefs), followed by Islam. For many years after Indonesia took over the territory, West Papua faced a violent separatist movement, but some calm has returned since the Jakarta government promised greater regional autonomy. The province's main industries include agriculture, fishing, oil production and mining.

Page 51: The Korowai spend their days in the forest collecting all they need to survive. Since wild pigs are a delicacy difficult to find, the Korowai eat almost any animal, as well as insects and fruit. West Papua. Indonesia. February and March 2010.

Opposite: Yali women wear a bag woven from orchid fibers. The bag, whether empty or in use, covers the woman's back and bottom and may even reach her knees. West Papua. Indonesia. September 2010.

Pages 54/55: The Korowai live in small family groups in tree houses, usually between 20 and 80 feet (6 and 25 meters) above the ground. However, when there is a dispute with neighbors or a nearby community, security demands that tree houses are built at heights of up to 130 feet (40 meters). West Papua. Indonesia. February and March 2010.

Pages 56/57: As this father and daughter demonstrate, the most important items of clothing for the Yali are skirts for the women and *kotekas*, or penis gourds, for the men. The skirts consist of four layers. The first layer is given to a girl when she is around four, with an extra layer added every four years. With four layers in place around the age of 16, the girl is ready to be married. As to the *koteka*, stone weights are tied to the bottom of the dried gourd to stretch it. String is also used to give it different shapes. It is sometimes waxed with beeswax or native resins and can be painted and decorated with shells and feathers. West Papua. Indonesia. September 2010.

Pages 58/59: The diet of the Yali people is composed of a large variety of vegetables. The most important is sweet potato, which is cultivated everywhere. There are individual and collective plantations of sweet potato. They also grow tarot, cassava, banana, and pandanus and collect insects and leaves from many different trees. The women carry large bags woven from orchid fibers, in which they put all they collect during the day. West Papua. Indonesia. September 2010.

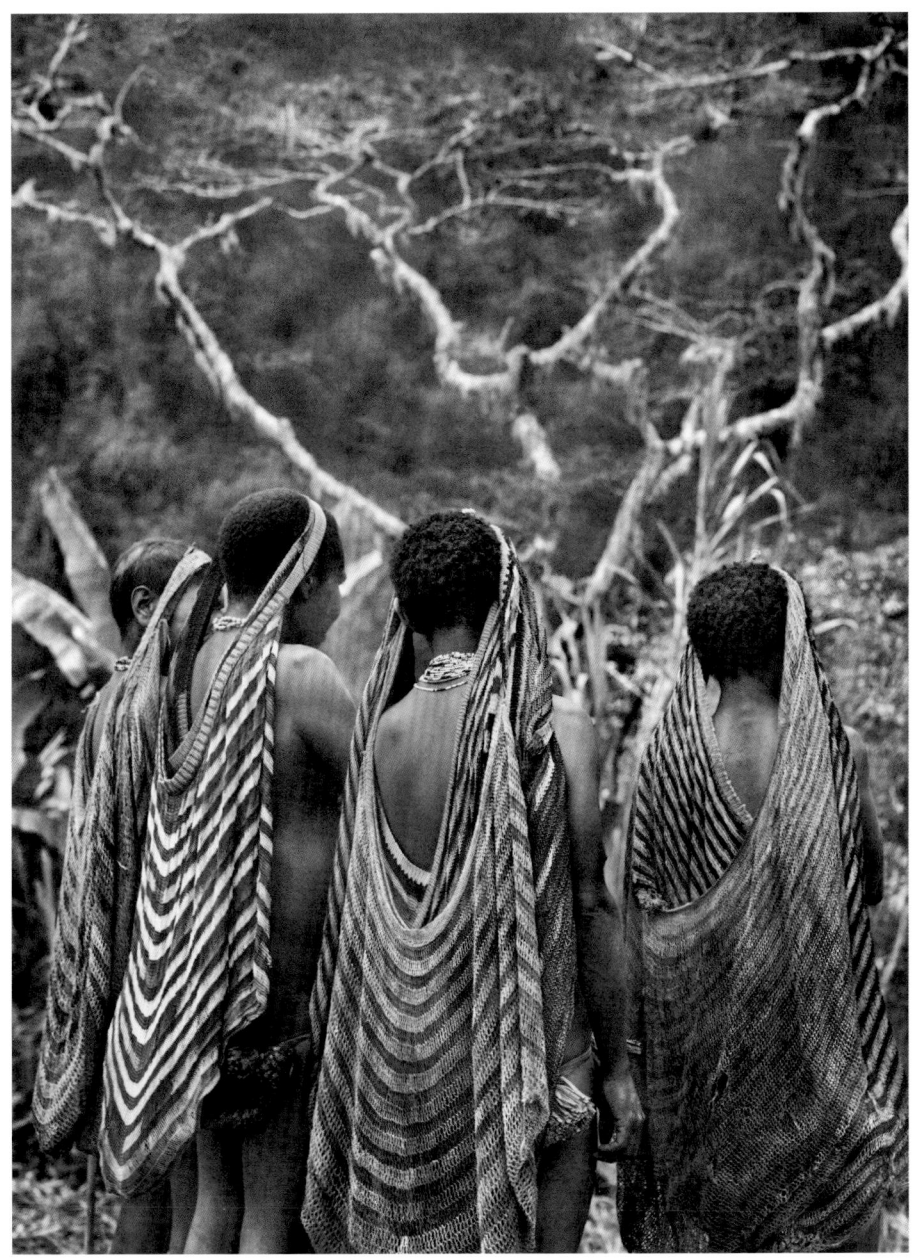

53

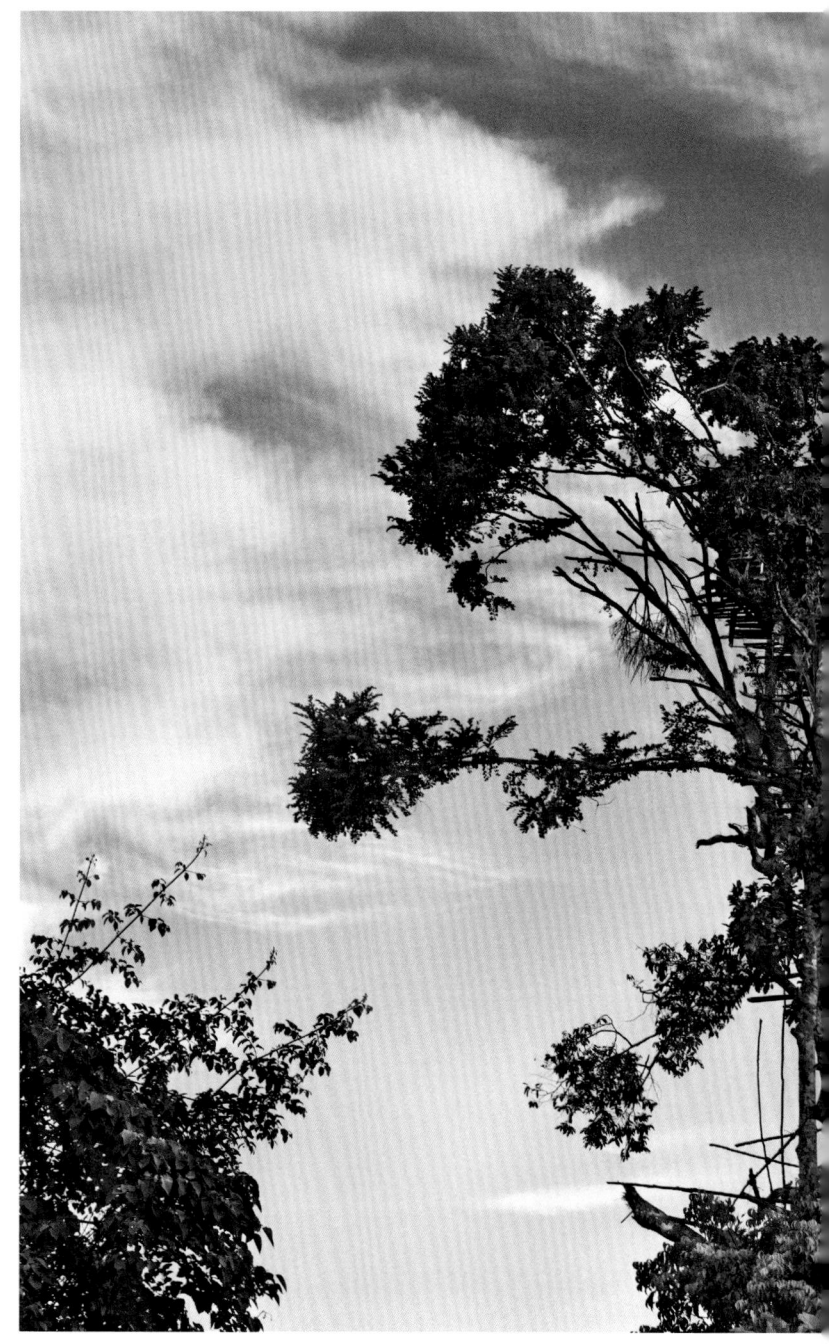

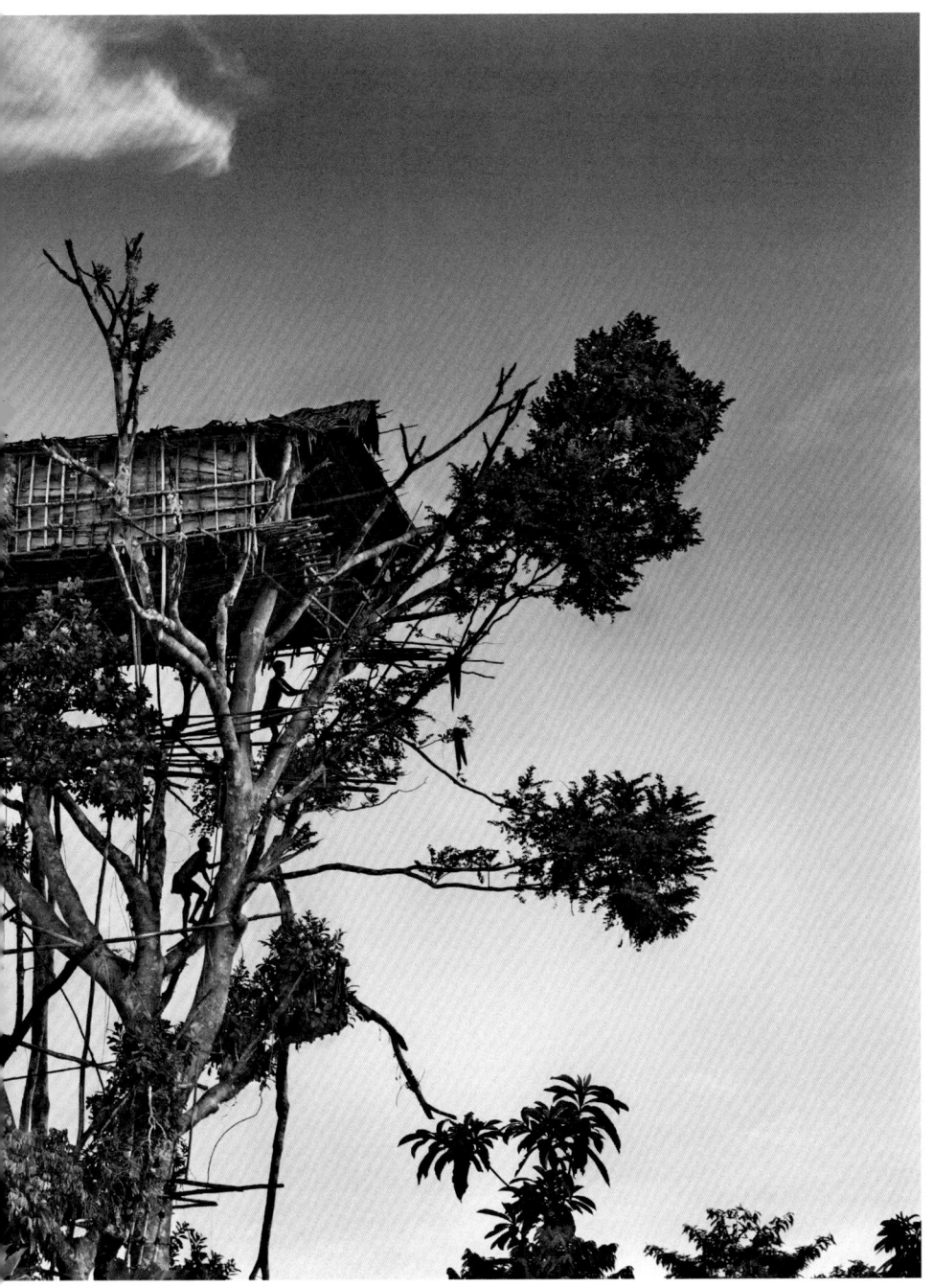

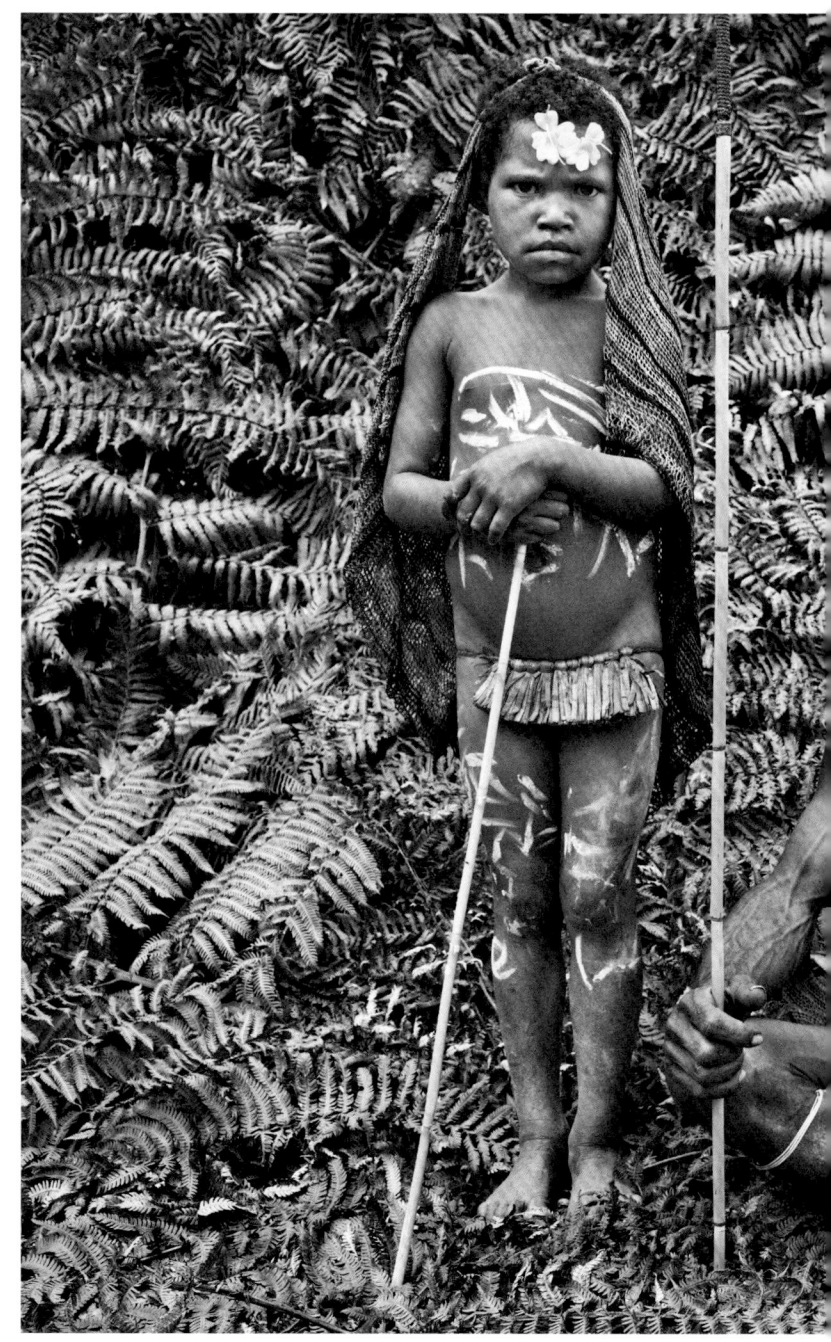

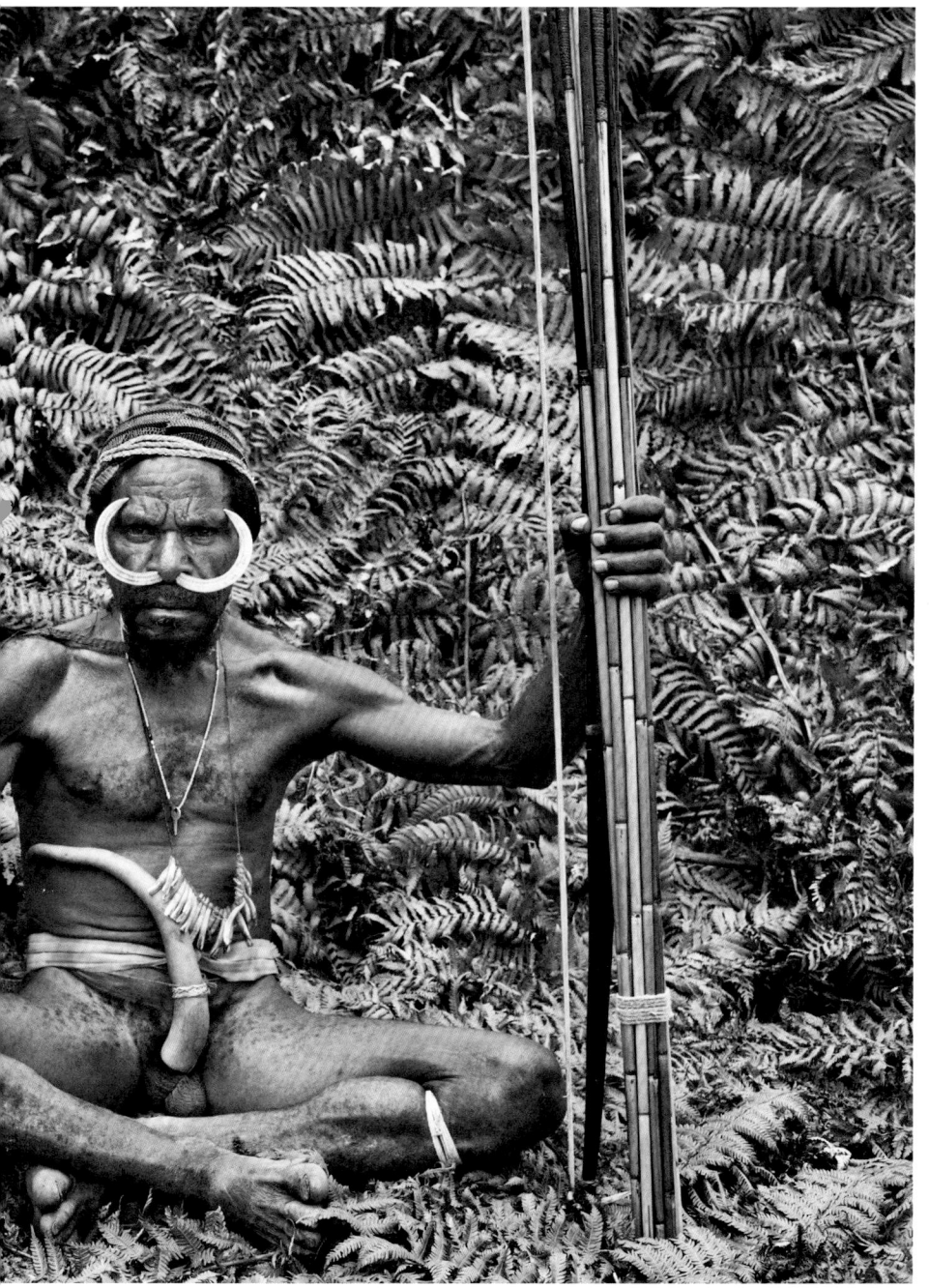

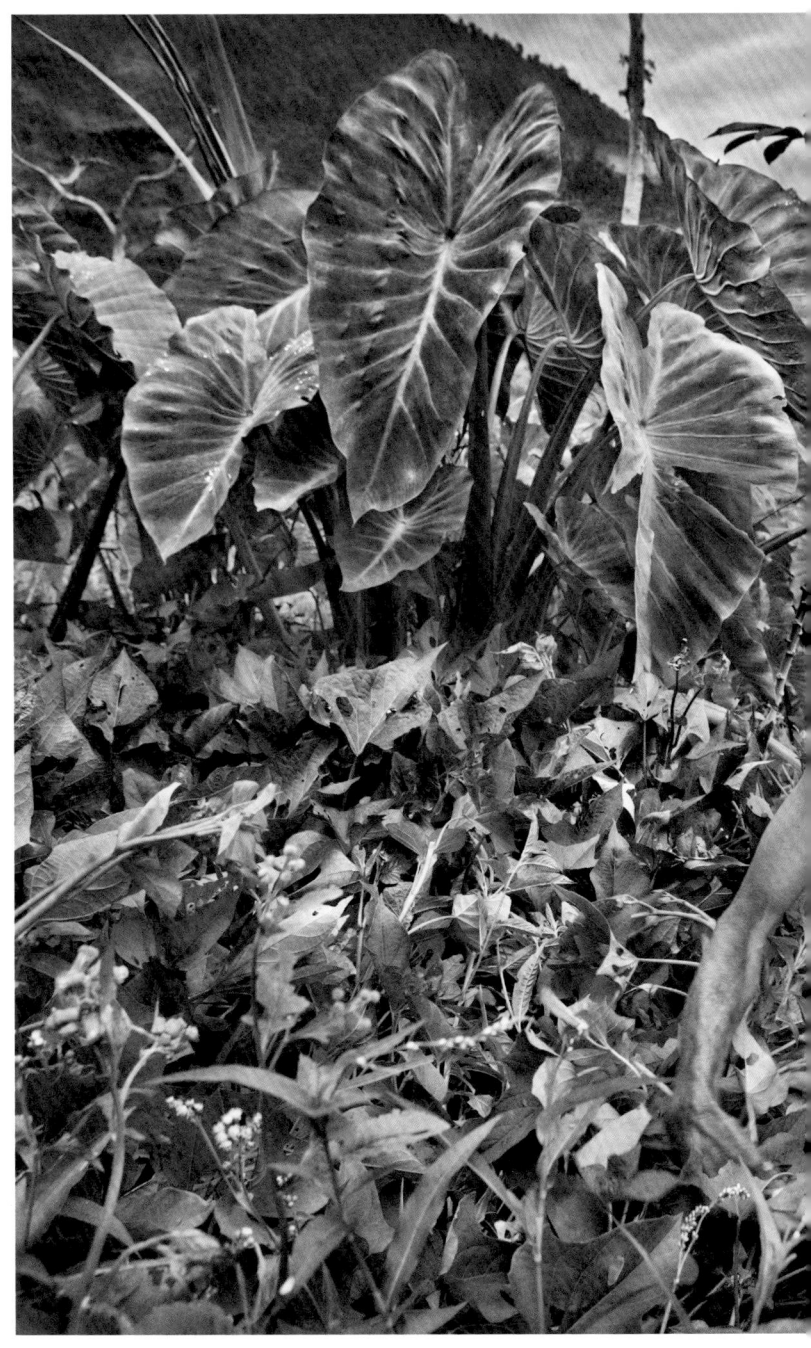

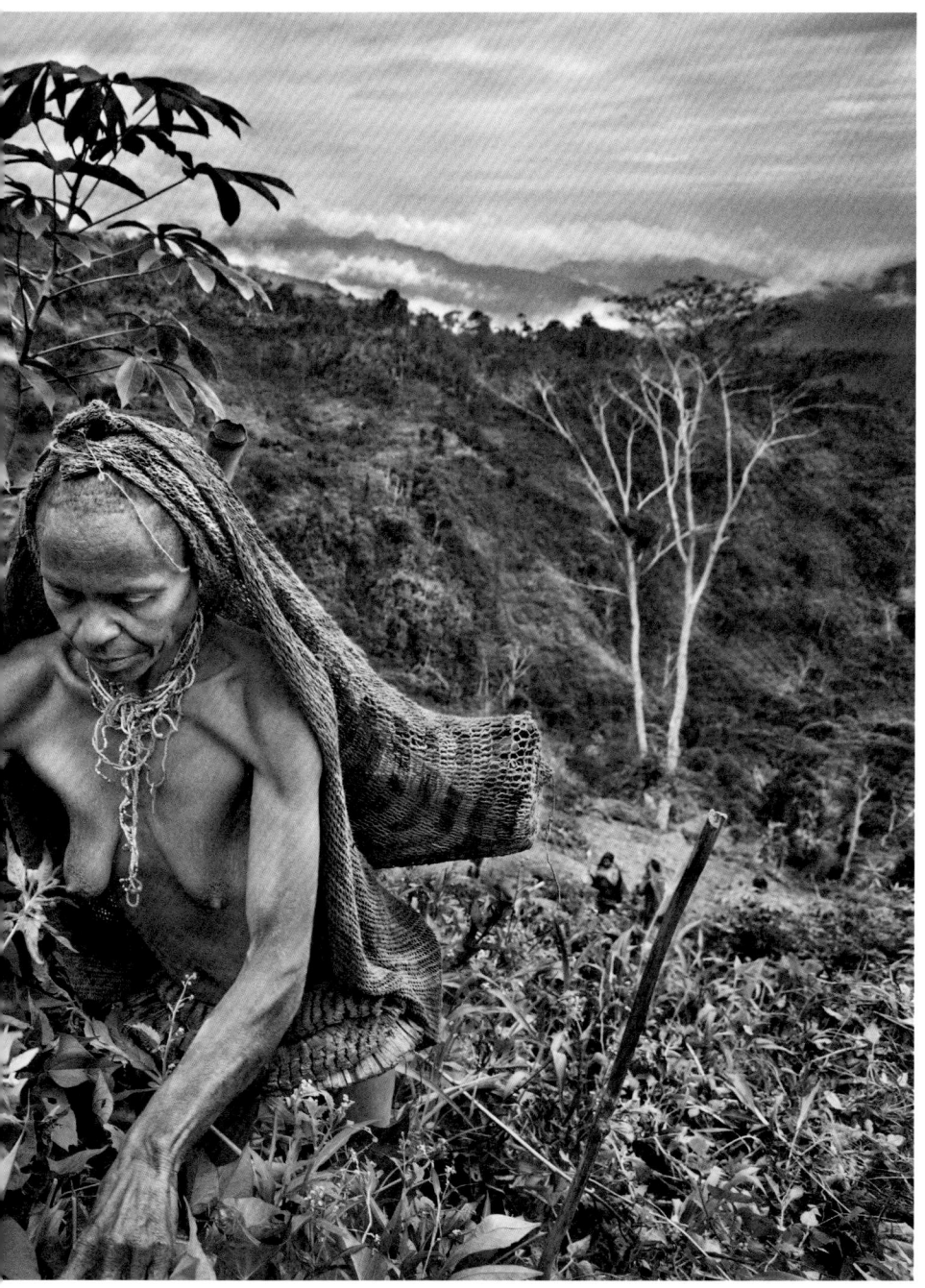

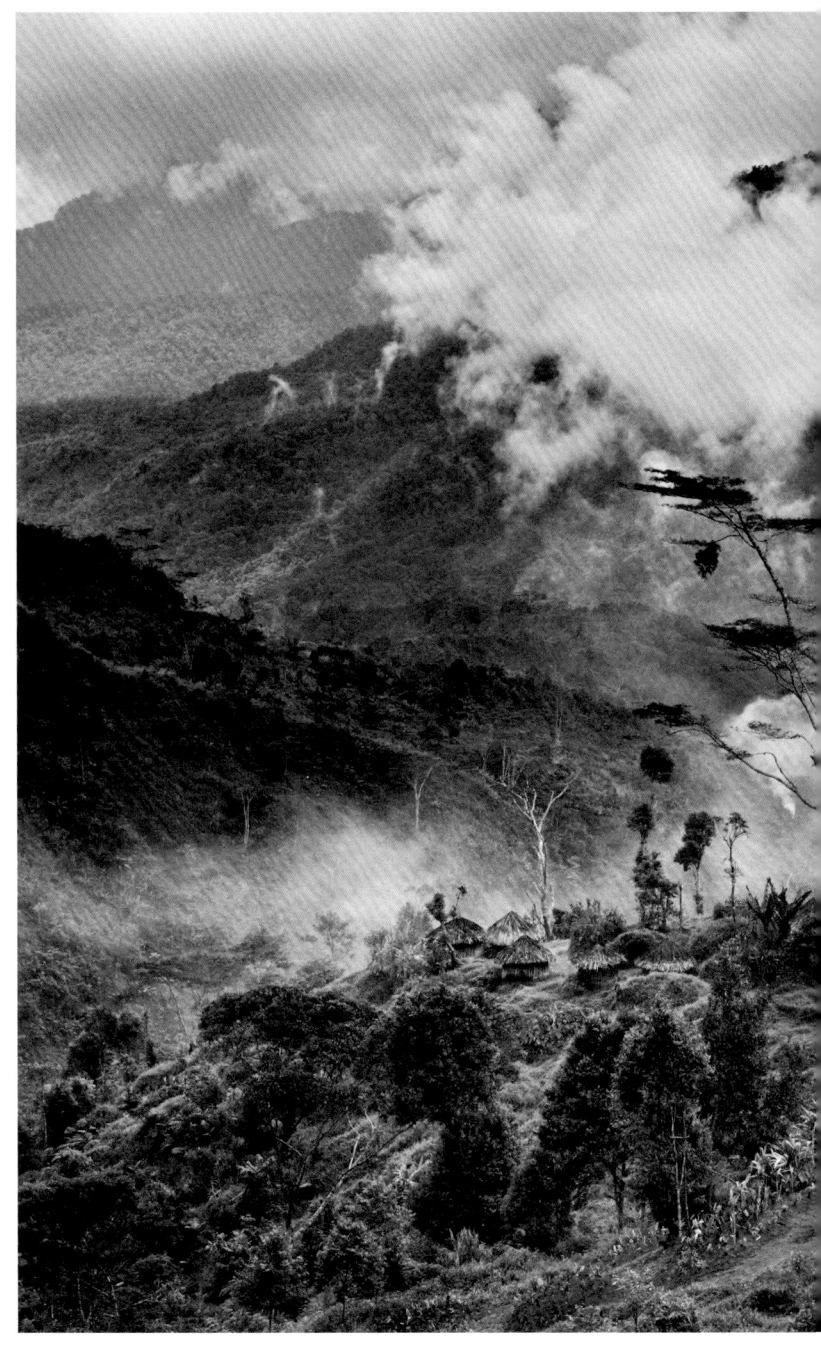

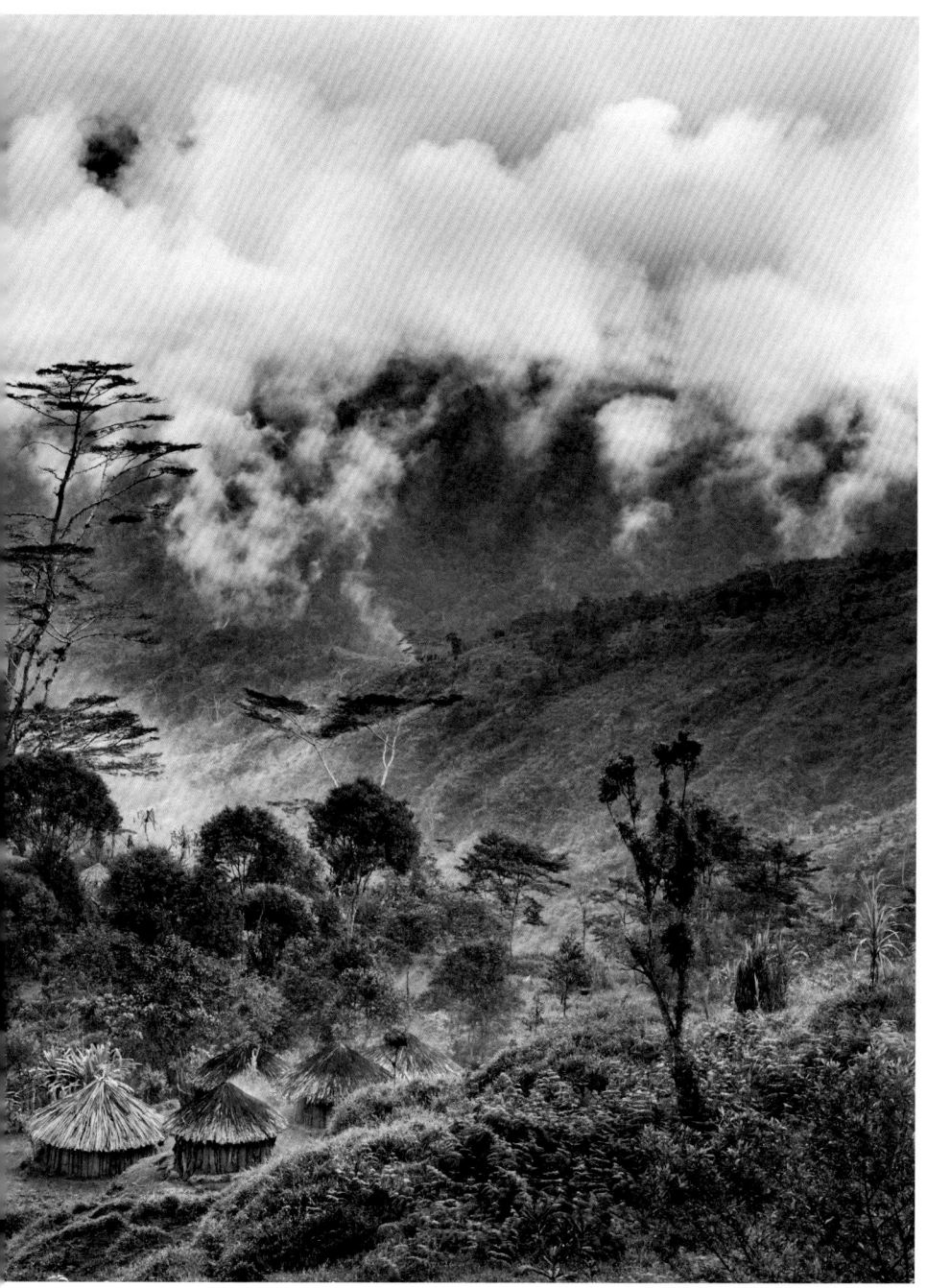

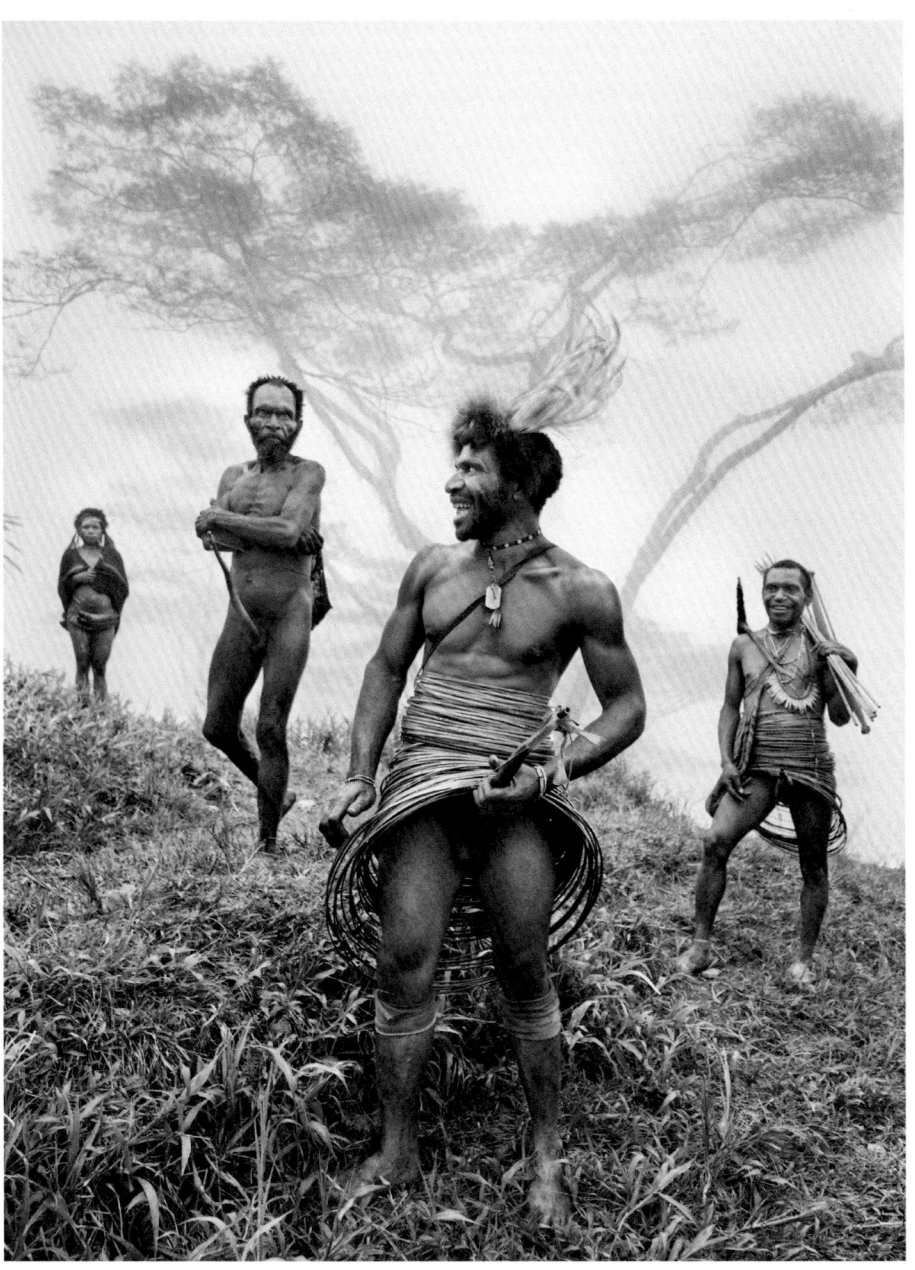

MADAGASCAR

Pages 60/61: In the mountains of West Papua, the Yali build round wooden huts, with roofs covered with pandan leaves. Women live separately in their own houses, while men live in community houses, known as *honai*. Yali settlements are traditionally located on ridgetops because, in the past, this offered some protection from enemies. This remote and spectacular landscape shielded the Yali from contact with the modern world until Christian missionaries penetrated the area in the 1970s. But even now, like many isolated peoples, the Yali have what to outsiders seems like a charmingly simple life. West Papua. Indonesia. September 2010.

Opposite: Men from several of New Guinea's ethnic groups, in the main those living in the highlands, cover and protect their genitals with the *koteka*, or penis gourd, usually made from a dried fruit, such as a calabash (*Lagenaria siceraria*) or a common swamp pitcher-plant (*Nepenthes mirabilis*). This is held in place by a small loop of fiber attached to the base of the *koteka* and placed around the scrotum. Another fiber wrapped around the chest or abdomen is attached to the main body of the *koteka*. The men in one group will usually wear similar *kotekas*: for example, the Yali favor a long, thin *koteka*, which holds up the rattan hoops worn around their waist. Other groups opt for different shapes and angles: pointed, straight out, straight up, at an angle, or in other directions. In practice, though, there is no correlation between the size or length of the *koteka* and the man's social status. West Papua. Indonesia. September 2010.

Pages 64 through 78
Located in the Indian Ocean off the southern coast of Africa, Madagascar is the world's fourth-largest island. This isolation explains its privileged place in nature, comparable in its endemic species, and diversity with a small continent. Scientists have defined it as a biological "hotspot" of great importance since most of its plant and animal species are endemic to the island. This endemism is accompanied by what experts define as a megadiversity of natural life. Lemurs are Madagascar's most famous flagship species, with 50 different kinds found only here. The island has three broad geographic zones. These are the highlands, a plateau region in the center of the island ranging in altitude from 2,200 to 4,500 feet (762 to 1,372 meters) above sea level; a narrow and steep escarpment that runs the length of the eastern coast and contains much of the island's remaining tropical rainforest; and a wide, dry plain that slopes gently from the western boundaries of the highlands toward the Mozambique Channel.

Today, Madagascar's rich ecosystems are highly endangered, due largely to incessant and numerous fires, for which a fast-growing population is largely responsible. But widespread agriculture, rice-growing and cattle-raising are also damaging the island's delicate ecosystems. Furthermore, large forested areas are regularly cut to provide firewood and charcoal for cooking. The central plateau region, for instance, is now almost entirely deforested. Surviving natural habitats are now to be found mainly in coastal areas to the east, west, and south. It is probable that 90 percent of Madagascar's natural forest has already been lost.

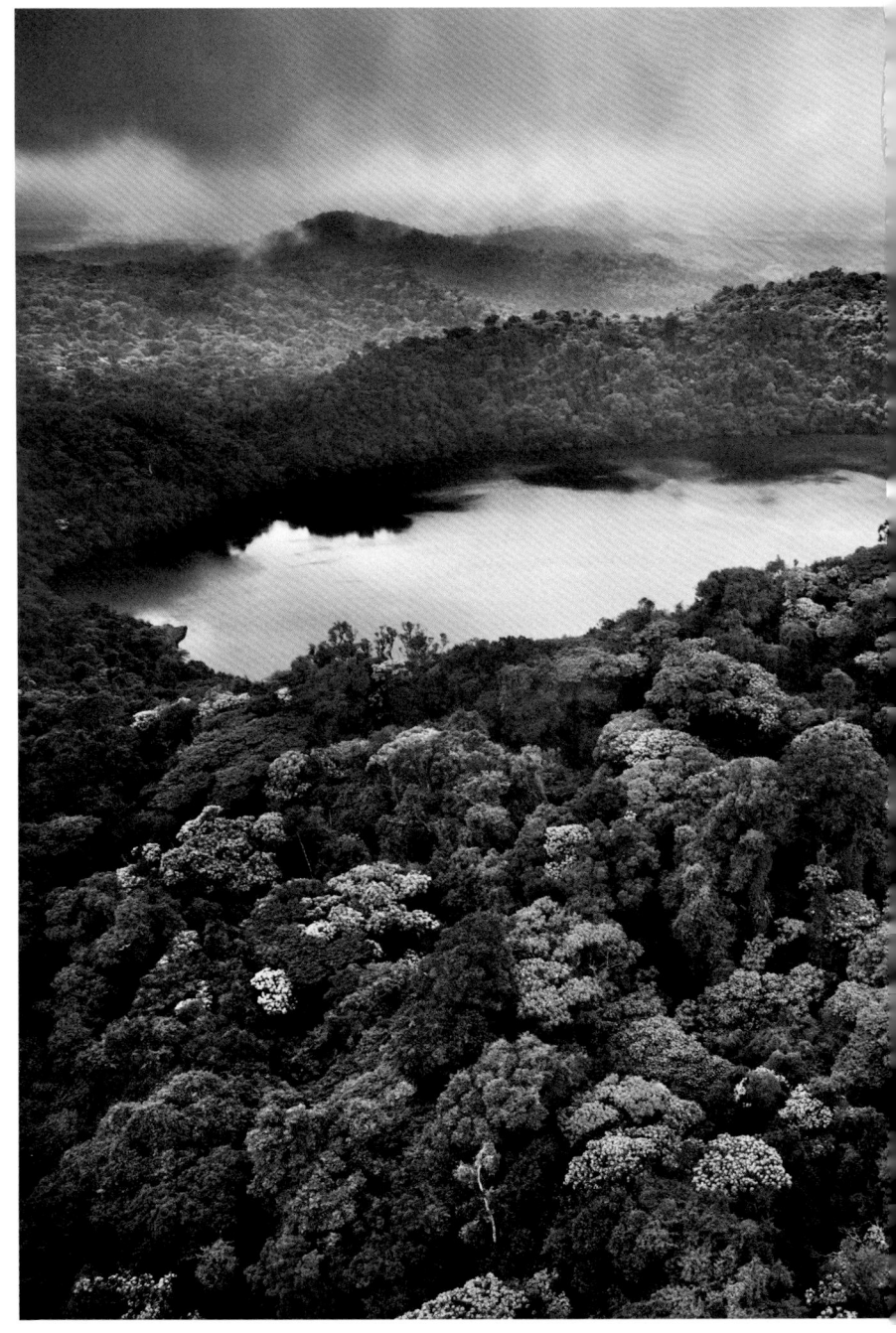

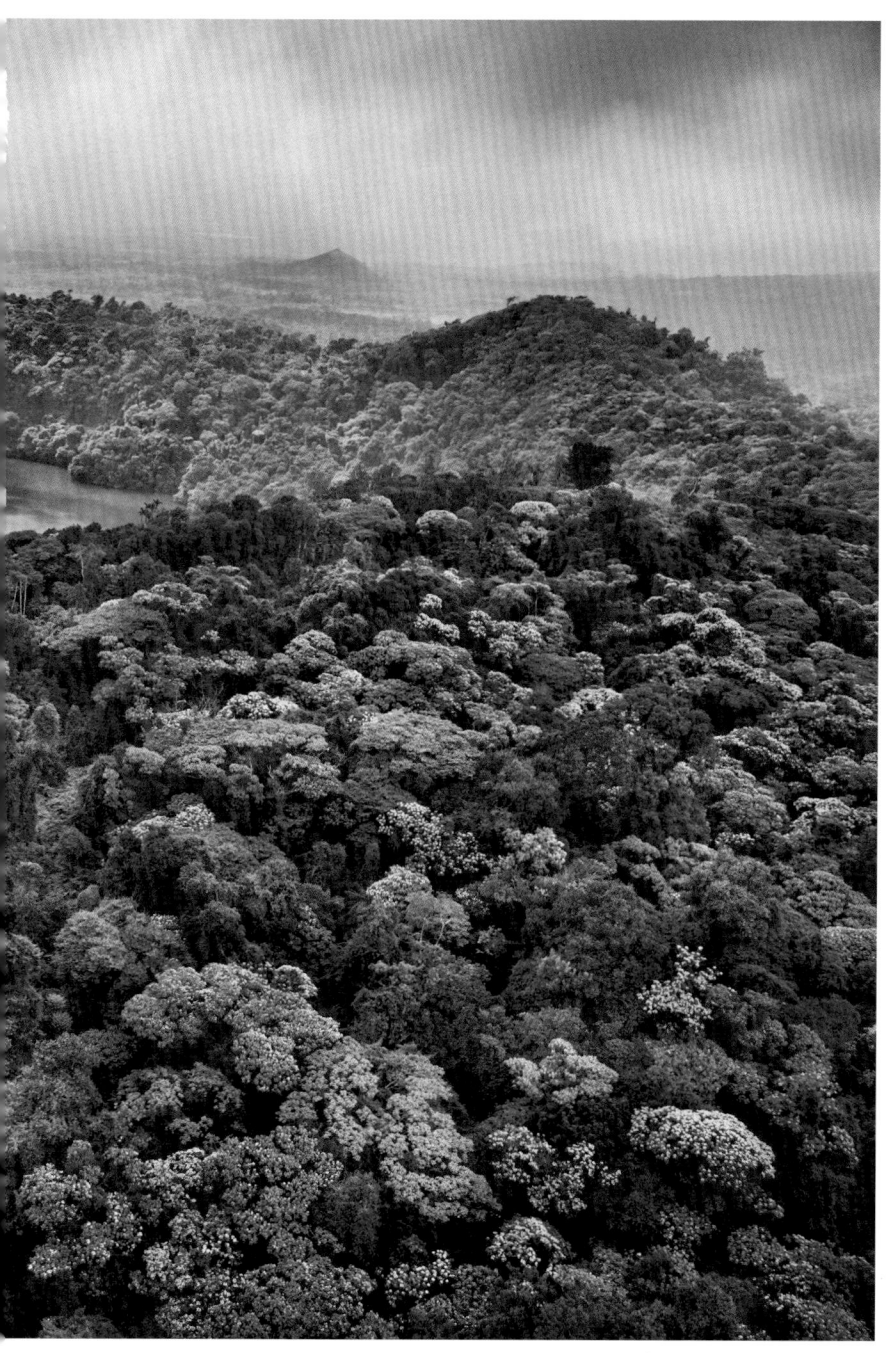

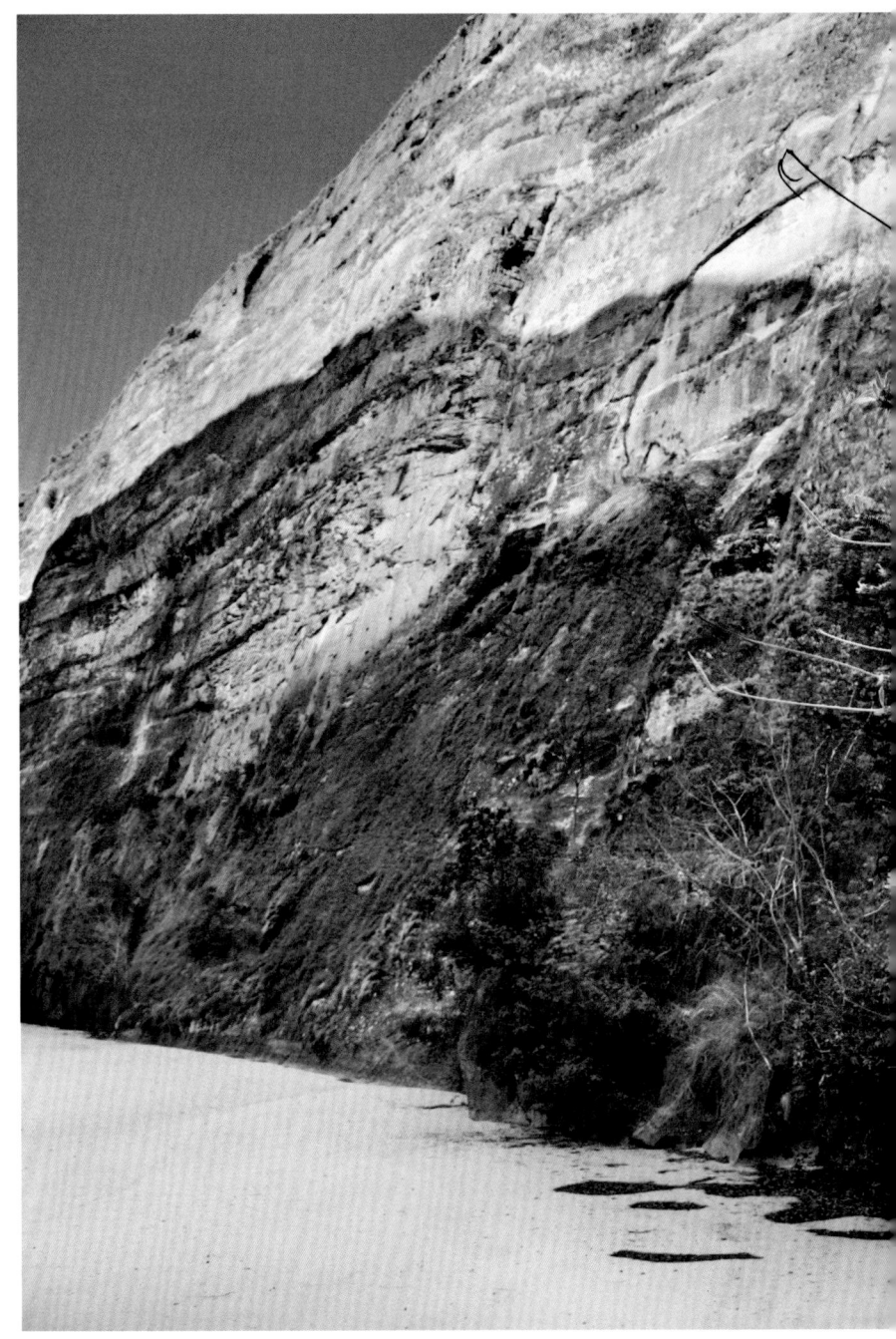

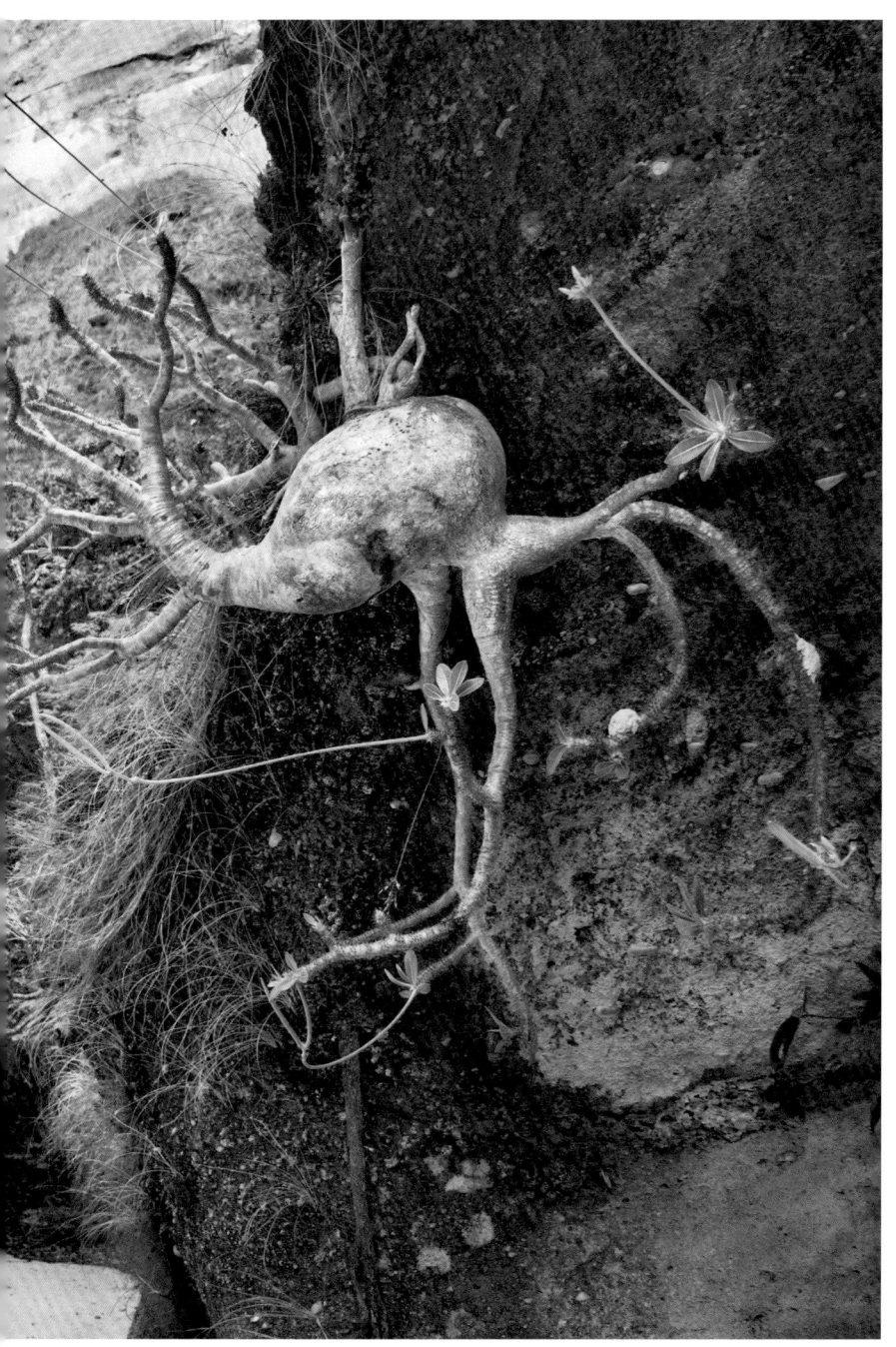

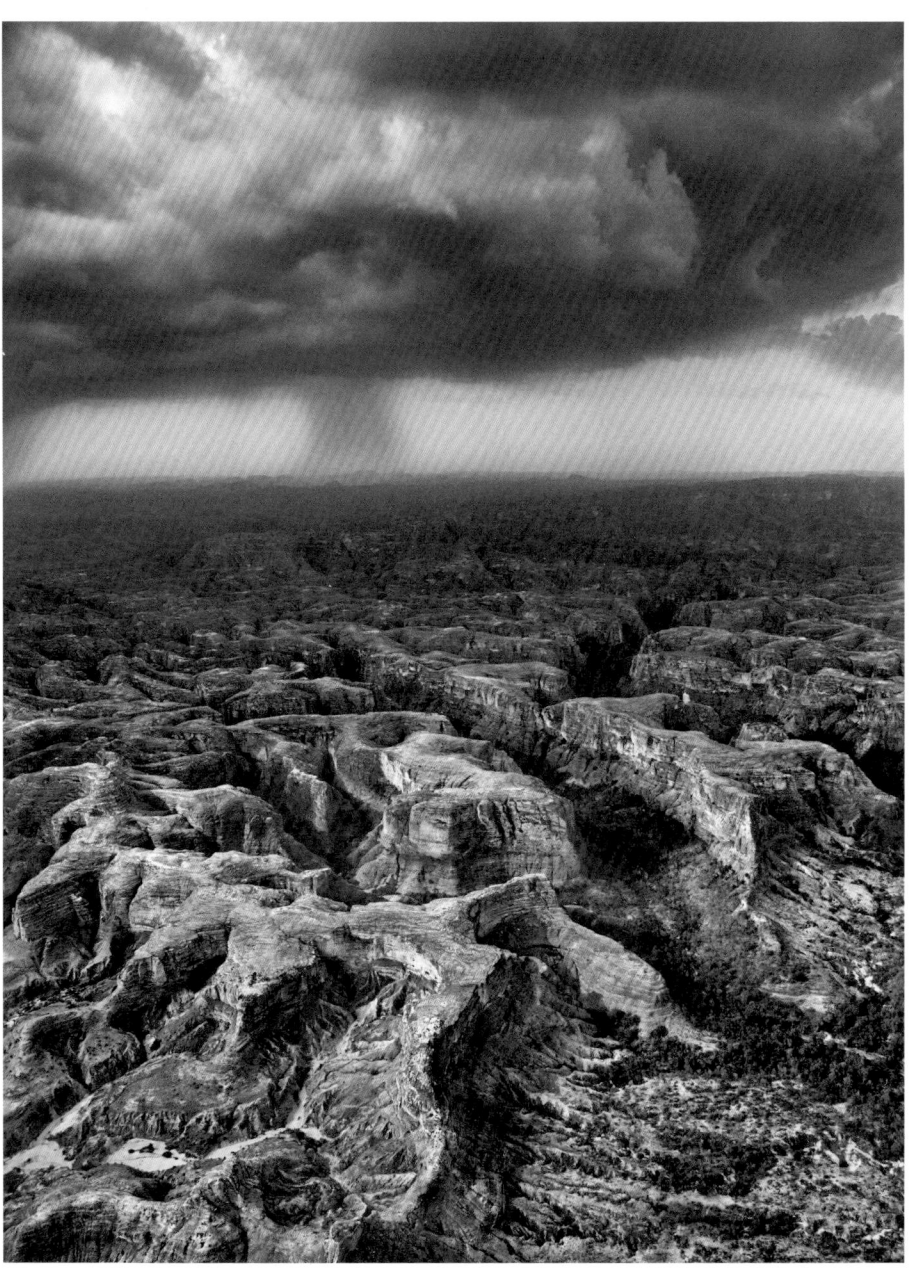

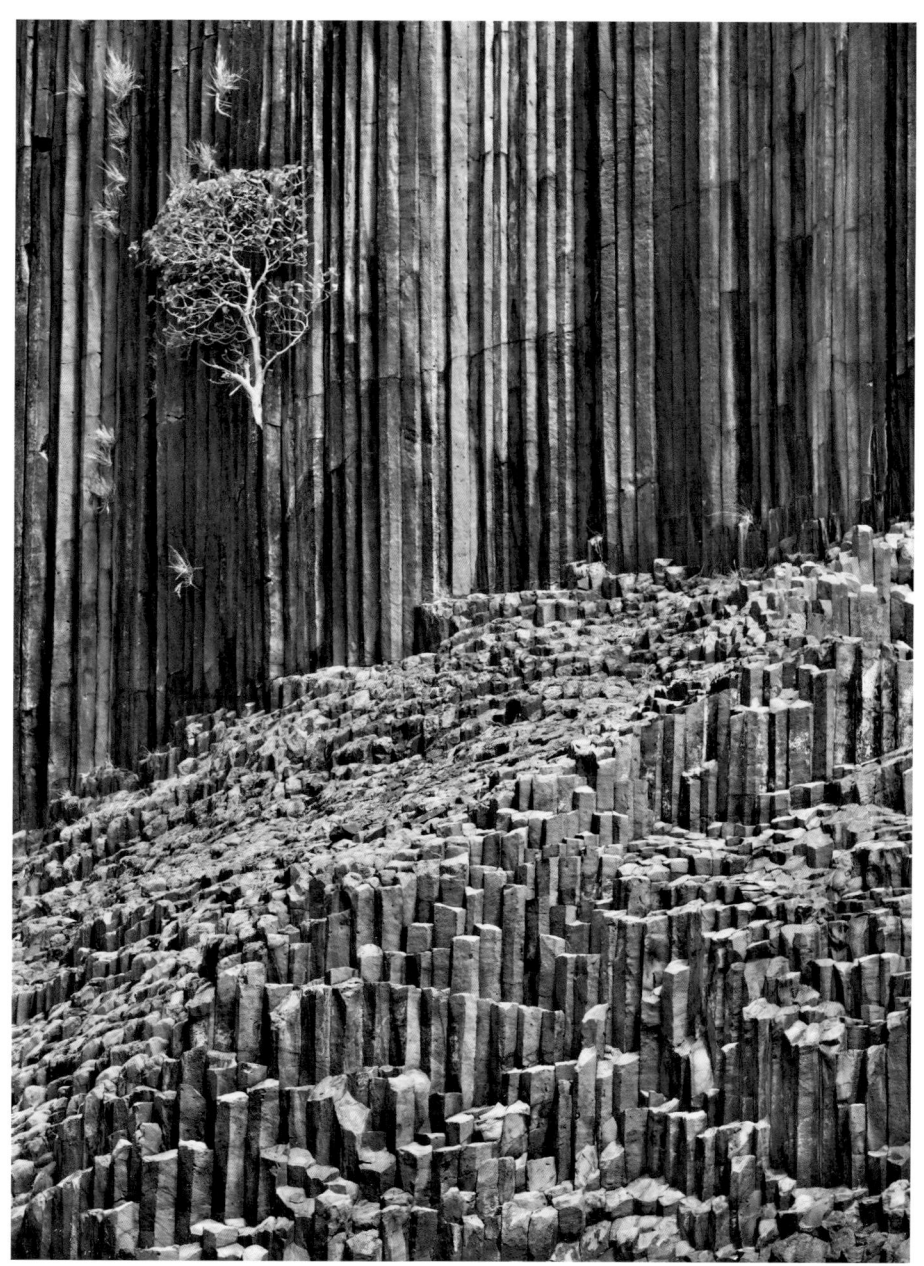

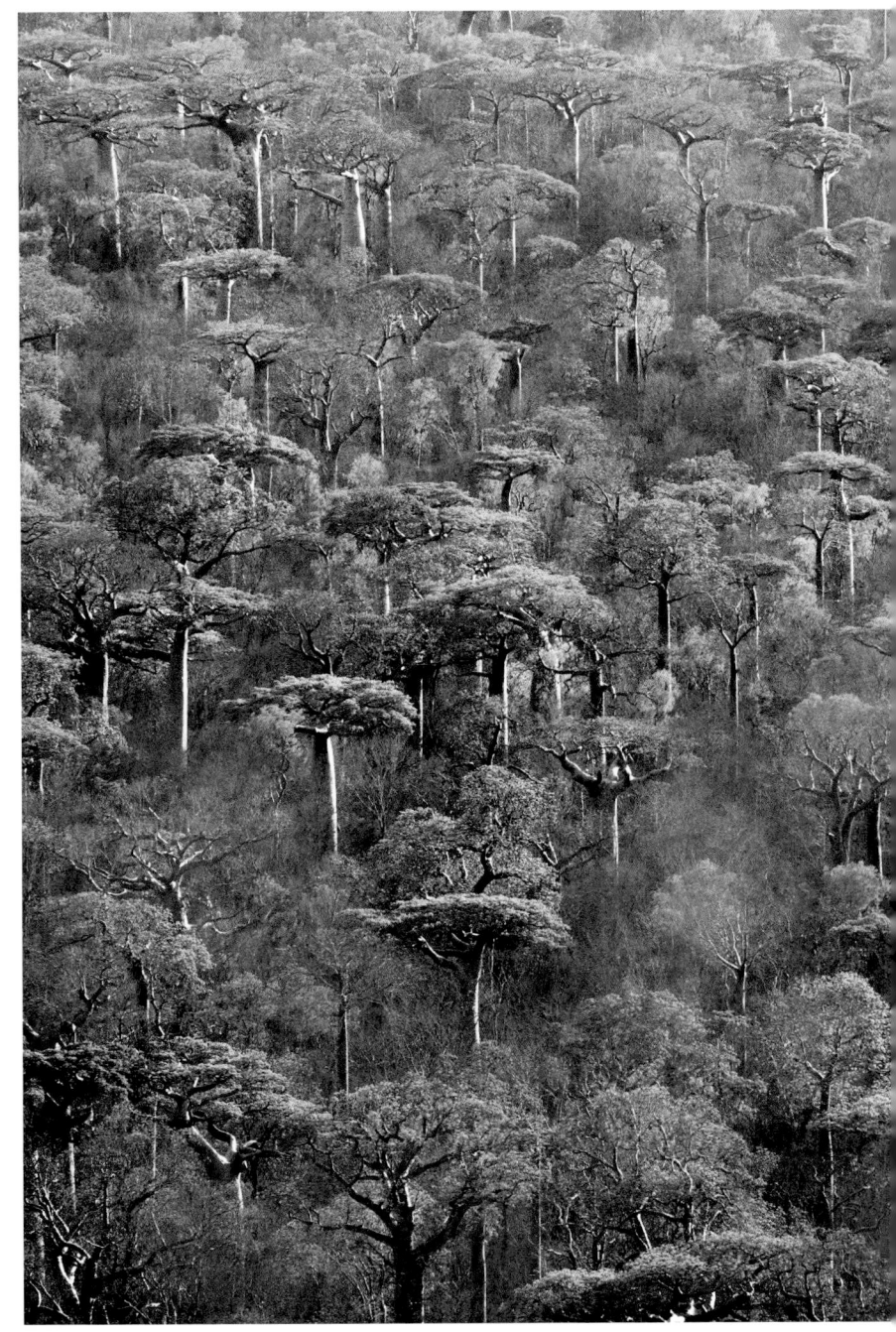

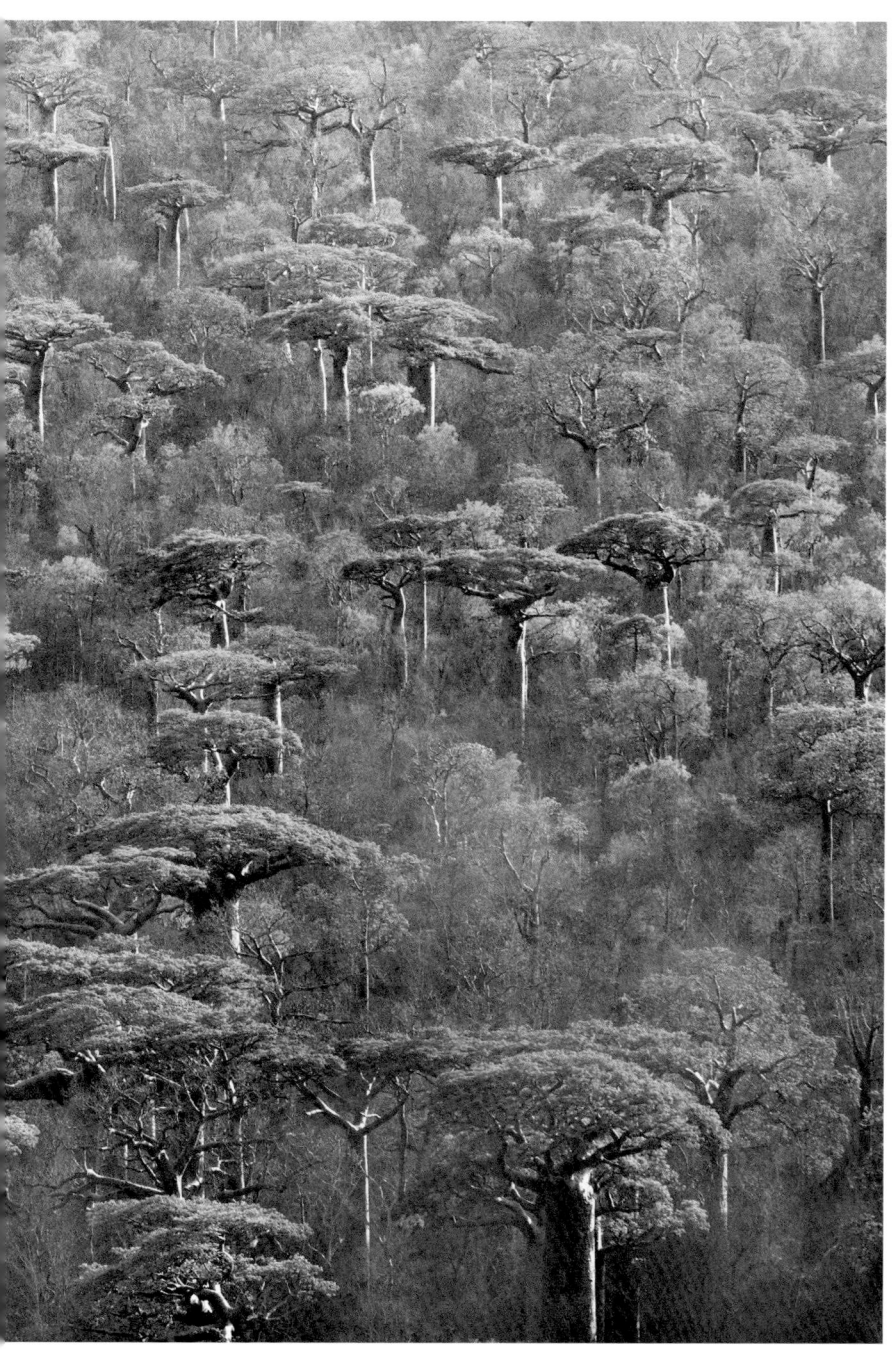

Pages 64/65: A crater lake in the rainforest of Amber Mountain National Park. Madagascar. November and December 2010.

Pages 66/67: Pachypodium plant (*Pachypodium rosulatum*) in the Makay range. Madagascar. November and December 2010.

Page 68: Thunderstorm in the Makay range. As a result of erosion over millions of years, this magnificent sandstone mountain range in the southern part of Madagascar harbors innumerable inaccessible canyons that have provided a unique refuge for biodiversity. Madagascar. November and December 2010.

Page 69: Basaltic organ pipes on Mitsio Island. The archipelago of Mitsio Island is situated off the northwest coast. Madagascar. November and December 2010.

Pages 70/71: Adansonia grandidieri, sometimes known as Grandidier's baobab, is a very strange-looking tree because its thick trunk seems out of all proportion with its toupee of branches, leaves, and fruit. This bloated trunk, though, can store a large amount of water, assuring the tree's good health in drought conditions. The baobab can also be found on the African mainland, although the Grandidier's is native to Madagascar and is the most widely exploited of the island's six kinds of baobab. Its seeds and fruit pulp, rich in vitamin C, can be eaten literally off the tree, while its seeds can be pressed into cooking oil. Using wooden pegs hammered into the trunk, local men climb the tree to collect its fruit. Fibers extracted from the tree's bark can also be made into strong rope without harming the tree. The trunk of a fallen tree can in turn be pressed into sheets of fiber for use as roof covering. Fortunately, most of these activities pose little danger to the baobab's survival, but it is nonetheless now considered an endangered species because of encroachment by farming land. No less alarming is that fires, seed predation, competition from weeds, and an altered physical environment have increasingly diminished the baobab's ability to reproduce. This photograph was taken about 62 miles (100 kilometers) northeast of the Makay range. Madagascar. November and December 2010.

Opposite: Helicopter tree (*Gyrocarpus americanus glaber*). Tsingy of Ankarana National Park. Madagascar. November and December 2010.

Pages 74/75: Baobab trees (*Adansonia rubrostipa*) on a mushroom island in Bay of Moramba. Madagascar. November and December 2010.

Pages 76/77: Bats (*Pteropus rufus*) on tamarind tree (*Tamarindus indica*) in the Berenty Reserve. It is a small private reserve of gallery forest along the Mandrake River, set in a semiarid spiny forest ecoregion of the far south of Madagascar.
The Madagascan flying fox (*Pteropus rufus*) is native to Madagascar. Its other common names include the Madagascar fruit bat and the Madagascar flying fox. It is one of many species of megabat and the largest bat that can be found on the island of Madagascar. With a wingspan of 40 to 50 inches (100 to 125 centimeters), it can weigh between 1 and 1 ½ pounds (500 and 750 grams). Its diet consists of flowers, fig leaves, and, of course, fruit. Because of the loss of its habitat, it is now considered a vulnerable species. Madagascar. November and December 2010.

Page 78: Crowned lemurs (*Eulemur fulvus coronatus*) in Ankarana National Park. Madagascar. November and December 2010.

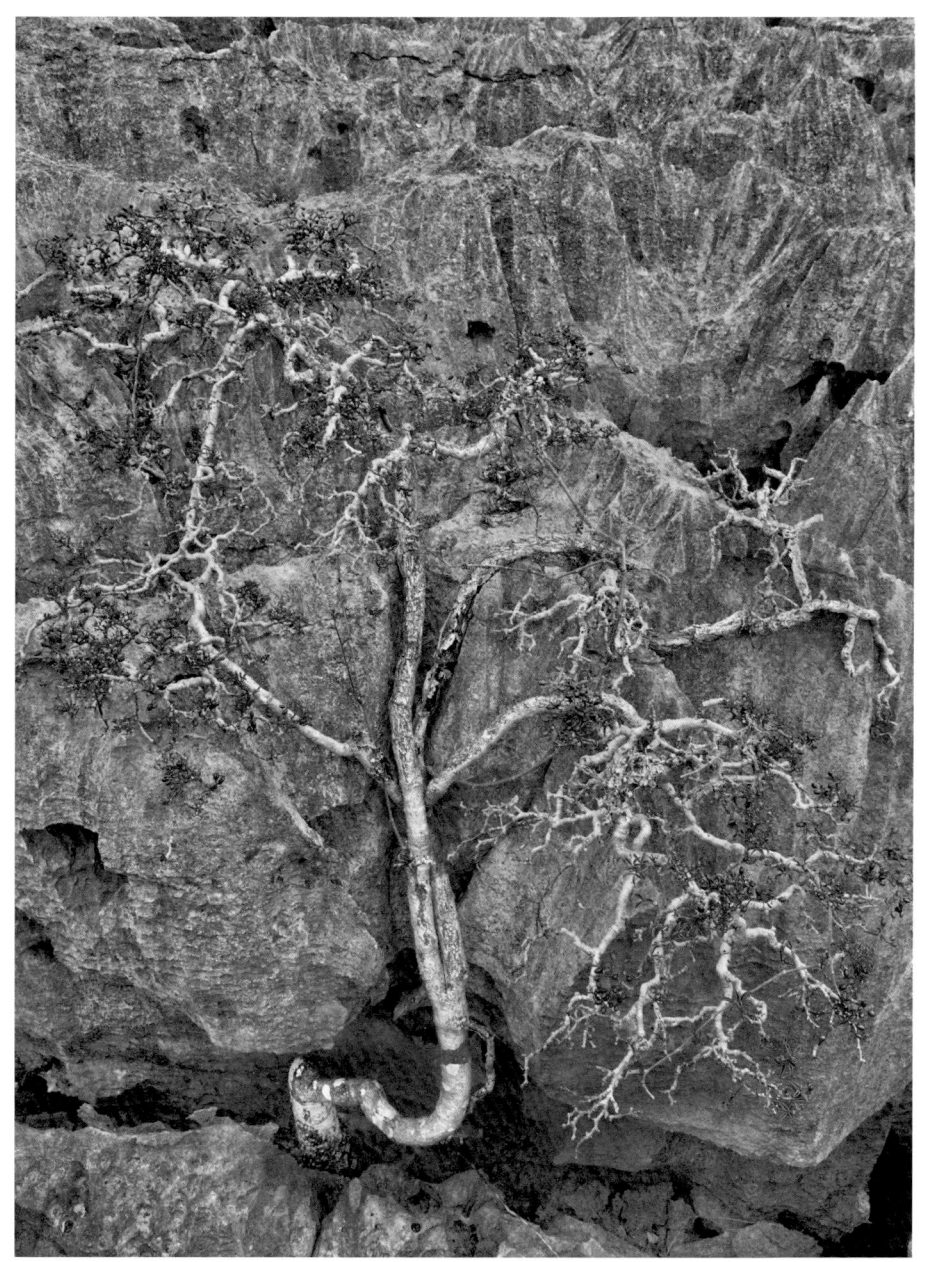

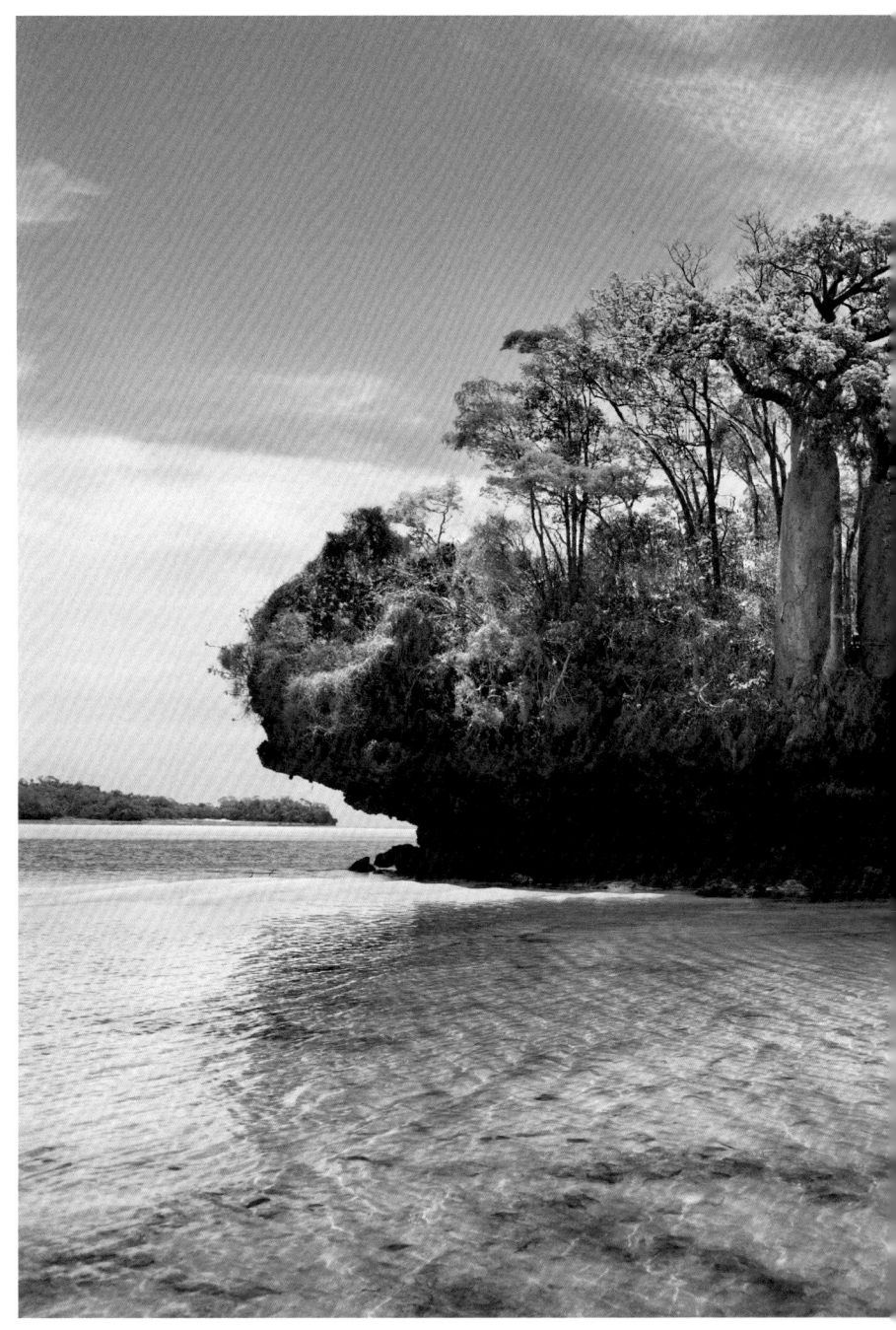

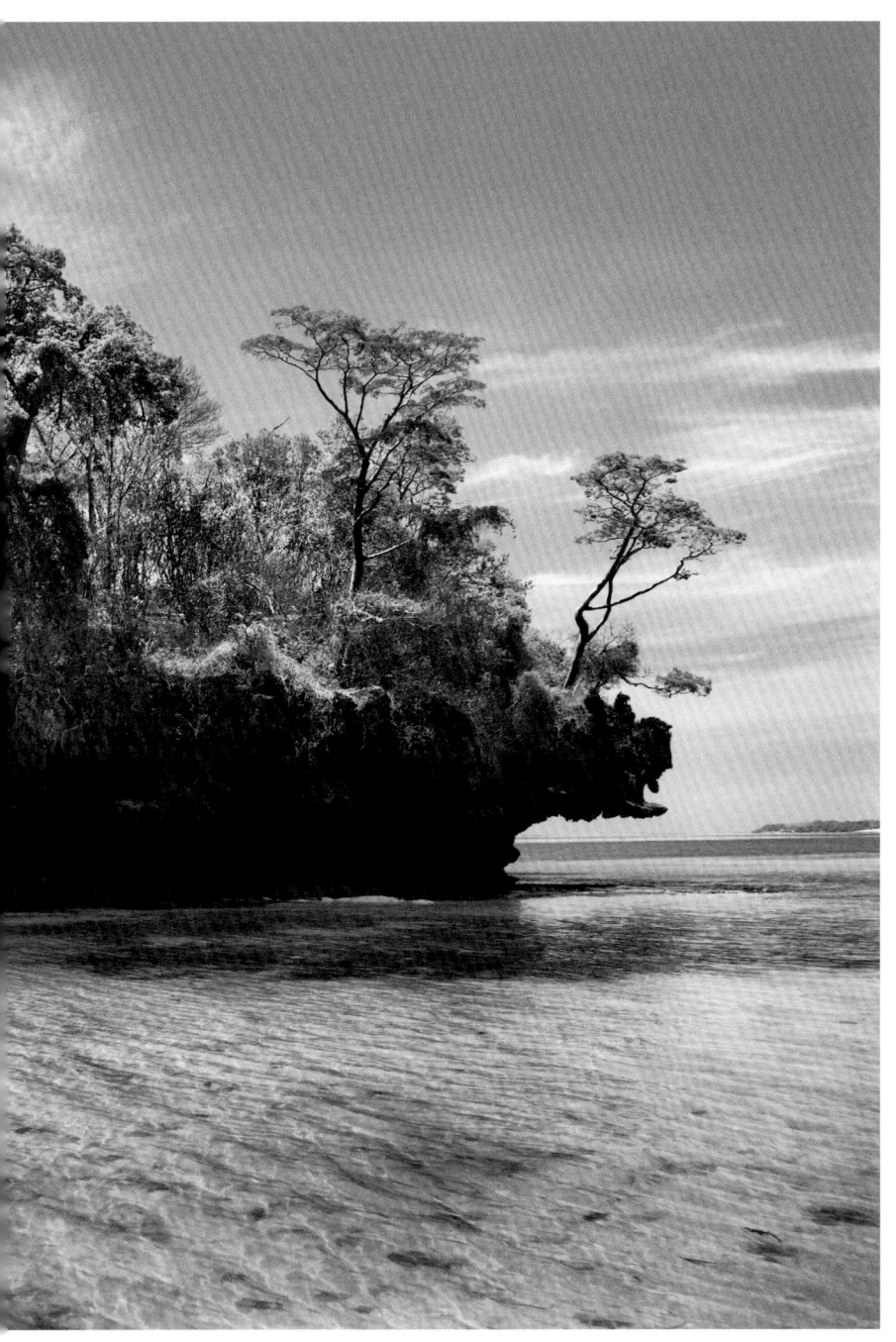

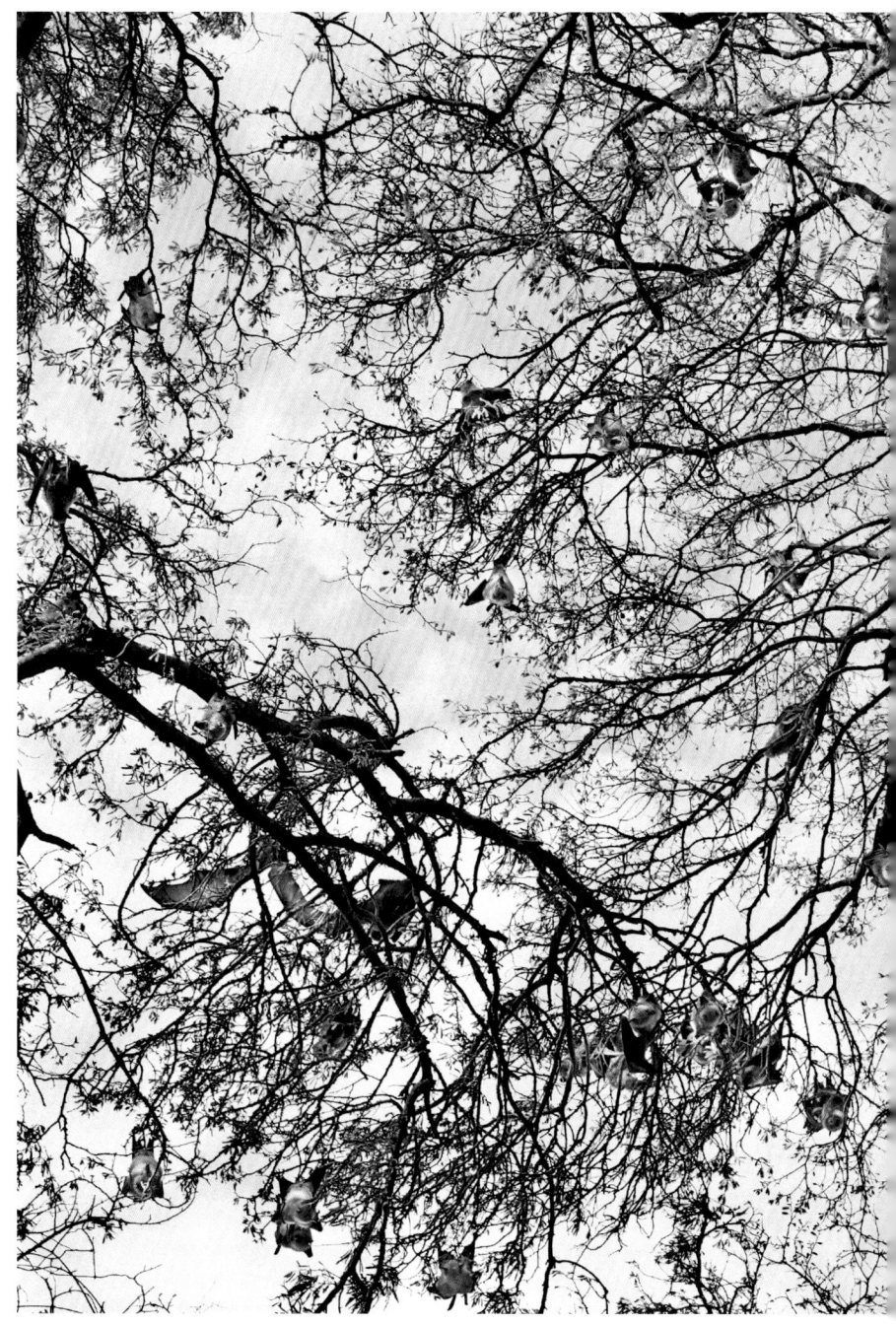

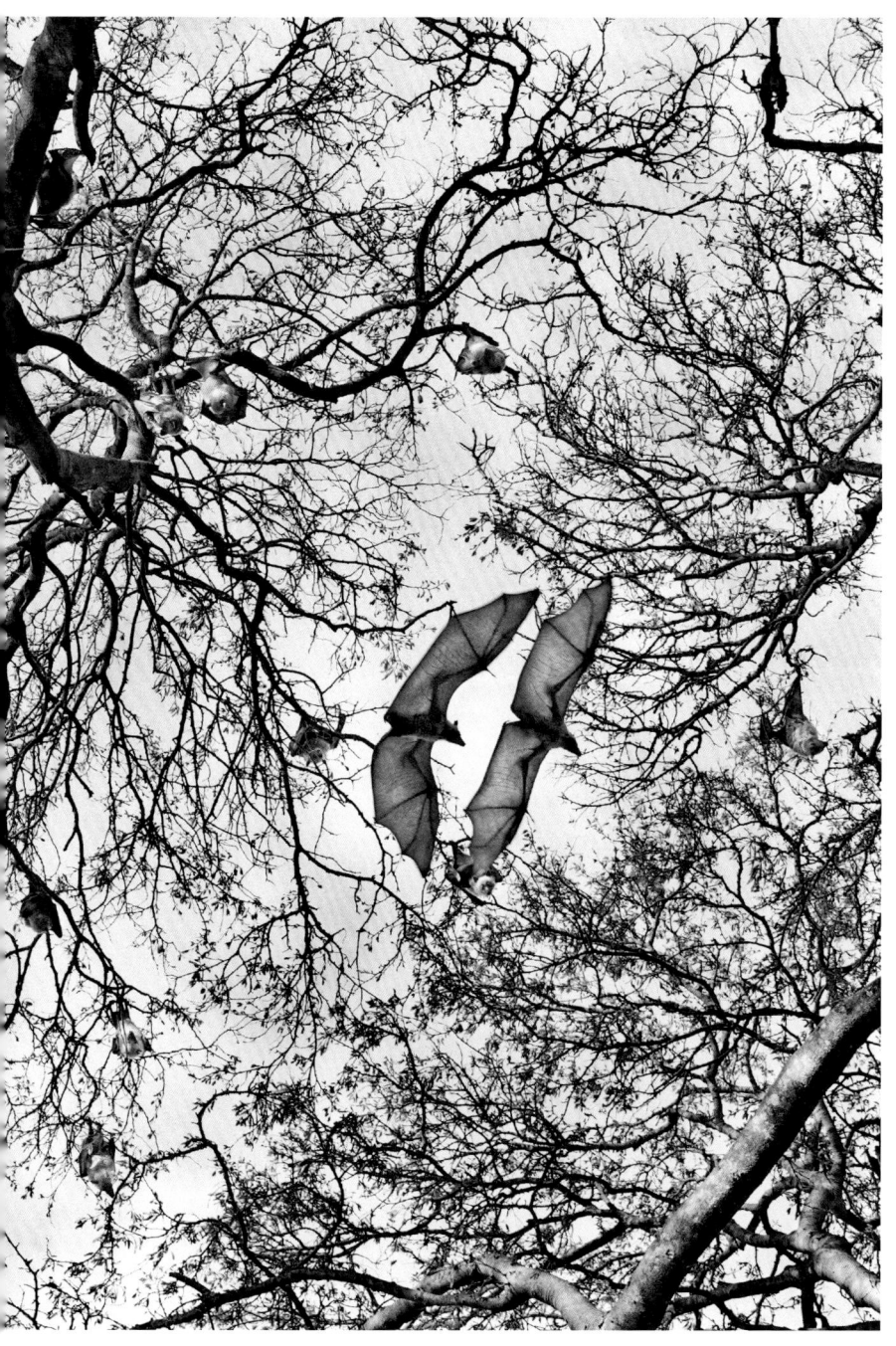

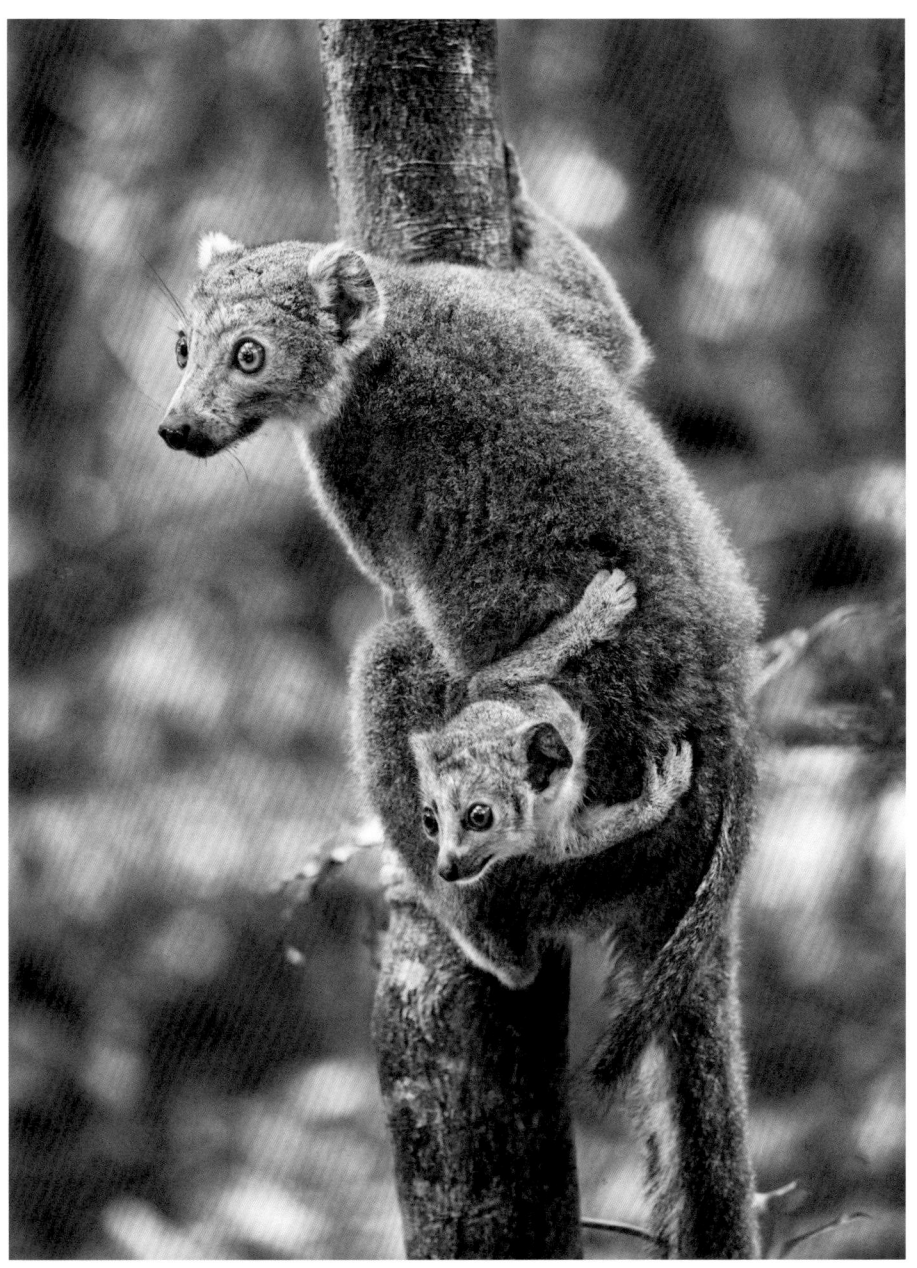

PAPUA NEW GUINEA'S HIGHLANDS

Pages 80/81

The highlands of Papua New Guinea are dramatic and beautiful, with fertile valleys, turbulent rivers and seemingly endless sawtoothed mountains. But they are also the country's most densely populated and productive region. It is therefore all the more surprising that it was only in the 1930s that the outside world first came face-to-face with the diverse and artistically inventive Indigenous peoples that live here.

The first European explorers to enter this rugged interior had expected to find an unbroken tangle of mountains. Instead, they came across broad, heavily cultivated valleys and a population of more than one million. They were still more surprised by the cultural chasm that separated them from these newly contacted peoples.

Since then, much has changed. The region's five provinces—Eastern Highlands (around Goroka), Simbu (around Kundiawa), Western Highlands (around Mount Hagen), Enga (around Wabag), and Southern Highlands (around Mendi)—now have the country's most extensive road system and a healthy economy based on coffee, tea, gold, and copper. All the photographs presented here are about the *singsing* festivals in the highlands. The *singsing*, a celebratory festival or dance, can happen for all sorts of reasons, and it is always spectacular, with highlanders in traditional costume and face paint dancing in formation and playing their *kundus* (an hourglass-shaped drum with lizard skin). The Enga Show, the Hagen Show, and the Paya Show are annual events that bring together thousands of performers. Body art and personal decoration, called *bilas*, are particularly sophisticated. While the Sepik people and other Papua New Guineans create beautiful carvings and artifacts, the highlanders use themselves as rustic canvases: they paint their bodies and dress up in feathers, pearls, and animal skins to represent birds, trees, or mountain spirits. On occasions, an important event, such as legendary battle, is reenacted at a *singsing*.

Page 80: Performer at the *singsing* festival of Paya. Western Highlands Province. Papua New Guinea. July and August 2008.

Page 81: Performer of the *singsing* festival of Mount Hagen. Western Highlands Province. Papua New Guinea. July and August 2008.

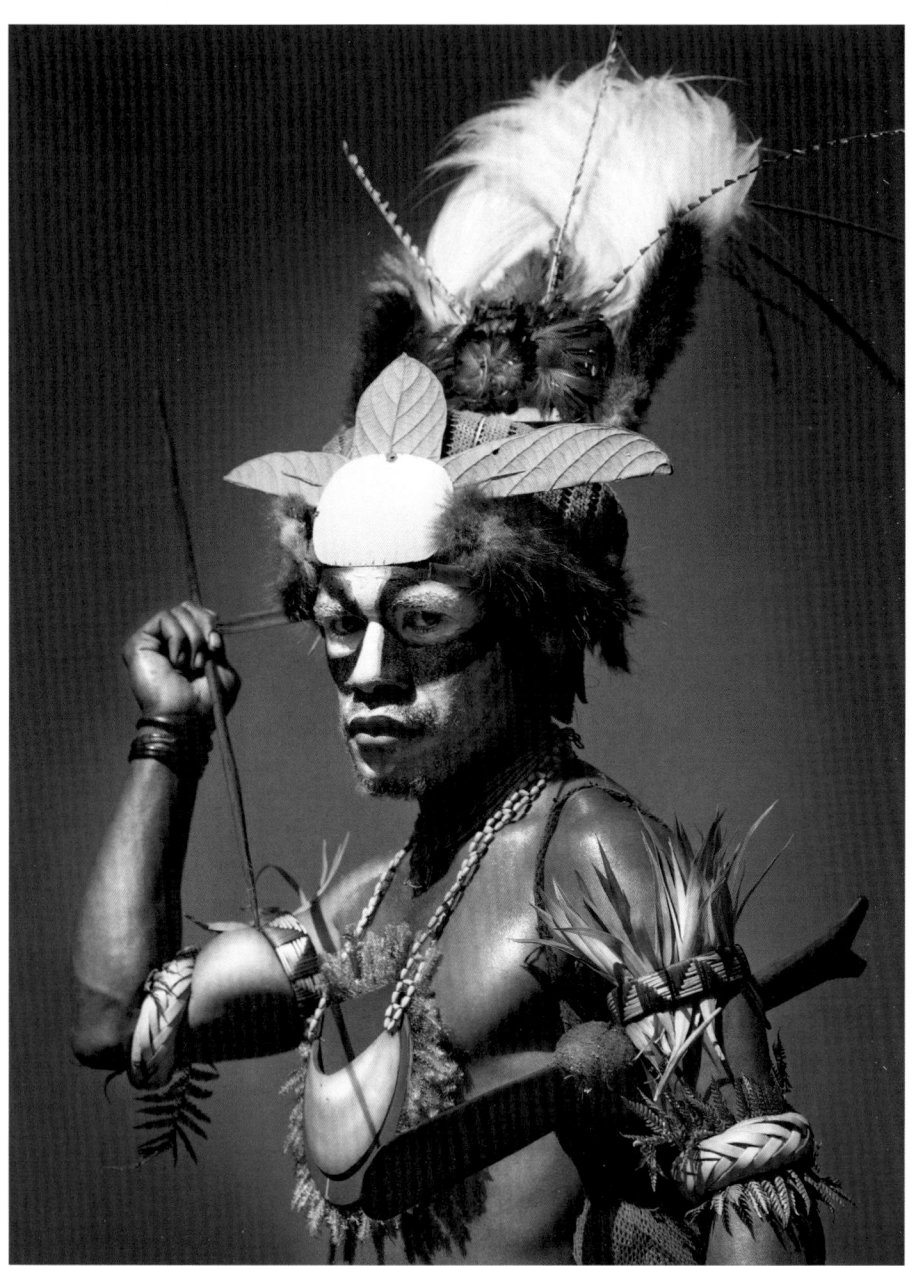

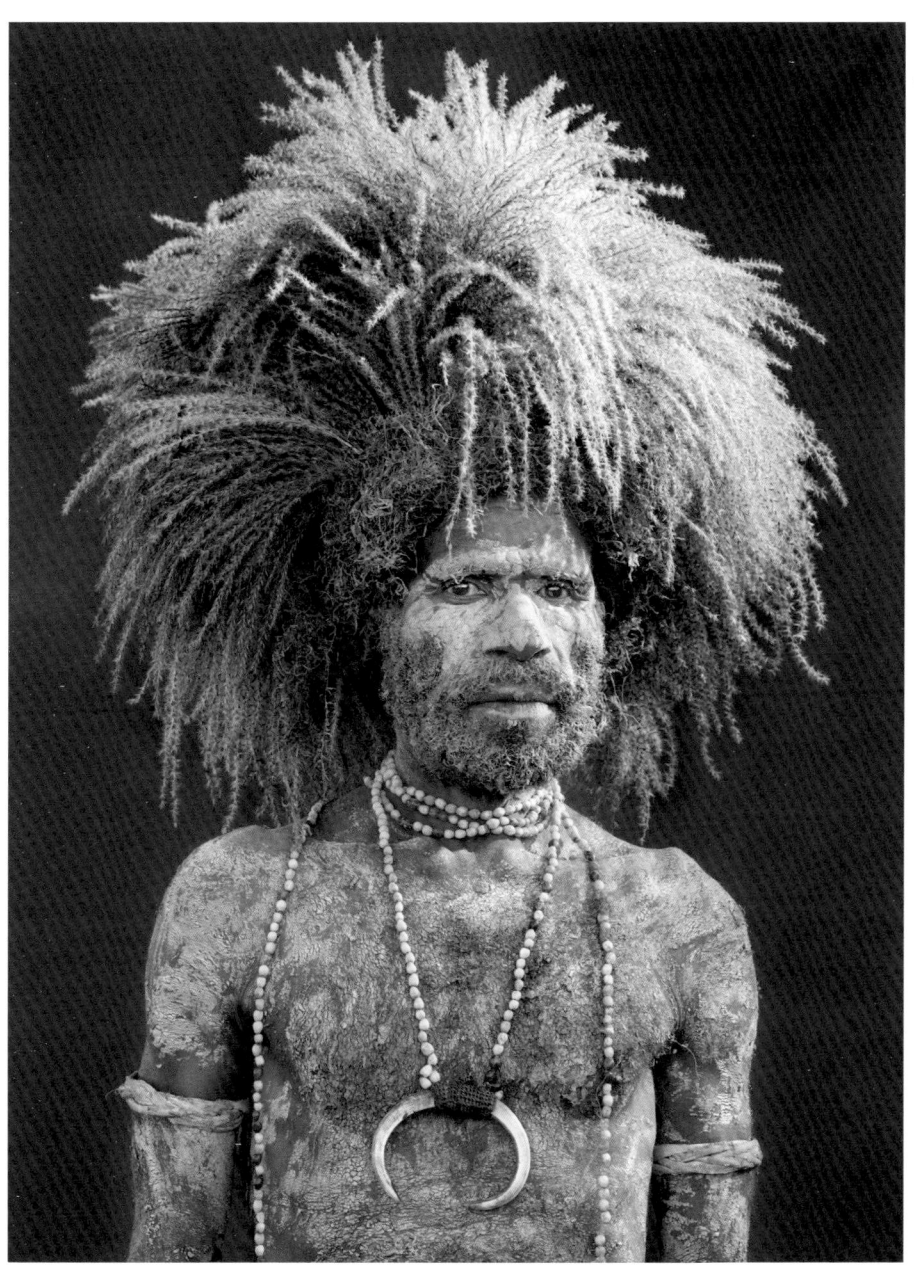

THE MENTAWAI, INDONESIA

Opposite

The Mentawai (also known as the Mentawei and Mentawi) are the native people of the Mentawai Islands, some 80 miles (130 kilometers) west of Sumatra. They live a seminomadic hunter-gatherer lifestyle in the coastal and rainforest environments of the islands. The people are renowned for their spirituality, body art, and their practice of sharpening their teeth, which they feel adds to their beauty. The Mentawai are among the very few traditional Indigenous groups remaining in Asia. They still build almost everything out of natural products from the rainforests, and their lifestyle and rituals have changed little in thousands of years. The Mentawai language belongs to the Austronesian language family. The largest and northernmost island is Siberut. Here, most Mentawai live in small settlements dotted along major rivers or close to the coast. They commute between their settlements and smaller dwellings some distance away on ancestral land. There, they raise pigs in the jungle and harvest seasonal fruits, such as durian, jackfruit, and other wild species. Chickens are usually raised close to the settlement, while sago palms are tended in low-lying swampy areas, usually beside a river. Flour ground from the sago palm heart and from the taro tuber is an important part of their diet. The Indonesian government has worked for decades to assimilate the Mentawai by luring them into government-controlled villages; today, only a handful of unassimilated clans live in the jungle. Led by *sikeireis* (Mentawai shamans), they live according to tradition in long communal houses called *umas*. While the modern world is moving ever closer, traditional clans take from it only what they need. All use metal objects such as axes and cauldrons, and some have started using plastic cups and pitchers. The government and various religious groups have forced assimilated Mentawai to wear modern clothes, but in the traditional *umas*, the men usually wear only tree bark loincloths and the women traditional dresses. They love to wear colorful necklaces and bracelets and tropical flowers in their hair. Shamans and their wives have their bodies entirely tattooed.

Opposite: The bark of a felled *baiko* tree is cut into strips, then plunged into water and pounded at length with a mallet without tearing it. The objective is to crush the fibers and to soften the bark. After drying in the sun, it is dyed red with sap from another tree, and worn by men around their hips; this loincloth is called the *kabit*. Siberut Island. West Sumatra. Indonesia. March and April 2008.

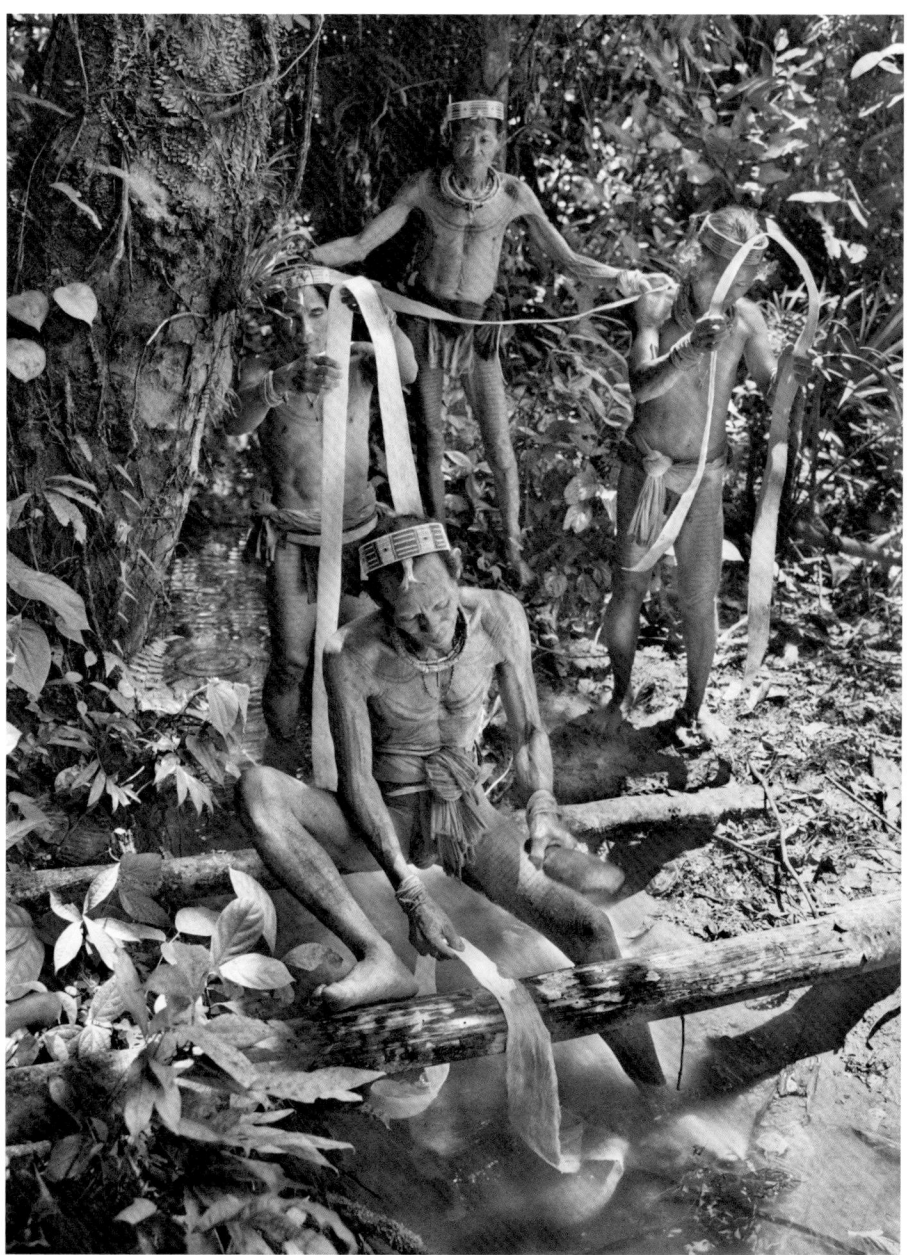

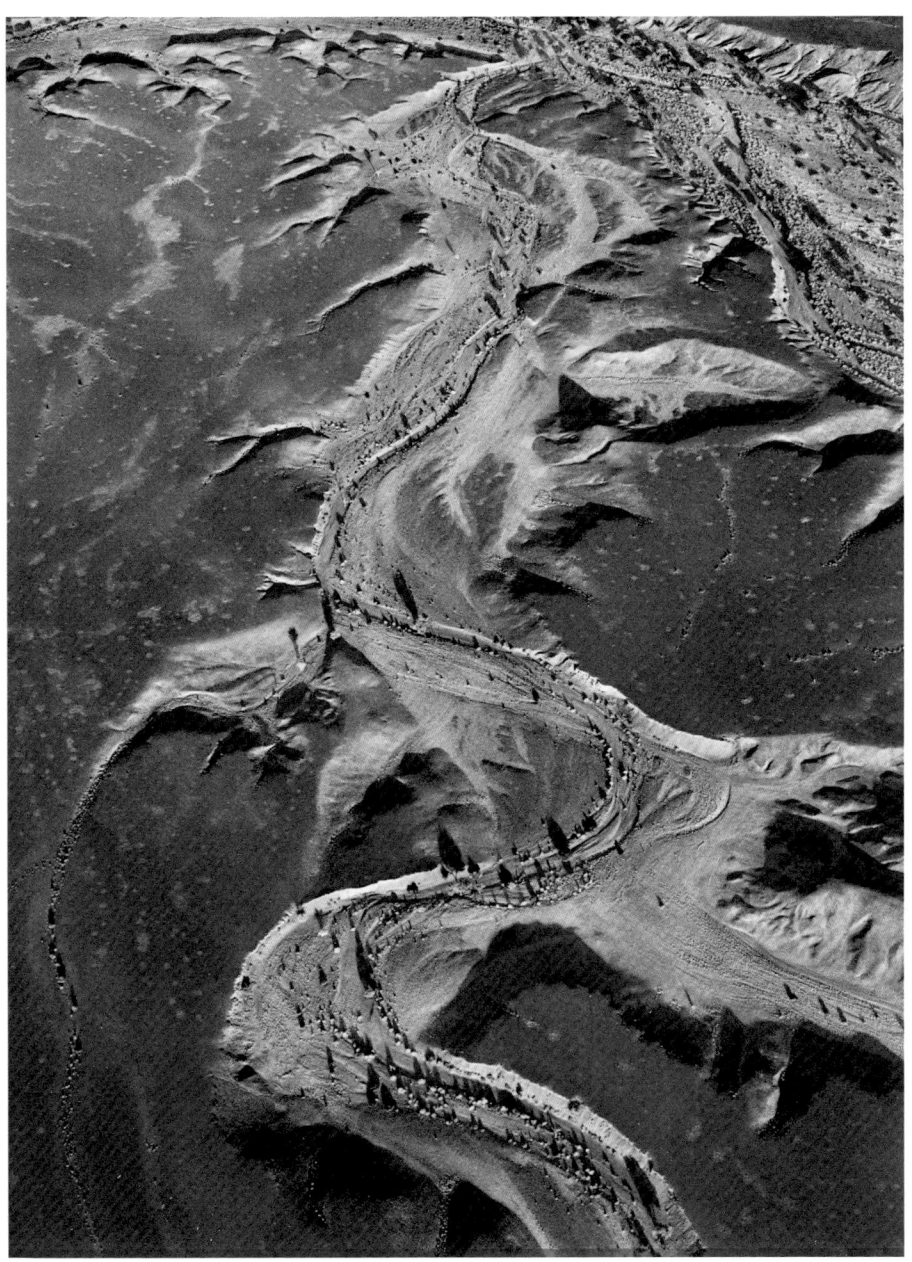

84

AFRICA

Since my first visit to Niger, in 1973, I have always felt a deep attachment to Africa. Even when assignments meant confronting crises of famine, drought, or war, I jumped at the chance to return. With *Genesis*, however, I had an altogether happier experience—that of recording a seemingly eternal Africa, one of ancestral tribes, majestic landscapes, and breathtaking wildlife. The continent may be vast and varied, yet its many ecosystems remain uniquely African.

The Sahara, which embraces ten countries and covers one-third of the entire continent, serves as an impressive gateway to Africa. Images of endless expanses of sand dunes may be familiar, yet every dust storm moves and reshapes their contours, much like a child playing in a giant sandbox. My trips to the deserts of southwest Libya and southeast Algeria were also full of surprises. I came across stunning oases and deep ravines where rivers once flowed. And we found evidence of human settlements dating back 16,000 years in rock art depicting the wildlife of the time, including elephants, rhinoceroses, antelopes, giraffes, and crocodiles.

At the other end of the continent, the Namib Desert, said to be the world's oldest desert, covers much of Namibia, with sand dunes up to 990 feet (300 meters) high stretching along the entire coastline. Heading north into Damaraland, we tracked down rare black rhinoceros, but found them too threatening to photograph at close quarters. Even elephants have their moods, as we discovered the day an agitated male charged us. Still farther north, we came across the Himba, a large nomadic group of cattle and goat herders. The men wear few clothes, but the women cover themselves with a mixture of butter, ash, and an ocher iron-ore powder that gives their skin a distinct reddish glow.

Cattle are a distinctive feature of many African savannas. For the Dinka of South Sudan, they are a symbol of wealth and power. In the rainy season, these seminomadic tribesmen grow maize, sorghum, and other cereals, and set up cattle camps for their herds. This is the time when the Nile floods and creates small lakes, which become rich pastures during the dry season. The Dinka then lead their cattle for hundreds of miles along these feeding grounds and build little villages and corrals where the herds shelter at night. They also burn cow dung and spread the ash on their bodies and on their cattle as protection from insects. One tradition has not survived: because of frequent warfare in the region, automatic rifles have now replaced bows and arrows. The cattle-herding tribes of southern Ethiopia are more isolated. Usually naked, they decorate their bodies and hair for ceremonies, while many women wear ceramic plates in their lower lips.

Some traditional peoples have suffered at the hands of traders, missionaries, and government officials. To make room for diamond miners, Botswana's government has driven the Bushmen of the Kalahari Desert from their ancestral lands. We spent time in the Ghanzi District with a small resettled community that keeps alive its age-old culture thanks to tourist groups. For a modest fee, they demonstrate how they hunt small animals, draw water from sand through a straw, and make fire by rubbing sticks. But, unable to return home, growing numbers of Bushmen now live in poverty in urban areas.

We came across hardier traditions during a 55-day-long hike across northern Ethiopia. We set off from Lalibela, an ancient Christian town famous for its churches carved out of red volcanic rock in the 12th century. On the mountain of Abune Yosef, 14,0000 feet (4,200 meters) above sea level, Christian services are held in cave churches built into hillsides, while centuries-old Bibles written on animal skins are still in use. These mountain people are skilled farmers, growing grains on ancient terraces and raising dairy cattle on high slopes. Beyond them lay the region long inhabited by Ethiopian Jews, the Falusha, although most have now migrated to Israel. Finally, in the Simien National Park, we found species I had never seen before, including the gelada baboon, the simien fox and the walia ibex.

Even on a continent synonymous with wildlife, perhaps no African animal is viewed with greater awe than the mountain gorilla. Only some 800 survive in a small area straddling Congo, Uganda, and Rwanda. Three groups live on the forested slopes of Virunga Volcanoes National Park, a safe distance from the park's two lava-spewing volcanoes. I came close enough to several family groups to identify the dominant males by the silver fur on their back. These gentle animals, some weighing up to 550 pounds (250 kilos), pay little attention to humans and spend most of their time looking after their families and feeding themselves.

For sheer variety of wildlife, few places match the Okavango Delta in Botswana, where the Okavango River—"the river that never finds the sea"—literally spills its water on to the land. When the delta floods and vegetation blooms, it draws some 400 species of birds, as well as the great beasts of Africa, from elephants, hippopotamuses, rhinoceroses, and buffalos to lions, leopards, cheetahs, zebras, and hyenas. Later, in Zambia, we saw the same spectacular display from the quiet of a balloon. And here, nature barely noticed we were watching.

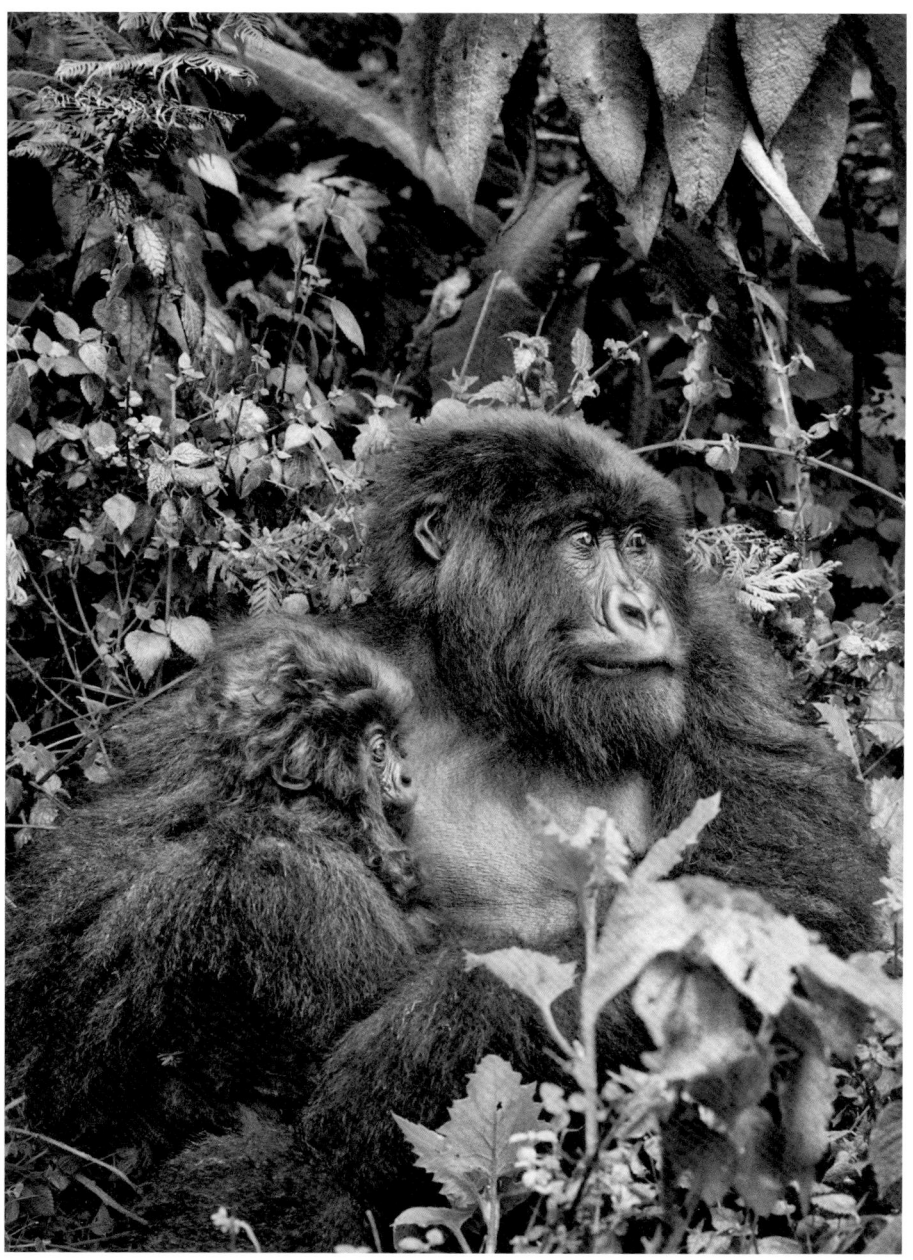

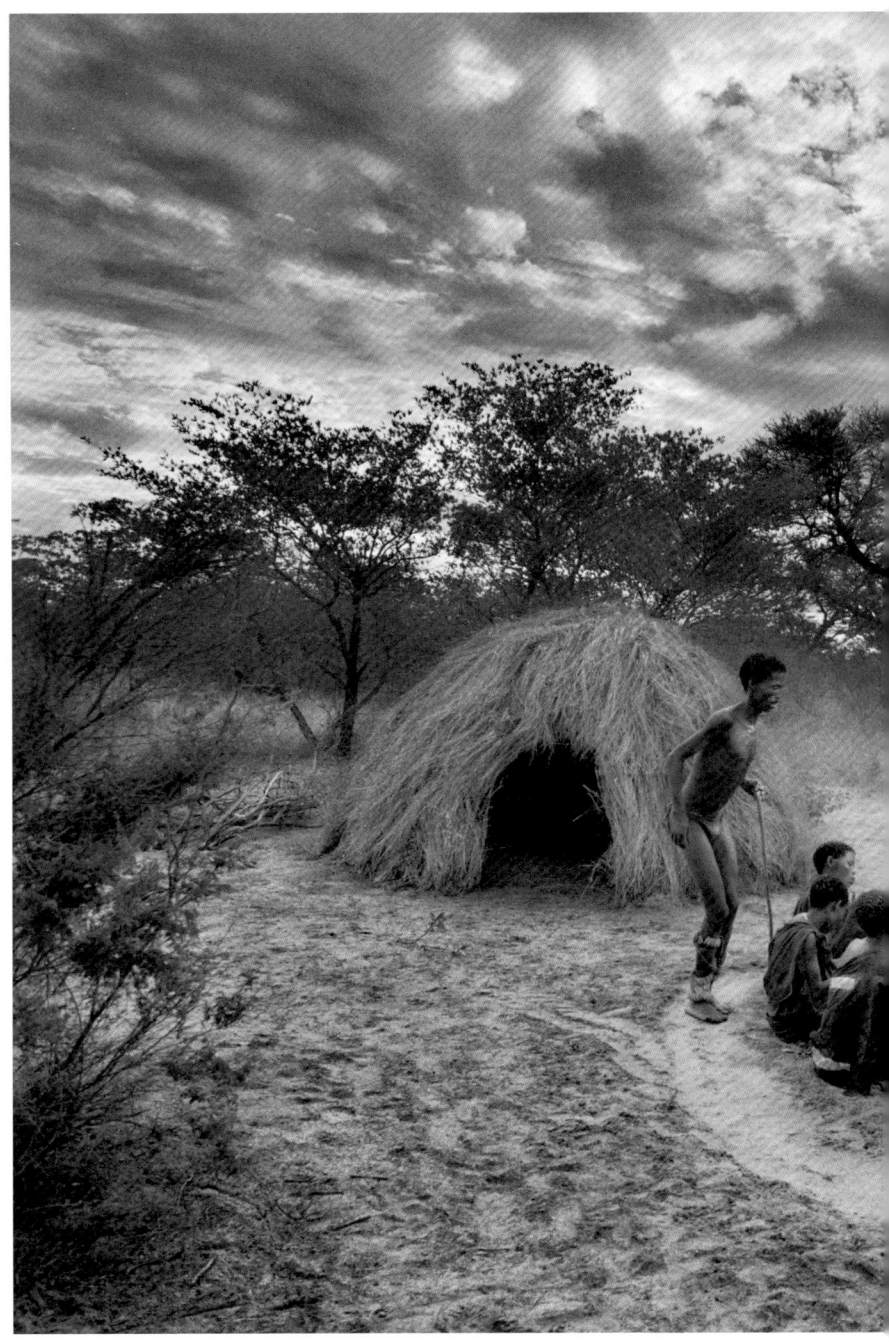

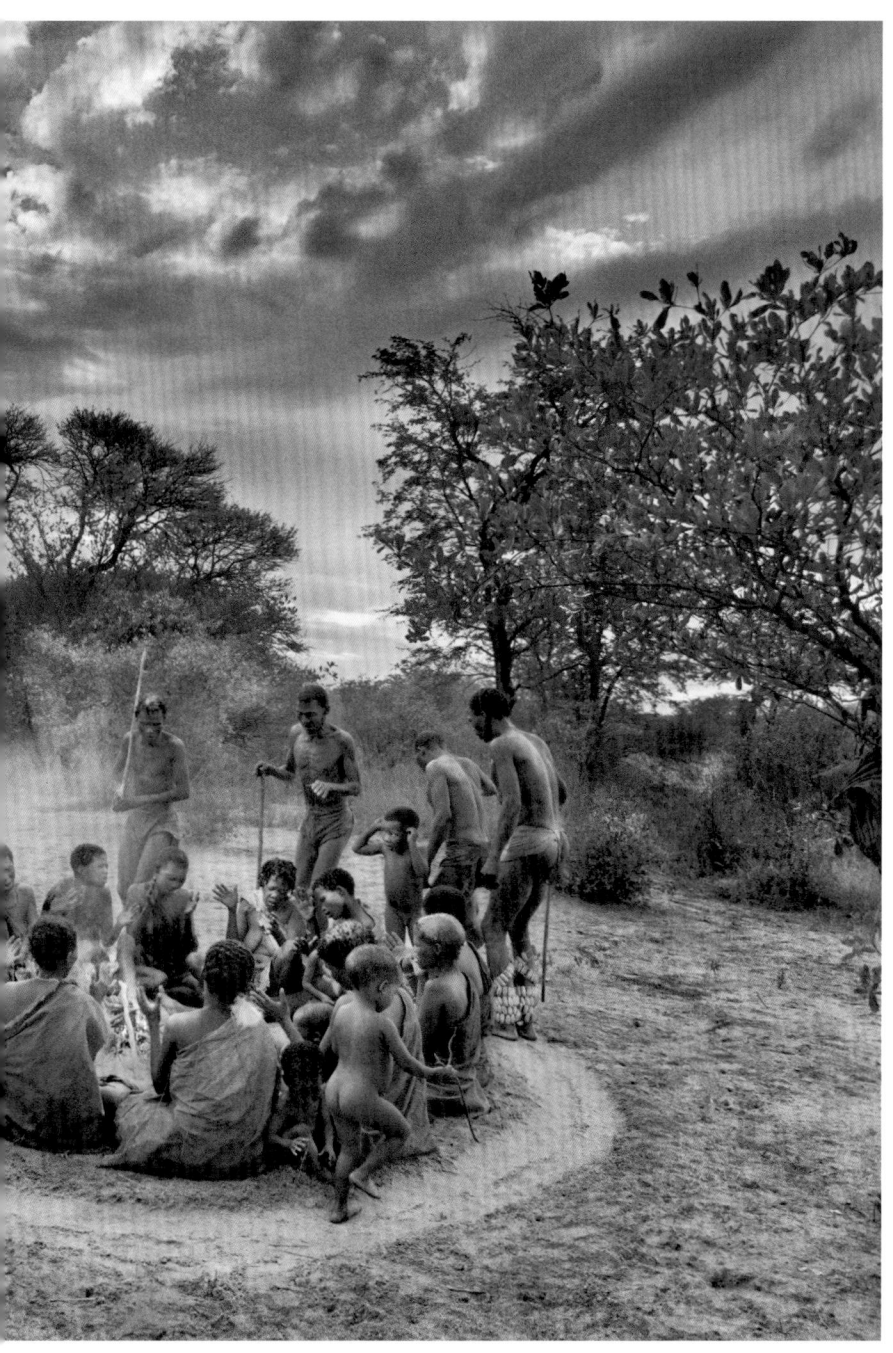

Page 84: In western Namibia, landscapes have been reshaped by water erosion, principally after storms release flash floods that eat away at the soil and cut ever-deeper gullies and river channels. However, since heavy rain is rare today, much of the area's lunar appearance dates back to far wetter, earlier times. Namib-Naukluft National Park, Namibia. October and November 2005.

Page 87: The mountain gorilla (*Gorilla beringei beringei*) is the rarest of the three species of gorilla, numbering only about 800, with roughly half in the volcanic region of Virungas and the rest in the Bwindi Impenetrable National Park in Uganda. For all their formidable size, with adult males weighing up to 550 pounds (250 kilos), gorillas are peaceful animals, preferring family life to anything more adventurous. Here, a female gorilla displays typical tenderness toward her infant. Family groups of young males, females, and their infants are led by a dominant silverback male, whose name derives from the saddle of gray hairs that develops across his back once he reaches full maturity. Young silverbacks often leave the group, opting for a solitary life until they can attract a female from a different group to form a family. Females sometimes transfer between groups and, in this way, inbreeding is avoided. Gorillas are vegetarians, with a diet that includes bamboo shoots, wild celery, thistles, nettles, galium, a leafy vegetable called *vernonia*, and various roots and vines. Unless a zoo succeeds in breeding these gorillas, every one seen in captivity is there as the result of a tragedy. Since adult gorillas are difficult to capture, their young are targeted. But they can only be taken if their parents are first killed. When the slain father is the silverback leader of the group, the entire family often falls apart and many gorillas end up dying from solitude. Virunga National Park. Rwanda. May and June 2004.

THE SAN PEOPLE

Pages 88/89 and 91
The Kalahari Desert in Botswana may look arid and hostile, but it is paradise to the San people (or Bushmen or Bochimans), among the earliest inhabitants of Africa. Over a period of 40,000 years, they have proven to be masters of survival. With its vast horizons, the Kalahari presents spectacular daytime cloud formations, particularly during the rainy season. And at night, the sky glitters with the most fabulous constellations, all of which have a name in the San language. Unfortunately, this immense natural cradle, home to one of just 14 "ancestral population clusters" from which modern man evolved, is no longer the exclusive territory of the San people. In several waves of evictions, from 1997 through 2002, Botswana's government has driven them from their ancestral land into overcrowded resettlement camps. These are truly sad places. Since there is almost no nearby wildlife, they are dependent on the government for food and water. Cut off from meaningful lives, San men grow depressed through tedium. The Botswana government claims that they moved the San in order to bring them development. The San are not persuaded. Why was development not brought to them where they had always lived? San lawyers have challenged their eviction, but so far, no court has authorized their return. In the meantime, the San people need permission just to enter their former game reserves and, even then, they risk detention and torture. The reality is that the government wanted to clear them out of the way so that Kalahari's important diamond reserves could be exploited without the bother of having to negotiate with traditional San communities. Nonetheless, a few small San groups still maintain their traditional way of life: encouraged by some nonprofit groups, several large, privately owned farms have allowed the San people to resume their hunter-gatherer practices; in exchange, the San people invite outsiders to observe how they hunt, build fires, cook, and construct their huts. These photos were taken during time spent with some 20 San men in the region of Ghanzi, Botswana, on the land of Trail Blazer Farm. They show how, despite the loss of their land, with their culture intact, they are ready to pick up where they left off in their beloved Kalahari.

Pages 88/89: The healing or trance dance is the San's most important mystical ritual. As the women sing and clap in rhythm, the men dance in a circle around them. During this dance, medicine men lay their hands on everyone present to draw out the "arrows of sickness." Dried seed pods are filled with small stones and, when tied to the legs of medicine men, rattle loudly as they dance. The frenzy of their trance, the San people believe, marks their entry into the world of spirits. Botswana. January 2008.

Page 91: Kalahari Desert in Botswana. January 2008.

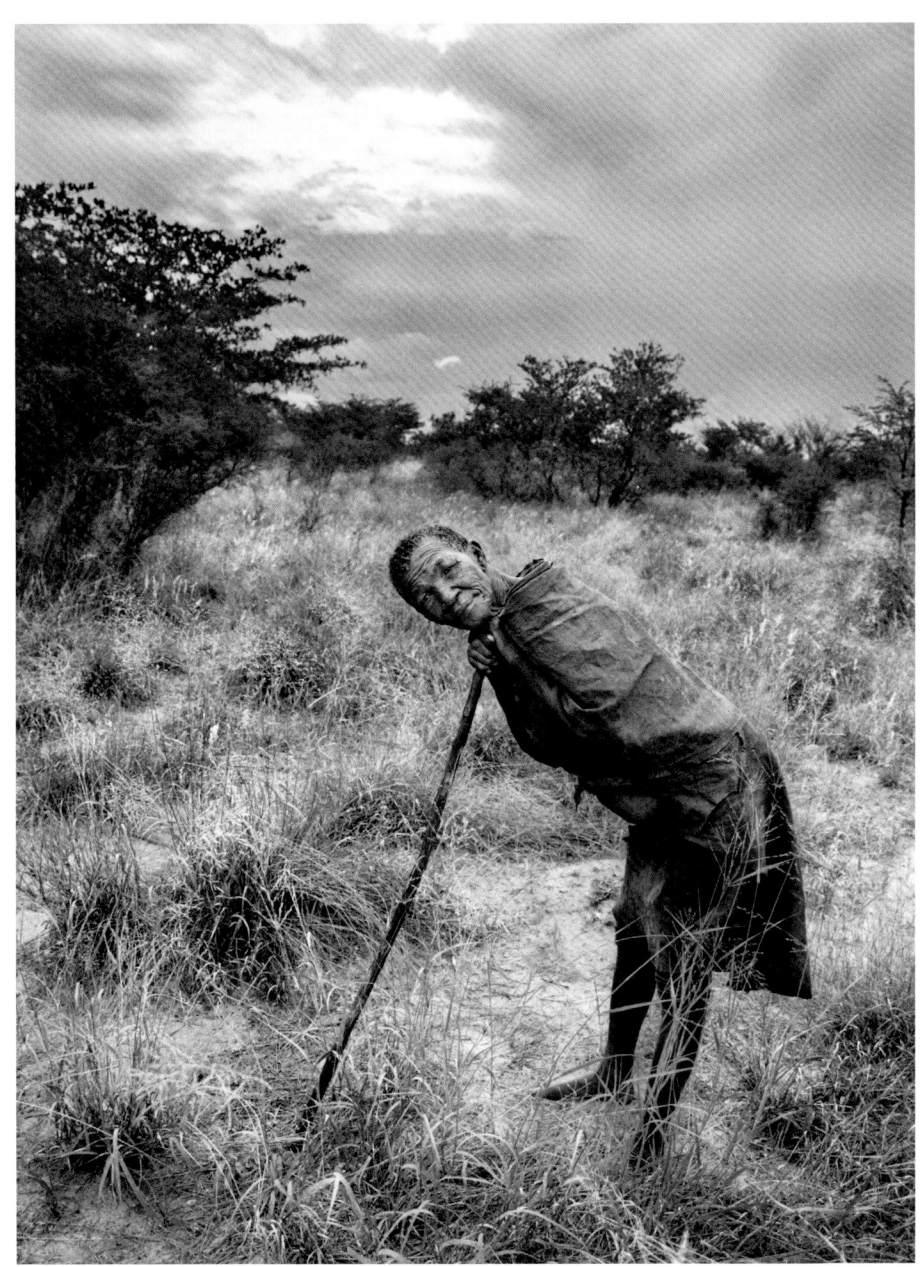

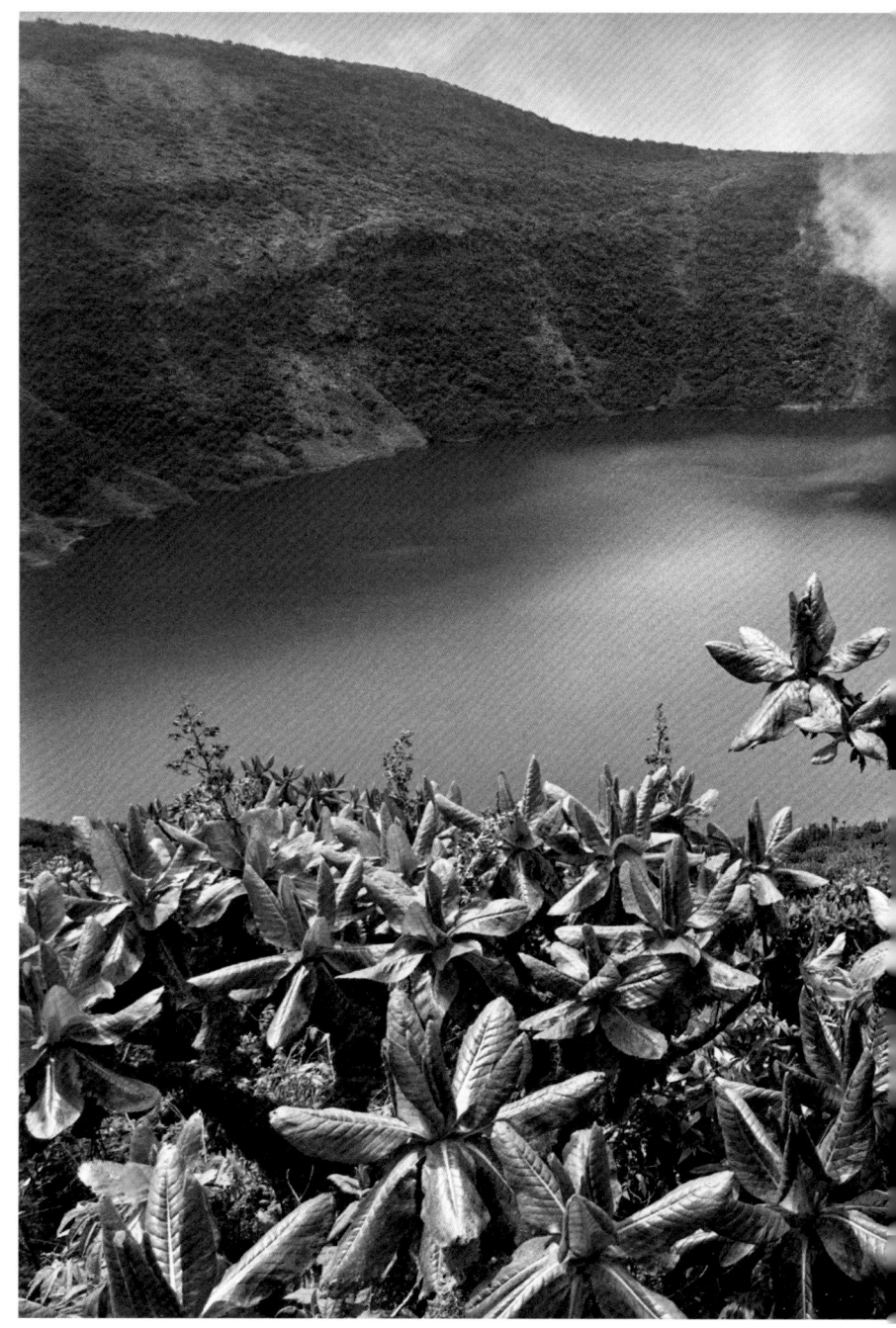

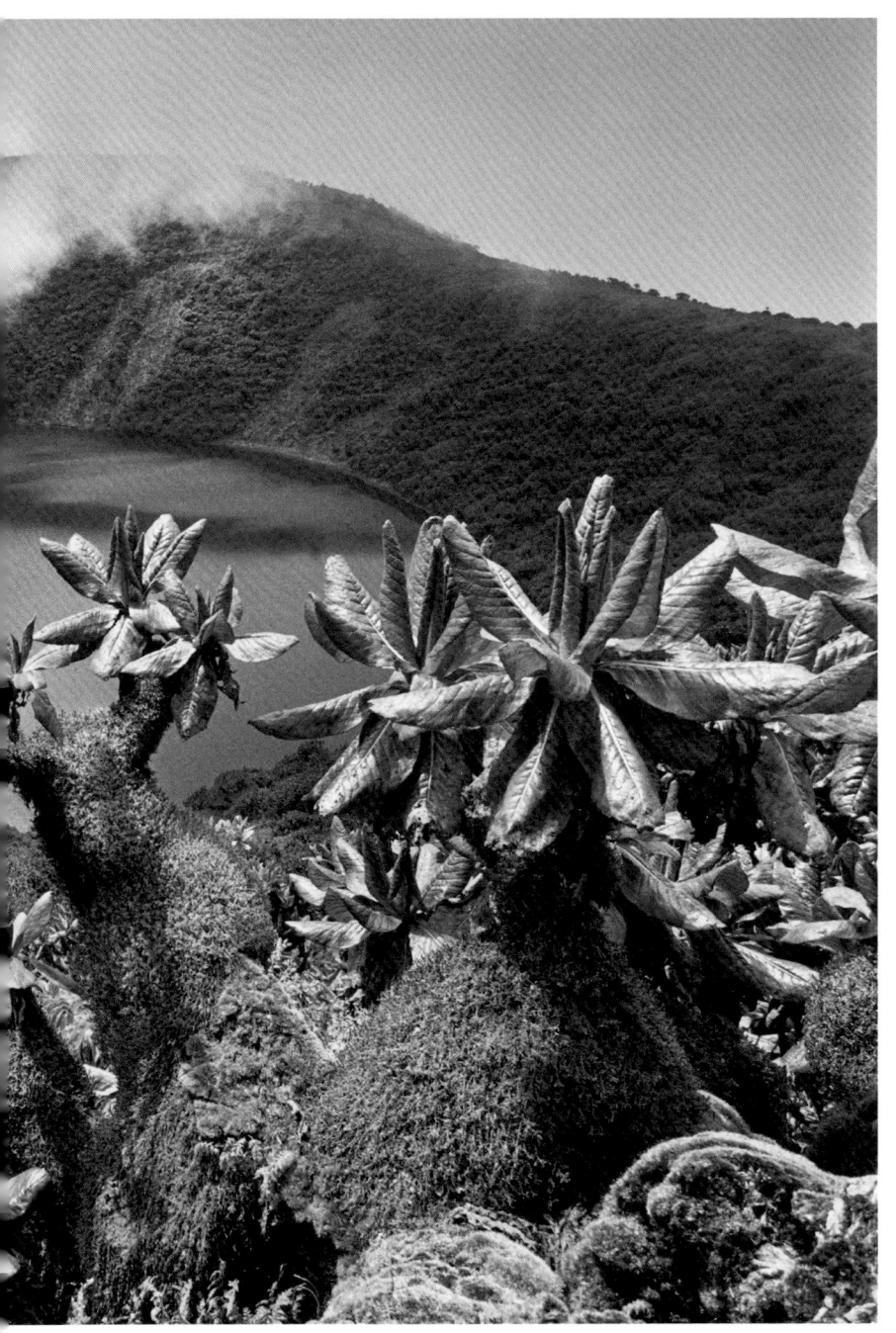

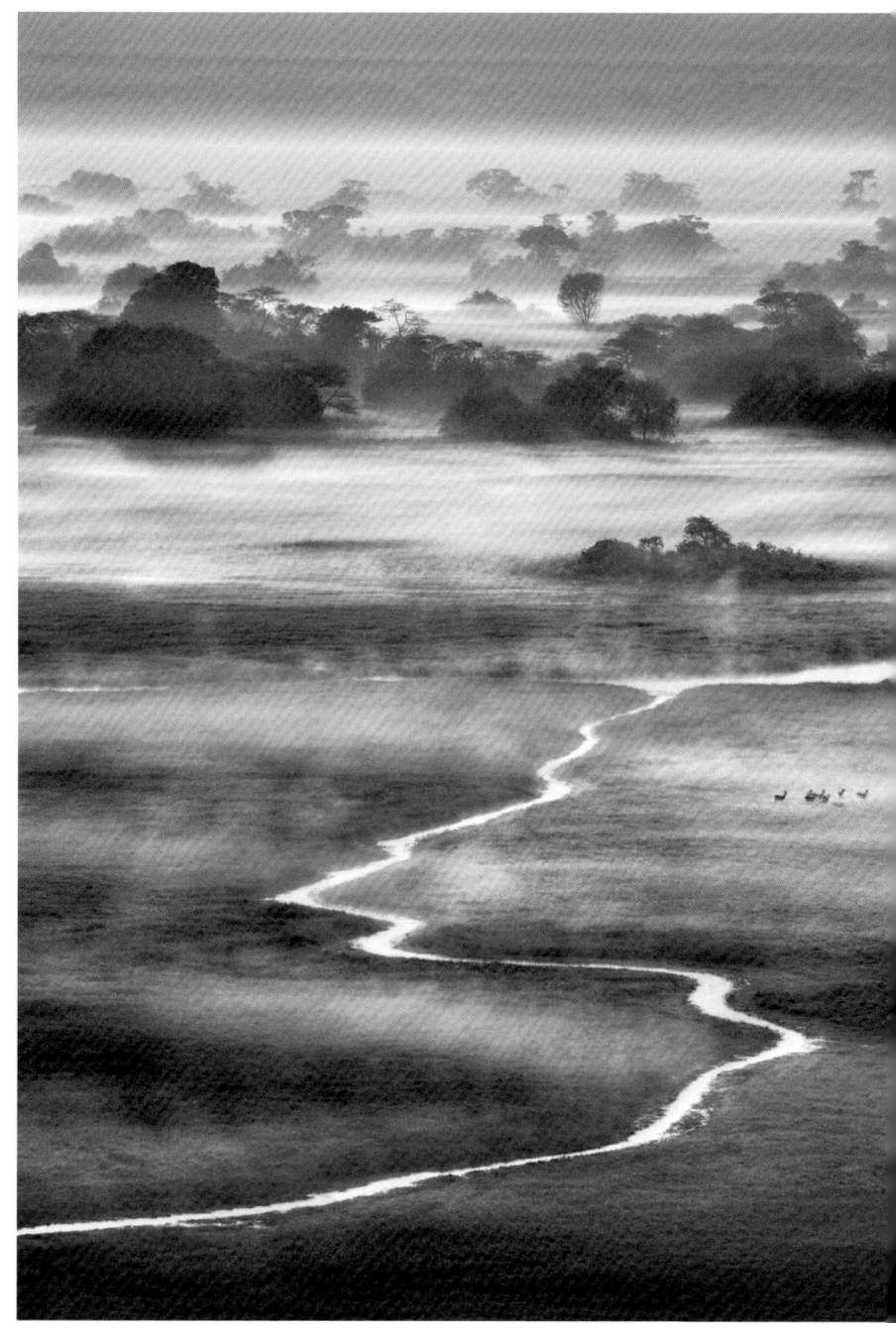

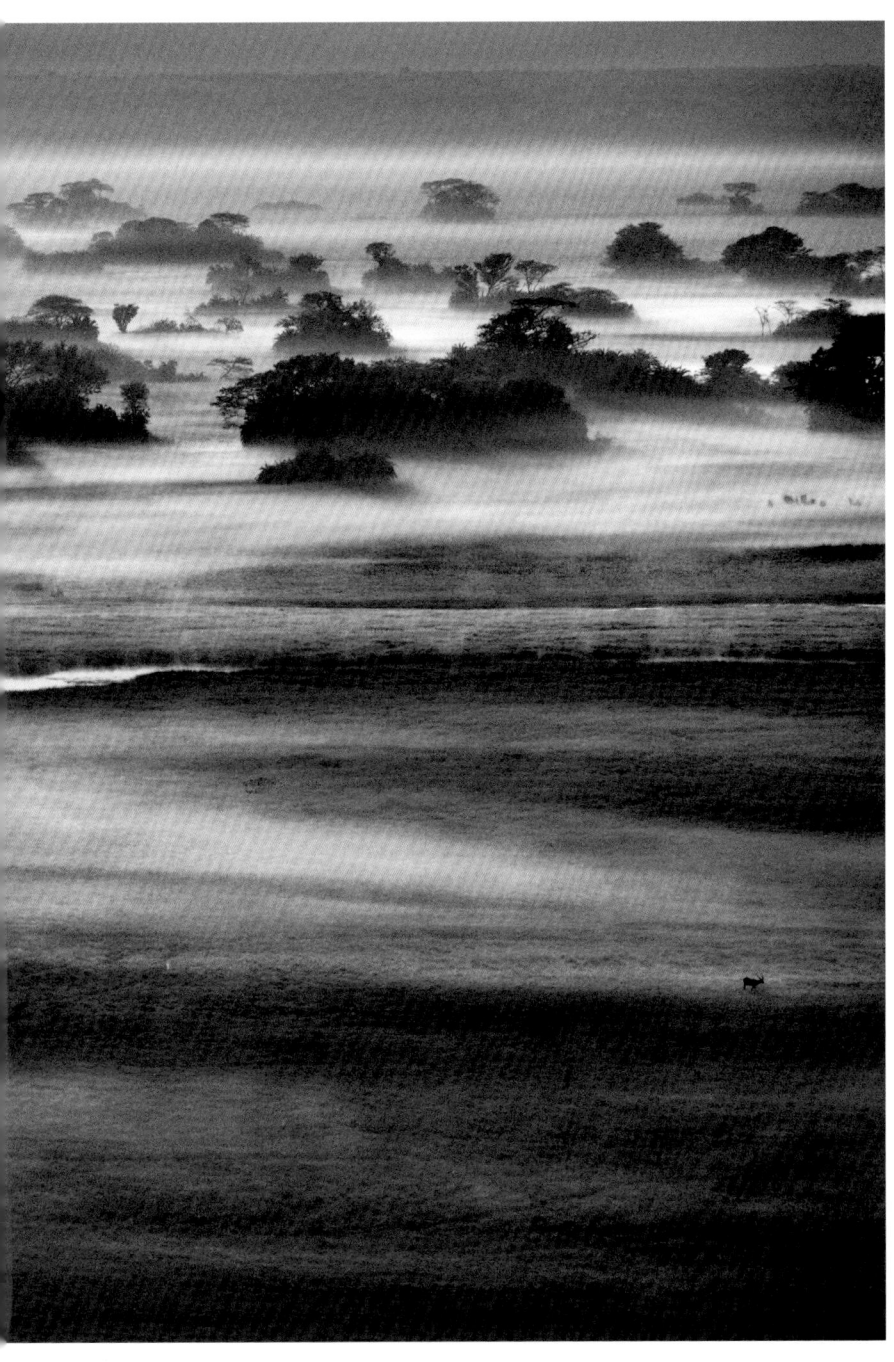

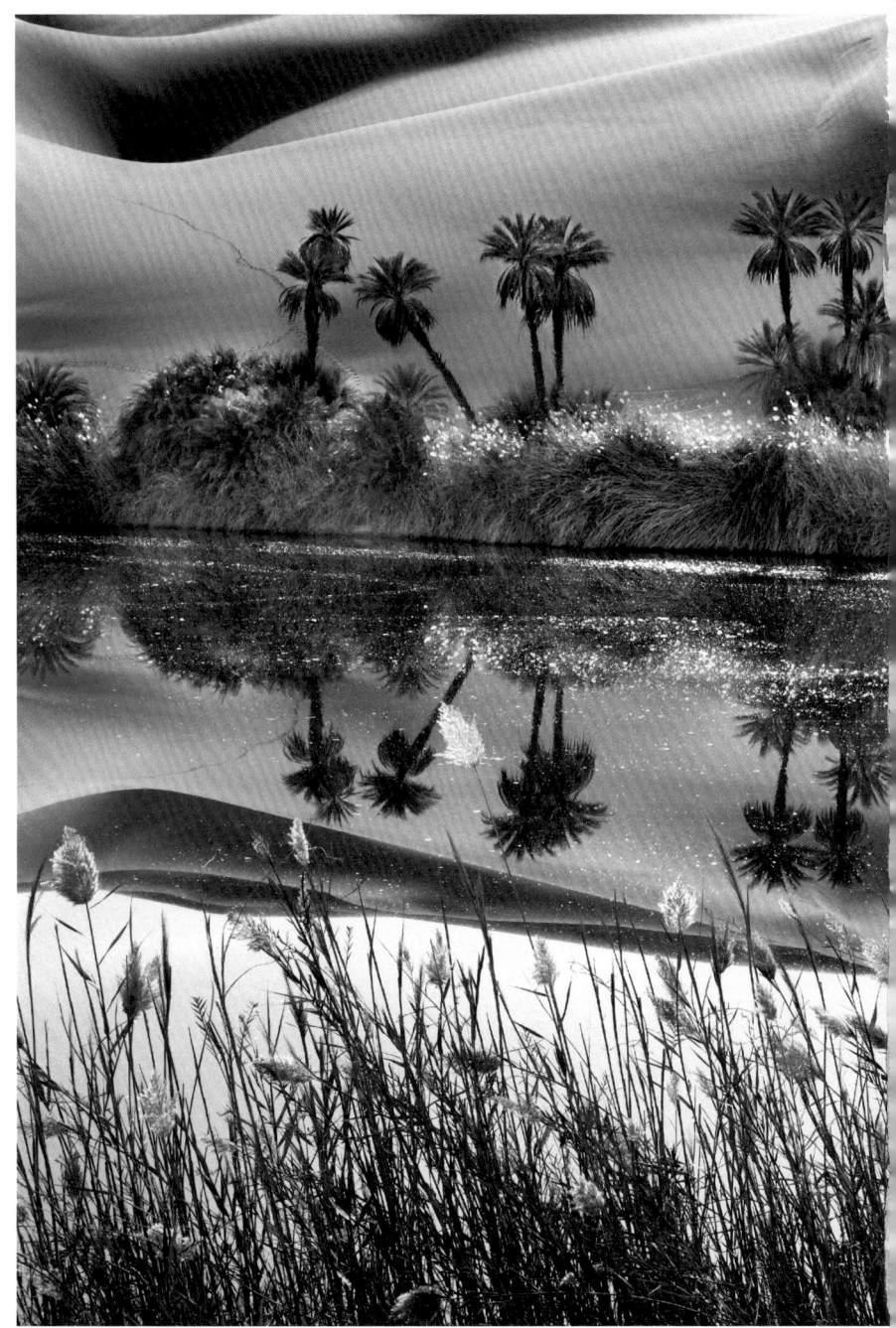

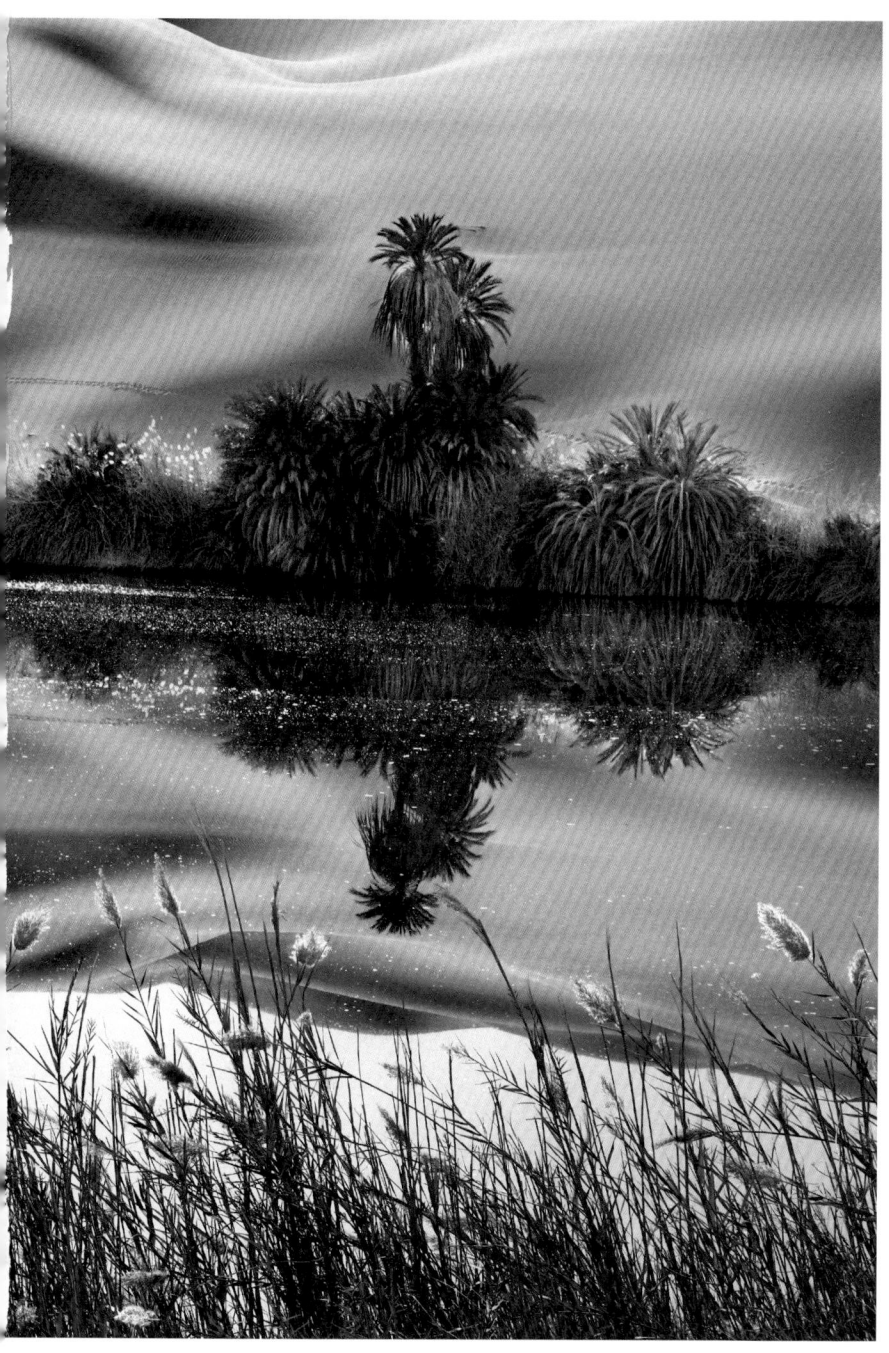

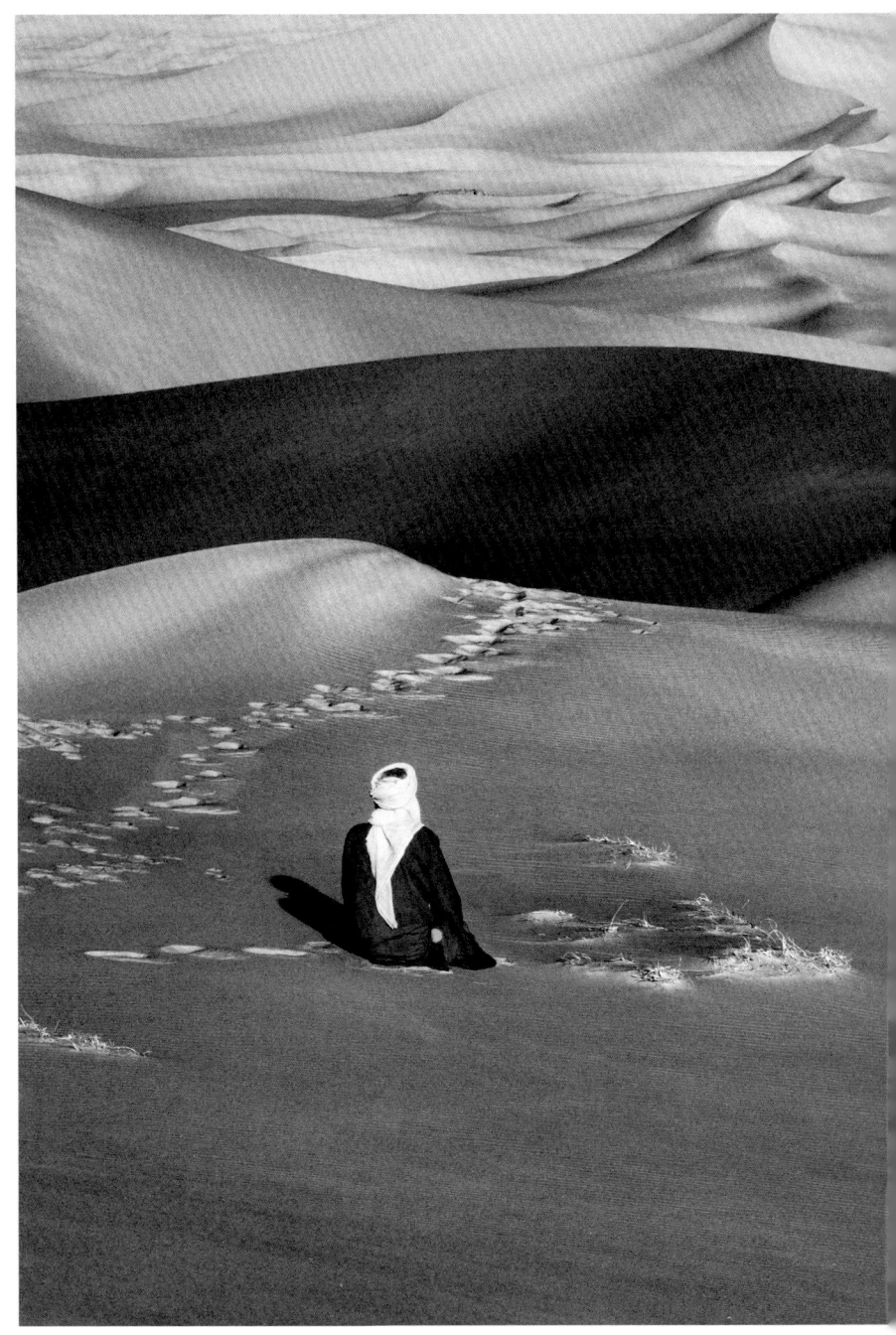

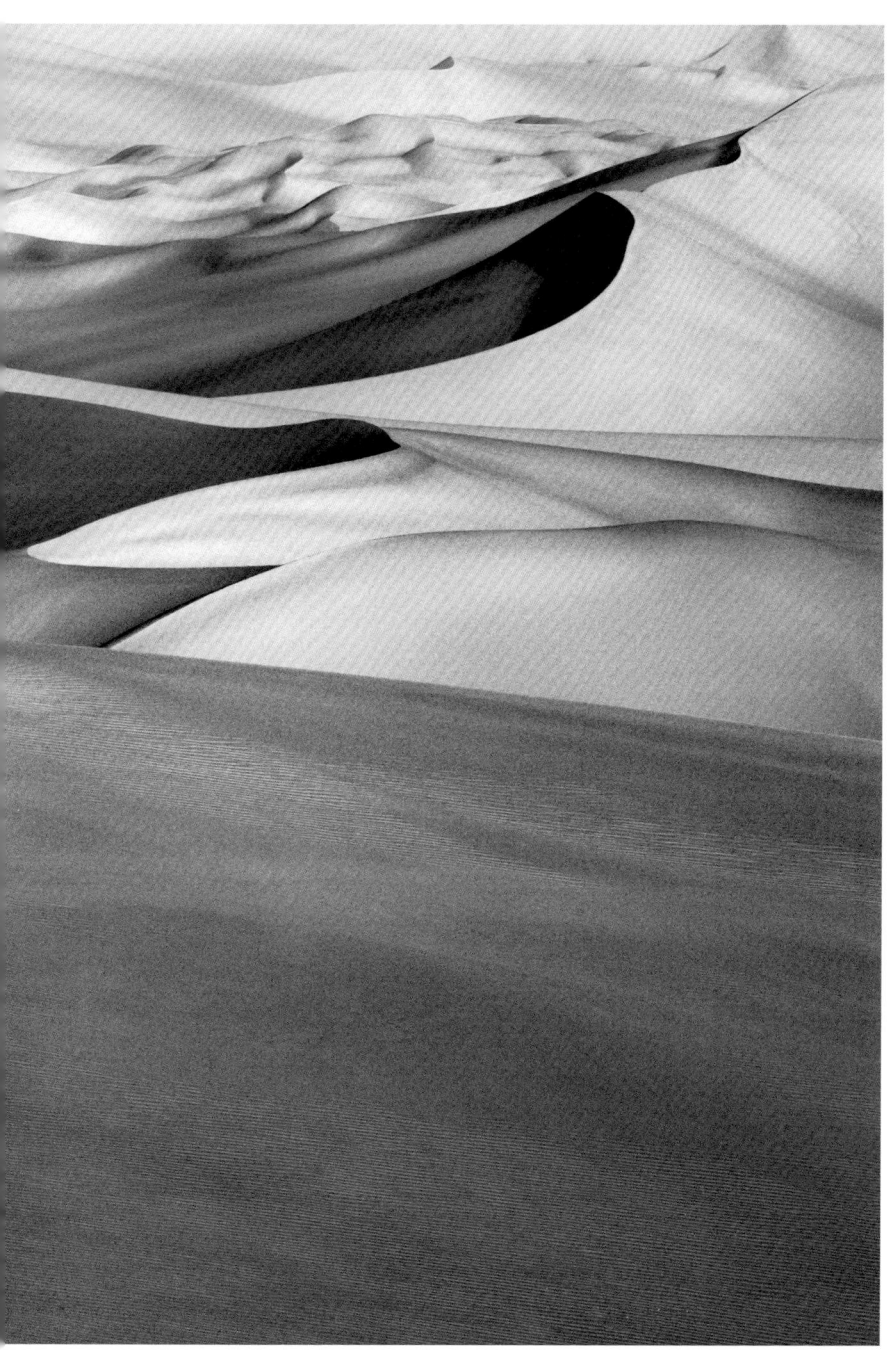

Pages 92/93: The lake in the crater of the 12,200-foot (3,711-meter)-high Bisoke volcano straddles the border between Rwanda and the Democratic Republic of Congo. Giant senecio plants (*Dendrosenecio erici-rosenii*), visible in the foreground, cover almost the entire top of this mountain. Rwanda. May and June 2004.

Pages 94/95: Nights can be chilly during the Zambian winter. At dawn, the water in lakes and small rivers, still warm from the previous day's sun, vaporizes and condenses to form strange and beautiful fog banks. Seen here from a balloon in the Kafue National Park, Zambia, at 5:30 a.m. July and August 2010.

Pages 96/97: The Erg Ubari is a vast expanse of sand dunes covering about 31,000 square miles (80,000 square kilometers). It has no fresh water, but it contains a number of salt lakes concentrated in an area known in Arabic as the "Ramla d'El Daouda," meaning the Dune of the Worm-Eaters. There are more than 20 of these lakes, although most have dried up after intense extraction of underground water for new agricultural projects. Libya. January and February 2009.

Pages 98/99: Large sand dunes in Maor, Tadrart. South of Djanet, Algeria. January and February 2009.

THE DINKA OF SOUTHERN SUDAN

Pages 101 through 105
Southern Sudan is far more ethnically diverse than northern Sudan. Three tribal groups account for around 30 percent of the region's inhabitants: the Dinka, with a population of over one million, followed by the Nuer and the Shilluk. But other groups are also important, including the Hamar, the Toposa, the Anuak, the Murle, the Bari, the Moros-Madi, the Lotuko, the Luo, the Acholi, the Lango, the Didinga, the Ber, and the Mundari. Most of these are known as Nilotic peoples because their languages are rooted in ancient Nilo-Saharan languages and because they live in the Upper Nile region. However, some groups have gone south to find pasture for their cattle and have assumed different identities, such as the Massai in Kenya and the Tutsi in Rwanda and Burundi.

These photos show Dinka in their cattle camps, in the region situated between Rumbek and Bor. During the rainy season, they live in villages and grow grain, such as millet, sorghum, and maize, while their cattle graze on plentiful grass. But during the dry season, when grass disappears from this semiarid region, the villages are abandoned and the Dinka set off in search of fresh pastures with their entire cattle herd, sometimes more than 5,000 strong. They bring few belongings but carry all the cereal they will need during the long months of drought. When they find an area with water and grass, they establish cattle camps. During the day, the animals may walk several kilometers to graze and drink, and at night they are driven back to the camps. The lives of the Dinka are inseparable from those of their cattle. Every morning, they use the urine of the cows to wash their faces but also to add to fresh milk as a preservative. They further collect cow dung, which, once dried in the sun, is burned at night and helps to chase away mosquitoes drawn by the cattle. They then cover themselves and their animals with the ash, which protects the skin against the stings of insects and parasites.

Opposite: In the village of Ger, a symbolic representation of horns is molded on the inside wall of a traditional home. Southern Sudan. February and March 2006.

Pages 102/103: Cattle camp of Amak at the end of the day, when the herd has returned to the camp for the night. This is the most active time at the camp. Several piles of burning cow pats can be seen here; the smoke keeps the insects away from the camp. Southern Sudan. February and March 2006.

Pages 104/105: Cattle camp of Kei. The Dinka choose the best bulls for mating and identify them by giving a distinct shape to the animals' horns as they grow. Southern Sudan. February and March 2006.

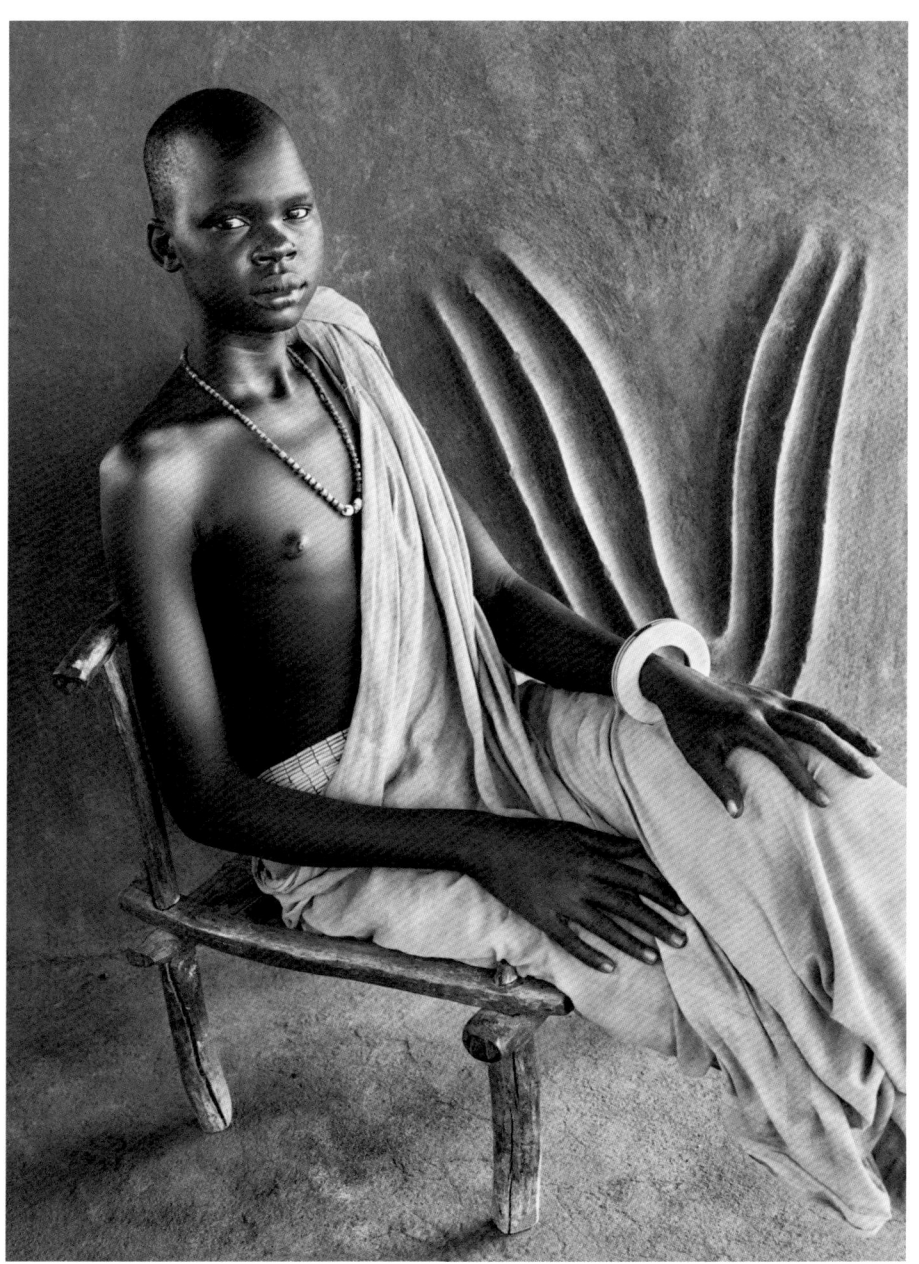

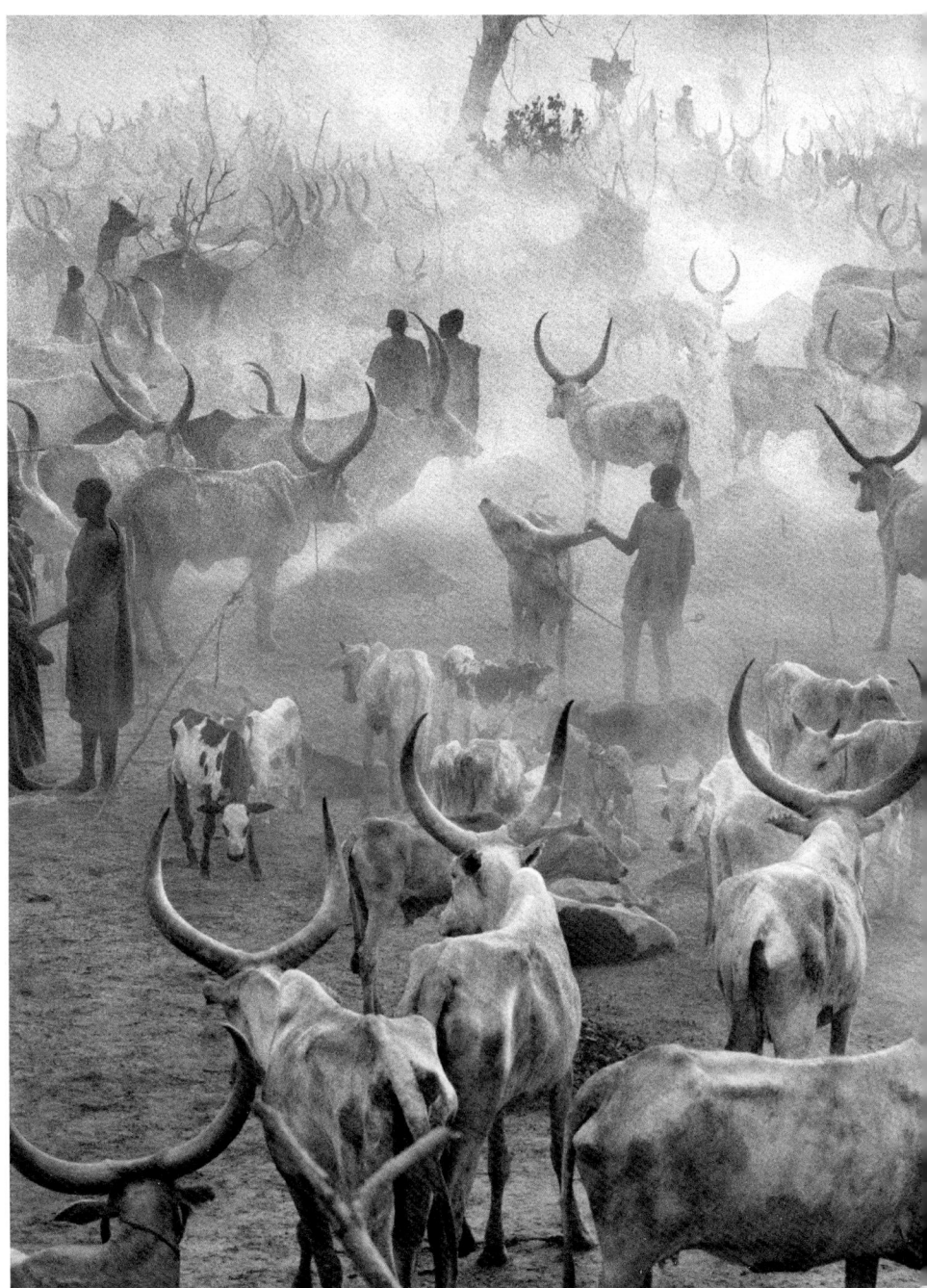

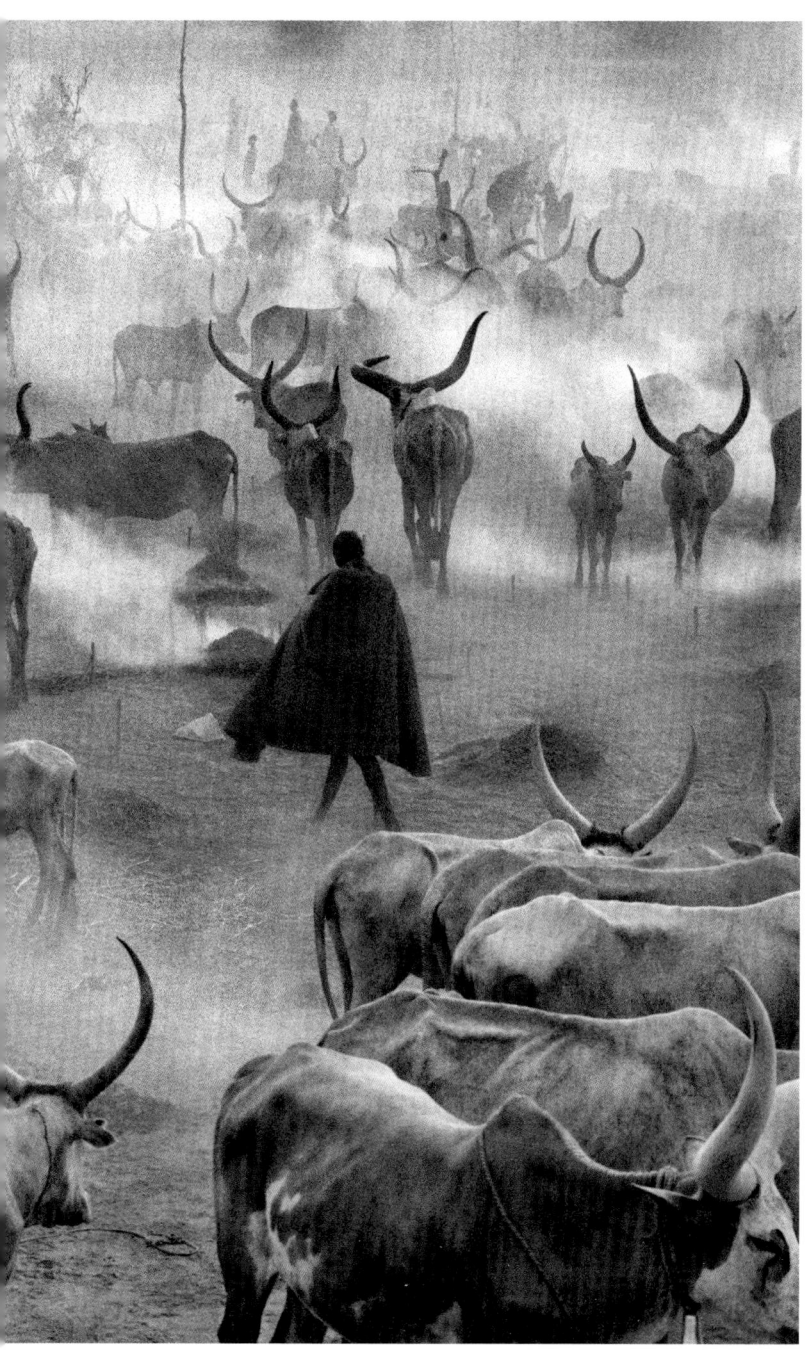

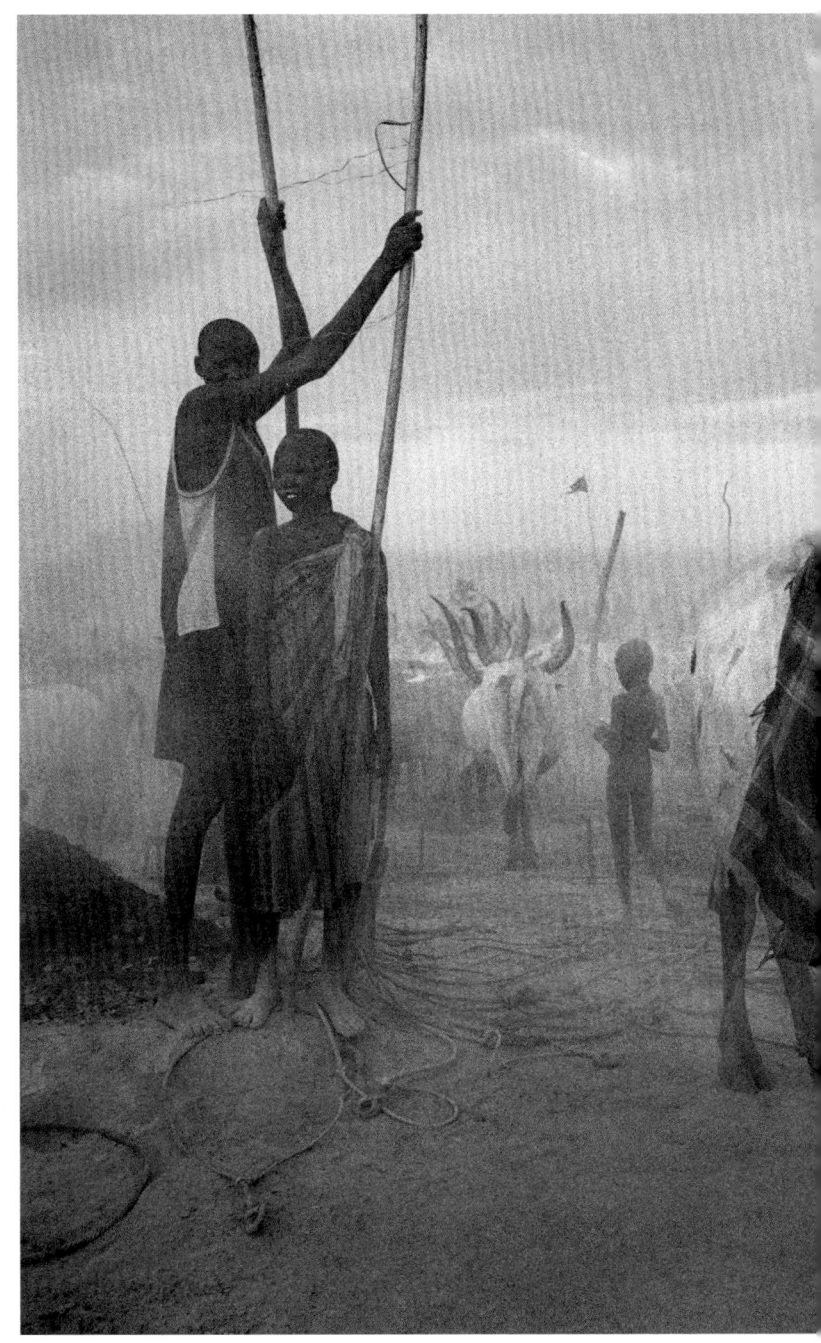

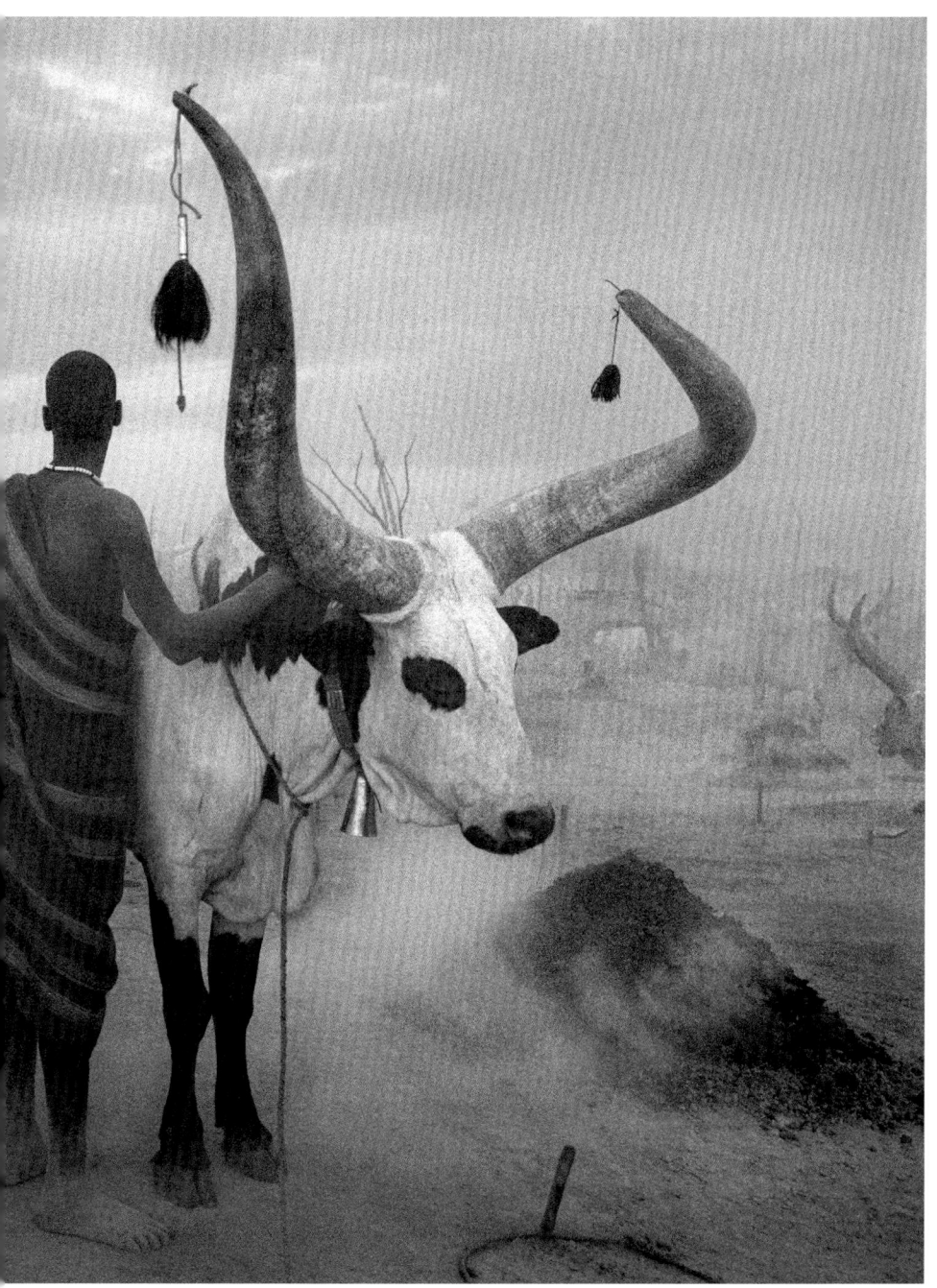

THE HIMBA

Pages 107 through 109
The Himba of Kaokoland in Namibia are seminomadic cattle herders who live in small groups, dependent on finding water and grass for their cattle. They are scattered across northern Kaokoland, where the proximity of the Kunene River makes living conditions adequate for both humans and livestock. The Himba have had a complicated history.

Known as the Herero in the 16th century, they migrated from the Moçâmedes Province of Angola towards the Kunene River. They called the land to their left "oka-oko," from which Kaokoveld and, later, Kaokoland, were derived. Later, when the main Herero group migrated to central and eastern Namibia, a smaller group remained in the arid and mountainous Kaokoland. In the mid-19th century, these Herero fell victim to marauding bands of cattle thieves and slid into deep poverty.

The Herero to the south began to call them "Tjimba-Herero," meaning "very poor Herero." Many "Tjimba" fled back across the Kunene River to Angola to seek refuge with the Ngambwe people, who called them "ova-Himba" ("beggars"). Over time, they rebuilt their cattle herds and, when they finally returned to Kaokoland, they retained the name of Himba.

Opposite: This Himba group in Orutanda was made up almost entirely of women since their men had gone in search of water and pastures with their cattle. Kaokoland, Namibia. October and November 2005.

Pages 108/109: A Himba group in Omuramba, near the Zebra Mountains in Kaokoland. Namibia. October and November 2005.

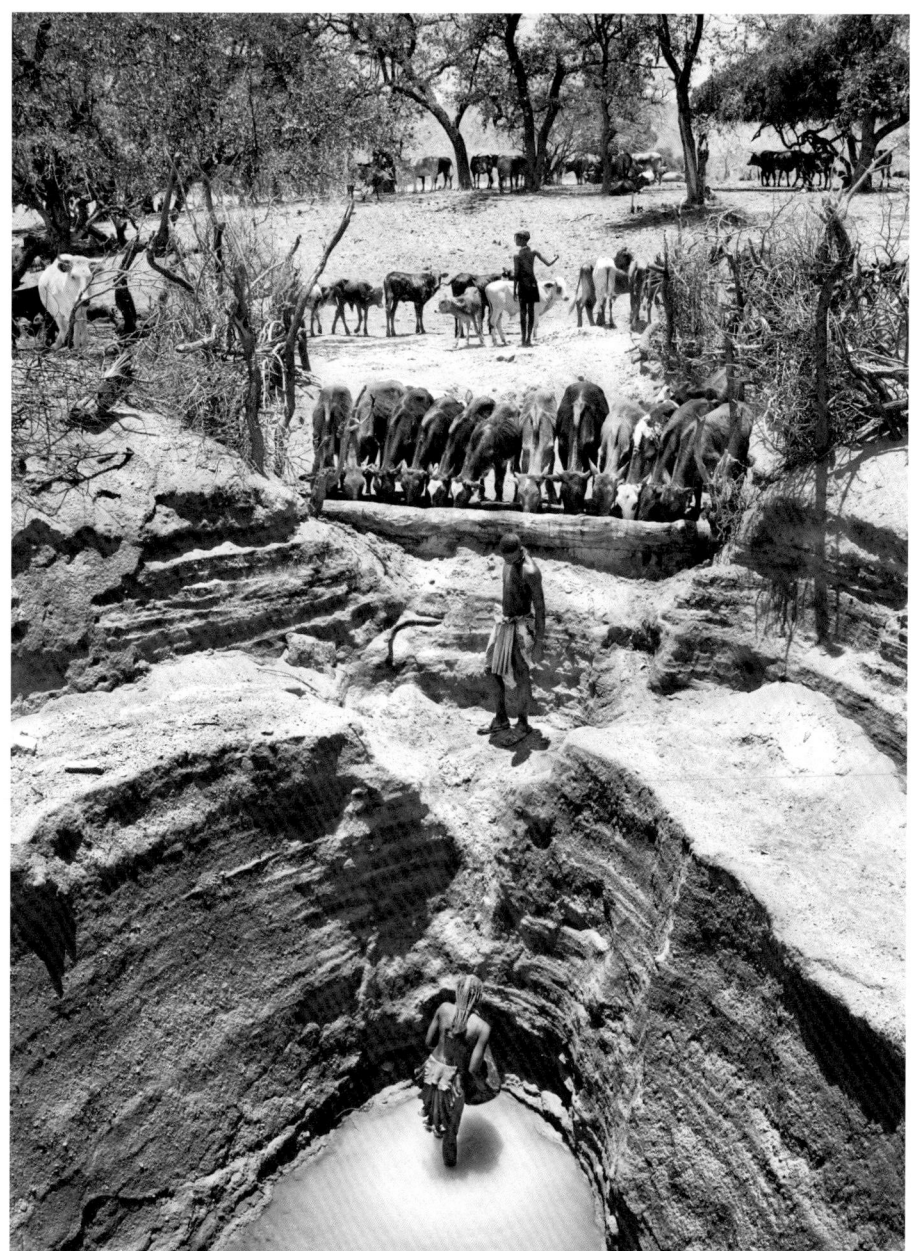

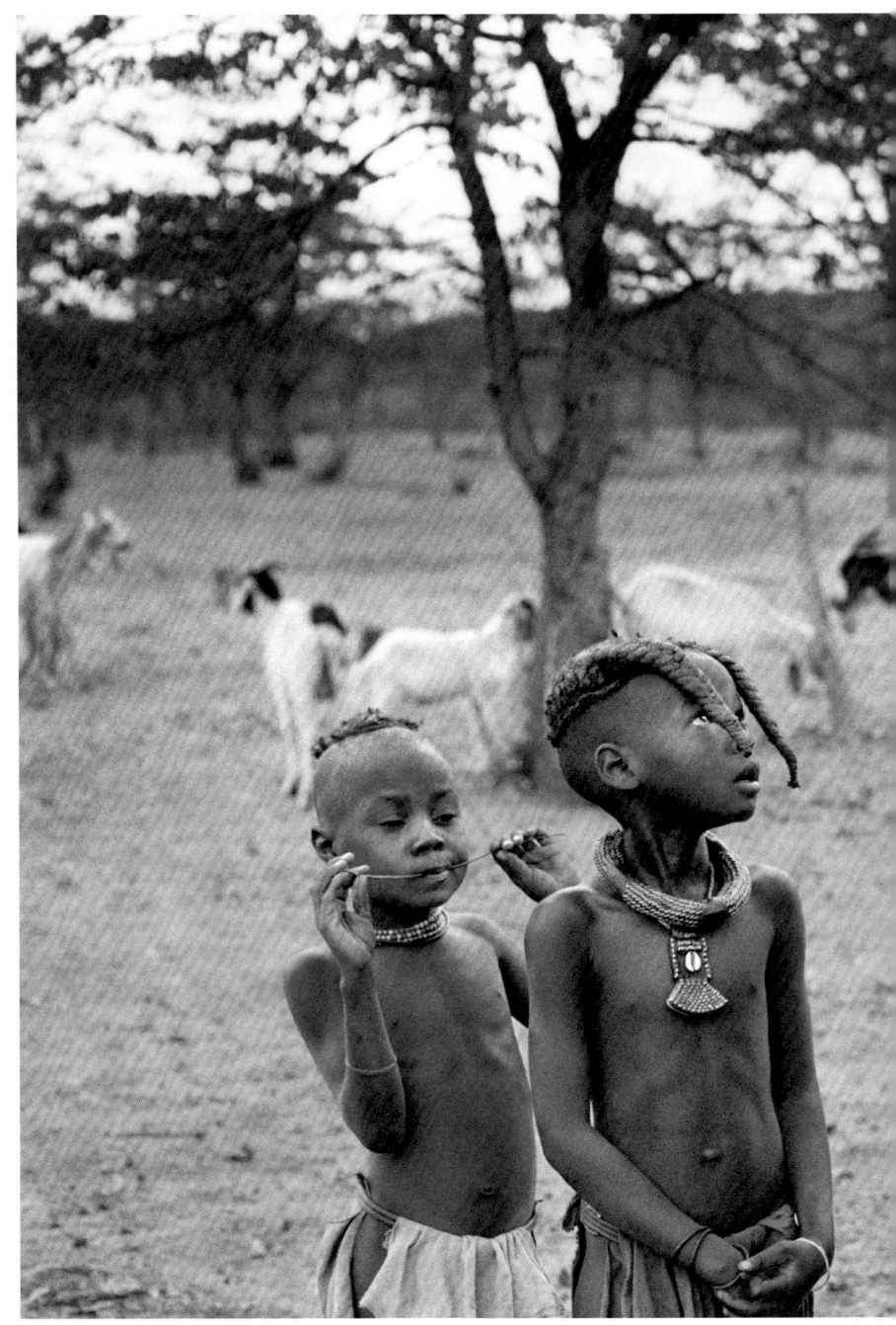

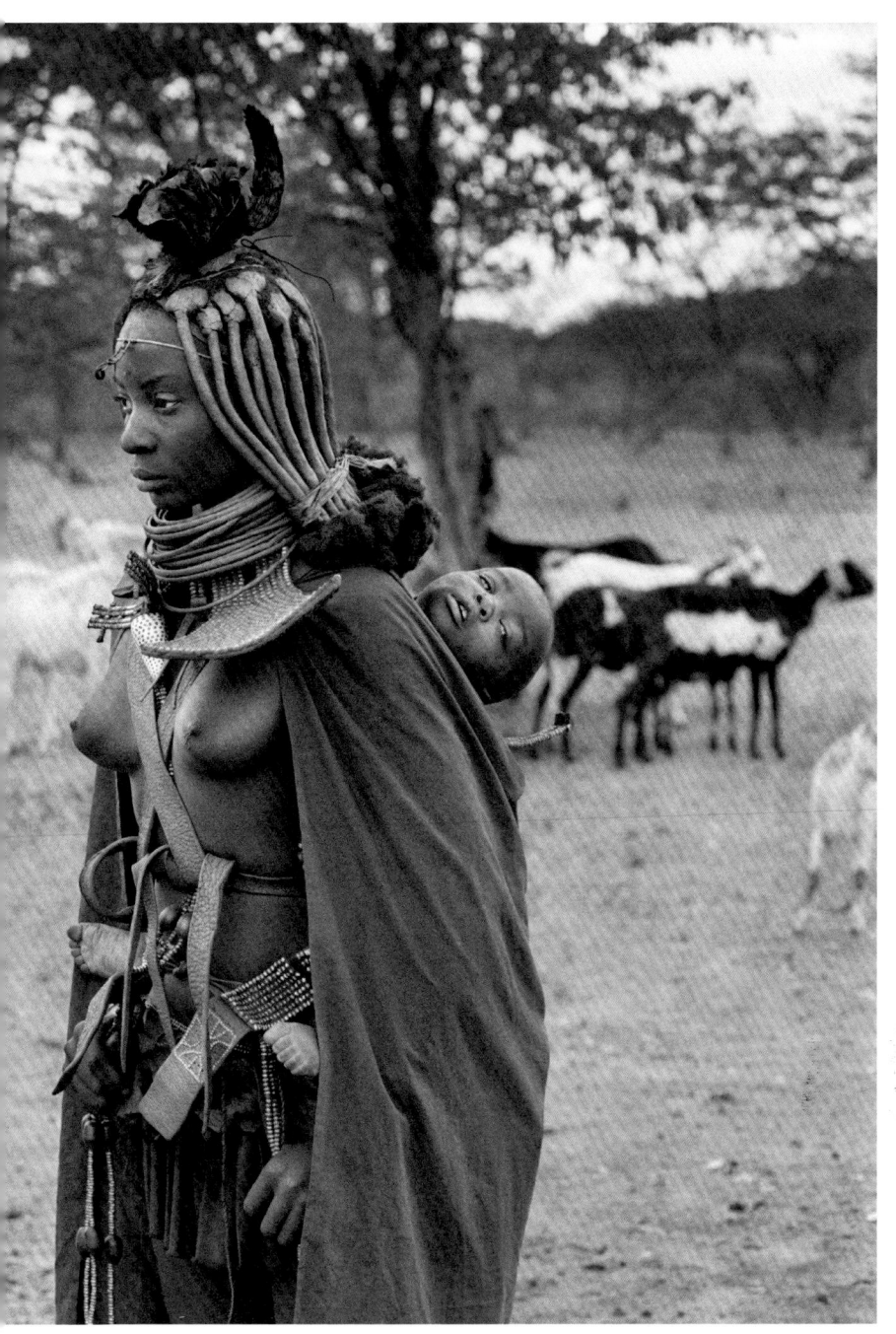

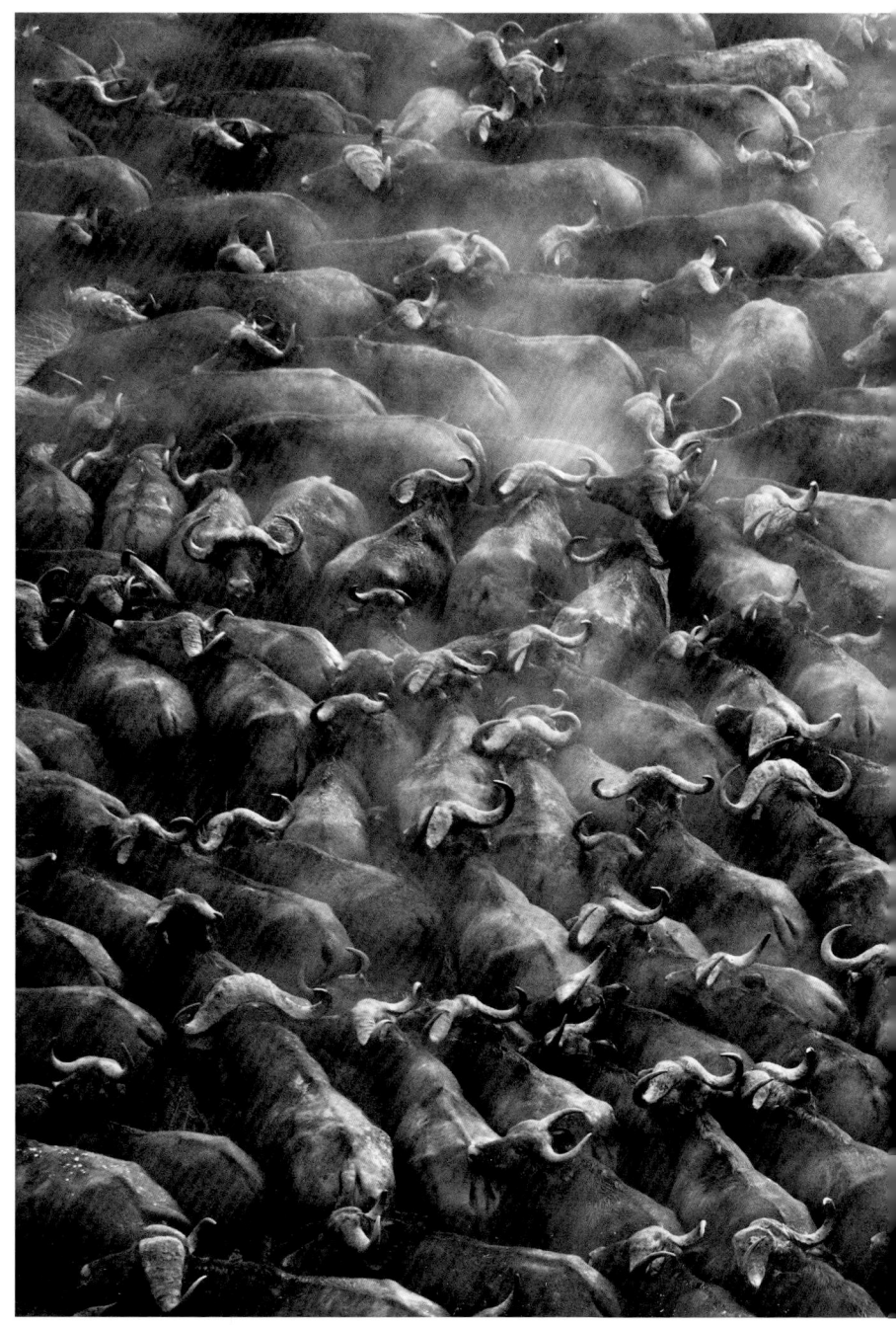

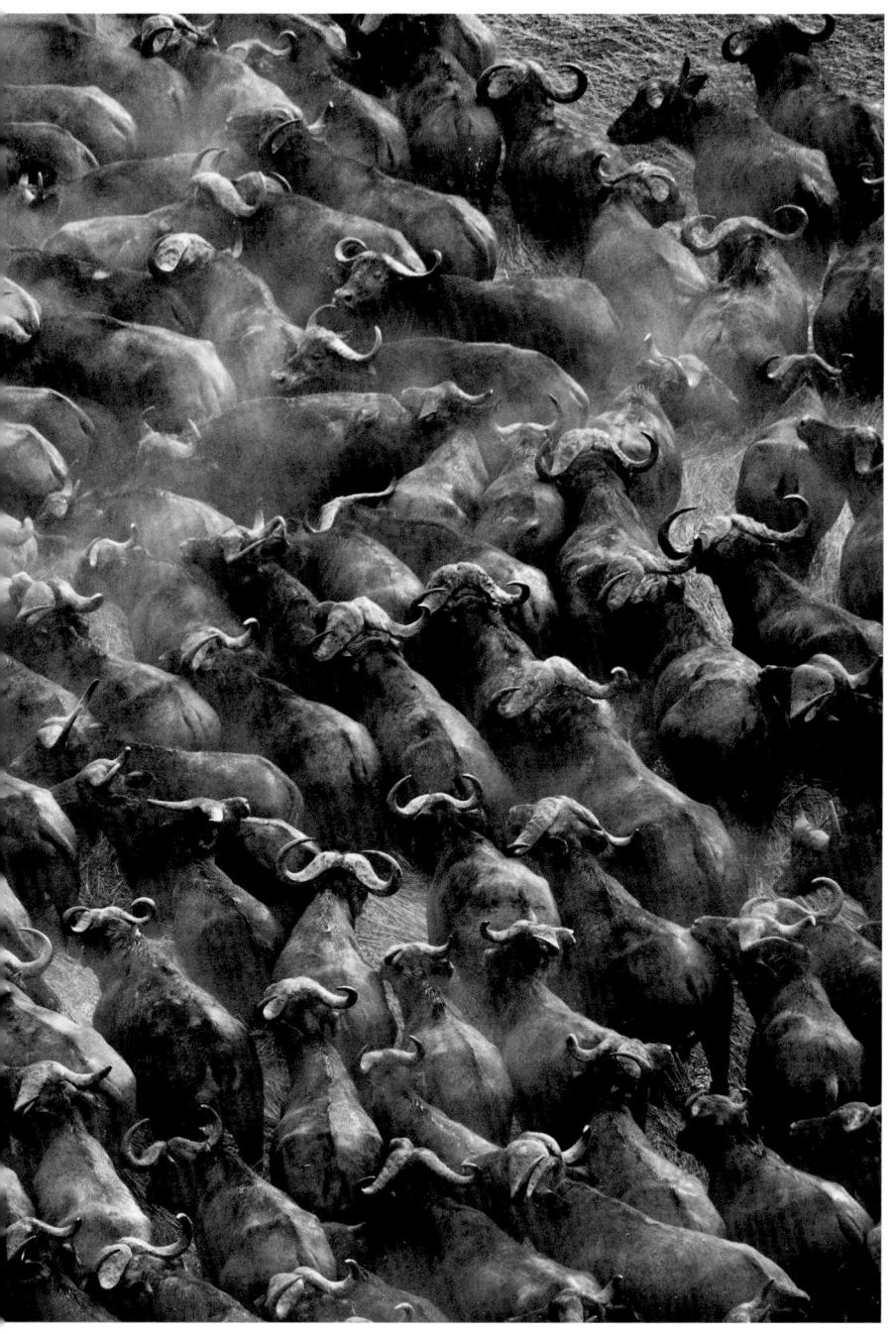

Pages 110/111 and opposite: Animals are understandably frightened when they hear a helicopter flying overhead, but in a balloon it was possible to come close to this herd of buffalos (*Syncerus caffer*) without disturbing them. Balloons, however, pose other problems. It is crucial to fly very early in the morning before spirals of hot air rising from the ground cause dangerous turbulence. There is also the risk that wind can send the balloon way off course. Kafue National Park, Zambia. July and August 2010.

Pages 114/115: African elephants (*Loxodonta africana*) are both diurnal and nocturnal, forming herds of as few as six and as many as 200 animals, with a cow as leader. Chobe River. Botswana. June and July 2007.

Pages 116/117: The lion (*Panthera leo*) is the largest of Africa's cat family, with males weighing between 400 and 530 pounds (180 and 240 kilos) and females between 265 and 400 pounds (120 and 180 kilos). Cubs are born at any time of the year after a gestation period of around 110 days. Here two brothers rest after a night of hunting in preparation for the following night's hunt. Young males are pushed out of the group by the male leader when they are strong enough to create their own group. Kafue National Park. Zambia. July and August 2010.

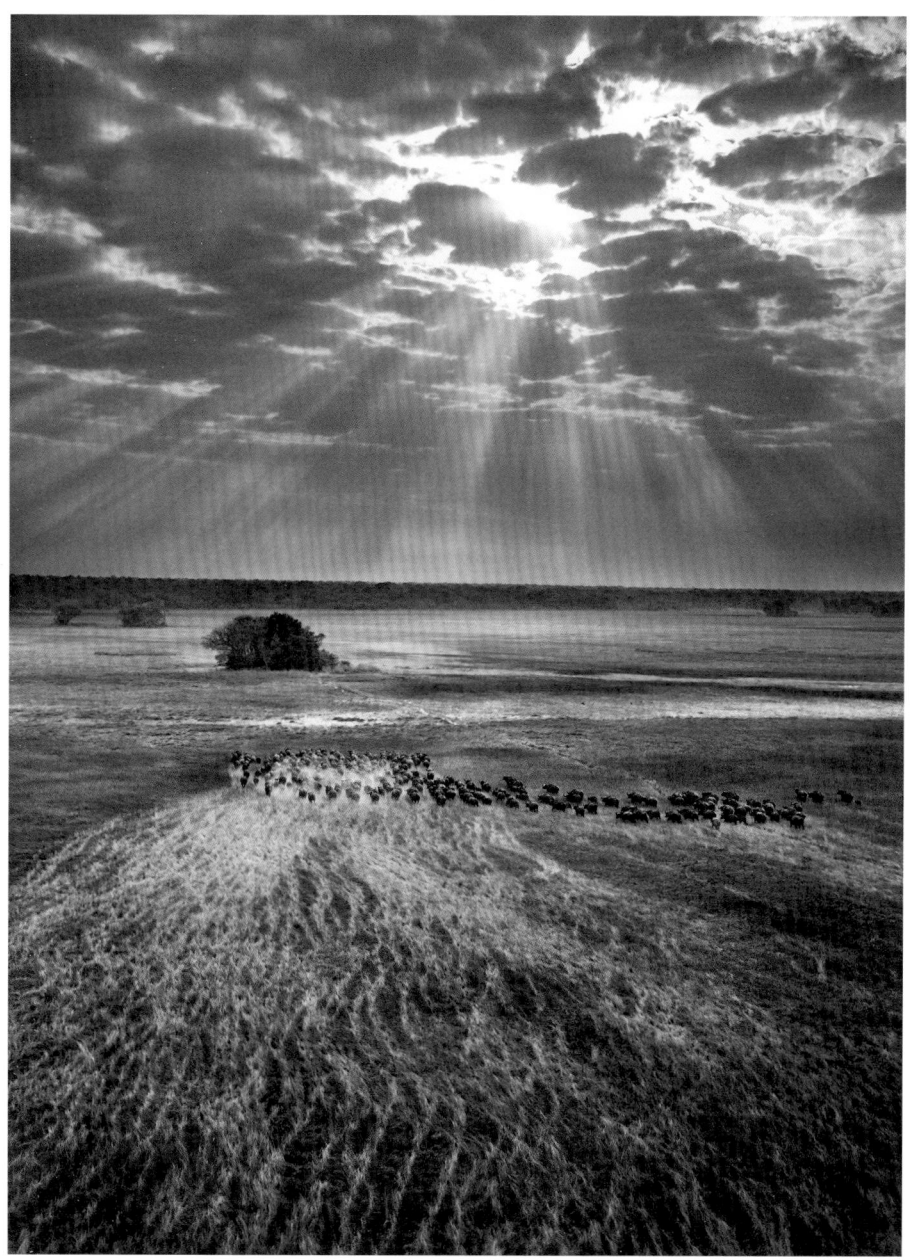

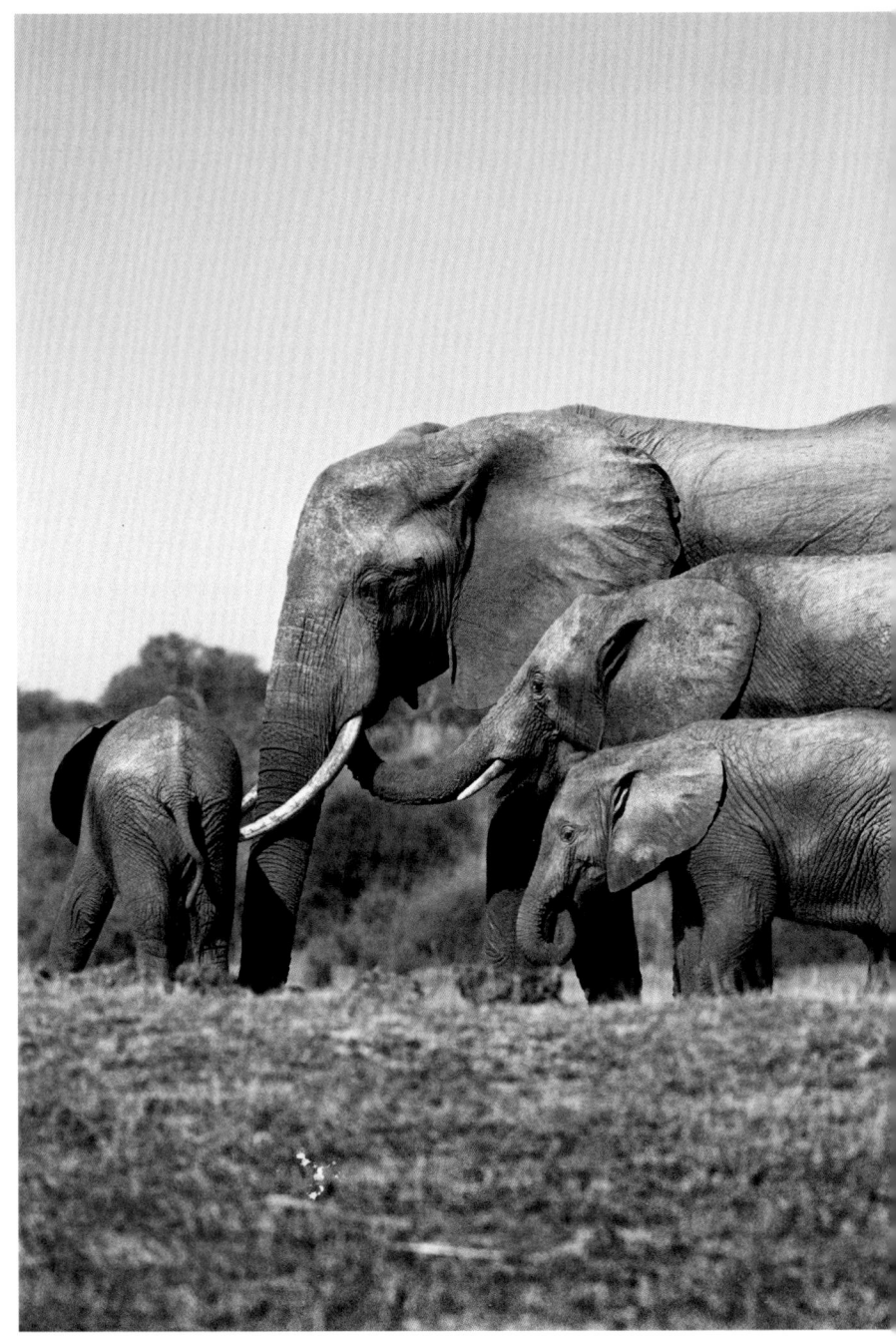

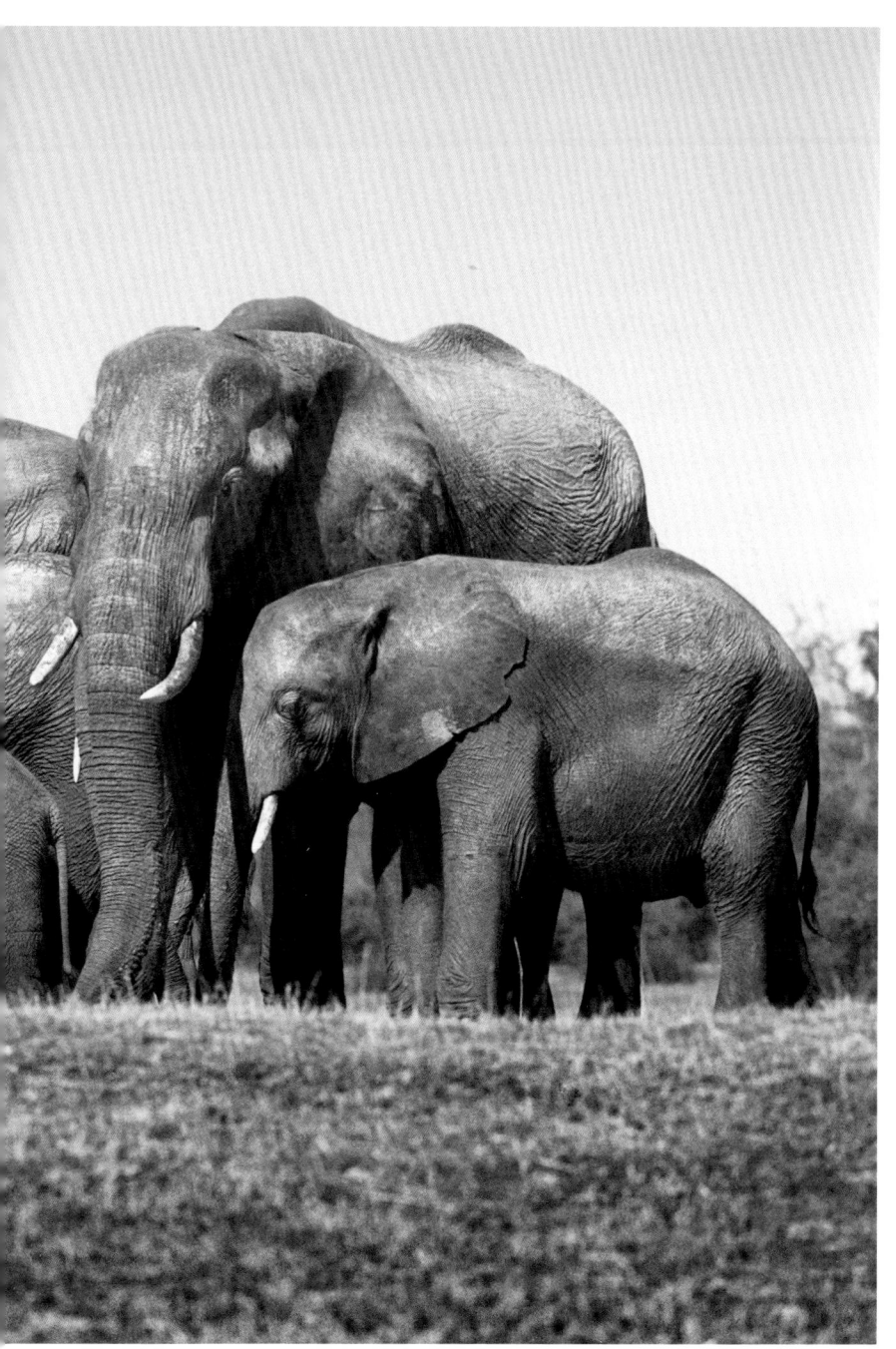

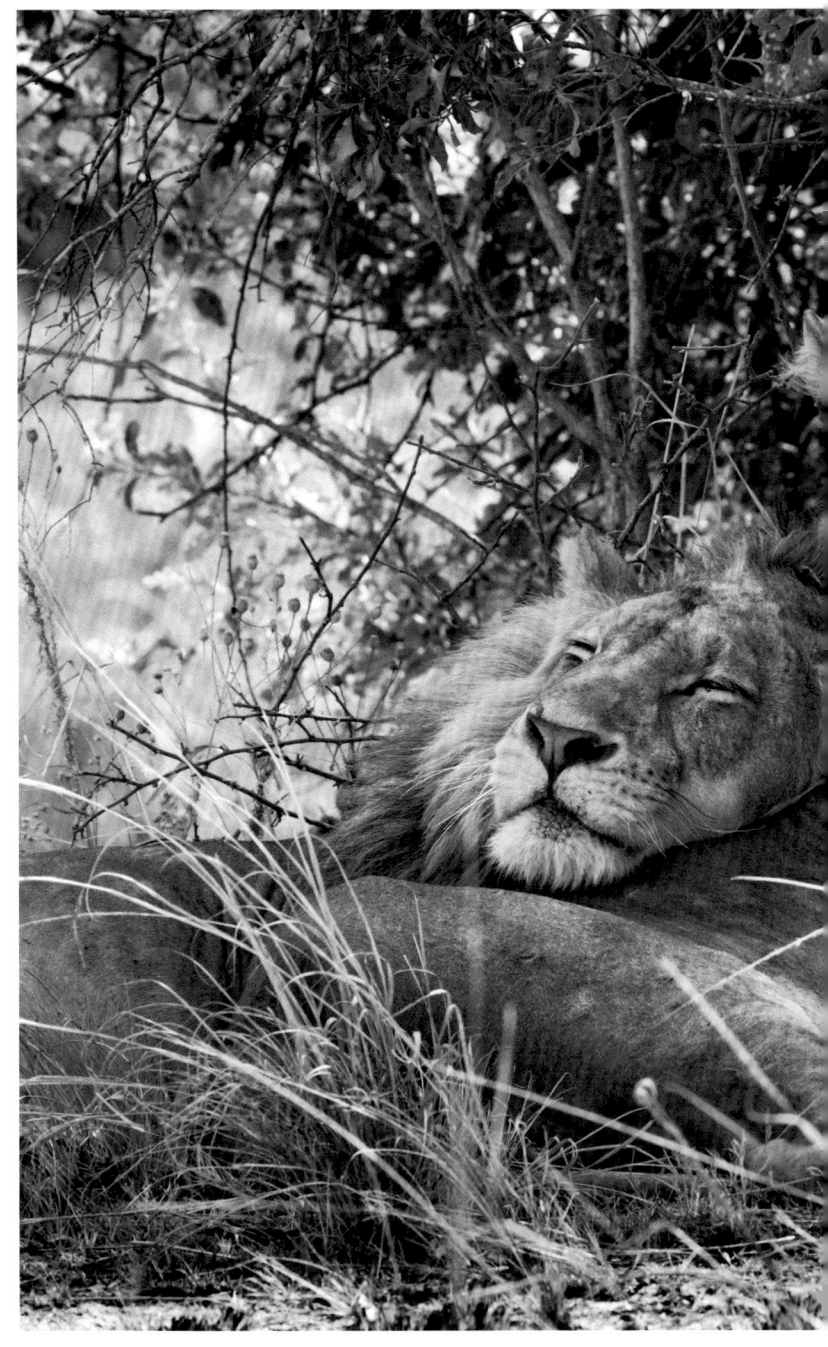

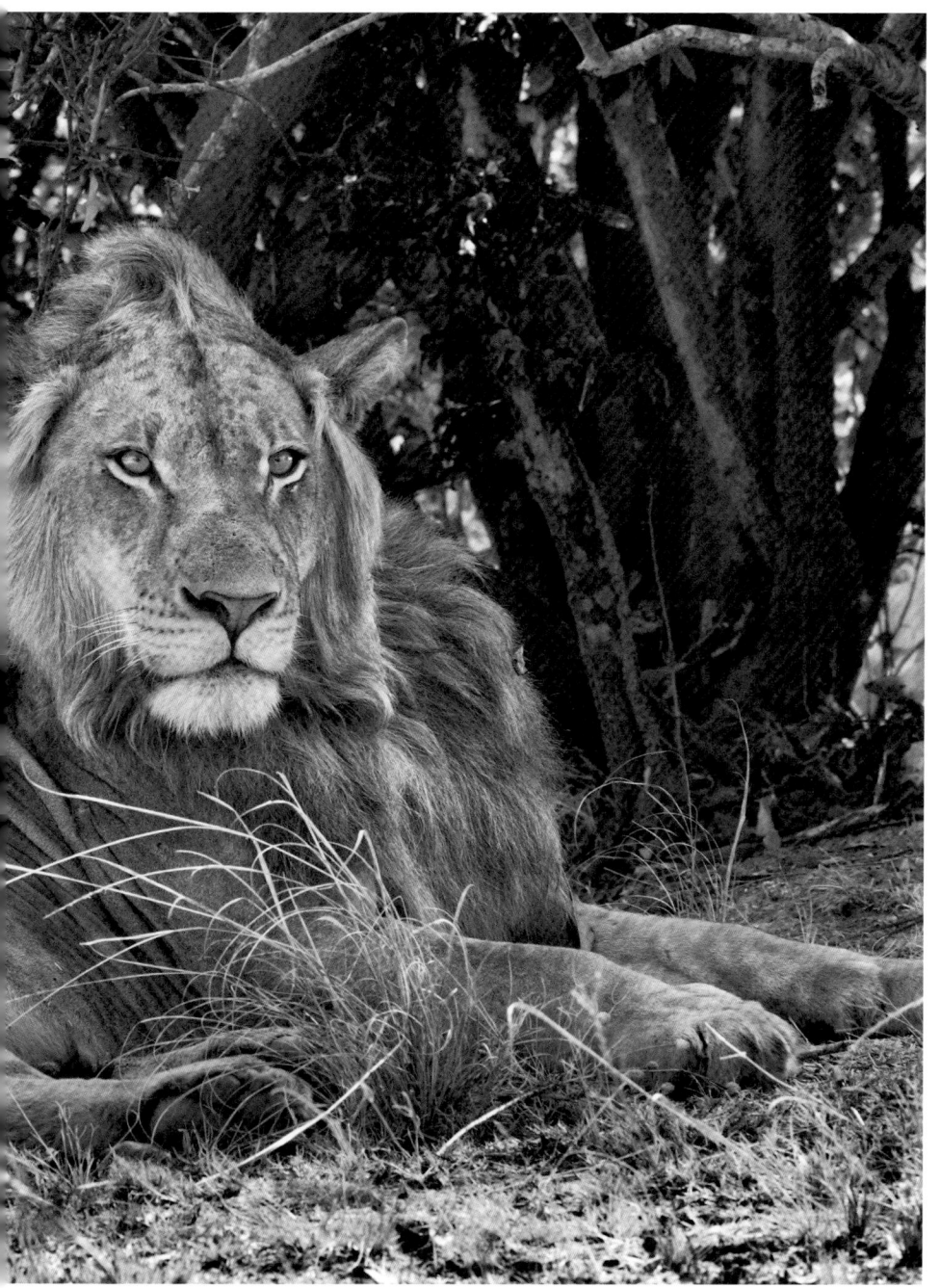

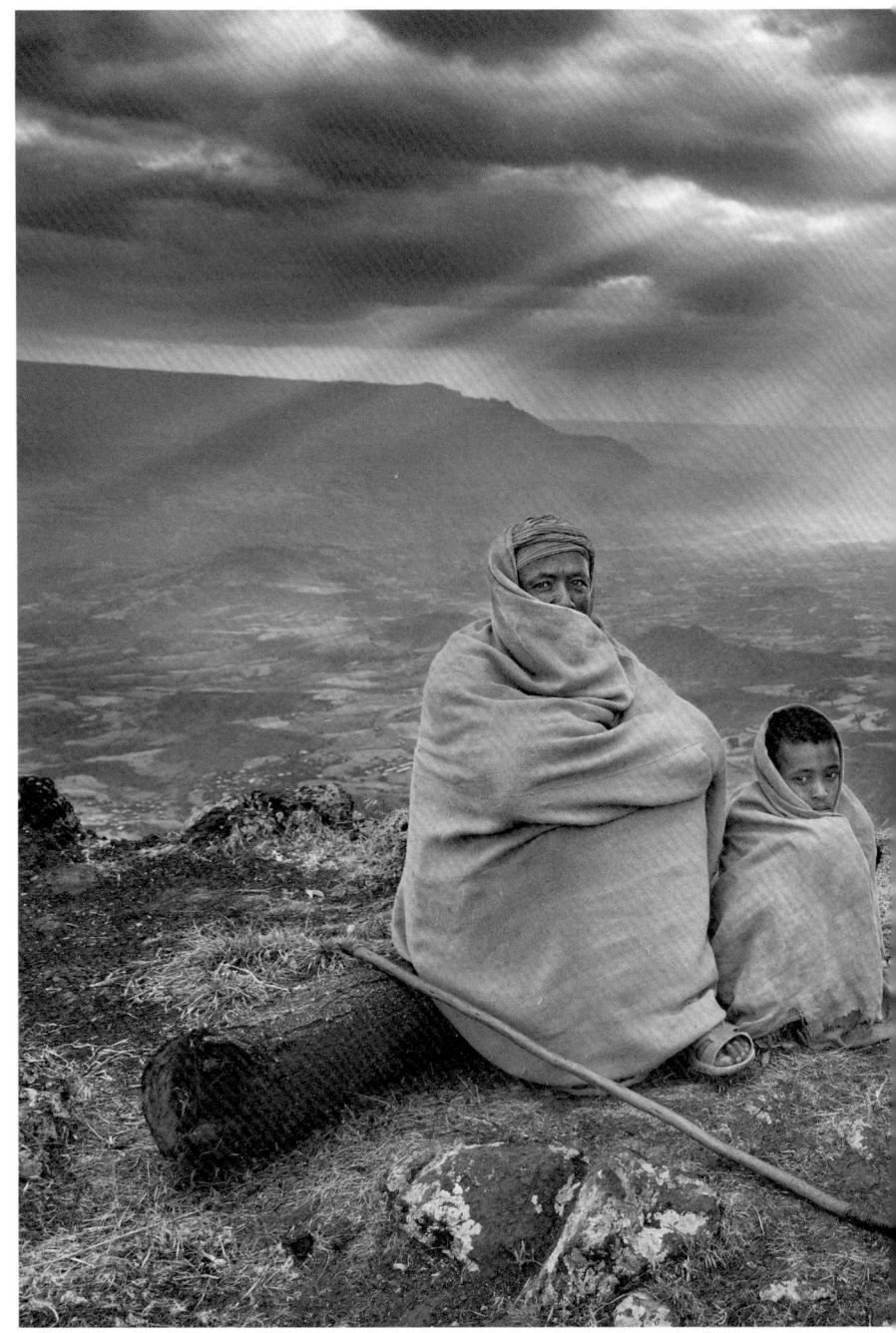

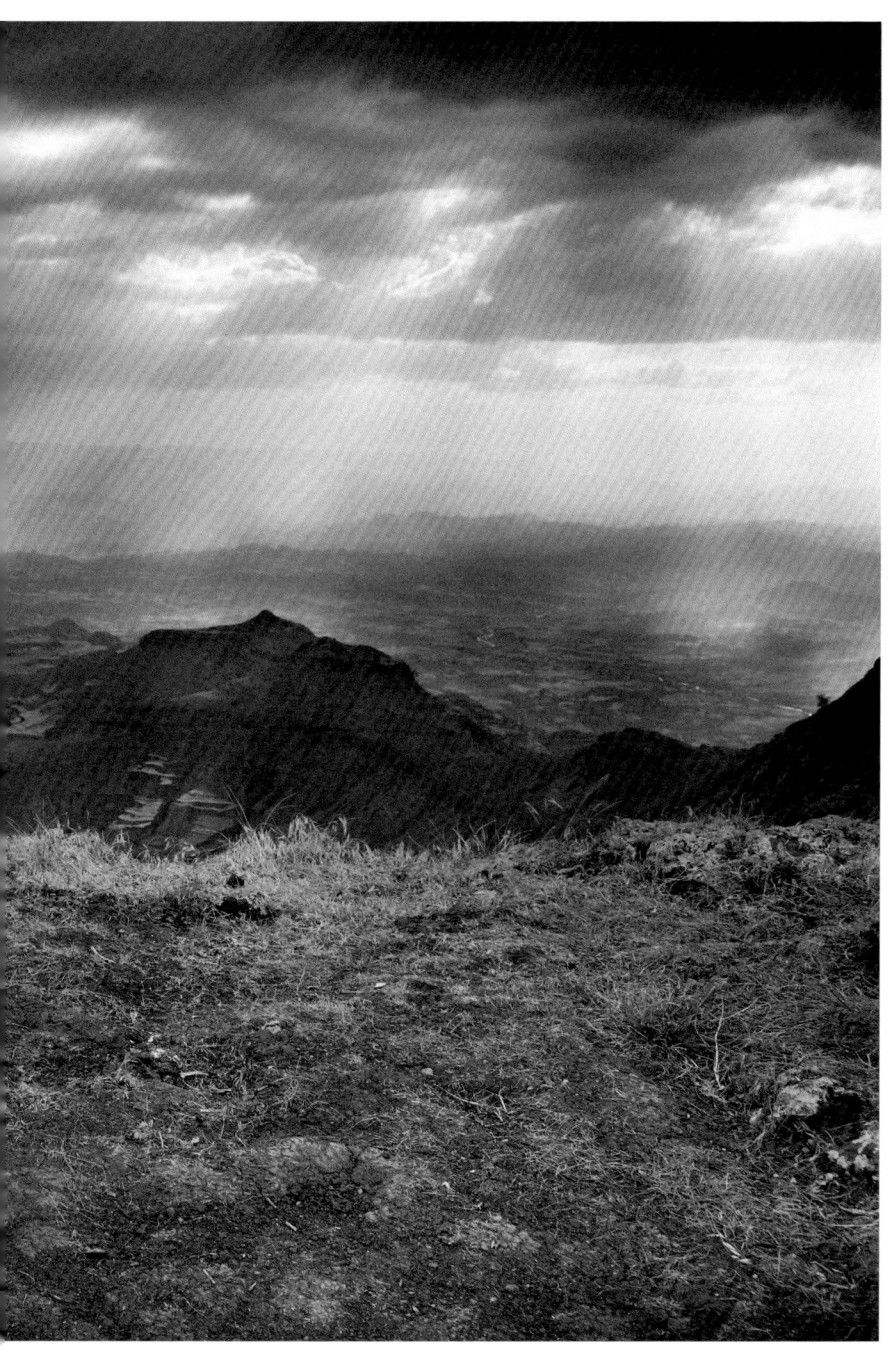

A JOURNEY THROUGH THE OLD TESTAMENT

Pages 118 through 123

Modern Ethiopia has been beset by political instability, war, and famine spawned by drought, but it is also a country that retains remnants of one of the world's oldest civilizations. This trip took me across an extraordinarily remote region of northern Ethiopia where, in many senses, time has stood still. It is here that you can find some of the world's oldest Christian communities, whose lives, farming practices, and ways of worship have changed little for centuries. It is also a rugged, mountainous area sliced into imposing canyons by rivers, which have carried away the soil to bring fertility to the Nile Valley far to the north. The region is so inaccessible that it can only be reached on foot. Unsurprisingly, the logistics involved in what turned out to be a 55-day-long hike of more than 500 miles (800 kilometers) were immensely complicated. To carry everything needed to work, eat, and sleep, I hired 15 donkeys, with each donkey accompanied by its owner. During the most difficult climbs, the owners would even carry some of the donkeys' burden in order to protect their most valuable possession. Even so, five donkeys died of exhaustion and, naturally, we compensated the owners for their loss.

Our journey began in Lalibela, one of Ethiopia's oldest Christian towns, famous above all for its 11 Orthodox churches carved out of red volcanic rock in the 12th century. From there, we headed northeast, taking a week to reach the high plane of Abune Yosef, 14,000 feet (4,200 meters) above sea level. On our way, we passed through Christian villages where a hole in a hillside announced the entrance to a cave church. Some ancient Christian traditions survive: for example, on Wednesdays and Fridays, they refuse to consume any product of animal extraction, such as milk or meat. Their Bibles and church documents are written on animal skins. Local priests are allowed to marry and they work in the fields like other farmers, but they enjoy the special status of being elders of the church. As we traveled west, the mountains slowed our progress, requiring long hikes up and down steep slopes in order to advance just a few kilometers on the map. But we kept coming across farming communities that grow grains on ancient terraces and raise cattle that provide milk for yoghurt and cheese; here, at least, we saw no evidence of hunger. In some areas, the patchwork patterns of cultivated fields stretch as far as the eye can see. Because many

languages and dialects survive in a relatively small area, a product of the isolation imposed by the mountainous terrain, we had to change guides every two or three villages. When we could, we also often spent two or three days in villages to give us time to explore nearby areas and to be accepted by villagers. And since on some days we walked as many as 22 miles (35 kilometers), we were glad for the rest. For the most part, families live in round huts, with walls made of wood and mud. Their sleeping quarters are on a wooden mezzanine, directly above their animals, whose body heat brings welcome warmth at over 9,800 feet (3,000 meters) above sea level. Our journey eventually led us into the region long inhabited by Ethiopian Jews, known as the Falusha or, more formally, as Beta Israel. The roots of this community remain mysterious, although legend has it that its members descended from Menelik I, said to be the son of King Solomon and the Queen of Sheba. In the 1980s and 1990s, about 85 percent of the 140,000 Falusha immigrated to Israel, but Judeo-Christian traditions and values continue in the home and in schools. Local Ethiopians also watch over the Jewish cemeteries. Finally, we reached the Simien National Park, a wonderfully unspoiled area that is home to many rare species, including the gelada baboon, the Simien fox, and the Walia ibex, unique to this area. Here, as during much of the journey, the developed world belonged to another age.

Pages 118/119: View of the valley that stretches from Lalibela to Makina Lideta Maryan. From this location, more than 9,800 feet (3,000 meters) above sea level, thousands of cultivated fields in the valley below resemble patchwork quilts. With no roads connecting them to the modern world, the people in this area live much as their ancestors did in biblical times. Ethiopia. October and November 2008.

Opposite: The Simien National Park. Massive erosion over the years on the Ethiopian plateau has created one of the most spectacular landscapes in the world, with jagged mountain peaks, deep valleys, and sharp precipices of some 4,900 feet (1,500 meters). The average altitude here is 13,000 feet (4,000 meters). Ethiopia. October and November 2008.

Pages 122/123: This village situated at the base of Abune Yosef is at an altitude of 12,970 feet (3,953 meters). Nights are very cold. People keep their cattle inside their houses at night to protect them from temperatures below freezing. Ethiopia. October and November 2008.

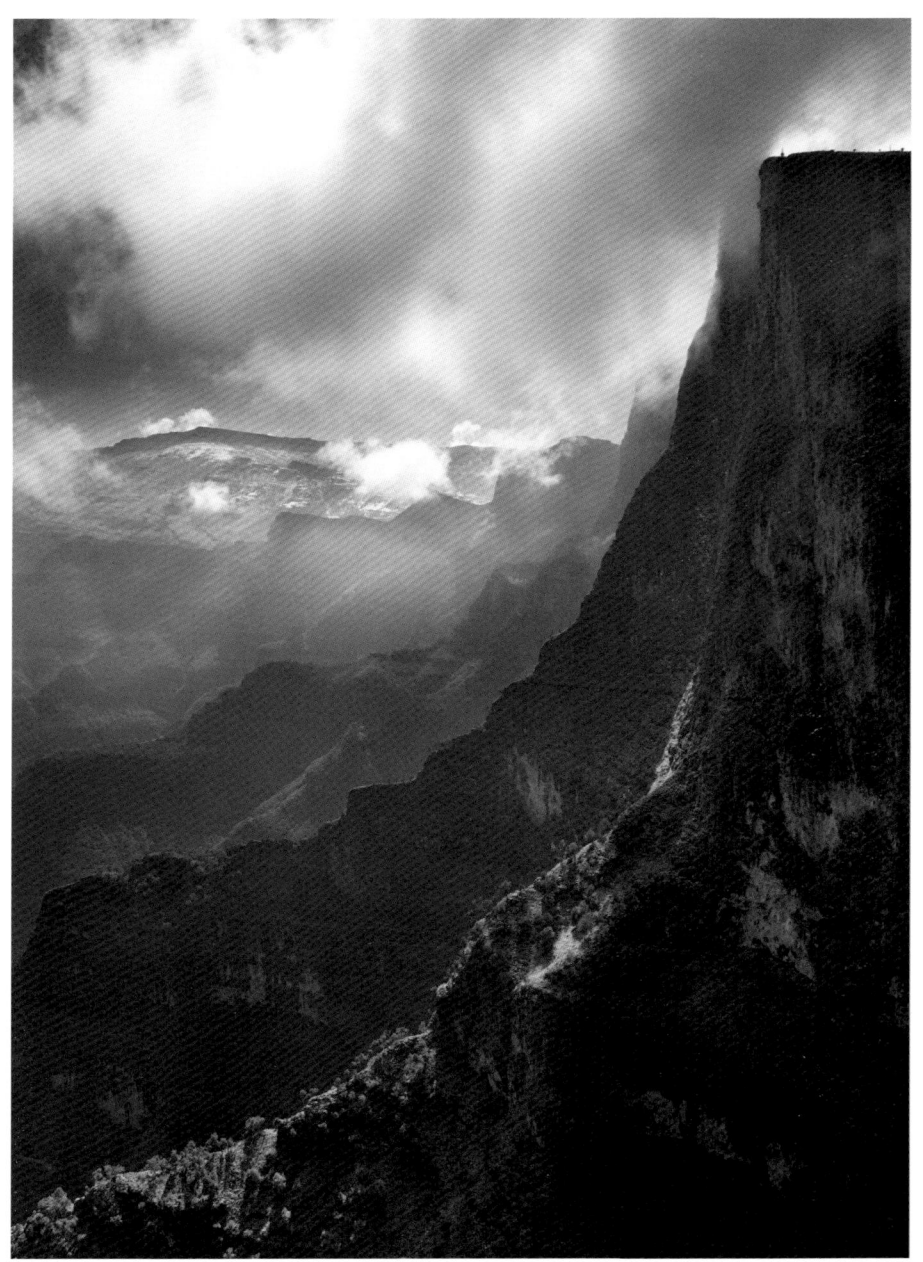

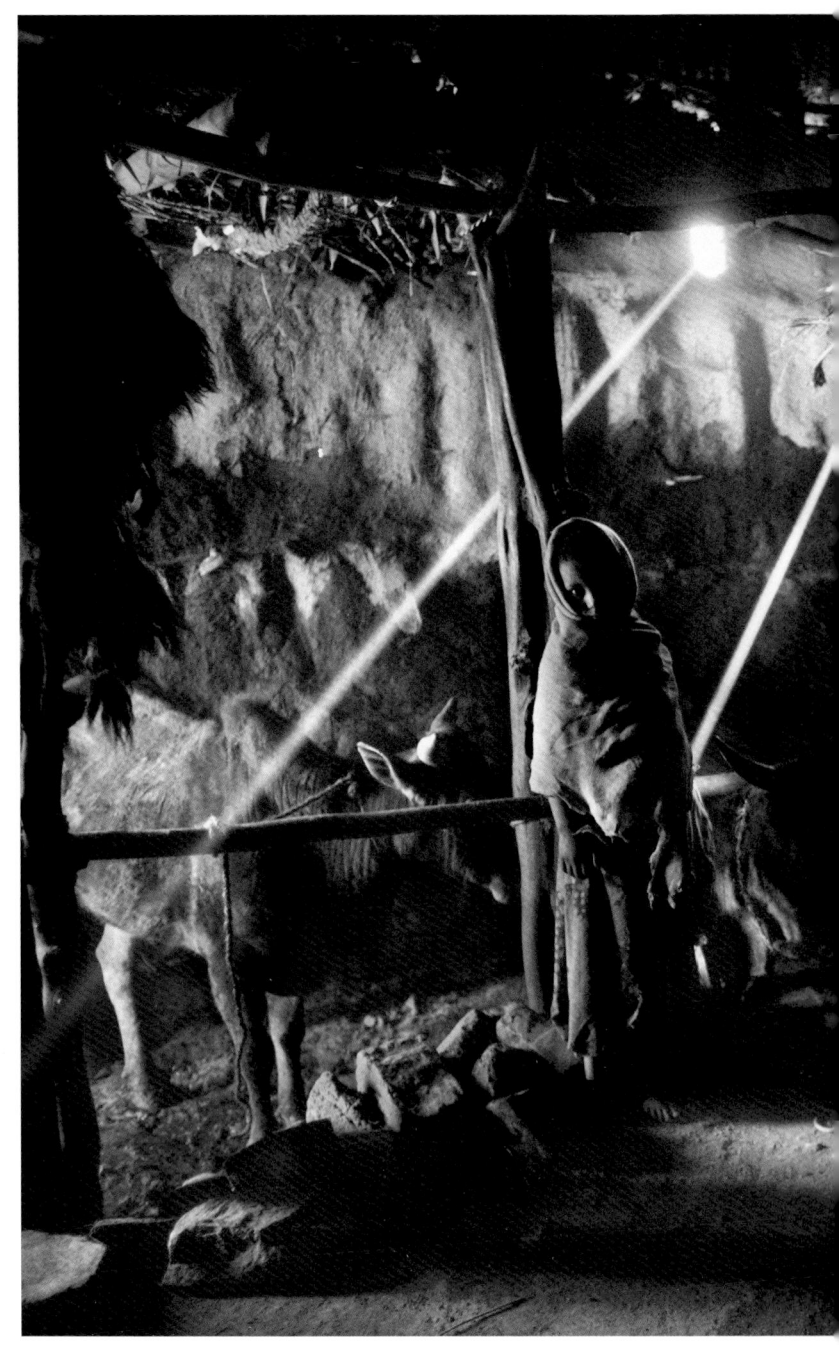

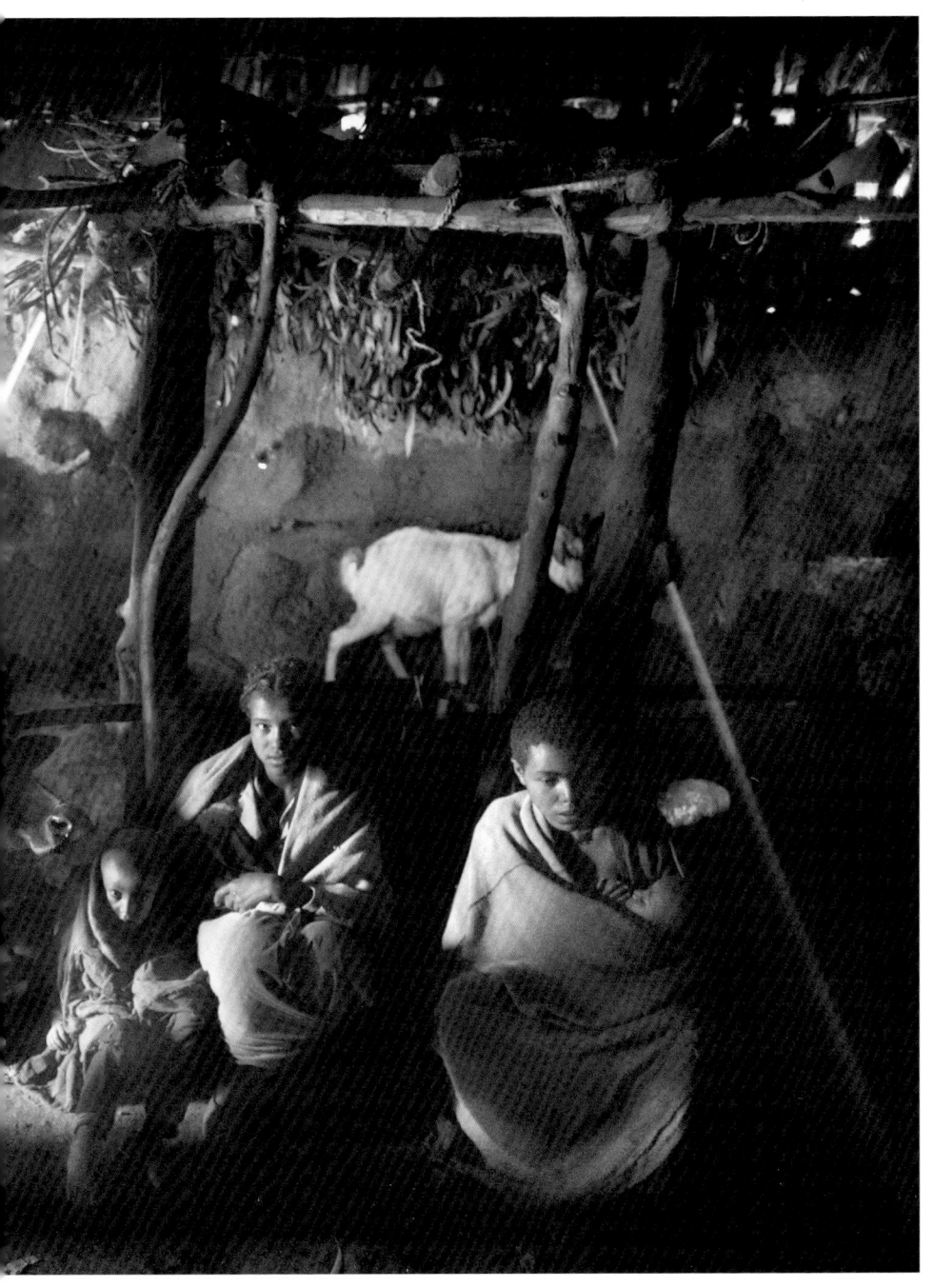

THE ETHNIC GROUPS OF OMO VALLEY, SOUTH ETHIOPIA

Pages 125 through 129

The plains of South Omo, which lie between the mountainous center of Ethiopia and the highlands of Kenya, are home to some of Africa's most culturally diverse and traditional ethnic groups. For the most part agropastoralists, their lives are little different from those of their ancestors. To spend time among them is to feel transported to another age.

As many as two dozen ethnic groups occupy South Omo, some numbering tens of thousands, others no more than 500, each culturally unique. These photographs were taken during visits to four different groups: the Hamer, the Nyangatom, the Mursi and the Surma.

The Hamer are famous for the elaborate hairstyles of their women. After rubbing their hair with a mixture of ocher, water, and a binding resin, they create copper-colored tresses known as *goscha*, which are considered a sign of health and welfare. The Hamer, who number around 50,000, are typical agropastoralists, cultivating sorghum, vegetables, millet, tobacco, and cotton as well as rearing cattle and goats.

The Nyangatom, whose semiarid territory spills into South Sudan, are famous for their warrior tradition and are often in conflict with neighboring groups, principally because of cattle rustling and competition for water and pastureland. They raise zebu cattle and grow cereals and tobacco.

The Mursi are a small ethnic group, numbering some 6,500, who live in the Mago National Park in southwest Ethiopia. Moving with the seasons between the plains and the Mursi Hills, they grow crops and rear cattle, with honey being a favorite delicacy.

The Surma, also known as the Suri, with a population of some 45,000, live in a territory covering southwest Ethiopia and South Sudan. Their most famous traditions are fierce stick fighting between the men and lip plates worn by the women. Once nomadic, the Surma now live in permanent settlements and cultivate their land, although males usually own some 30 to 40 head of cattle as proof of their wealth and importance. Occasionally, wars are fought with their traditional enemy, the Nyangatom, with automatic weapons increasingly used on both sides.

Opposite and pages 128/129: Mursi and Surma women are the last women in the world to wear lip plates. No anthropologist has been able to explain with certainty the origin or the function of this practice. Some say that this mutilation, unaesthetic to the eyes of the slavers, was imposed by men to protect their women from slavers' raids. Only women belonging to a high caste have the right to wear lip plates, which they display proudly when they walk around the village in the company of their husband and sons. Mursi village of Dargui in Mago National Park, near Jinka. Ethiopia. September and October 2007.

Pages 126/127: Surma men practice stick fighting known as *donga* in order to develop an aggressive spirit, to learn agility and endurance and to display their virility as future warriors. For this, the fighters paint their bodies with white symbolic figures designed to protect them from supernatural forces. Using long sticks as weapons, their aim is to dominate and neutralize their adversary, with winners celebrated by the women. Although *donga* is only one of several rites of passage from adolescence to manhood, it is the most violent: blood is spilled, heads and ribs are cracked, and occasional deaths are reported. Surma village of Tulgit. Omo National Park. Near Maji. Ethiopia. September and October 2007.

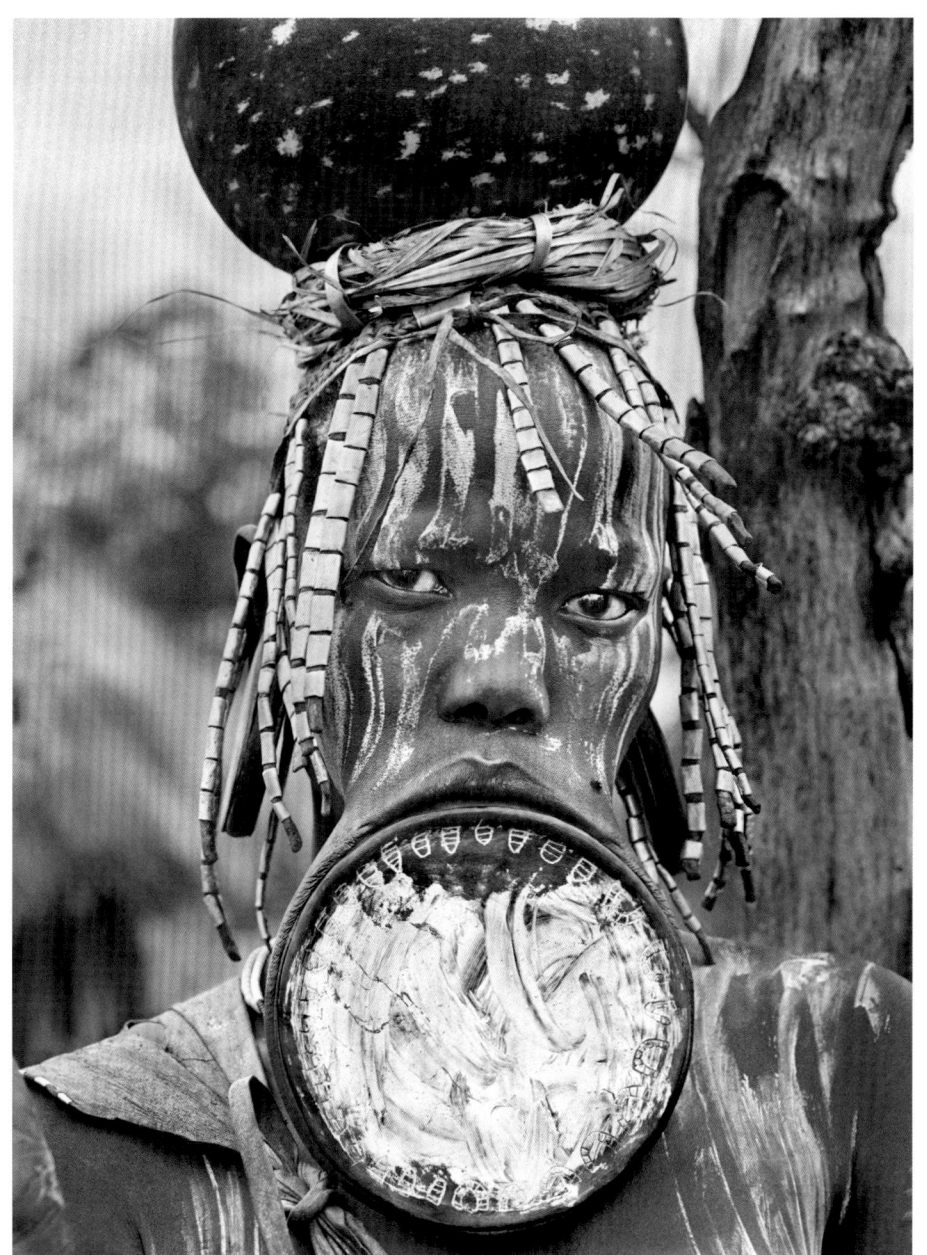

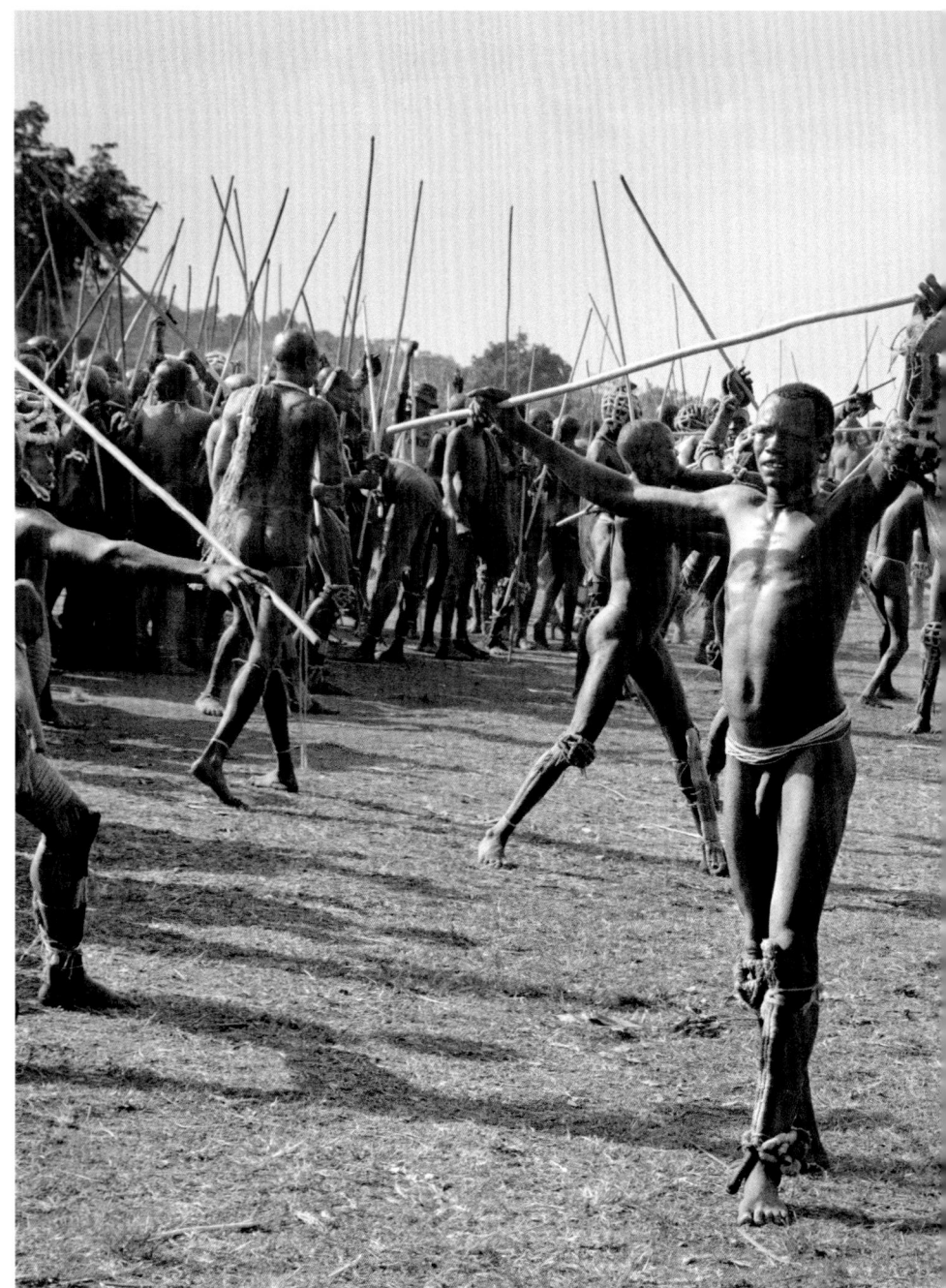

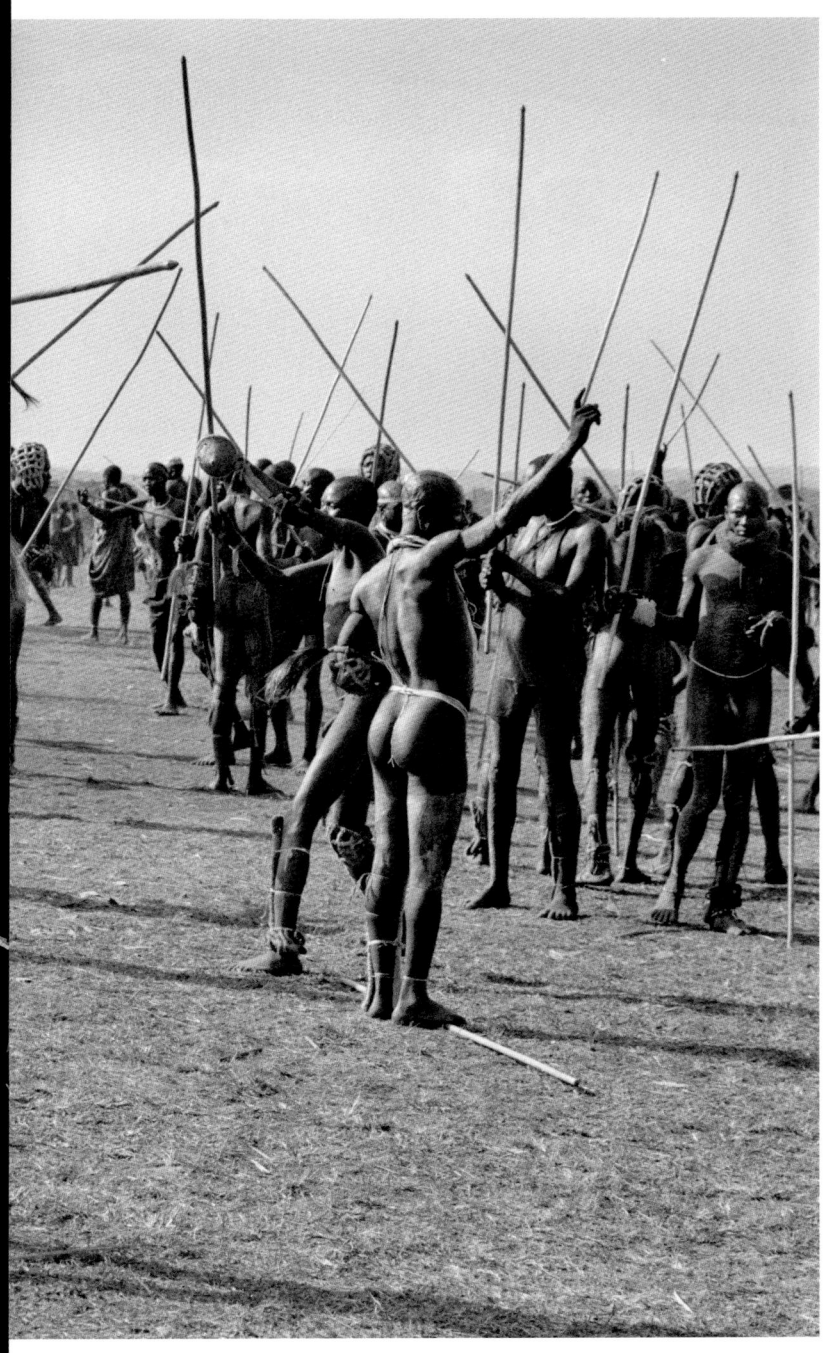

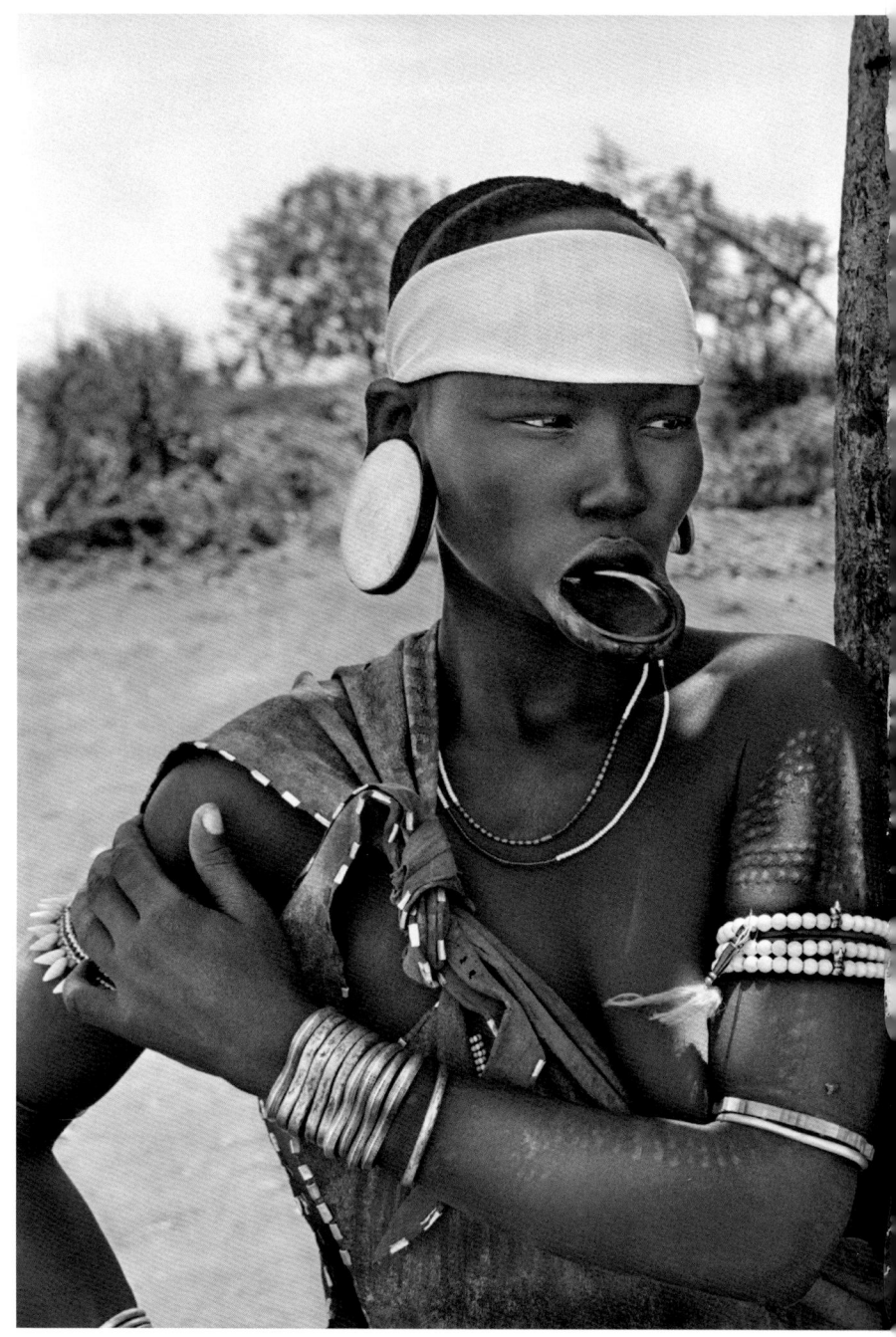

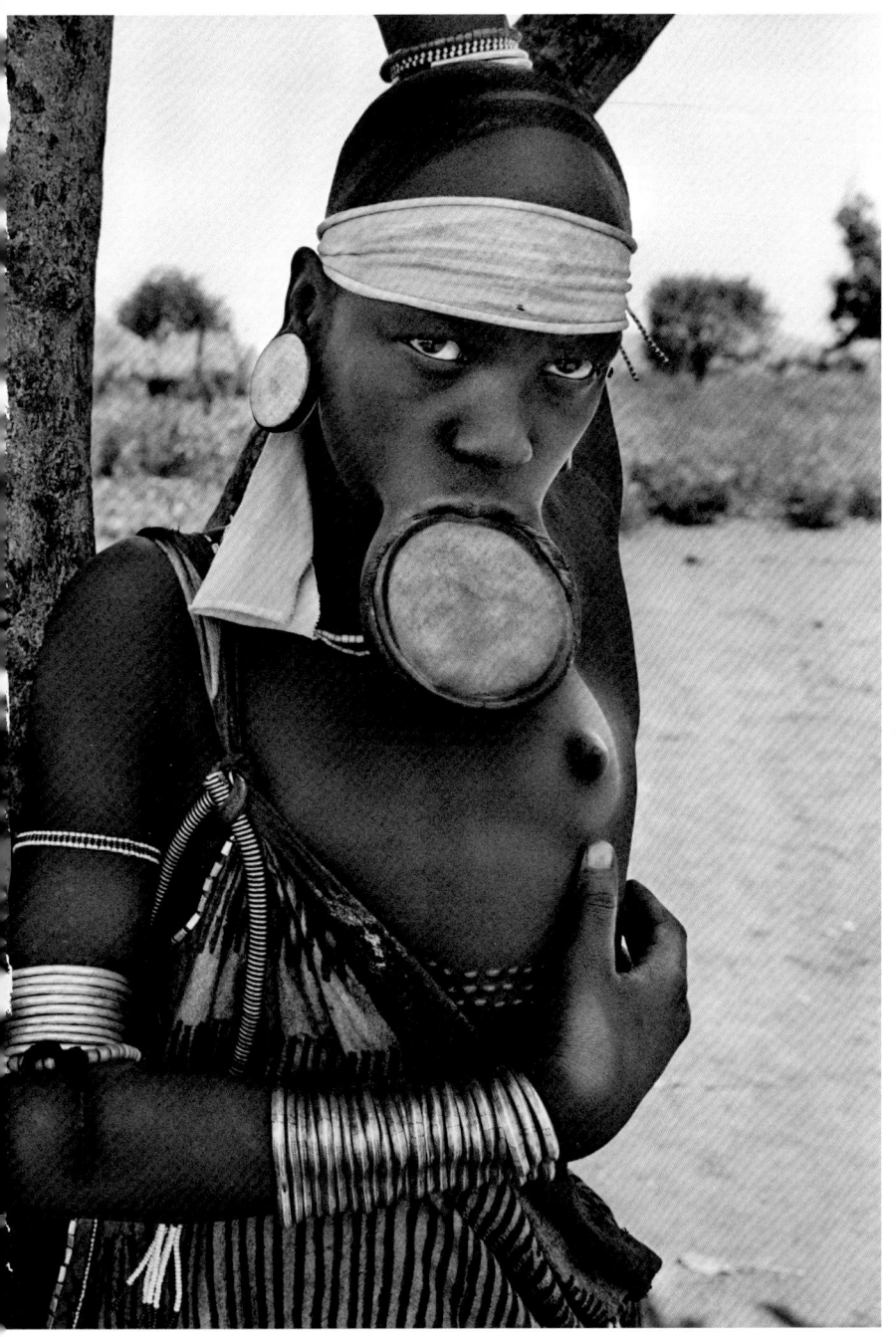

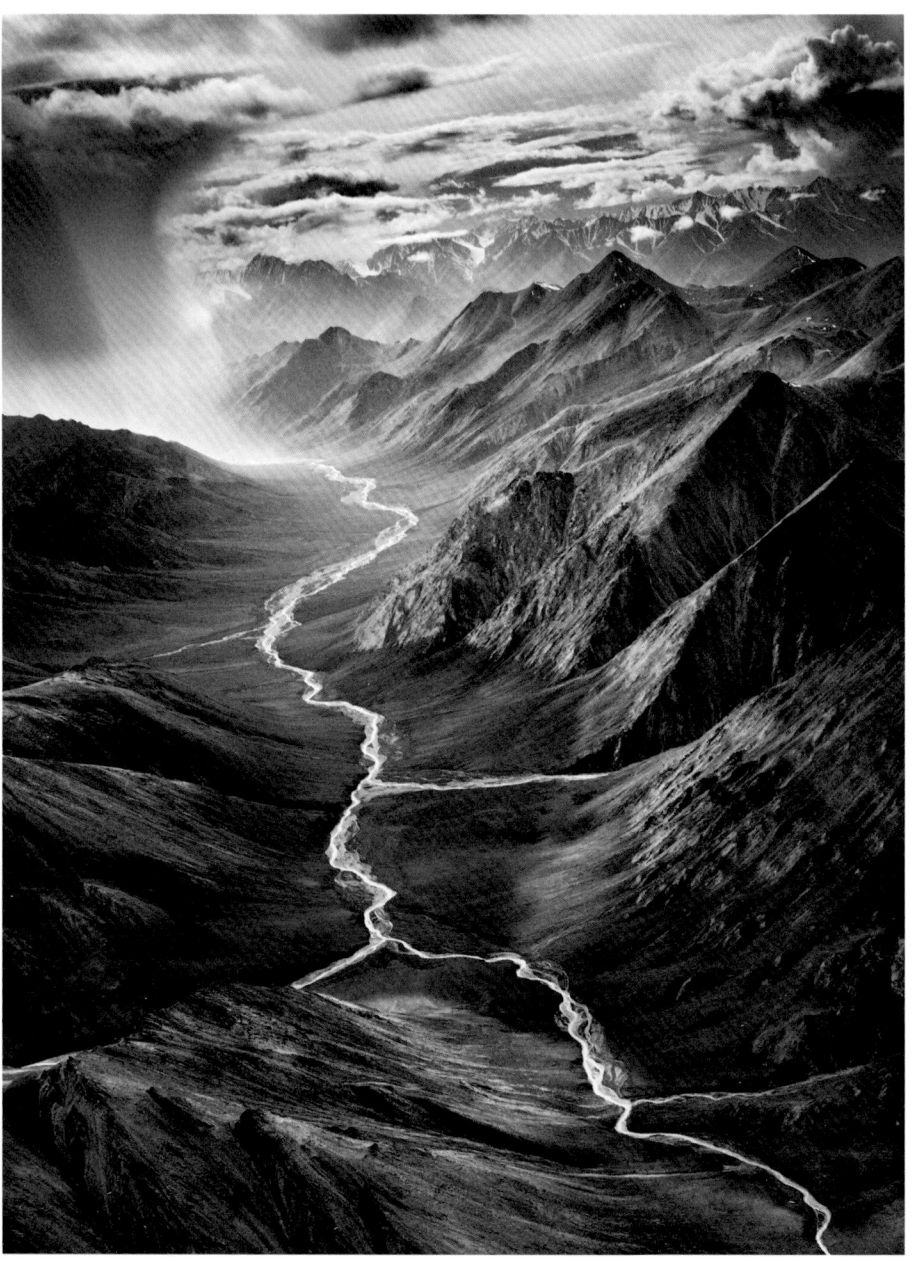

NORTHERN SPACES

The North Pole stands on ice, surrounded by hundreds of kilometers of frozen ocean, but the Arctic Circle itself is ringed by the northernmost regions of the Americas, Europe, and Asia. As a result, the Arctic ecosystem reaches well into Alaska, Canada, Greenland, Scandinavia, and Russia. In some areas, the ice gives way to permafrost and tundra; in others, volcanoes, glaciers, and canyons recall the geological convulsions that marked the formation of the earth. Yet, for all this, tenacious animals and peoples have chosen to live there.

The Kamchatka Peninsula in eastern Russia has always intrigued me, not least because, as the home base of the Soviet nuclear submarine fleet, it was off-limits to foreigners (and most Russians) throughout the Cold War. Its 780-mile (1,250-kilometer)-long coastline faces the Bering Sea, but I was most drawn to its wild interior, with its 160 volcanoes, 29 of them still active. It was thrilling to fly above and around them as their cone shapes and white peaks came in and out of view amid ever-changing cloud formations. Above the ice-covered summit of the Kronotsky volcano, I peered down from 13,000 feet (4,000 meters) into its smoking crater. Later, we trekked through lava-filled valleys with hot springs and dark lakes. It was there that we came across awesome brown bears, the monarchs of the peninsula's rich fauna.

Some 1,200 miles (2,000 kilometers) to the northeast, the Arctic National Wildlife Refuge in Alaska seems almost as rugged from the air as Kamchatka, with snow-capped mountains and valleys etched by glaciers and rivers. Photographing on the ground, however, proved difficult because the terrain is steep and rivers are too fast and cold to cross on foot. Even in midsummer, the temperature was well below zero. The porcupine caribou, the area's most emblematic animal, usually flees when it smells approaching human beings. But in the end, we were able to follow tens of thousands of these elegant creatures during their annual migration to the coastal plains to breed.

Adjacent to southeast Alaska is Canada's Kluane National Park and Reserve, which is dominated by the Saint Elias Mountains and includes Mount Logan, Canada's highest peak. Its huge icefield, glaciers, and rivers make it virtually inaccessible on foot. Our good fortune was that, during the month we worked there, we had two weeks of good weather for aerial photography. It meant that, on long summer days, we could work up to 11:00 p.m. One of many unforgettable sights was that of glaciers spreading like the fingers of a hand then darkening as they gather up rocks and stones in their steady slide down steep valleys.

To gain an understanding of how human life survives inside the Arctic Circle, we sought out the Nenets, a nomadic people in northern Siberia numbering some 42,000. They spend the winter within reach of towns where some of their families now live. But from mid-March, they set off with their large herds of reindeer into the Yamal Peninsula, where by the summer the animals can feed off shrubs, grasses, and lichens which they find by burrowing into the tundra. We accompanied one group with some 6,000 reindeer in temperatures far below zero. It was an extraordinary adventure. While some reindeer pulled sleds loaded with food and the poles and fur needed to build overnight shelters, dogs kept the main herd on track. On the day we crossed the Ob River onto the peninsula, we traveled 32 miles (52 kilometers), no fewer than 47 of them across the frozen river; on other days, we were trapped by snowstorms and struggled to stay warm.

Still inside the Arctic Circle but 2,400 miles (4,000 kilometers) to the east is Wrangel Island, which we reached after a 30-hour-long boat ride from the town of Pevek on the eastern Siberian coast. I had been told it was a treasure trove of biodiversity and, above all, a favorite breeding ground for polar bears. Instead, our first encounter was with the detritus of what had once been a Soviet air base, including abandoned fuel barrels and wrecks of cars and planes. Fortunately, a large part of Wrangel remains unspoiled and even the unpleasant Soviet legacy is slowly being cleaned up. However, our visit proved frustrating. The island is home to large numbers of musk oxen, but they were hard to photograph because they fear humans. Walruses also once came in their tens of thousands to Wrangel, but they have apparently been disoriented by warming oceans and we found only a few hundred of them. The scarcity of polar bears was still another disappointment: in the end, we saw only a handful.

But we were amply rewarded by our trip to the national parks of the American Southwest, truly among the most beautiful places I have ever seen. The parks are spread across the Colorado Plateau, but we decided to explore Utah and Arizona. Naturally, this included the Grand Canyon. We worked first from the air, then from the water, taking an eight-day-long boat ride down 280 miles (450 kilometers) of the Colorado River. We were there in the late spring, but snow was still falling at the top of the canyon. Bryce Canyon in Utah is, in turn, memorable for the elaborate spires formed there by millennia of erosion of its limestone rock. As we watched nature's Gothic city change colors with the path of the sun, condors and eagles observed us from the skies.

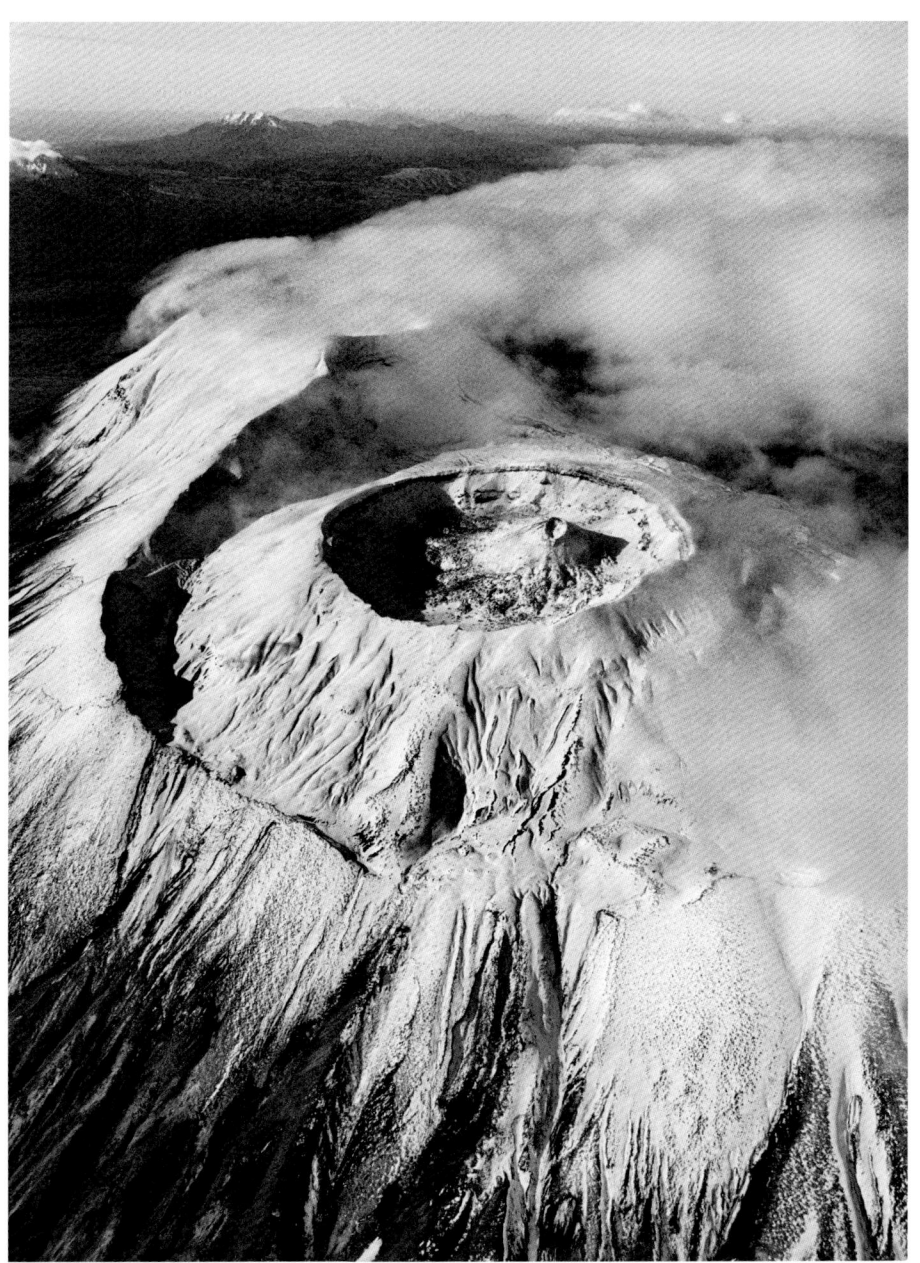

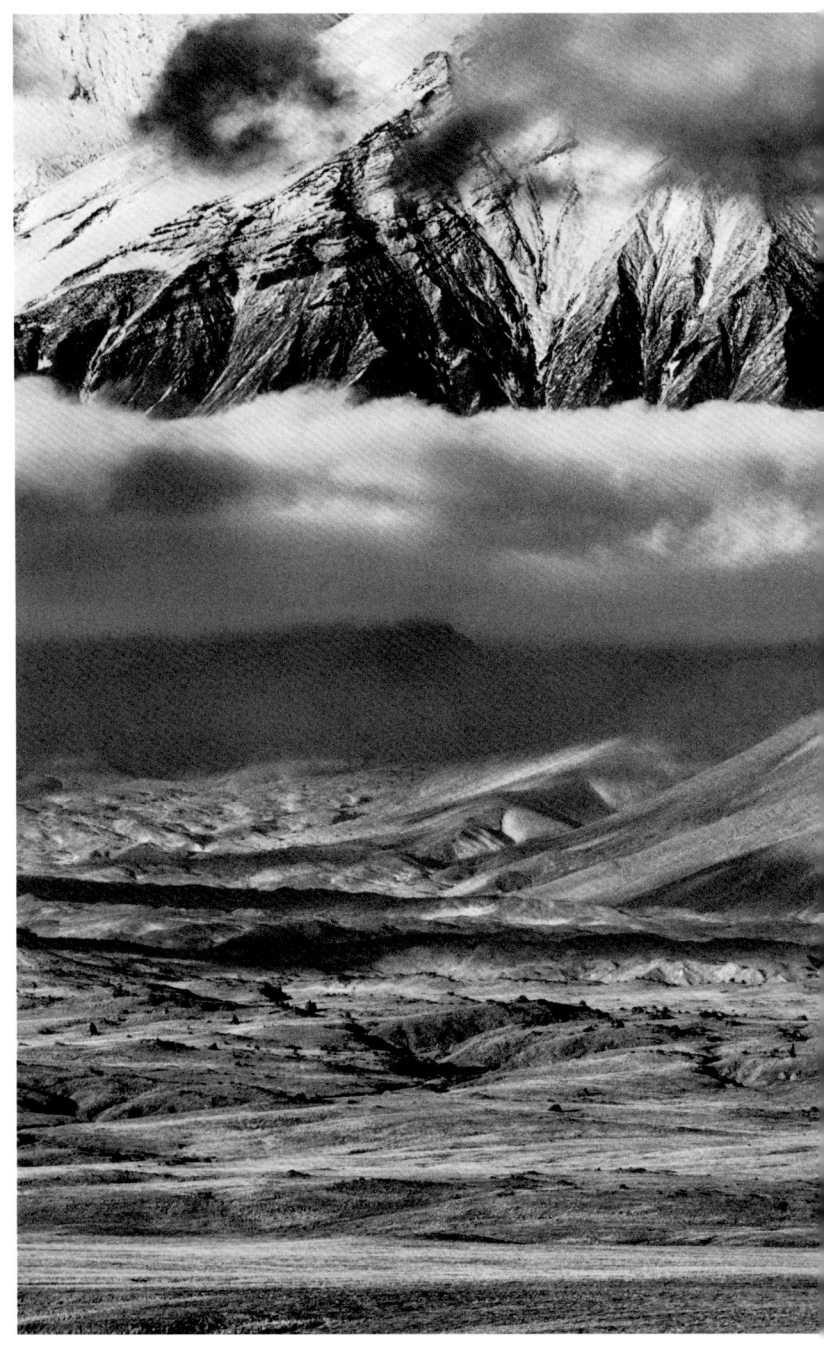

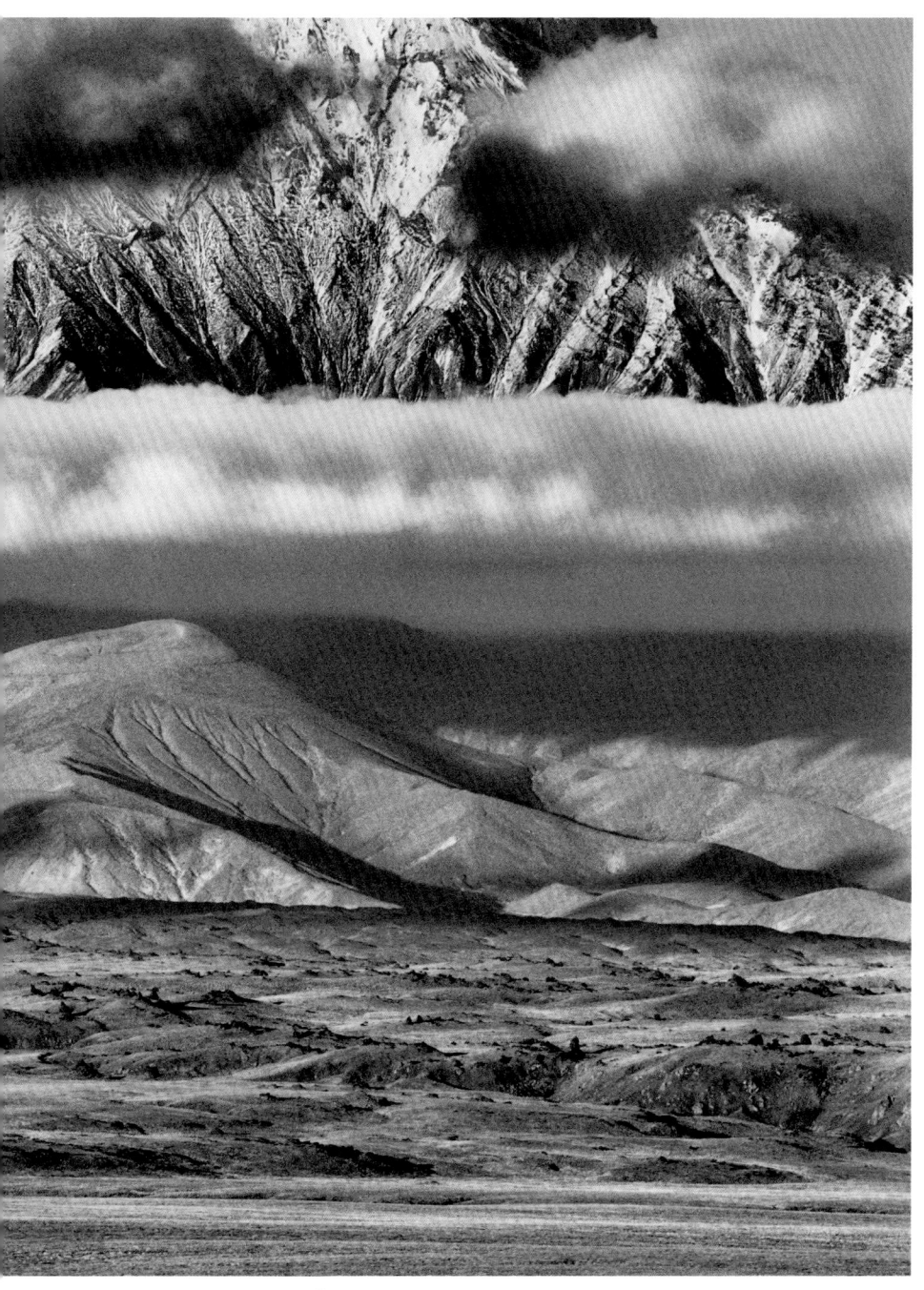

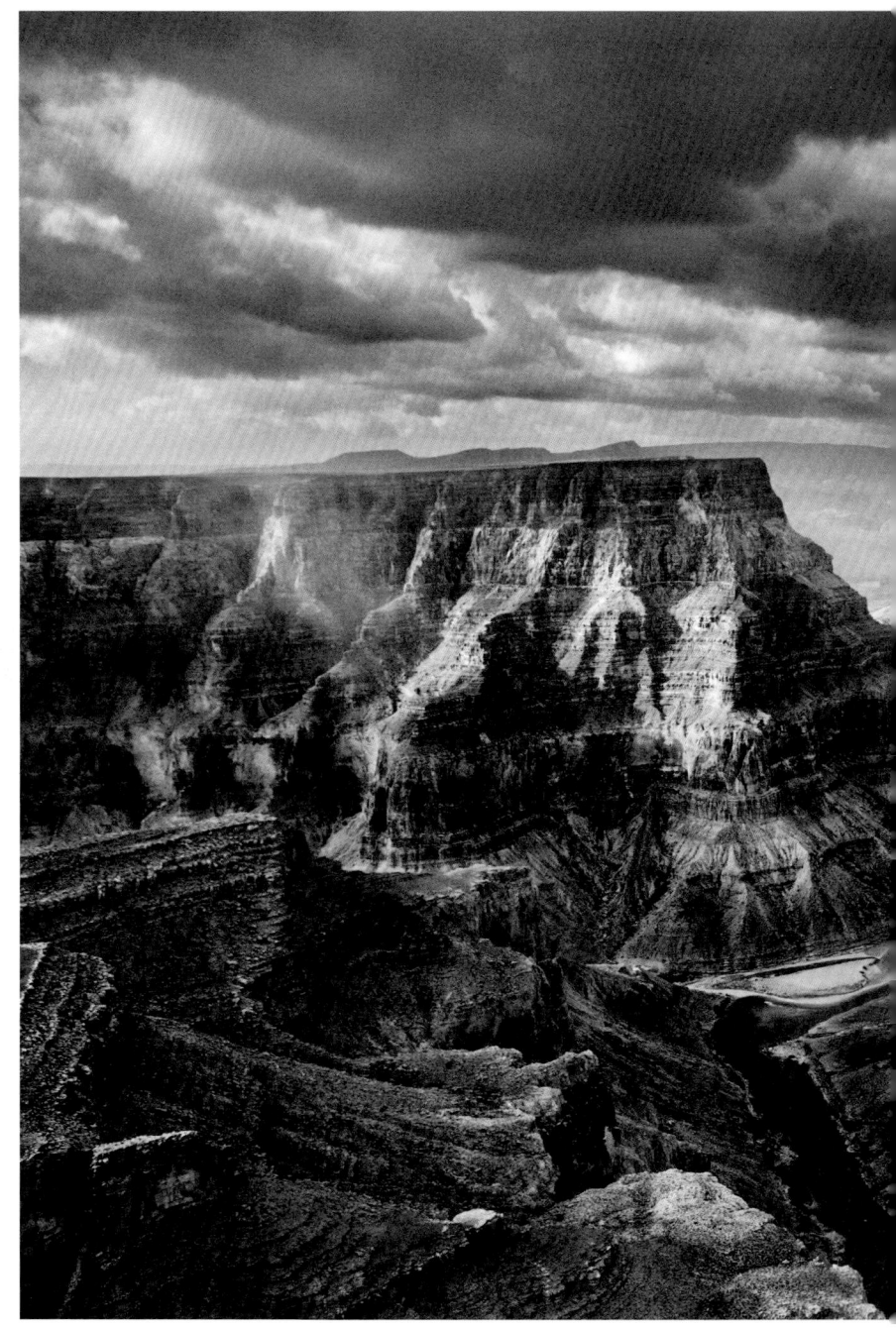

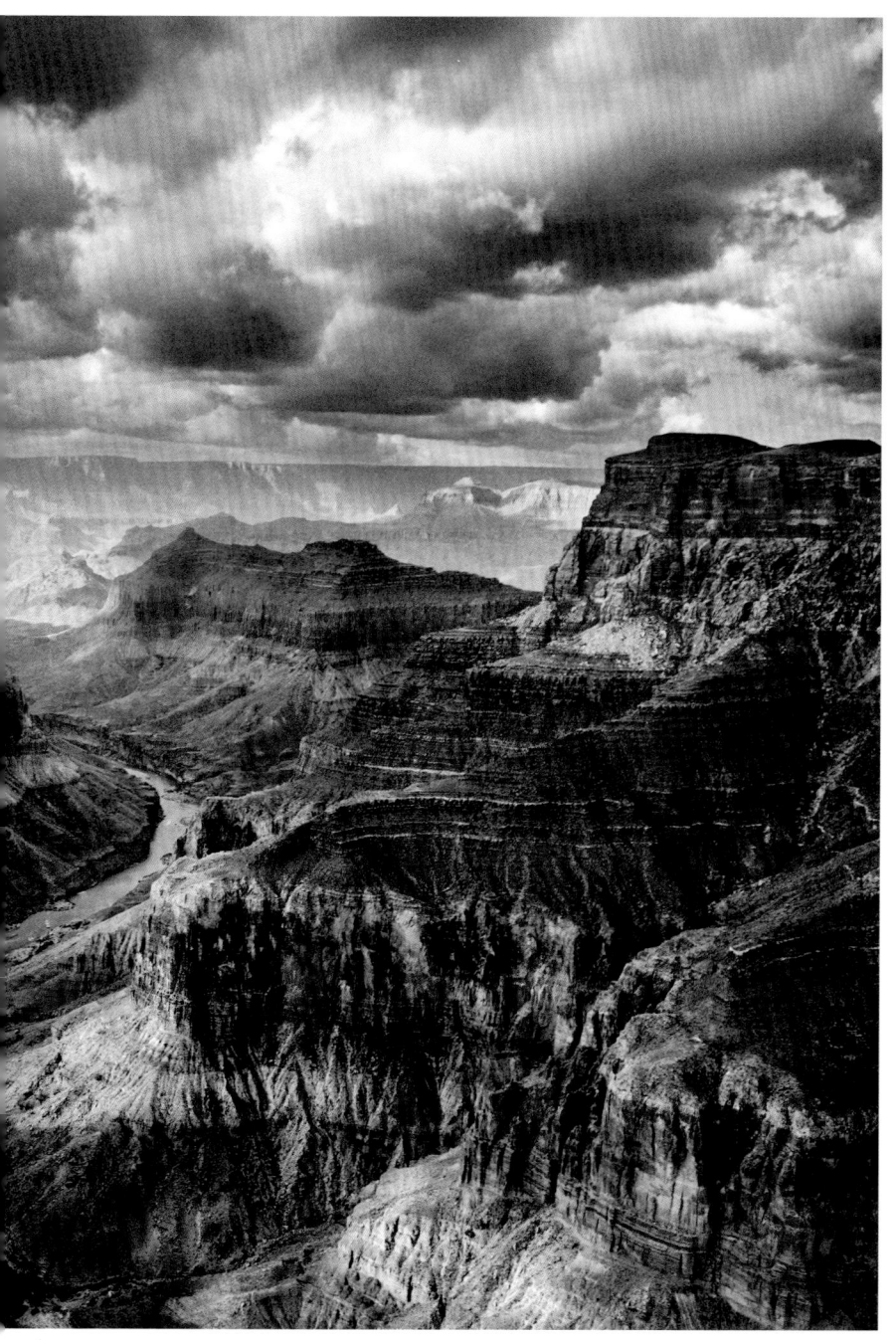

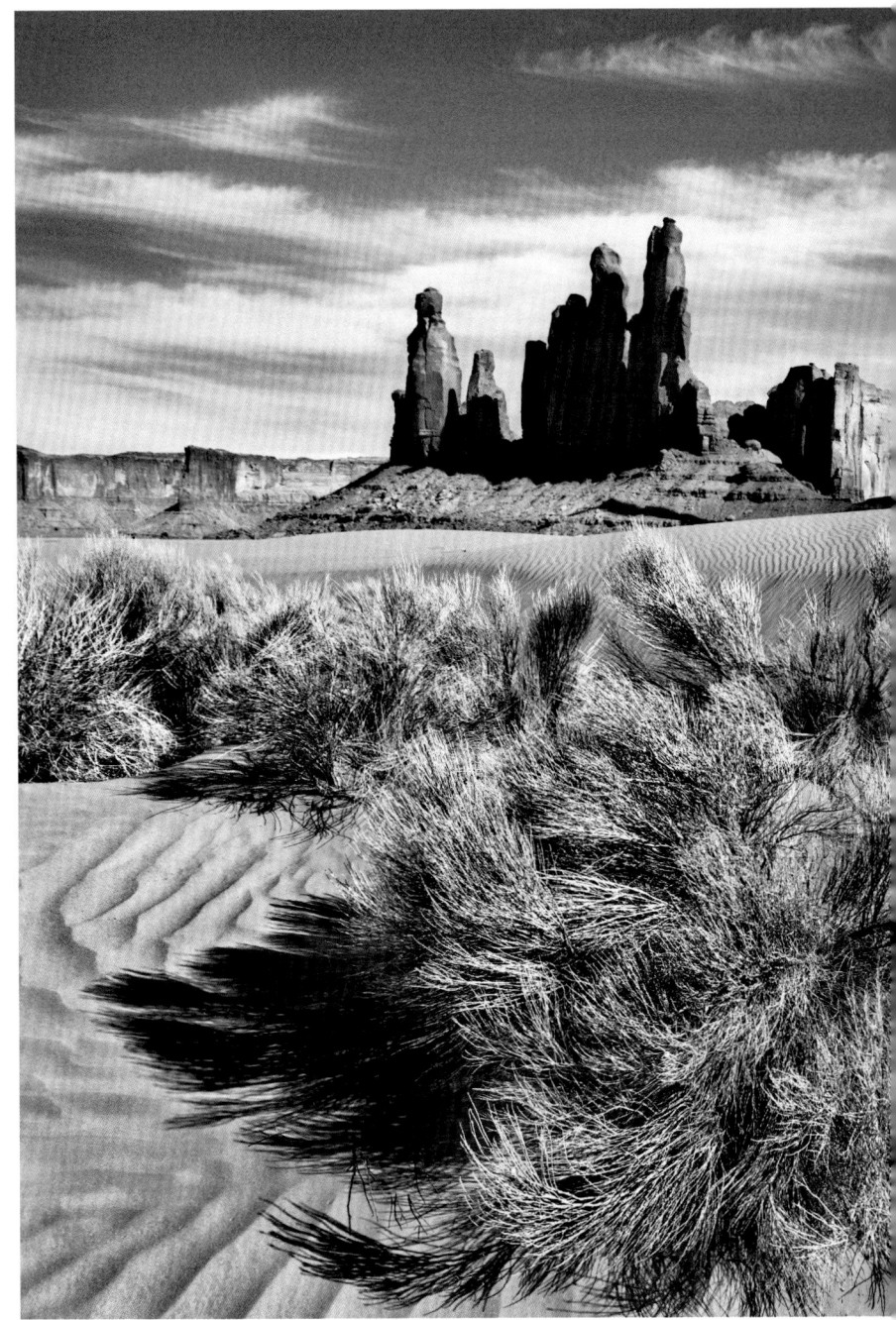

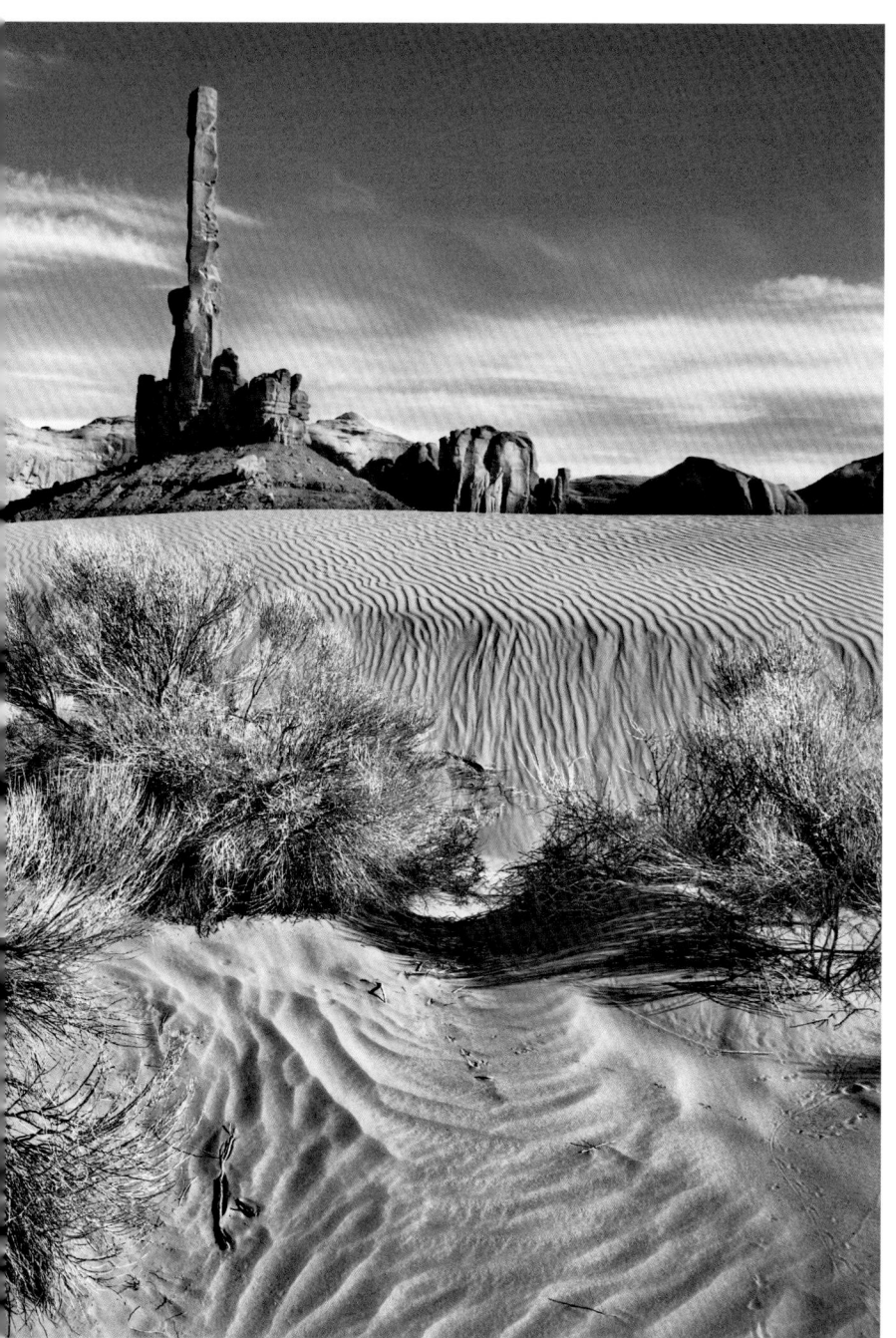

Page 130: The Arctic National Wildlife Refuge (ANWR) in northeastern Alaska is the largest wildlife refuge in the United States, covering no fewer than six ecozones and stretching some 200 miles (300 kilometers) from north to south. Along its northern coast, barrier islands, coastal lagoons, salt marshes, and river deltas of the Arctic coastal tundra provide a marvelous habitat for migratory water birds. Coastal land and sea ice are sought by caribou seeking relief from insects during the summer and by Arctic bears for hunting seals and breeding during winter. This photograph was taken in the eastern part of the Brooks Range, which rises to over 9,800 feet (3,000 meters); the rugged stretch of mountains is sliced by deep river valleys and numerous glaciers. The immense variety of microclimates results from the collision of cold air from the Arctic and hot air coming from the Yukon River region of central Alaska. Alaska. USA. June and July 2009.

Page 133: Krasheninnikov Volcano (6,089 feet / 1,856 meters). This distinctive-looking volcano is named after Stepan Krasheninnikov, a famous Russian naturalist and ethnographer who came to Kamchatka with Vitus Bering's second Alaska expedition in 1740. Its two adjoining cones rise from the center of an enormous ancient caldera, visible here as a dark circle. There is no record of Krasheninnikov's last eruption. Kamchatka. Russia. September and October 2006.

Pages 134/135: A tundra valley extends between Tolbachik and Kamen Volcanoes. In the background, a line of clouds separates a "small" crater some 2,600 feet (800 meters) high from the huge base of Kamen Volcano, which rises 15,000 feet (4,579 meters) above sea level. Kamchatka. Russia. September and October 2006.

Pages 136/137: View of the confluence of the Colorado and the Little Colorado from the Navajo territory. The Grand Canyon National Park begins after this junction. Arizona. USA. April, May, and June 2010.

Pages 138/139: Monument Valley Navajo Tribal Park. This is a breathtaking part of the Colorado Plateau. The fragile pinnacles of rock are surrounded by kilometers of mesas and buttes, shrubs, trees, and windblown sand. The floor is largely siltstone, or sand derived from it, deposited by the meandering rivers that carved the valley. The valley's vivid red color comes from iron oxide exposed in the weathered siltstone. The darker, blue-gray rocks in the valley are in turn colored by manganese oxide. Utah and Arizona. USA. April, May, and June 2010.

Opposite: Bryce Canyon National Park. Bryce Canyon is not in fact a canyon but a giant natural amphitheater created by erosion along the eastern side of the Paunsaugunt Plateau. Bryce is famous for its extraordinary geological structures, known as *hoodoos*, formed by frost weathering and water erosion of the river and lake bed sedimentary rocks. Utah. USA. April, May, and June 2010.

Pages 142/143: Bryce Canyon National Park during a snowstorm. Utah. USA. April, May, and June 2010.

Pages 144/145: Bighorn Creek in the western part of the Kluane National Park. Canada. May and June 2011.

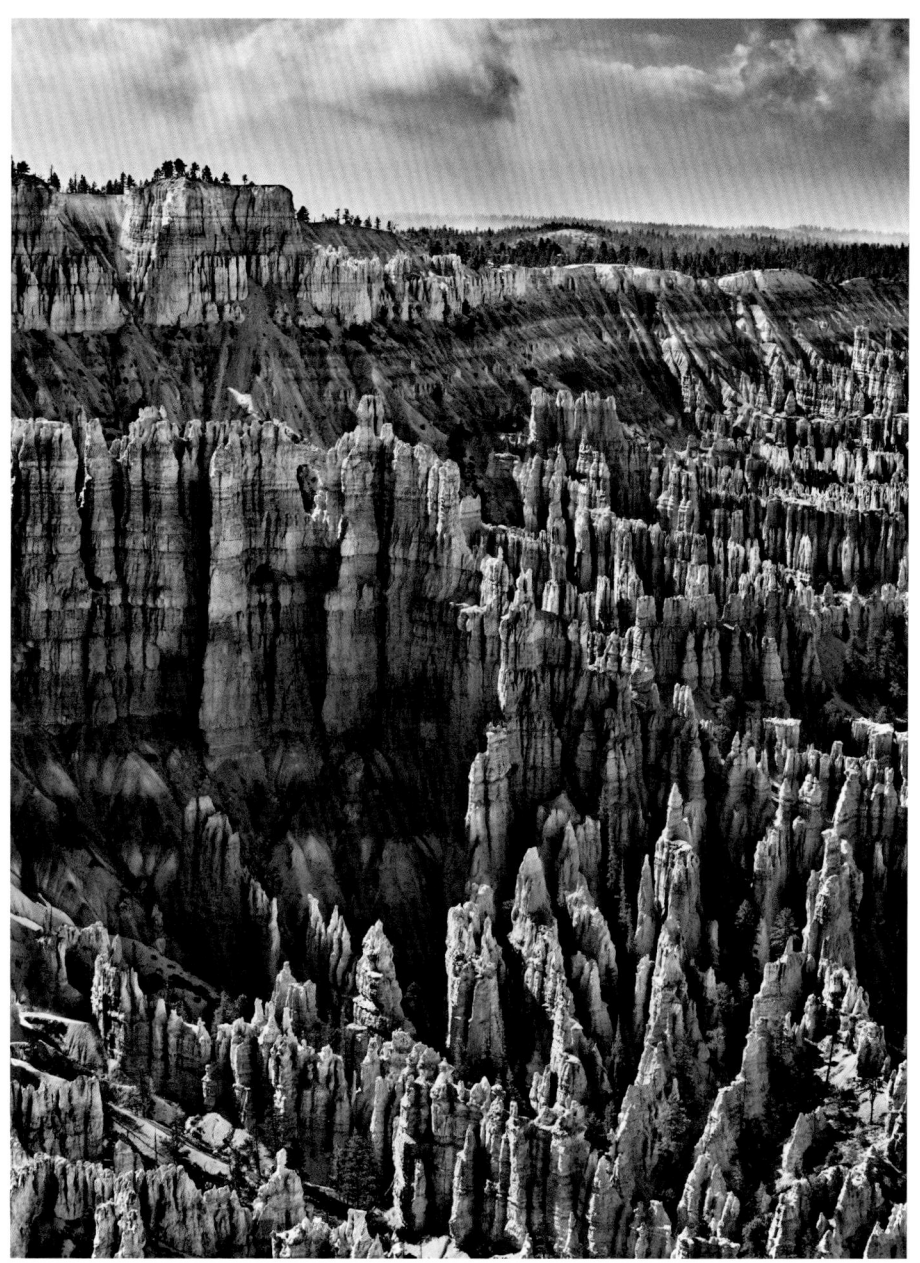

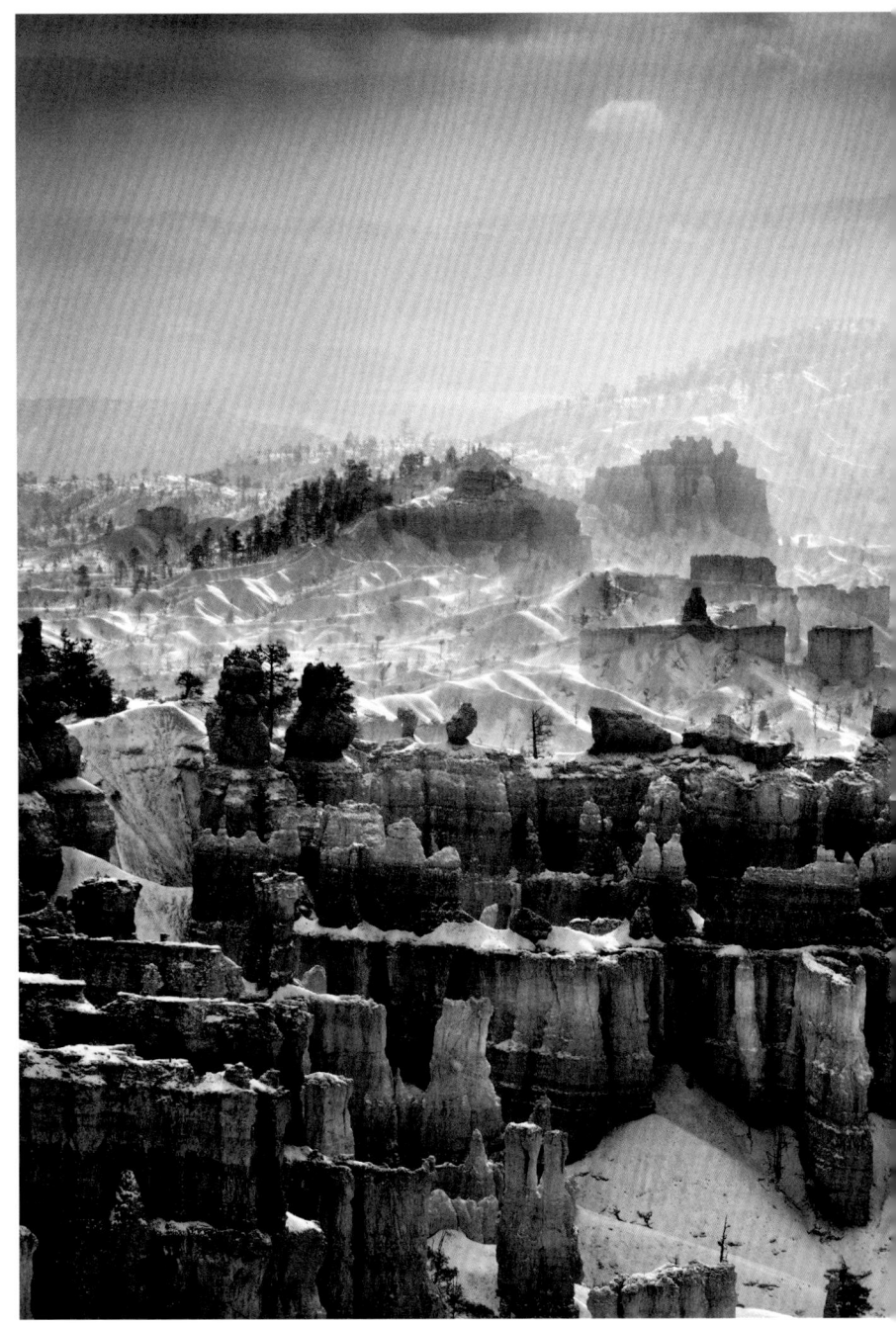

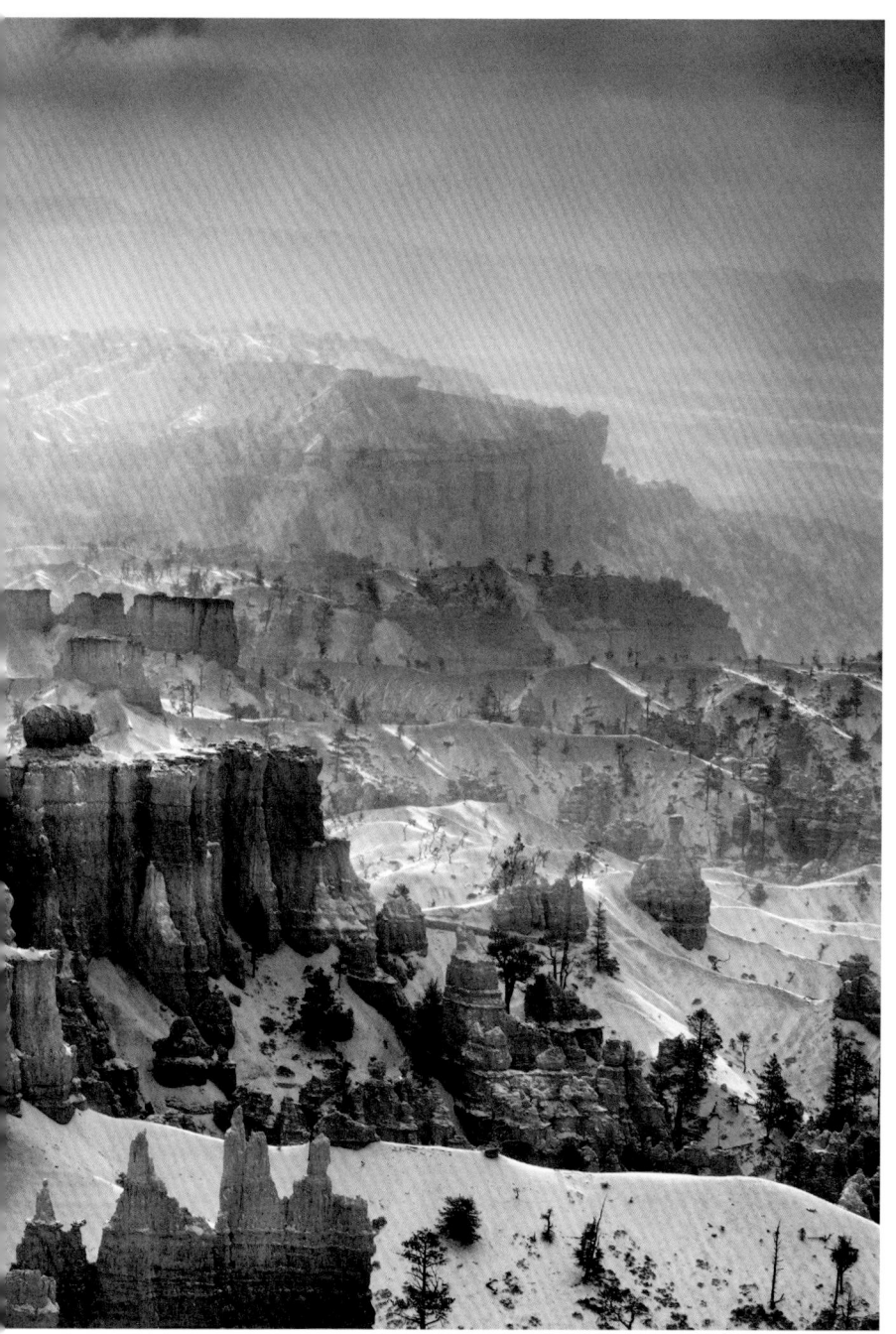

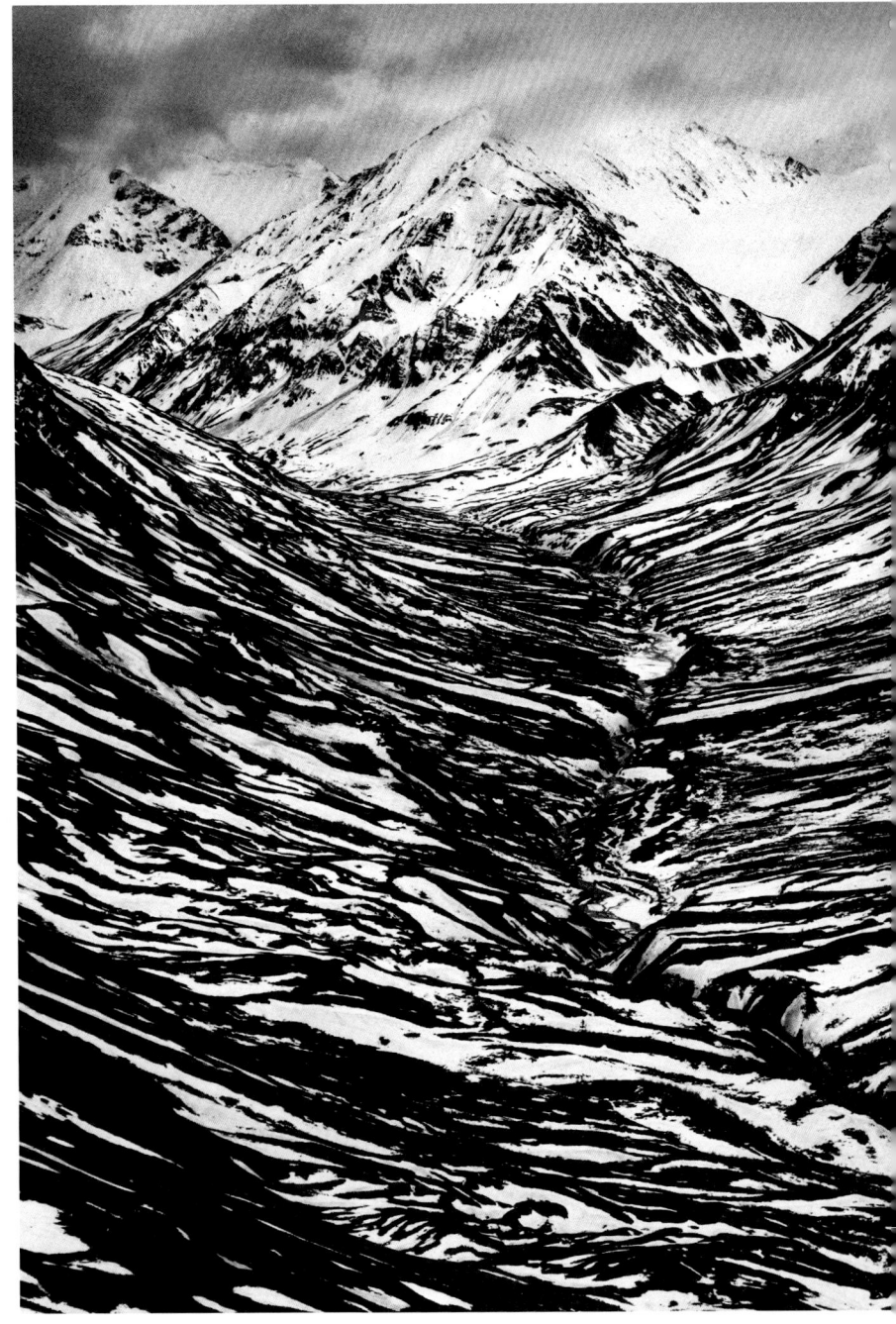

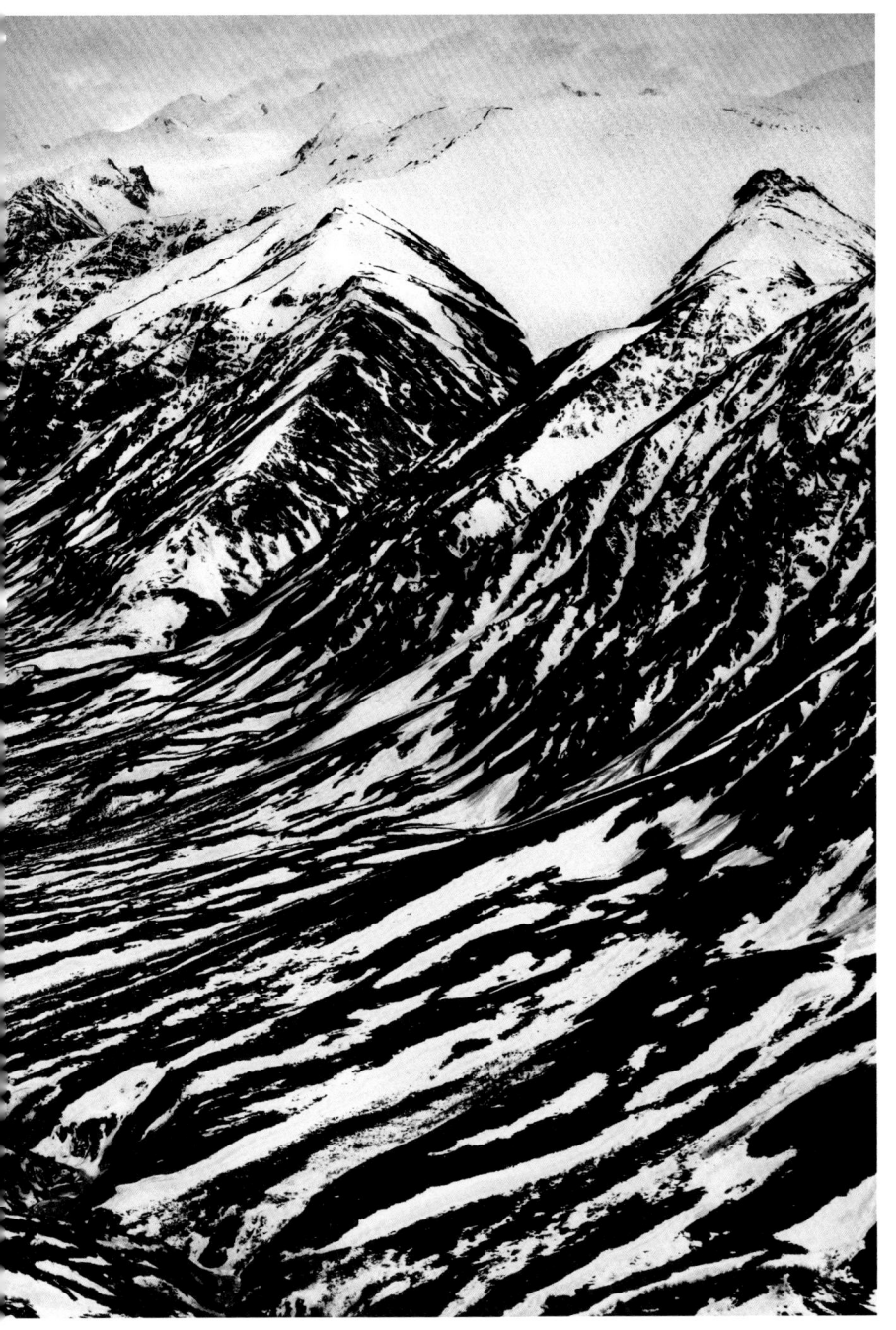

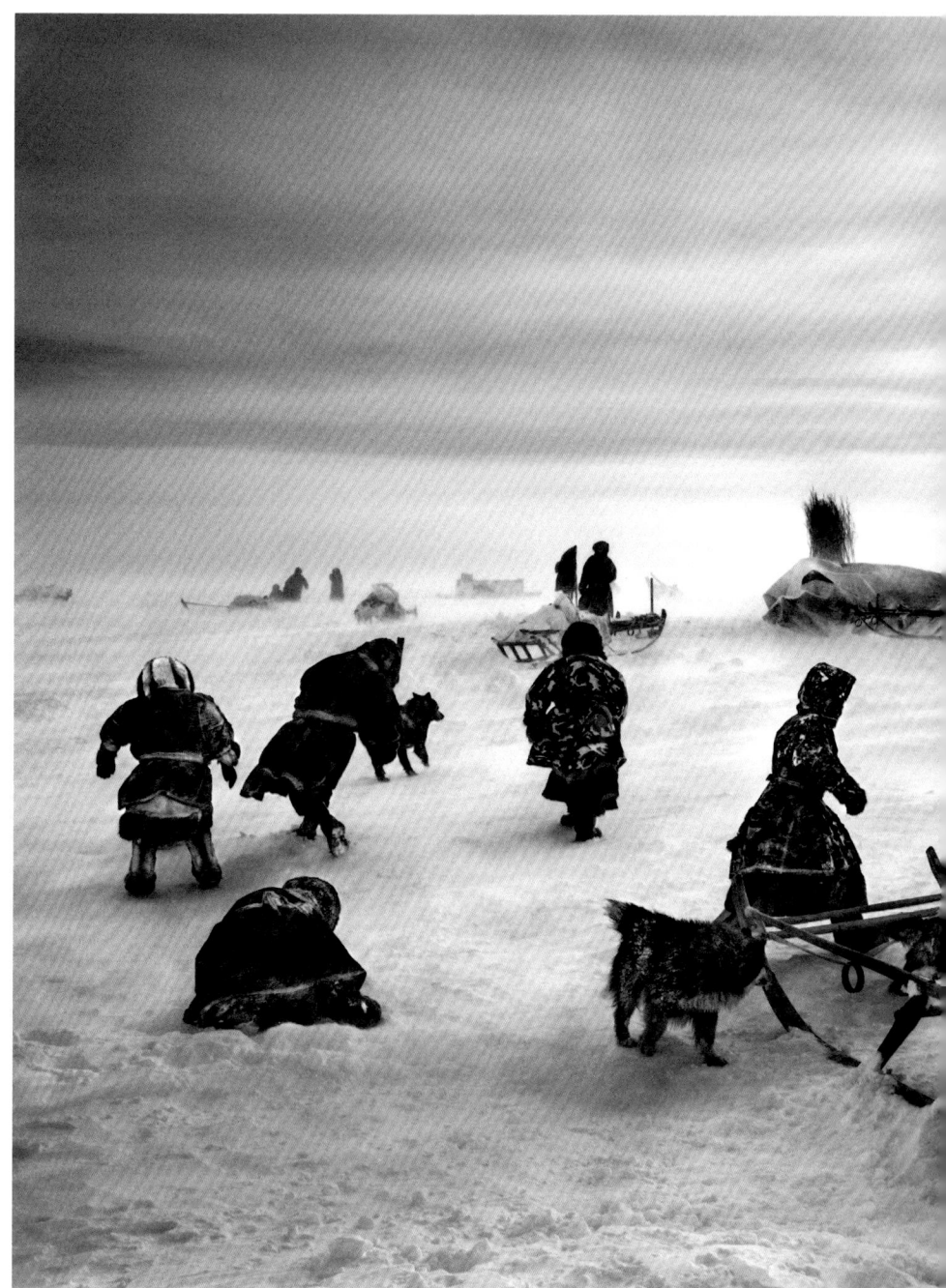

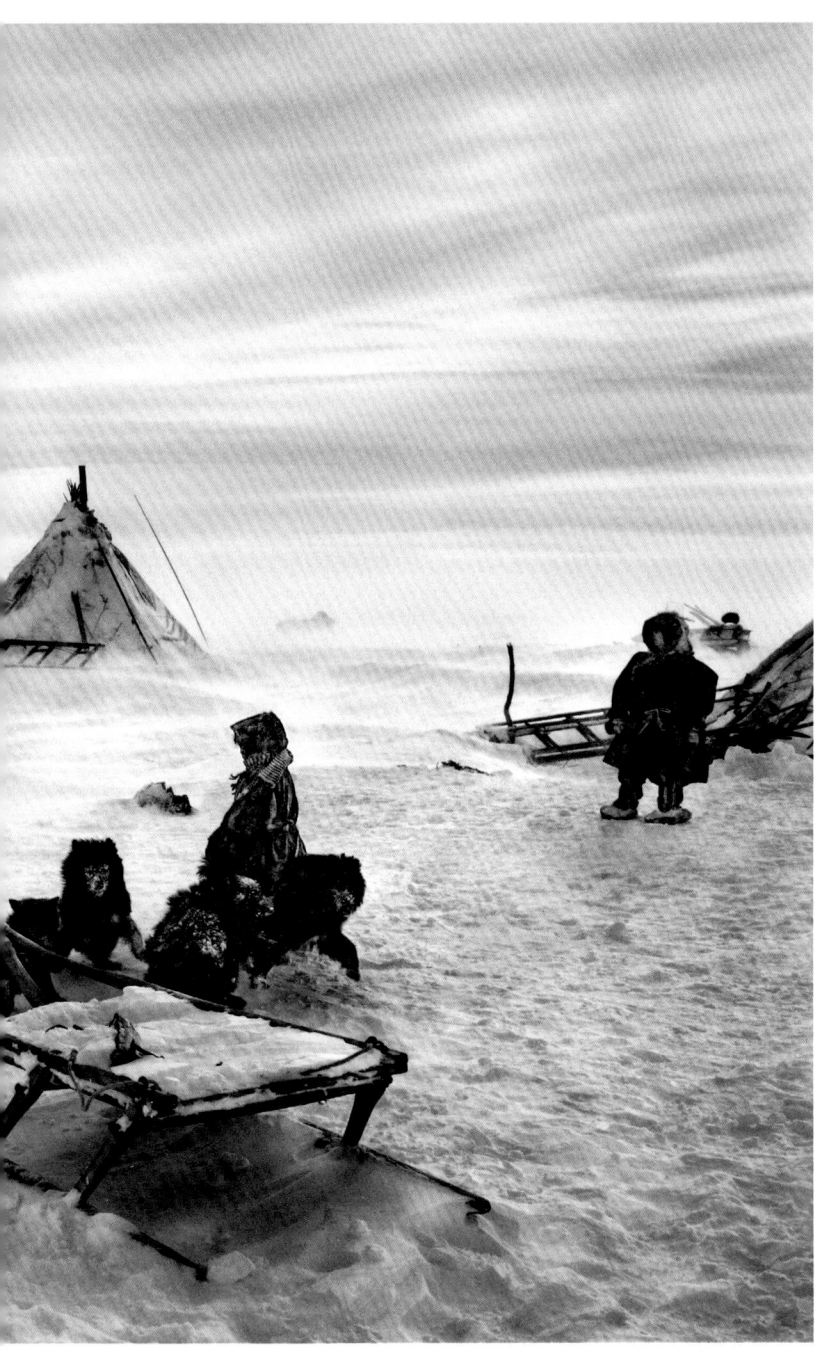

THE NENETS

Pages 146 through 153

The Nenets are an Indigenous people numbering some 42,000 who live in the Yamalo-Nenets Autonomous District of Russia's northern Siberian region. Their culture and way of life are defined by the reindeer (*Rangifer tarandus sibiricus*). They spend winters in their own communities near the Kanin and Taymyr Peninsulas, around the Ob and Yenisey Rivers, with a few now settled in small towns like Kolva. Then, in the summer, they lead their reindeer herds northward into the Arctic Circle, where the animals are skilled at digging under the tundra for grasses and other hardy vegetation. The Nenets travel on sledges drawn by reindeer, while they breed the Samoyed dog to help them herd their reindeer (this dog has also been used by Europeans during Arctic expeditions). Even in the summer, they live with the danger posed by tundra wolves, which prey on reindeer herds. During their migration north, the Nenets fish through holes in the ice. Their ability to live in such conditions is bolstered by a shamanistic and animistic belief system that stresses respect for the land and its resources.

But they have not been shielded from political and environmental change. As part of its nationwide collectivization program, the Soviet government tried to force this nomadic population to become sedentary. Many had to settle in villages and place their children in state boarding schools, weakening their cultural identity and, in some cases, even stripping them of their native tongue. Today they face a different threat. In some areas, such as the Yamal Peninsula, development of oil and gas fields is damaging reindeer grazing land. Climate change is also affecting the Nenets since they can only cross some areas of the Arctic Circle when they are frozen—and melting ice is shrinking the effective length of winter.

Pages 146/147: North of the Ob River, about 62 miles (100 kilometers) inside the Yamal Peninsula, fierce winds keep even daytime temperatures low. When the weather is particularly hostile, the Nenets and their reindeer may spend several days in the same place, doing repair work on sledges and reindeer skins to keep busy. The deeper they move into the Arctic Circle, the less vegetation is to be found. Inside the Arctic Circle. Yamal Peninsula. Siberia. Russia. March and April 2011.

Opposite: This portrait of a young girl illustrates both the beauty of and the importance given by the Nenets to their clothes. Her main coat is made of the inside of reindeer skins, while her hood is made with the fur of blue fox. Yamal Peninsula. Siberia. Russia. March and April 2011.

Pages 150/151: The larger sledges are driven by the women, with as many as 10 sledges forming a long caravan. The men drive smaller sledges since they go faster: it is the men's job to regroup the herd around the camp each morning and, often with the help of dogs, to keep the reindeer moving in a single direction throughout the day. Yamal Peninsula. Siberia. Russia. March and April 2011.

Pages 152/153: Crossing the Ob River to enter the Arctic Circle involves traveling some 31 miles (50 kilometers) over ice. Yamal Peninsula. Siberia. Russia. March and April 2011.

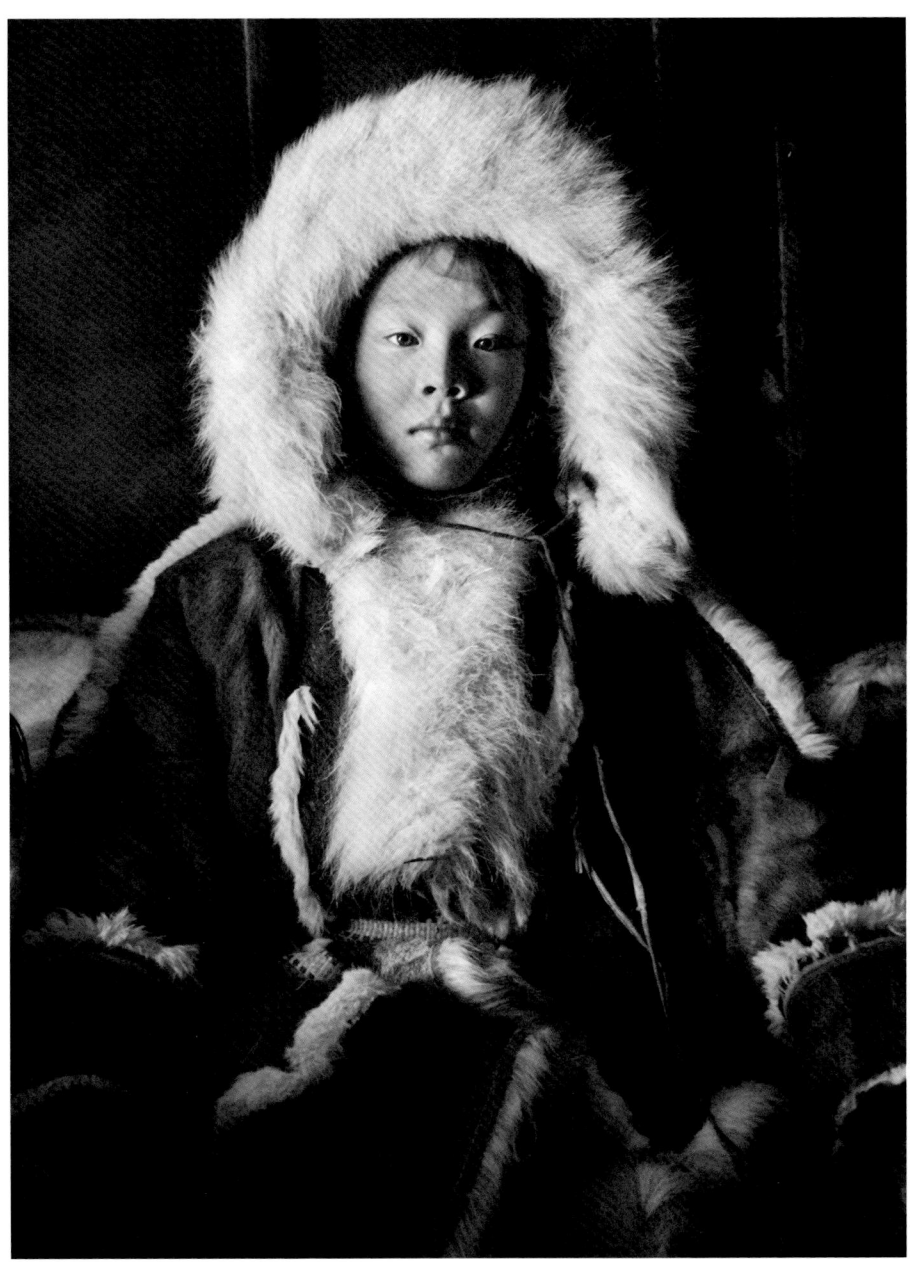

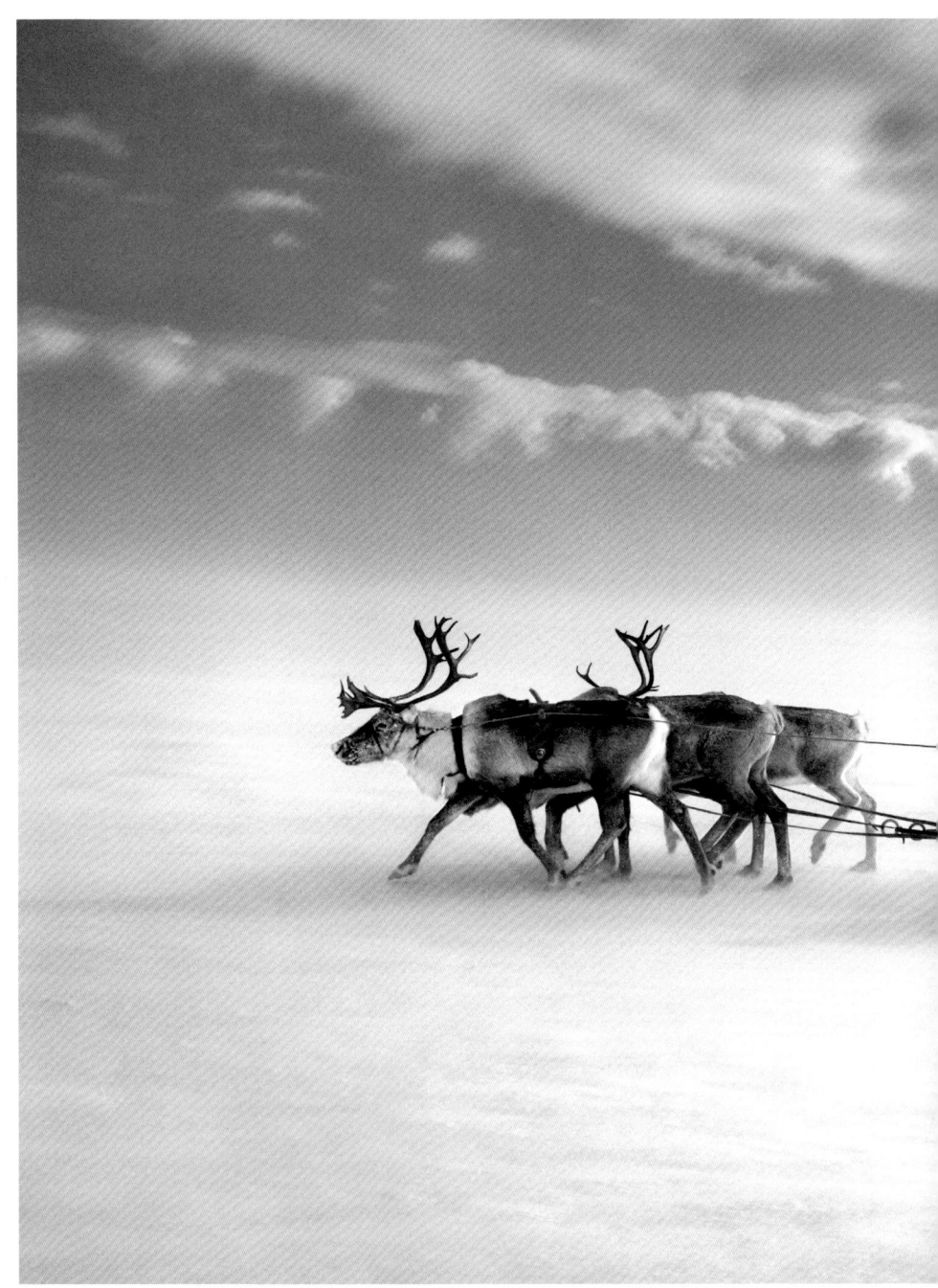

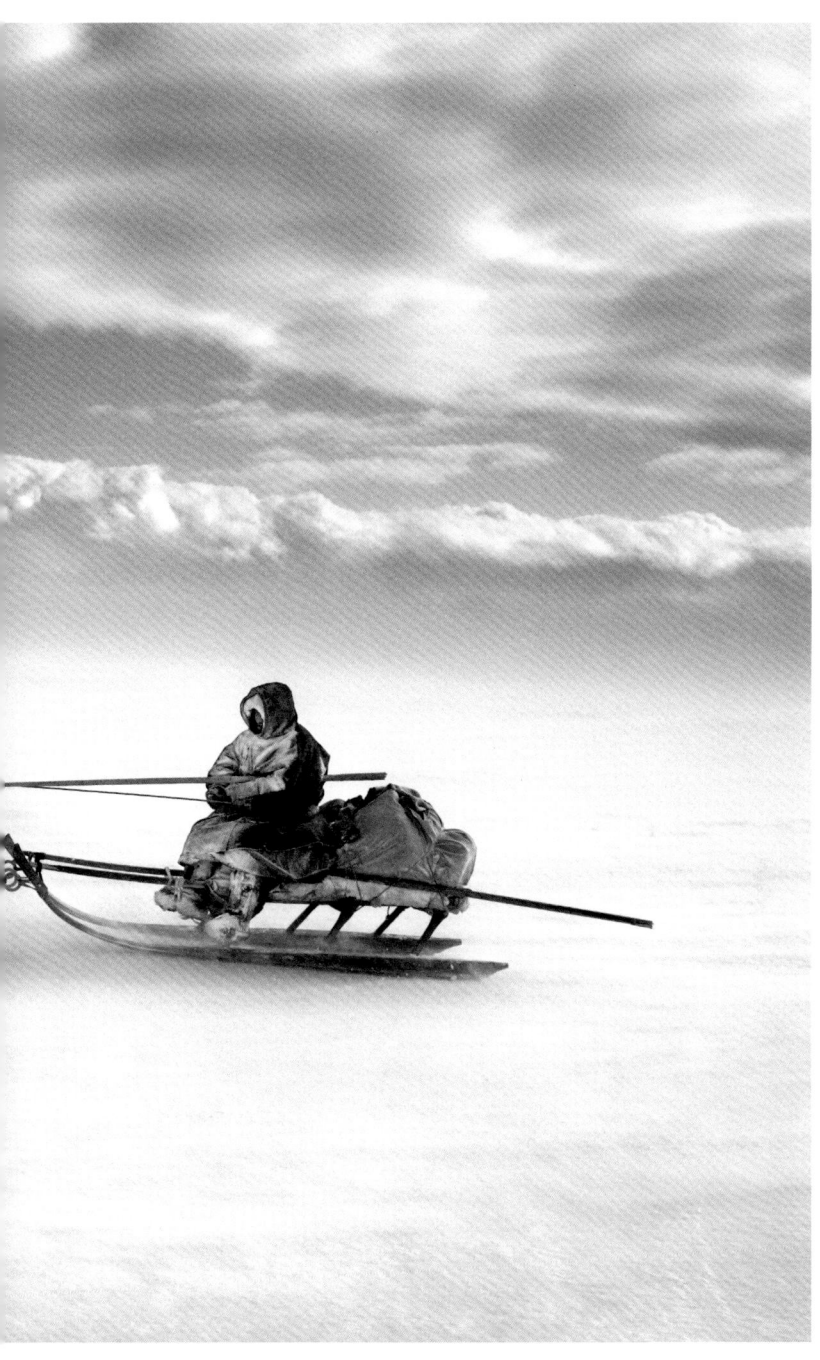

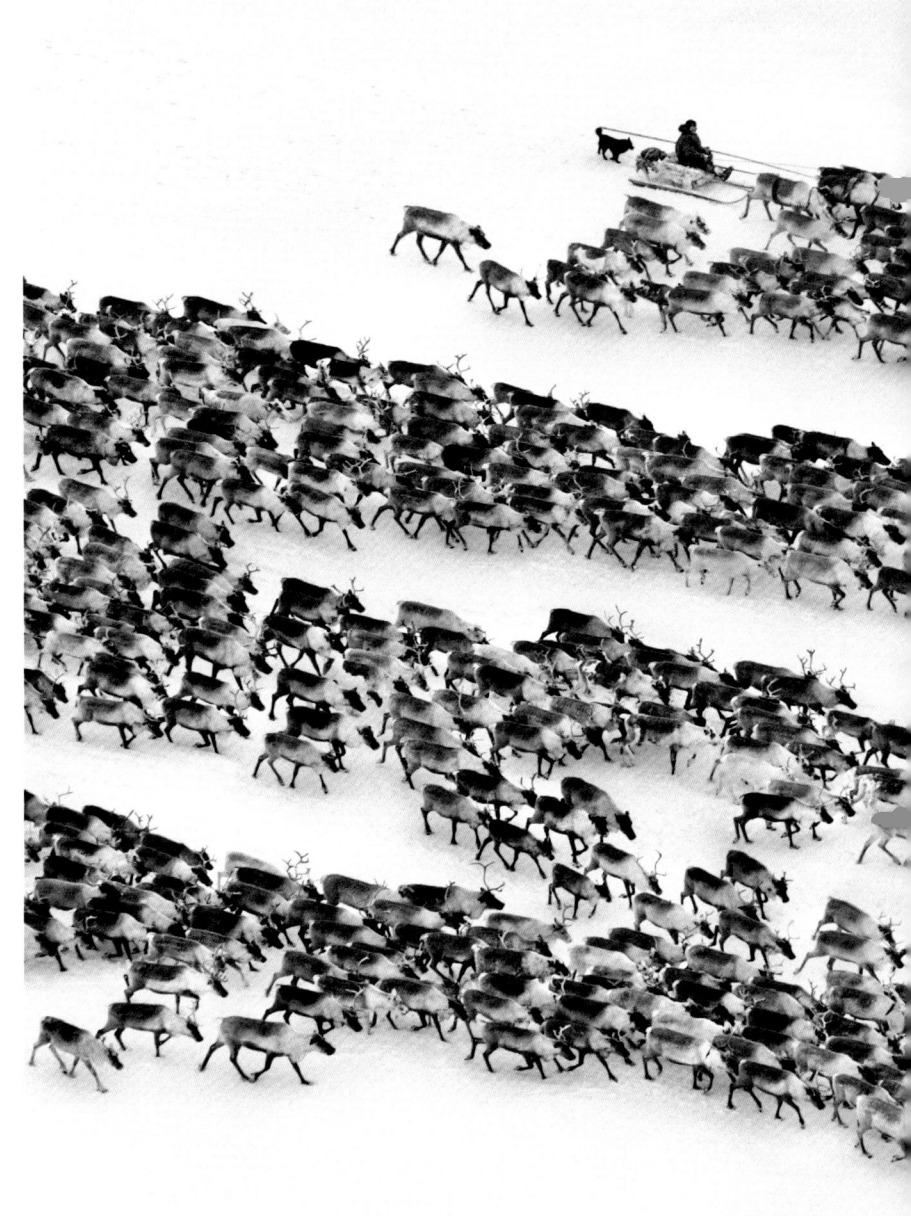

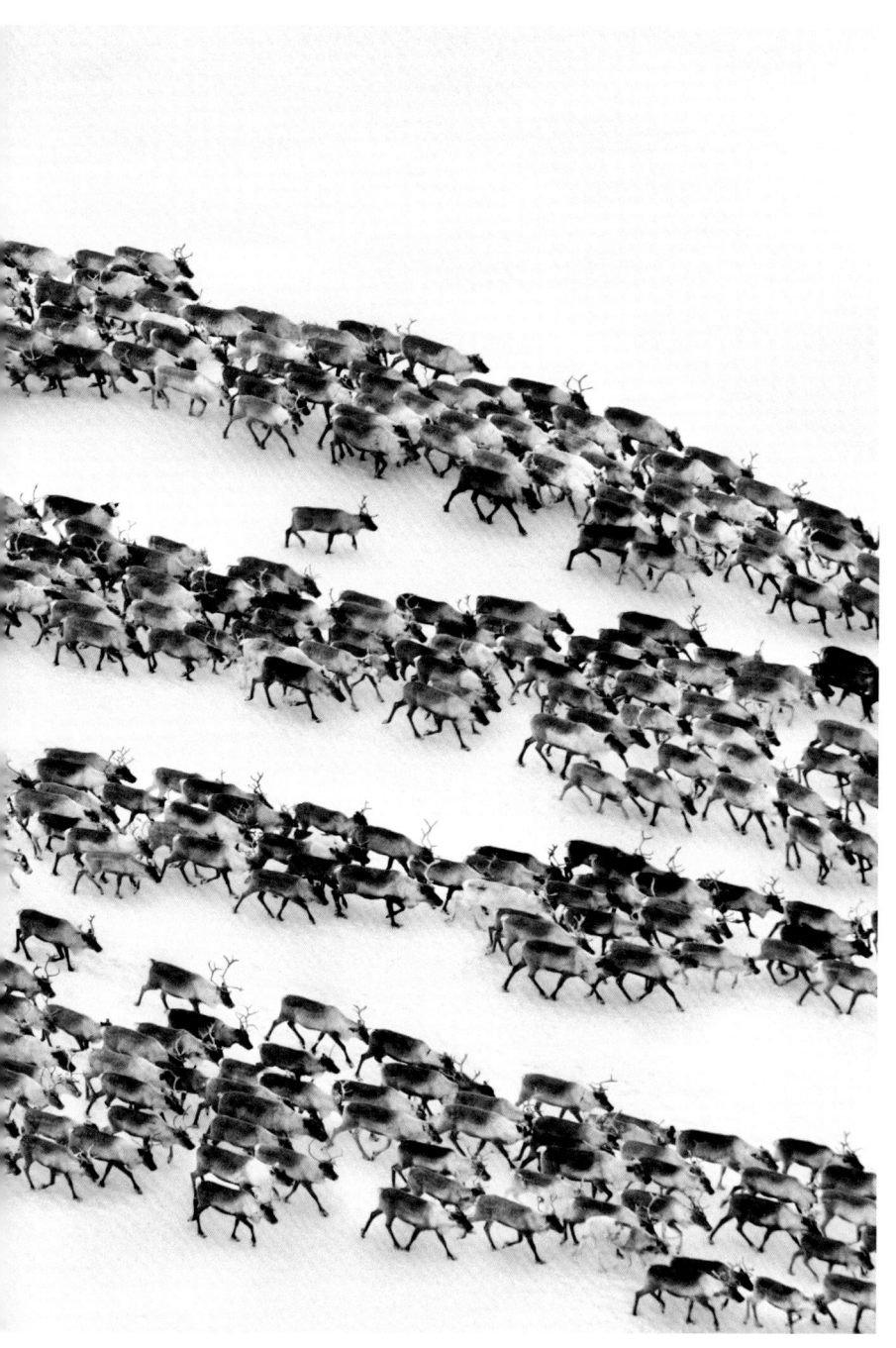

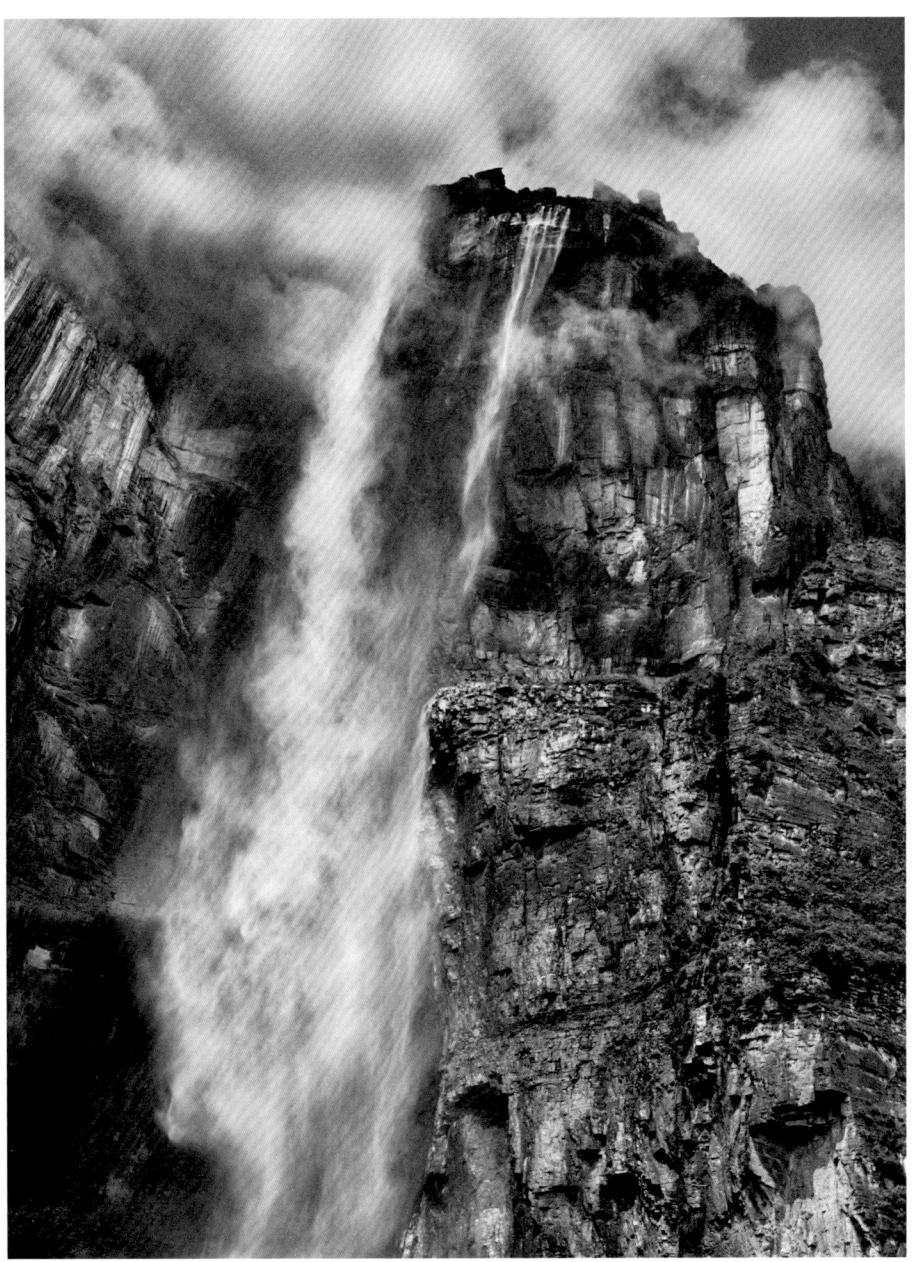

AMAZONIA AND PANTANAL

From space, the Amazon River and its tributaries resemble a giant tree of life. Indeed, the entire Amazon basin represents life in myriad ways: as a global lung, as the source of 20 percent of the world's fresh water, as home to uncounted species of flora and fauna, and as a refuge for scores of Indian tribes. On its peripheries, though, logging, cattle farming, mining, and urbanization are slowly eating away at the jungle. Burned forest and cleared land have now left vast scars on what was once an uninterrupted carpet of green.

I know and love the Amazon region. This time I wanted to fly over the river, which Brazilians only call the Amazon, after the dark Rio Negro and the paler Rio Solimões meet at Manaus. From there, we headed northwest up the Rio Negro over land so flat that the river is sometimes 12 miles (20 kilometers) wide, leaving long fingers of islands covered by dense vegetation. What may appear in a photograph to be a static landscape is in fact ever-changing, depending on the changing seasons and the flow of water coming down from the Andes.

The Amazon rainforest spreads far beyond Brazil's borders, but what drew me to the Canaima National Park in southeast Venezuela were tabletop mountains known as *tepuis*, nearly 10,000 feet (3,000 meters) high, which rise abruptly from the jungle. Formed some four billion years ago, they are among the world's oldest geological formations. Climbing to the top of several *tepuis*, I was stunned to see how erosion had carved rocks into ghostly shapes, some evoking prehistoric animals, others deserted cities. And, everywhere, there are waterfalls, as if the very mountains were weeping. At the Angel Falls, the highest on earth, the water plunges more than 3,200 feet (970 meters). No wonder Arthur Conan Doyle chose this setting for his 1912 novel *The Lost World*.

People have lived in the Amazon forest for more than 10,000 years, although many tribes have disappeared in the wake of road-builders, loggers, missionaries, and imported diseases. One exception are the Zo'é, first "contacted" only two decades ago. Thanks to Brazil's National Indian Foundation (FUNAI), I had the good fortune of being allowed to spend several weeks observing a way of life that has changed little over millennia. These gentle hunter-gatherers live in small communities and wear no clothes. Adults have a small wooden plug piercing their lower lip. I followed them into the jungle when they went hunting for monkeys and fish with bows and arrows, and watched them grind manioc root into flour. They now own a 2,400-square-mile (6,250-square-kilometer) reserve; even so, curious about the outside world, a few tribesmen have recently visited nearby towns.

Some 930 miles (1,500 kilometers) away, on the southern edge of Amazonia, Indian tribes in Mato Grosso state have more contact with modern society, although they enjoy the protection of living in the Xingu Indigenous Park, a reserve the size of Belgium created in 1961. My interest was to see how much of their traditional way of life had survived. I concentrated on three tribes living in the Upper Xingu Basin—the Waura, Kuikuro, and Kamayura—who speak different languages and have distinct ethnic backgrounds. Some tribesmen understand Portuguese and wear Western clothes, but they also take immense pride in their rituals and ceremonies.

The two months I spent in the Xingu coincided with preparations by the Kuikuro and Waura tribes for the funeral ritual of the *Kuarup*, which celebrates life, death, and rebirth. For this, a large amount of food and drink is prepared for guests from other villages, while near-naked bodies are painted and intricate feather headdresses are worn. The *Kuarup* climaxes with daylong chanting, dancing, and wrestling. The Kamayura tribe was holding the Amuricumã, an annual festival in which women assume power and, along with preparing the food, engage in the Dance of the Women. The Kamayura also boast the only female shaman in the Upper Xingu.

Still further south is the Pantanal, the largest wetland in the world, which is mainly located in Brazil but also spreads into Bolivia and Paraguay. During the rainy season, 80 percent of the region floods, and streams and rivers disappear into lakes. We traveled mostly by boat through a world owned by a remarkable variety of animal life, from river otters, anteaters, marsh deer and tapirs to capybaras, anacondas, caimans, and jaguars.

The air, in turn, belongs to crowned eagles, macaws, parrots, toucans, herons, hawks and giant storks known locally as the *tuiuiu*. Cattle have been introduced in some places, although nature occasionally protests. Where rain has washed away soil from cleared land, silted rivers have now permanently flooded pastures and bankrupted cattle farmers.

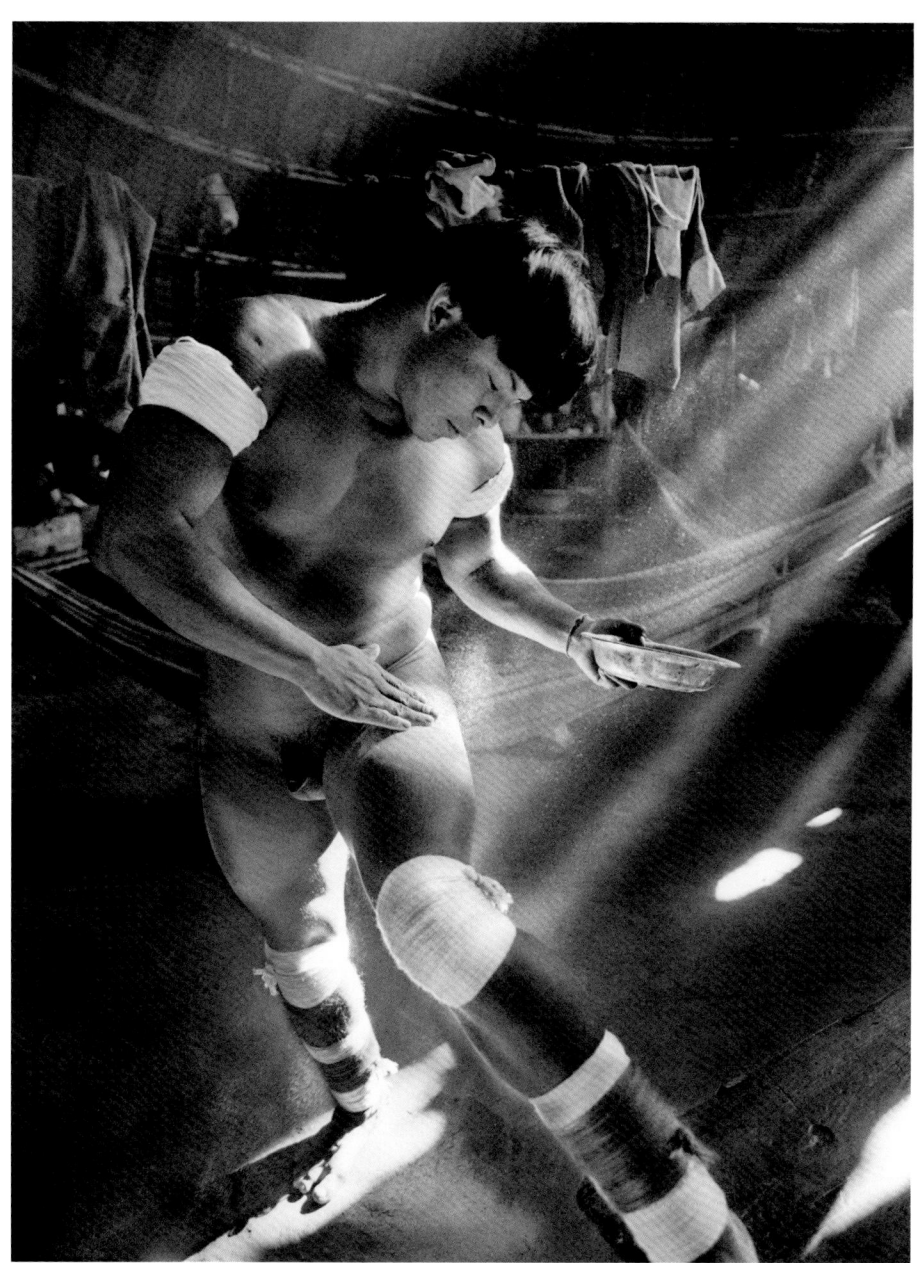

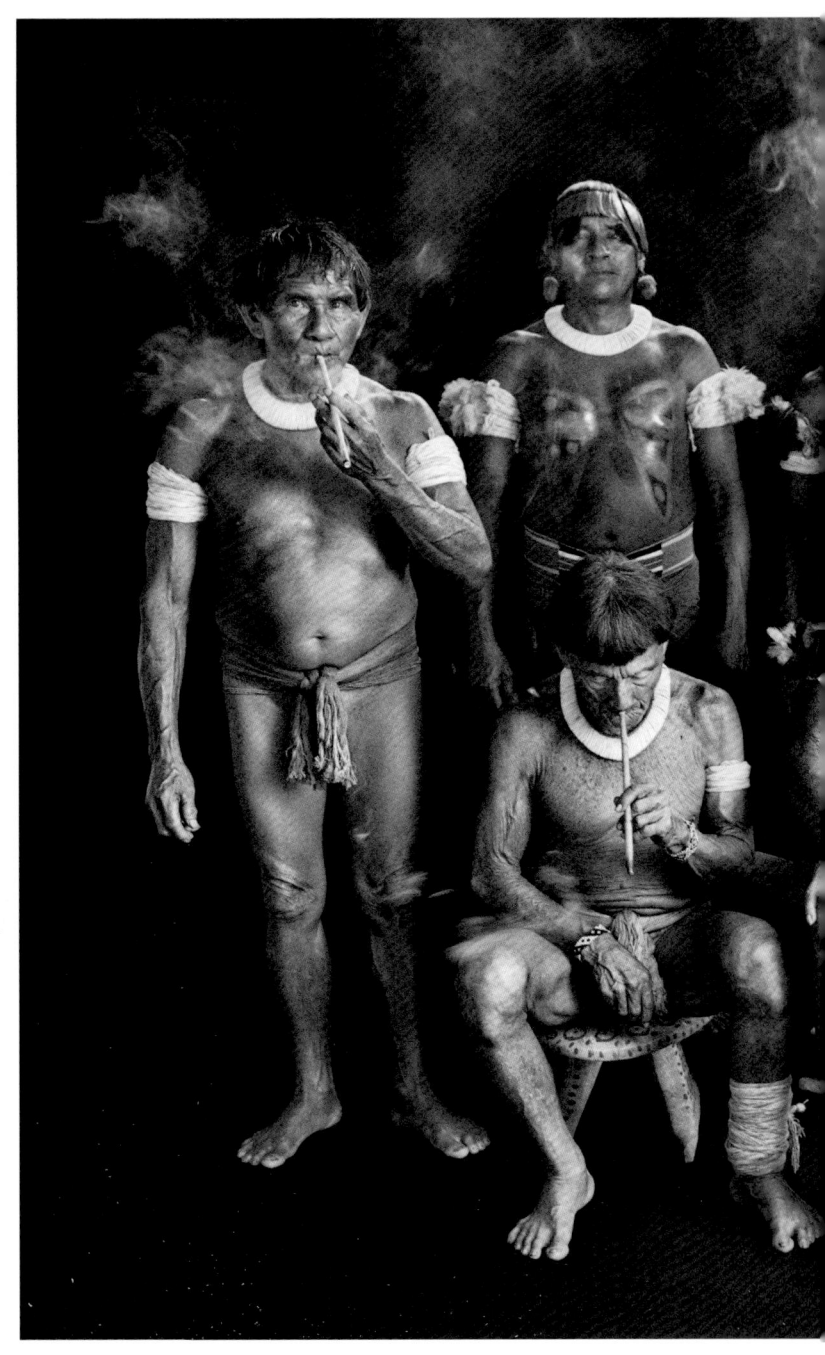

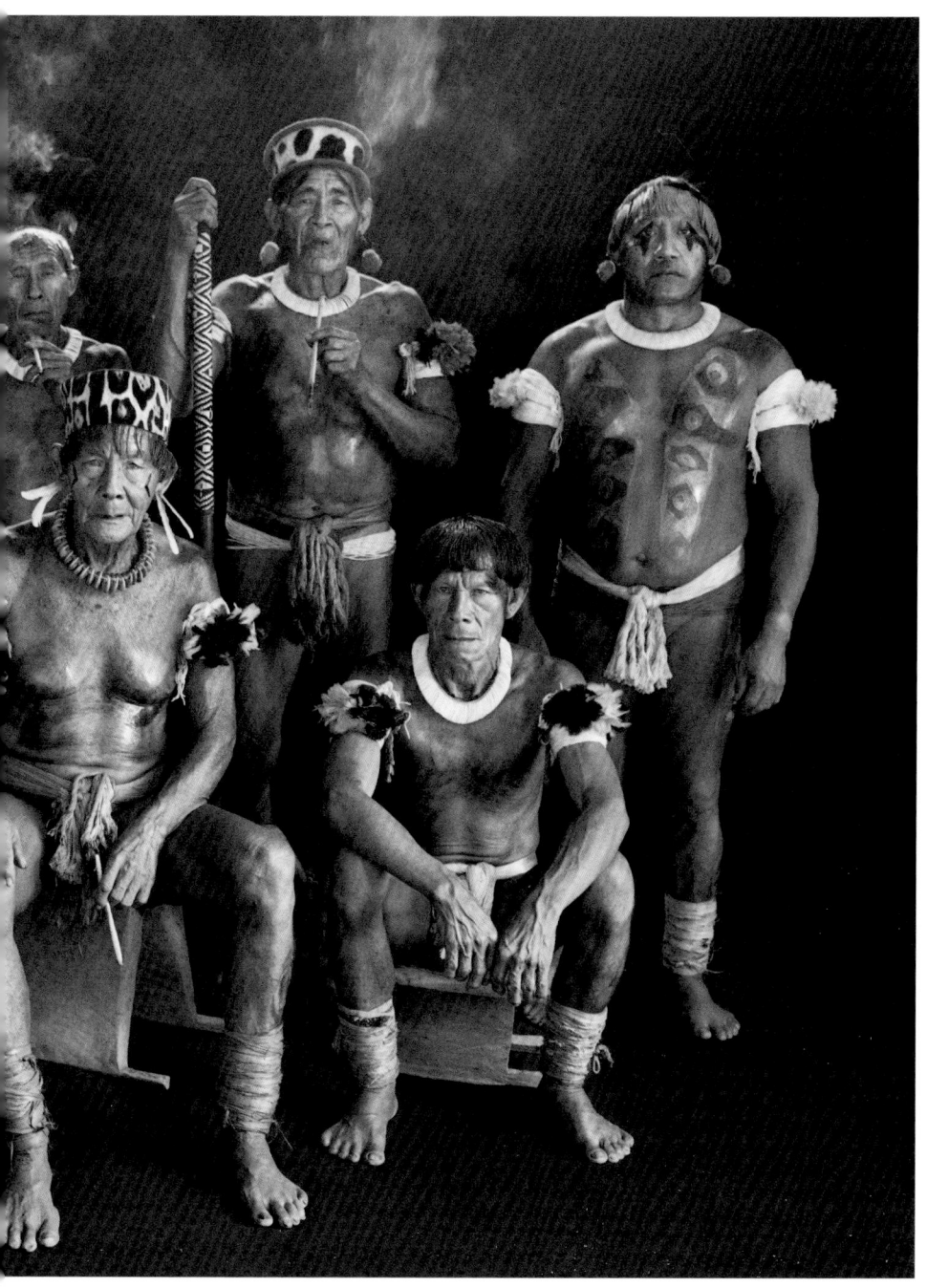

Page 154: Known in English as the Angel Falls, the Salto Ángel is the world's tallest waterfall, tumbling 3,200 feet (979 meters) from a flat-topped mountain called Auyantepui, or Devil's Mountain, in the Indigenous Pemon language. The waterfall is in the central portion of this *tepui* and drops into what is known as the Cañón del Diablo, or Devil's Canyon, with the water flow eventually reaching the Churún River. The waterfall takes its name from an American bush pilot, Jimmie Angel, who flew over the falls in 1933. Four years later, he landed on Auyantepui's plateau in a four-seat plane while searching for gold. Unable to take off from the marshy terrain, Angel, his wife and two companions trekked across the *tepui* before climbing down an almost vertical cliff to safety. Their widely publicized 11-day odyssey drew attention for the first time to the existence of the waterfall. Venezuela. November and December 2006.

THE ALTO XINGU INDIANS

Pages 157 through 163

The Upper Xingu Basin in the state of Mato Grosso lies between the equatorial forest of southern Amazonia and the savannah of central Brazil. The Xingu River, which flows north into the Amazon near Belém, gives its name to this beautiful region in which flora, fauna, and soil present all the characteristics of Amazonia even though it lies more than 620 miles (1,000 kilometers) to the south. The Upper Xingu Basin is home to an ethnically diverse population, with the 2,500 inhabitants of 13 villages speaking languages with distinct Carib, Tupi, and Arawak roots. While they occupy different land and preserve their cultural identities, they coexist in peace. Even more unusually, they join each other's important ceremonies, such as the *Kuarup*, the *Amuricumã*, the *Takuara*, and the *Jawari*, with their ritualistic dancing, chanting, and speeches.

Unfortunately, this cultural and environmental harmony is threatened by damage to the areas adjacent to the National Xingu Park. The biggest worry is pollution of streams, which pass through soya plantations and carry toxic chemicals into the Xingu River. This is already affecting fishing by the region's Indigenous peoples, for whom fish is a central part of their diet. In fact, the Mehinaku tribesmen believe their fish diet accounts for their passivity: "We do not eat animals that have hot blood so our food is sweet and as a result our guts are never warmed up for aggression." No less alarming, the Upper Xingu region is recording among the highest rates of deforestation in Brazil. In addition, construction of several hydroelectric dams upstream on the Xingu could decimate the ecosystem of the river and its tributaries and undermine an entire culture that depends on the purity of its waters. Brazil. July, August, and September 2005.

Page 157: A Kamayura athlete paints his body to participate in the final day of the *Kuarup* as a guest of the Waura group village. Upper Xingu, Mato Grosso, Brazil. July, August, and September 2005.

Pages 158/159: In this group portrait of all the Kamayura shamans, the man wearing a jaguar skin hat in the center is the most important traditional priest of the entire Xingu region. His name is Takumã Kamayura, and he is the former chief of the Kamayura people. Only shamans are permitted to smoke in the Upper Xingu since it is considered a sacred act that allows them to enter into contact with the divinities. Mato Grosso, Brazil. July, August, and September 2005.

Opposite: As with this Kamayura villager, the Indigenous groups of the Upper Xingu attribute their pacifism to their overwhelming diet of fish. Mato Grosso, Brazil. July, August, and September 2005.

Pages 162/163: Approximately 1,500 miles (2,400 kilometers) long, the Juruá River is one of the Amazon's longest tributaries. It rises in Peru's Ucalayi Highlands and is navigable for 1,120 miles (1,800 kilometers) before it joins the Solimões River. But once it enters the flat, forested lowlands known as the Amazon depression to the west of Manaus, it wiggles like a worm, curving to the left and right in order to advance barely half a mile. Even traveling downstream, boat skippers need immense patience. Amazonas, Brazil. August and September 2009.

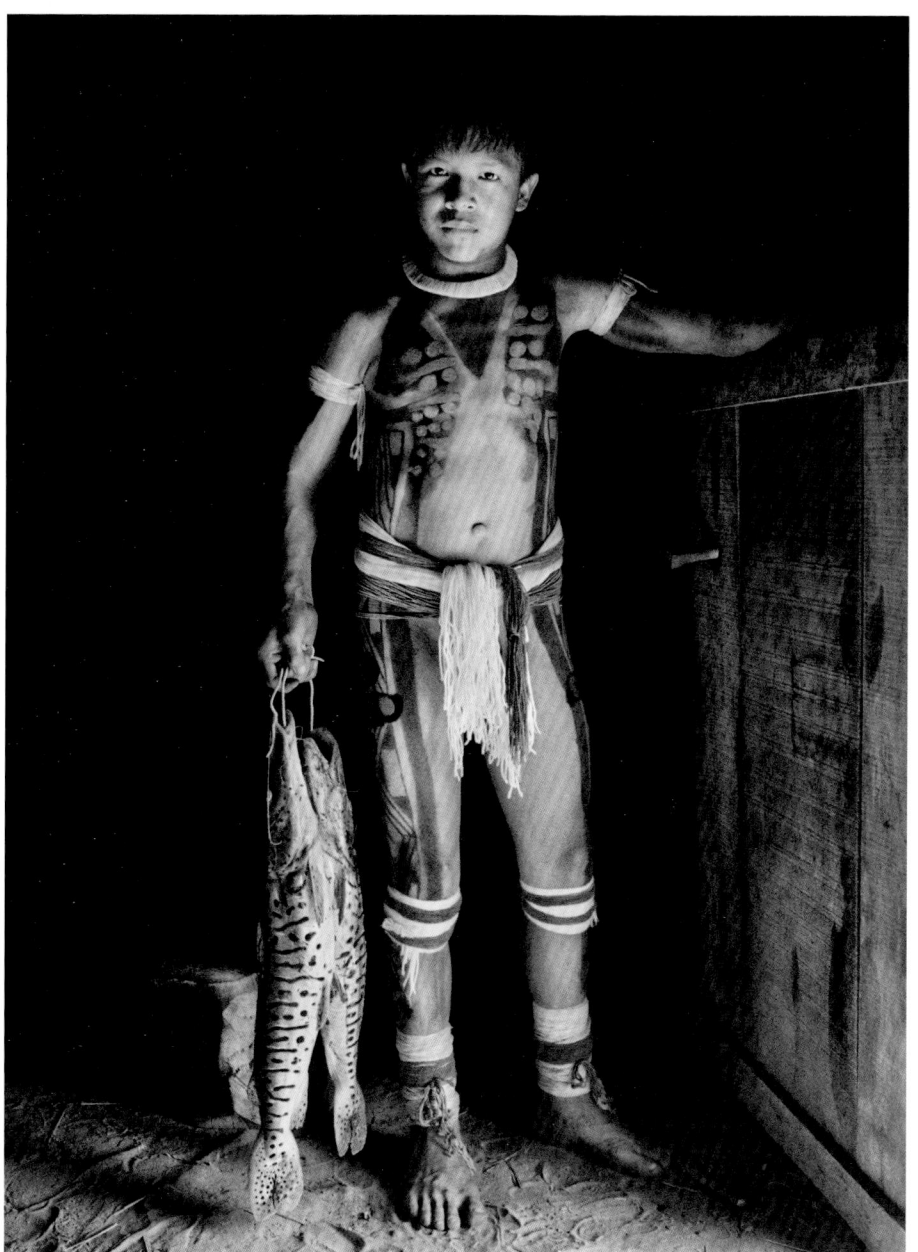

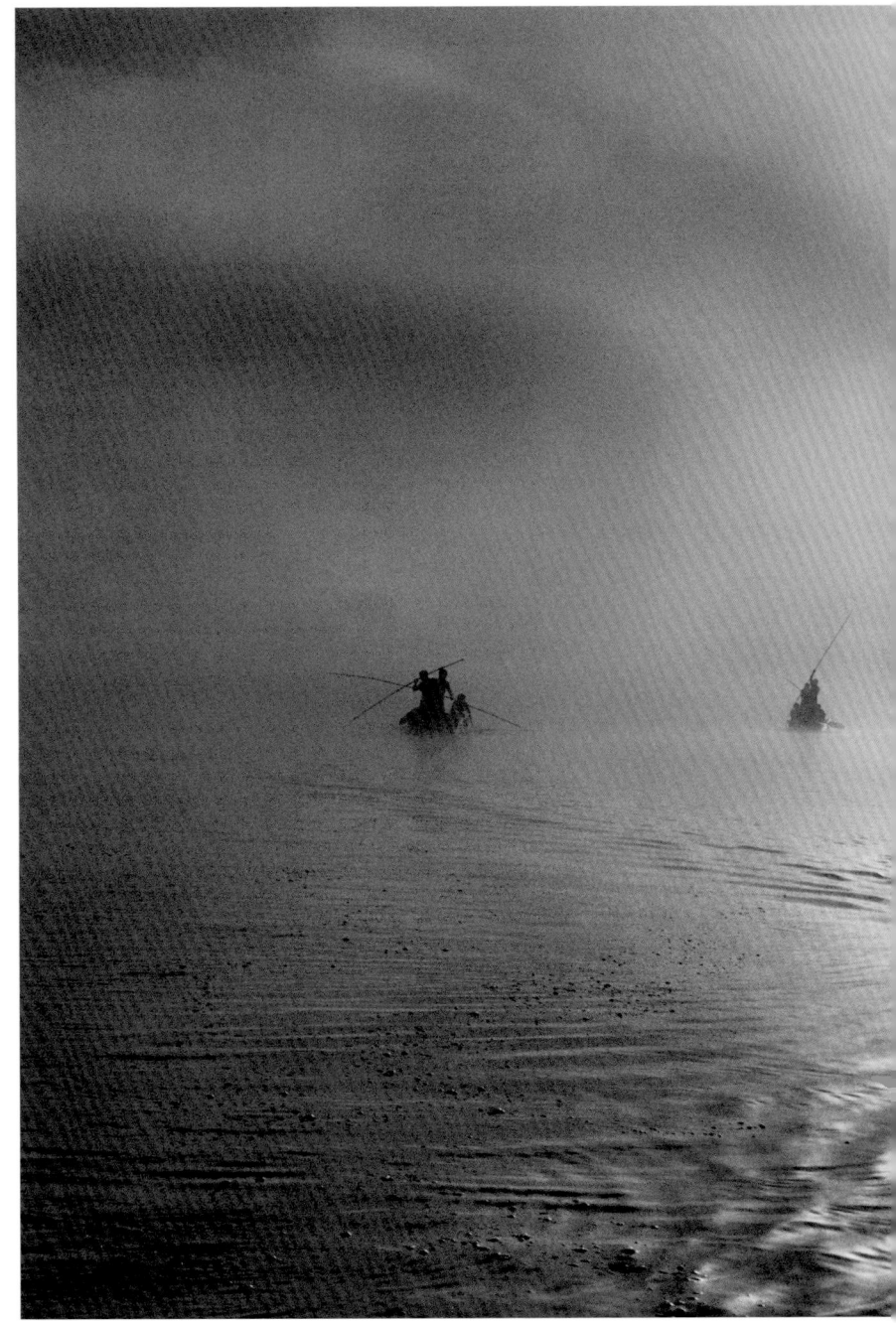

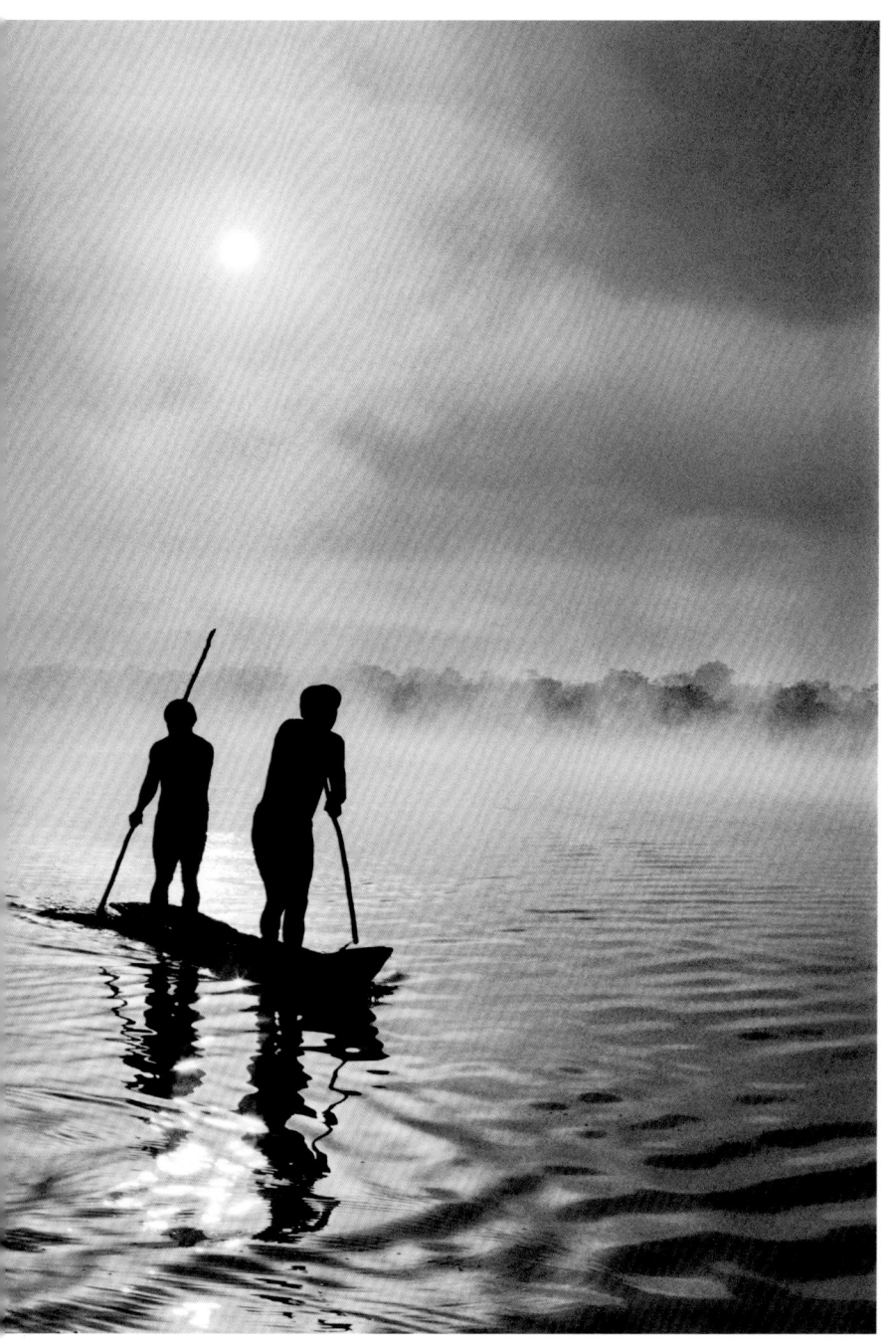

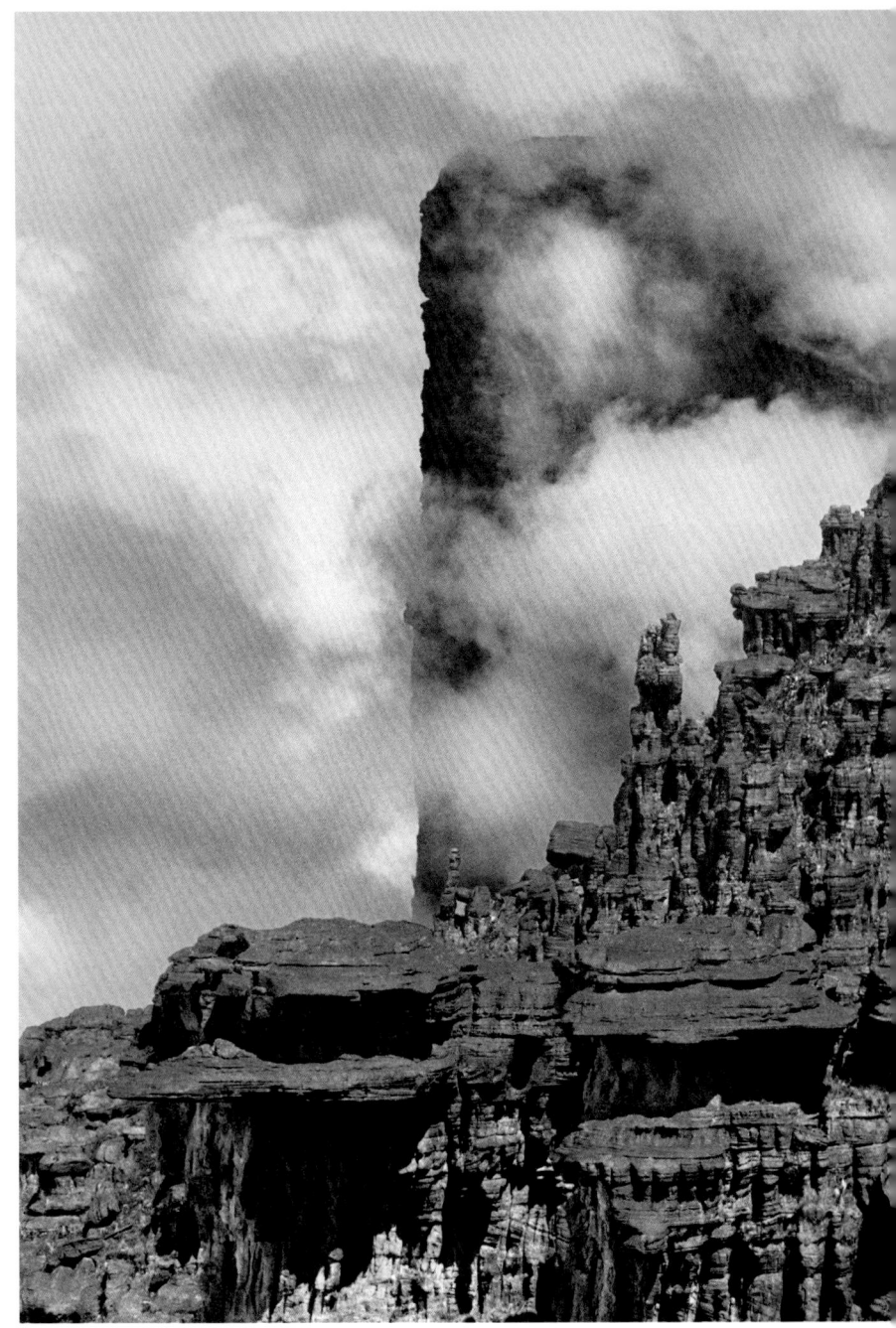

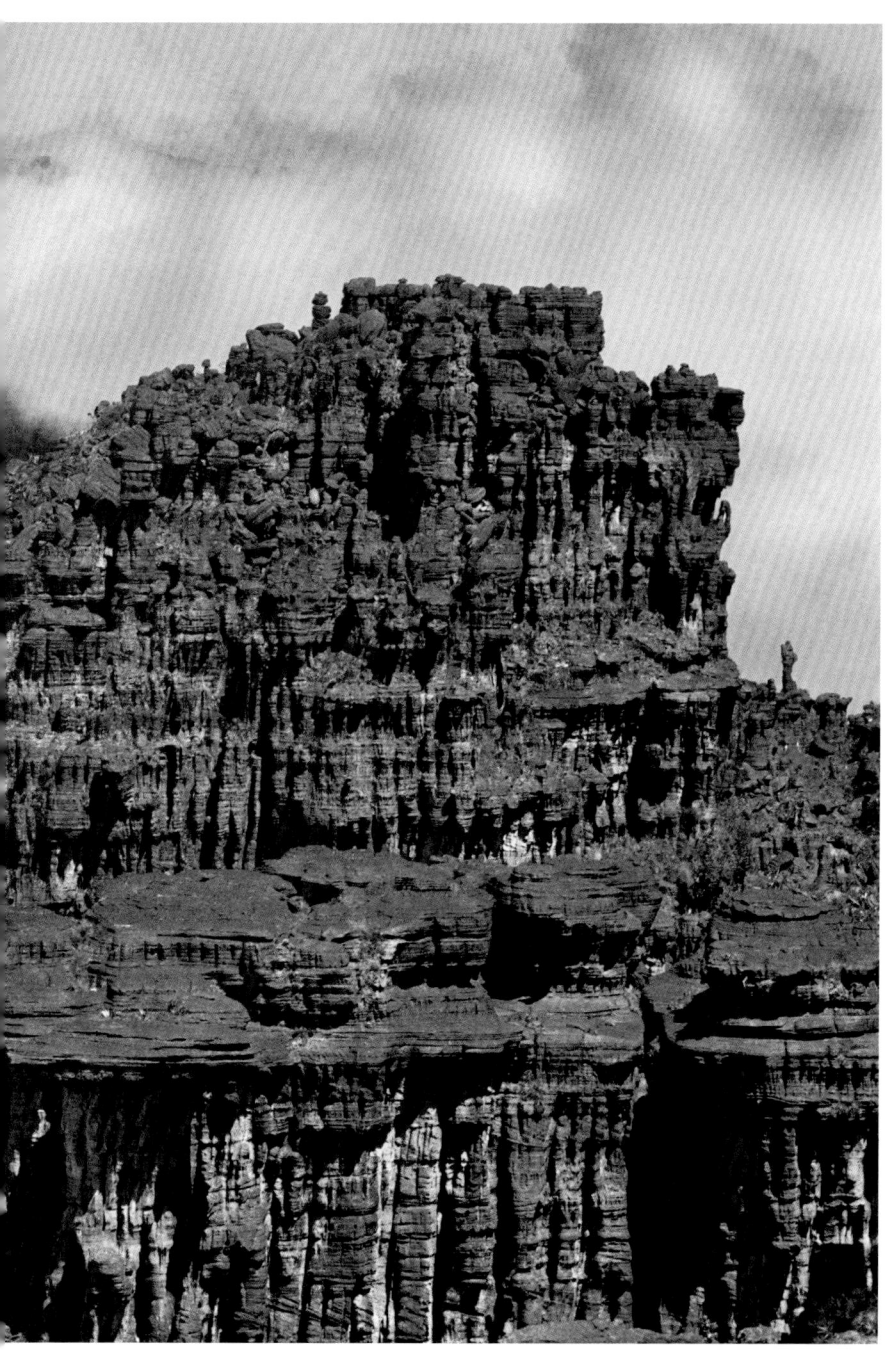

Pages 164/165: On the plateau of the Kukenan *Tepui*, wind and water erosion has sculpted bizarre shapes from the ancient rocks. *Tepui* is the Pemon Indian name given to the 115 or so flat-topped mountains in a region straddling southeastern Venezuela, southwestern Guyana, and northern Brazil. This *tepui* covers an area of 8 square miles (20.6 square kilometers) and stands 8,800 feet (2,680 meters) above sea level. In the background, partly hidden by clouds, the Roraima Tepui rises to a height of 8,933 feet (2,723 meters). Venezuela. November and December 2006.

THE PANTANAL FAUNA

Pages 167 through 172

The Pantanal, which takes its name from the Portuguese word *pântano*, meaning bog, swamp, or marsh, is a region bursting with natural life. One of the world's largest wetlands, it sprawls across the Brazilian states of Mato Grosso and Mato Grosso do Sul, spilling into Bolivia and Paraguay and covering an area estimated at between 54,000 and 75,000 square miles (140,000 and 195,000 square kilometers). Because the level of its waters rises and falls with the seasons, the Pantanal's cycles of life are also constantly in flux. During the rainy season, flooding of about 80 percent of the area nurtures an astonishing diversity of aquatic plants and animal species. Its ecosystem hosts some 1,000 bird species, 400 fish species, 300 species of mammal and 480 different kinds of reptile. Among its rarest fauna are the marsh deer (*Blastocerus dichotomus*) and the giant river otter (*Pteronura brasiliensis*). Endangered animals include the maned wolf (*Chrysocyon brachyurus*), the bush dog (*Speothos venaticus*), and the yacare caiman (*Caiman yacare*), while the hyacinth macaw (*Anodorhynchus hyacinthinus*) and the crowned solitary eagle (*Harpyhaliaetus coronatus*) are also threatened. In contrast, several species prosper. The jaguar (*Panthera onca*) is very much at home in the Pantanal, while the yellow anaconda (*Eunectes notaeus*), the red-footed tortoise (*Chelonoidis carbonaria*), and the green iguana (*Iguana iguana*) are relatively common. Brazil. September and October 2011.

Opposite: The biguatinga, or anhinga (*Anhinga anhinga*), is a large aquatic bird with an 33-inch (84-centimeter) wingspan as well as a long, straight bill and a very slender neck, which make it an effective fisher. Here, a biguatinga has just caught a lambari (*Astyanax bimaculatus*) in the Cuiabá River, close to Porto Jofre in northern Pantanal. Mato Grosso, Brazil. September and October 2011.

Pages 168/169: The Arara azul (*Anodorhynchus hyacinthinus*) or hyacinth macaw. With their 3-foot (95-centimeter) wingspan, these stunning macaws can be seen gliding in pairs over the forest canopy, their eyes alert to their favorite food, palm-tree fruits. Their feathers are a rich violet-blue, with bare skin below their beak and around the eyes providing little splashes of yellow. Caiman Ecological Reserve. Pantanal, Mato Grosso do Sul, Brazil. September and October 2011.

Pages 170/171: The jaguar (*Panthera onca*), the largest cat of the Americas, is to be found mainly in the Amazon rainforest although also in the Pantanal and its adjoining plain known as the Gran Chaco. Jaguars vary in size between 44 and 73 inches (112 and 185 centimeters), with the average male weighing 265 pounds (120 kilos) (although some in the Pantanal weigh as much as 330 pounds / 150 kilos). In the cat family, only lions and tigers are larger. This jaguar was seen beside the Tagoarira River, in the region of Porto Jofre. Encontro das Águas National Park. Pantanal, Mato Grosso. Brazil. September and October 2011.

Pages 172/173: The Pantanal, one of the world's largest wetlands, covering a vast area of western Brazil and spilling into Paraguay and Bolivia, is home to an estimated 10 million yacare caimans (*Caiman yacare*). At the end of the dry season, they concentrate in small lakes, such as seen here at the Porto Alegre estate in the region of Porto Jofre, where 5,000 to 8,000 are gathered. Measuring between 7 and 10 feet (2 and 3 meters) long, they feed on fish, mollusks, and shellfish. Although the Pantanal boasts the largest population of caimans on Earth, they have been declared a threatened species because of uncontrolled hunting, mainly in Paraguay and Bolivia. Pantanal. Mato Grosso, Brazil. September and October 2011.

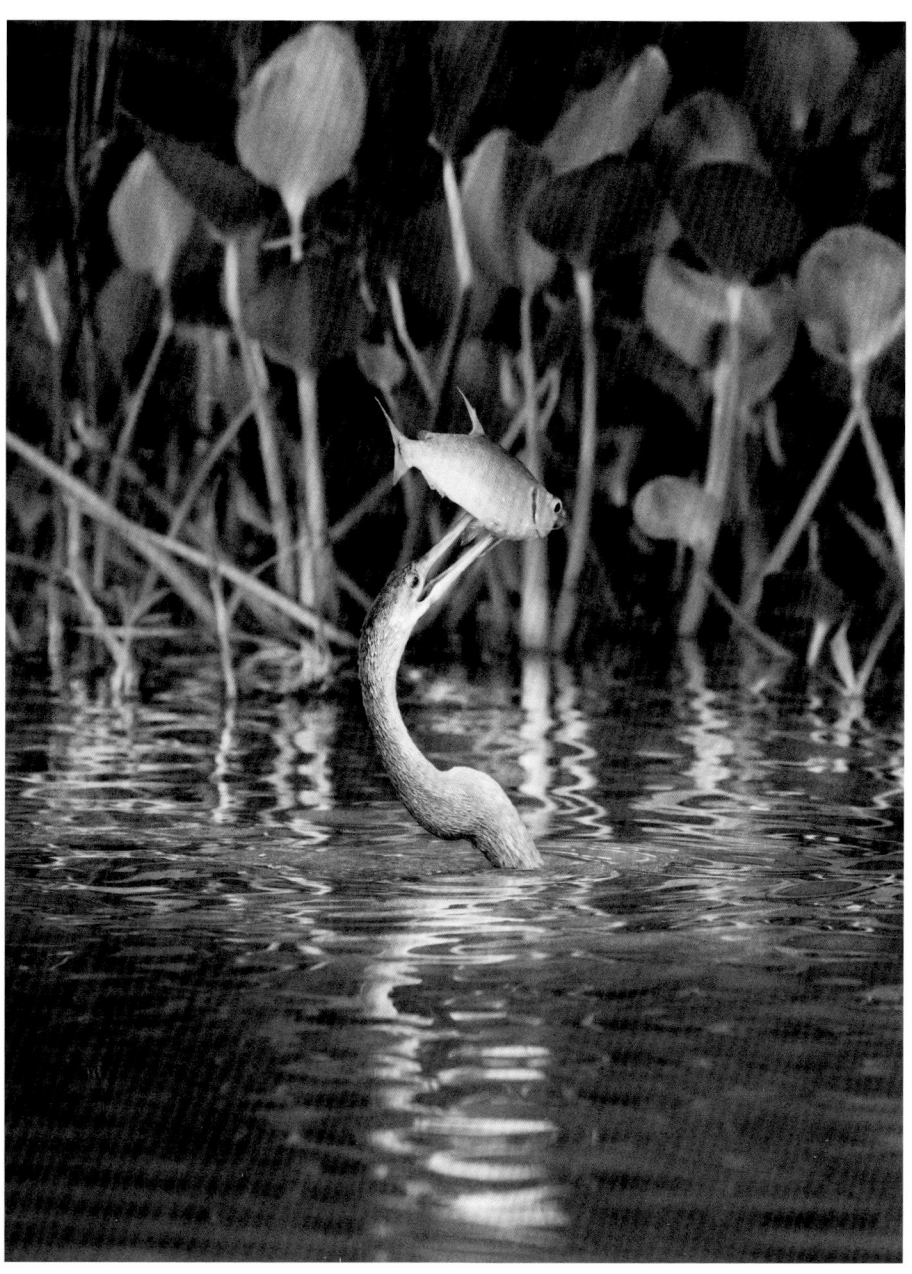

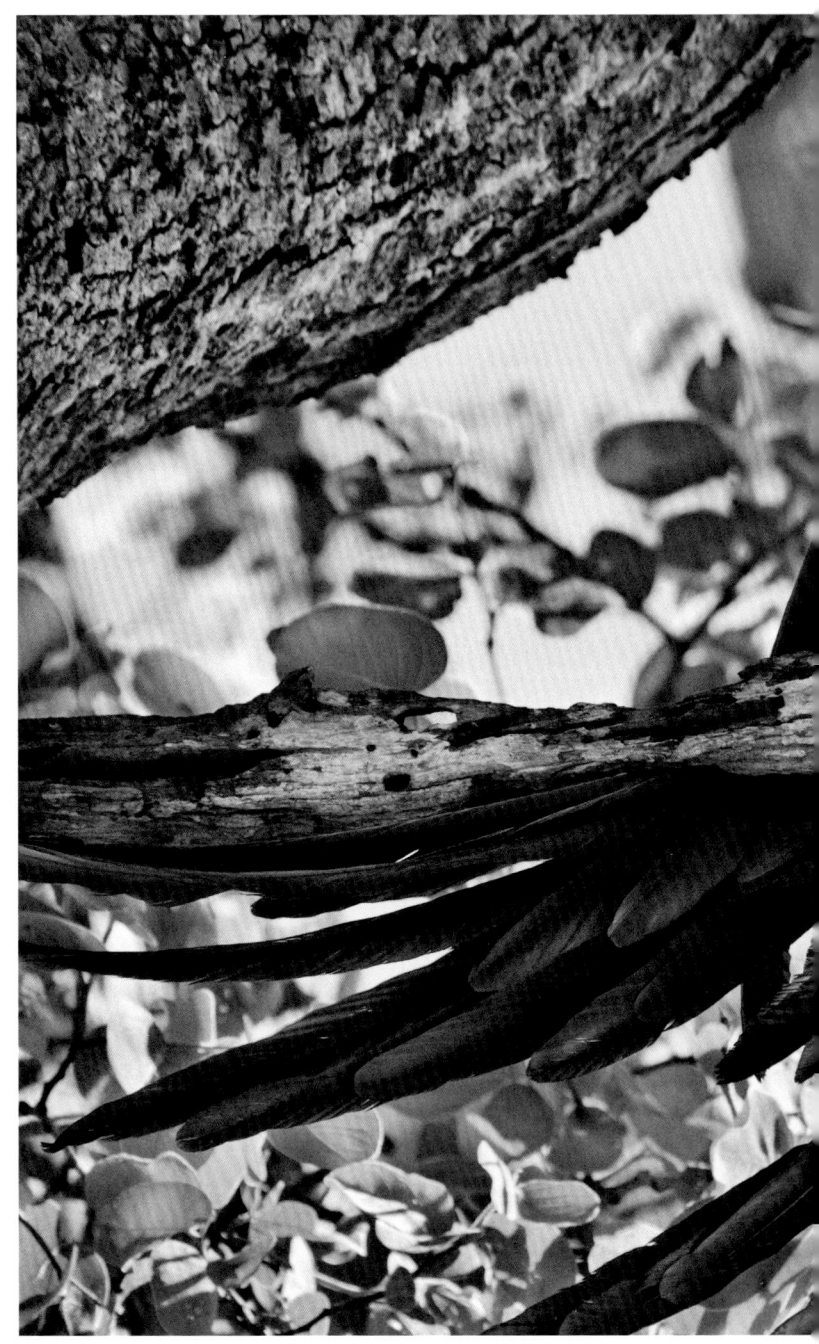

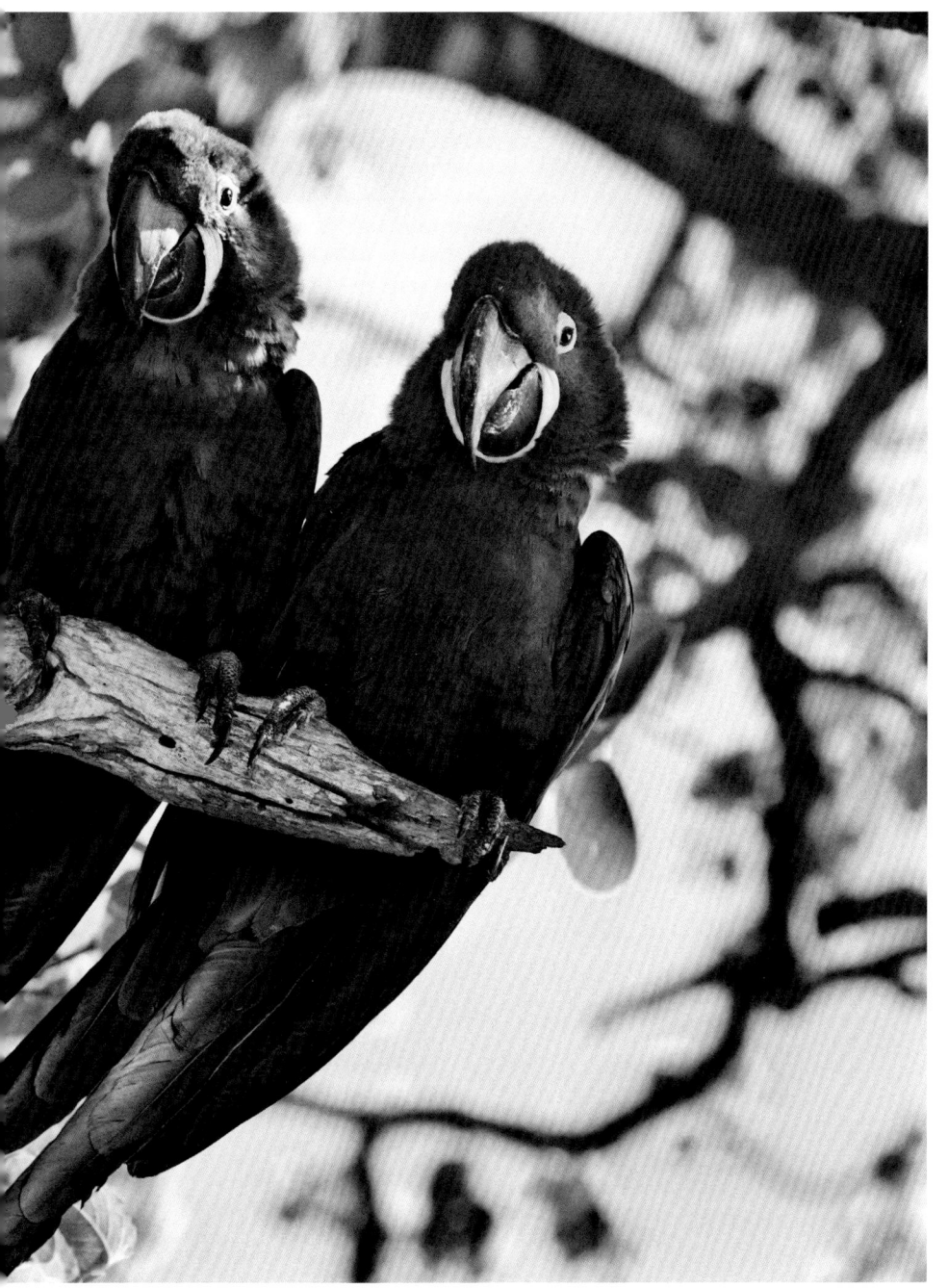

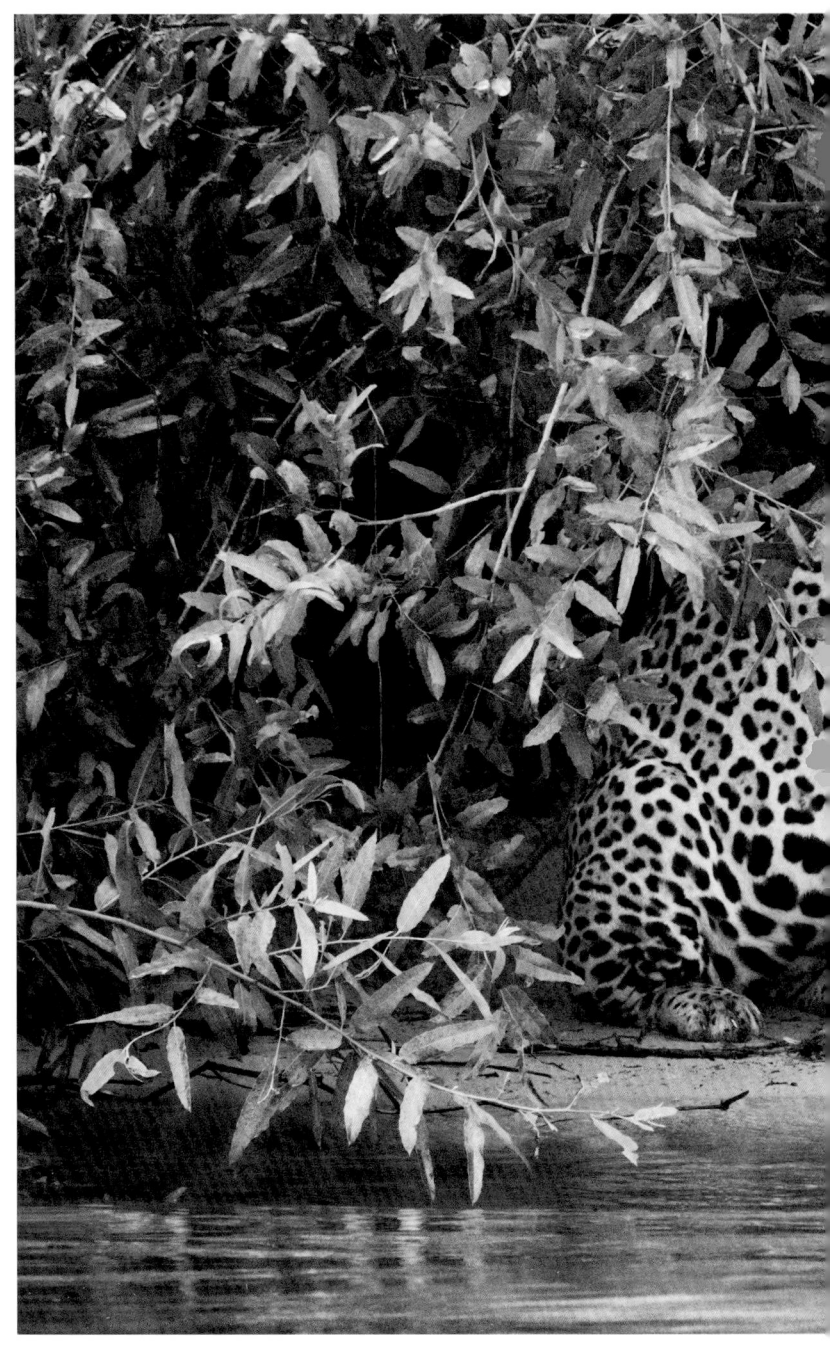

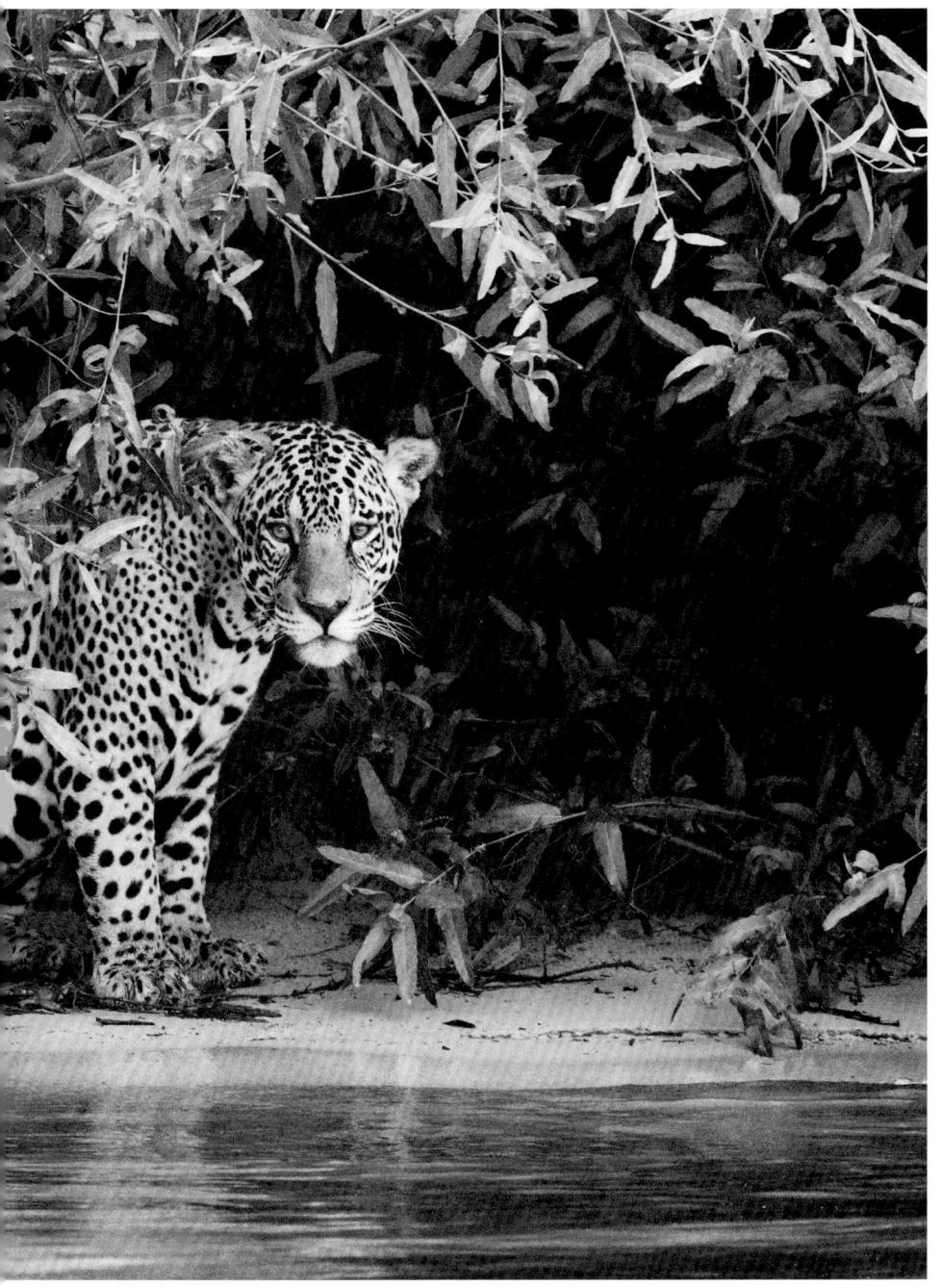

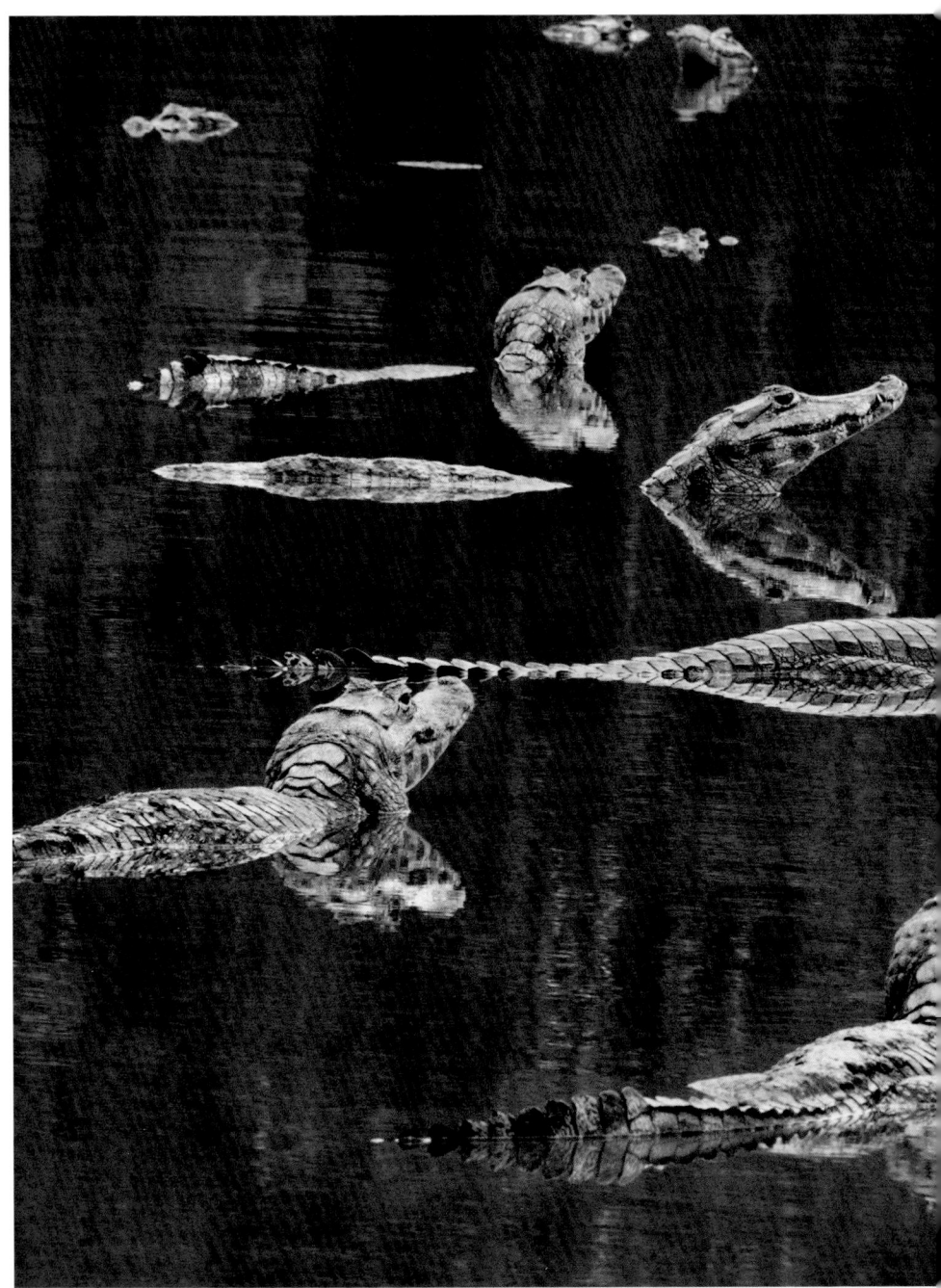

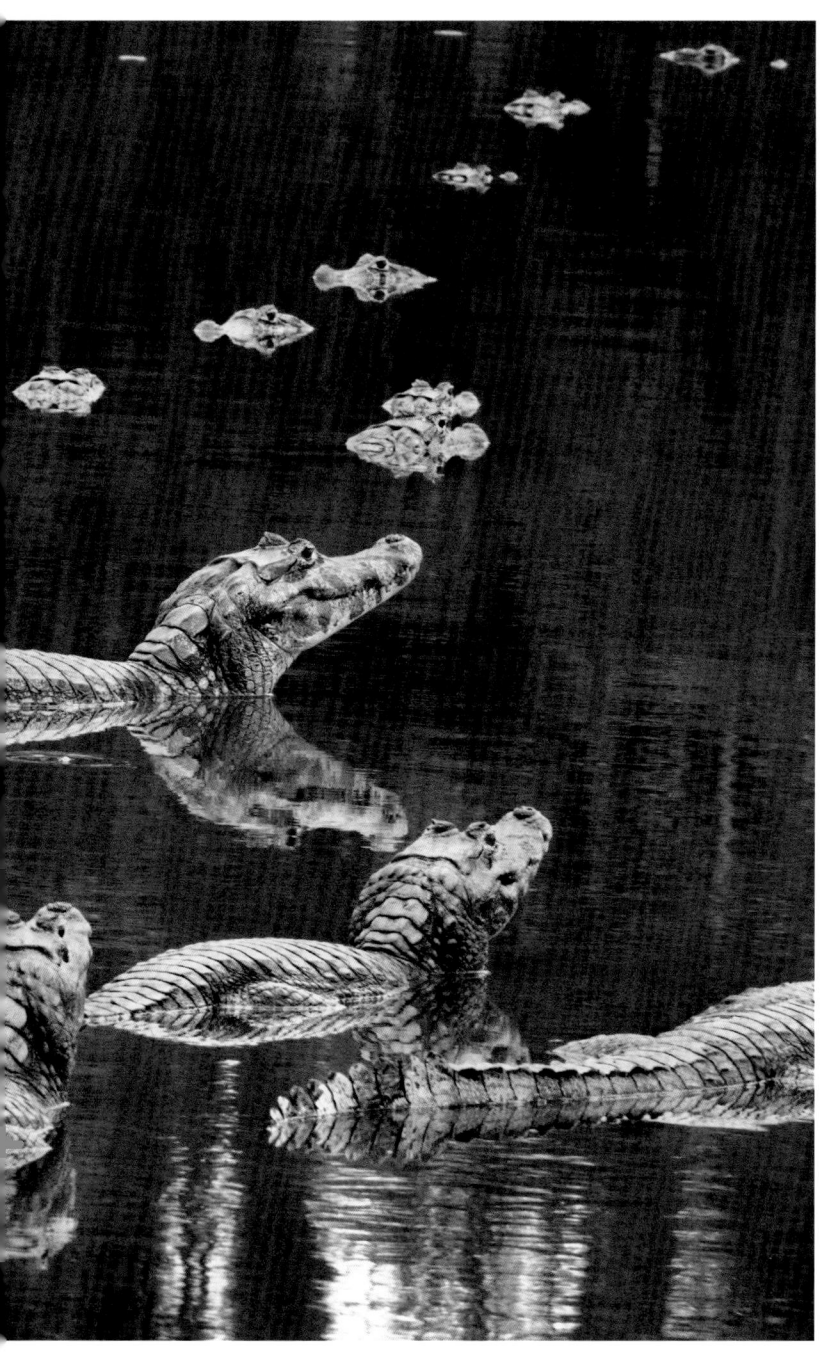

THE ZO'É

Pages 175 through 179

The Zo'é live deep in the rainforest of the northern Brazilian state of Pará in an area stretching between the Erepecuru and Cuminapanema rivers, both northern tributaries of the Amazon. Since they belong to the Tupi-Guarani linguistic group, traditionally settled near the Atlantic coast, it seems likely that the Zo'é migrated west several thousand years ago. They were contacted in 1987 by American evangelists from the New Tribes Mission. Intent on converting the Indians to their version of Christianity, they began by handing out presents such as clothes, machetes, and mirrors, and by building the first landing strip in the area. But within three years, the FUNAI, the Brazilian government agency responsible for protecting Indigenous peoples, expelled the New Tribes Mission from the Zo'é lands. FUNAI subsequently created the so-called Ethno-environmental Front for the Protection of Cuminapanema with the specific mandate of preventing any further invasion of Zo'é territory. In 2009, the Zo'é were granted ownership of 2,400 square miles (6,240 square kilometers) of land in the form of a protected reserve. Further protection is provided by a 12-mile (20-kilometer)-wide band of land around the perimeter of the reserve, which can only be crossed with special permission. Pará, Brazil. March and April 2009.

Opposite: Zo'é hunting practices vary with the season. This photograph was taken during the rainy season in March and April. Since this is not a good time for fishing, the Zo'é hunt monkeys, who are much sought after for their meat. Then, in June, they begin hunting wild pigs. Pará, Brazil. March and April 2009.

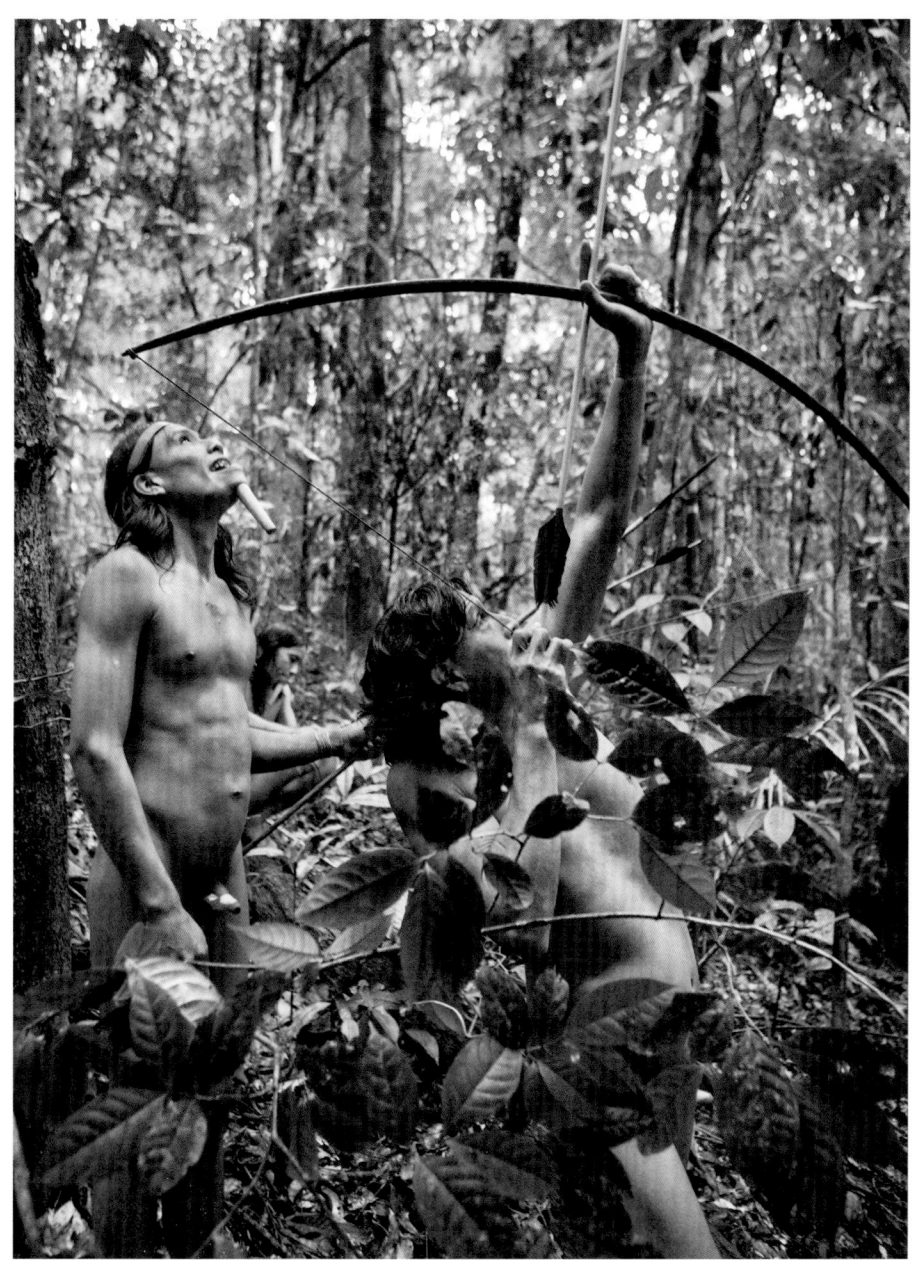

Opposite: The Zo'é, an isolated Indigenous people in the northern Amazon region, place great importance on their cleanliness. All the paths and trails from their settlement lead to water sources; their excursions, whether for hunting, fishing, or gathering, are regularly interrupted by breaks for bathing in brooks and streams. Pará, Brazil. March and April 2009.

Pages 178/179: Typically, the women in the Zo'é village of Towari Ypy use the red fruit of the *urucum* (*Bixa orellana*) to color their bodies. It is also used in cooking. The *urucum* is a shrub or small tree originating from tropical regions of the Americas. It has long been used by American Indians as body paint, especially for the lips, thus earning the nickname of "lipstick tree." Pará, Brazil. March and April 2009.

Pages 180/181: The Roraima Tepui, which straddles the borders of southeastern Venezuela, Brazil, and Guyana, has a surface of almost 14 square miles (35 square kilometers) and rises to a height 8,933 feet (2,723 meters). The photograph shows its best-known feature, its prow, which reaches into Guyana. *Tepui,* a Pemon Indian word for mountain, is now commonly used to describe a particular type of flat-topped mountain to be found in this region of South America. Varying in height between 3,300 and 9,800 feet (1,000 and 3,000 meters), the mesa or plateau of *tepuis* often have a unique ecosystem characterized by endemic animals and plants. Venezuela. November and December 2006.

Page 182/183: The waterfalls of Ichun-Prarara, located on the Ichun Plateau in the heart of Venezuela's Amazon rainforest, are very isolated and difficult to reach. Venezuela. November and December 2006.

Pages 184/185: The *Warime* ceremony of the Piaroa people in Venezuela symbolizes the birth of the world. It portrays earlier times of humanity and demonstrates how, thanks to their strength and vitality, they have survived until today. This ceremony, which takes place once a year, is also a harvest festival. This *Warime* is being held in the basin of the high Carinagua River. Venezuela on the border with Colombia. November and December 2006.

Pages 186/187: Sometimes the mesas of the *tepuis* resemble well-cultivated gardens. *Tepui,* a Pemon Indian word for mountain, is now commonly used to describe a particular type of flat-topped mountain found in southeastern Venezuela and across its borders with Brazil and Guyana. Seen on top of the Roraima Tepui, the *Orectante sceptrum* (of the *Xyridaceae* family) is a plant common to *tepui* plateaus. Venezuela. November and December 2006.

Pages 188/189: Approximately 1,500 miles (2,400 kilometers) long, the Juruá River is one of the Amazon's longest tributaries. It rises in Peru's Ucalayi Highlands and is navigable for 1,120 miles (1,800 kilometers) before it joins the Solimões River. But once it enters the flat, forested lowlands known as the Amazon depression to the west of Manaus, it wiggles like a worm, curving to the left and right in order to advance barely half a mile. Even traveling downstream, boat skippers need immense patience. Amazonas. Brazil. August and September 2009.

Pages 190/191: The Anavilhanas, the name given to around 350 forested islands in Brazil's Rio Negro, form the world's largest inland archipelago. Covering 390 square miles (1,000 square kilometers) of Amazonia, they start 50 miles (80 kilometers) northwest of Manaus and stretch some 250 miles (400 kilometers) up the Rio Negro, as far as Barcelos. Their formation dates back to the last Ice Age, when changes in the flow of rivers entering the Rio Negro produced accumulations of sediment that, over time, formed sandbars and islands. Since water levels change with the seasons by as much as 65 feet (20 meters), the Anavilhanas are themselves ever-changing, with channels, sandbars, and lagoons appearing during the dry season and some small islands vanishing when waters rise. Many of the larger islands, though, are self-contained parcels of rainforest. Amazonas. Brazil. May 2009.

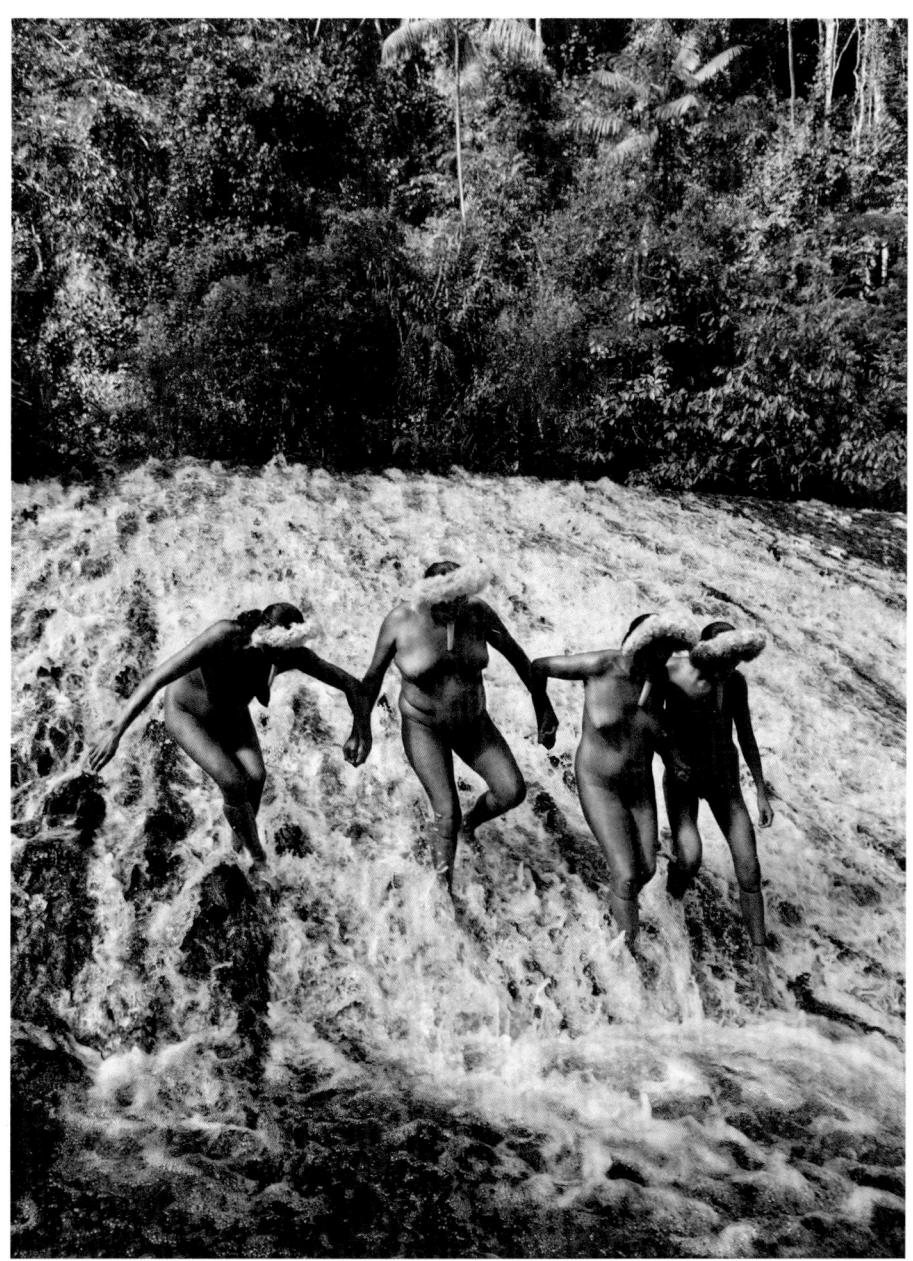

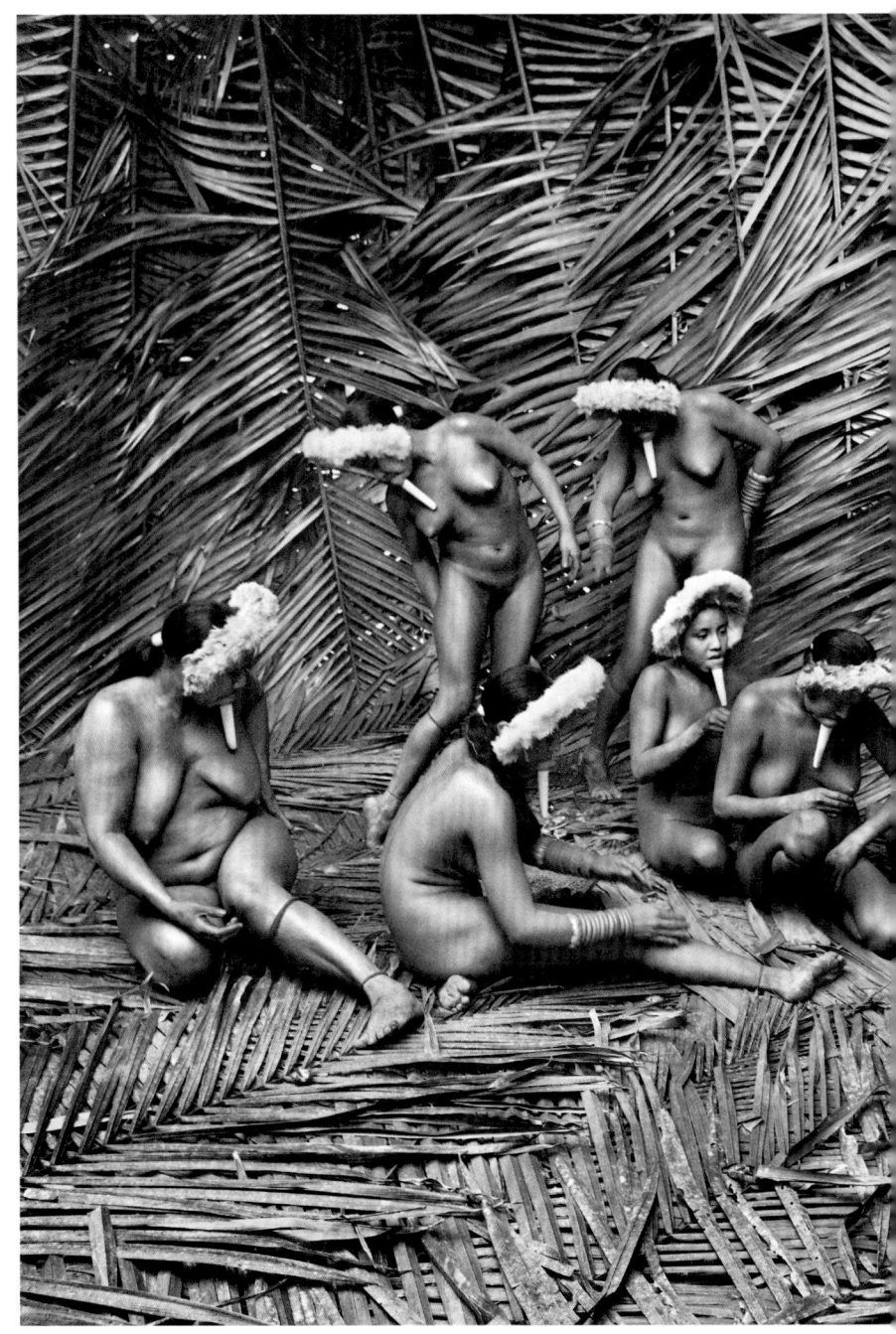

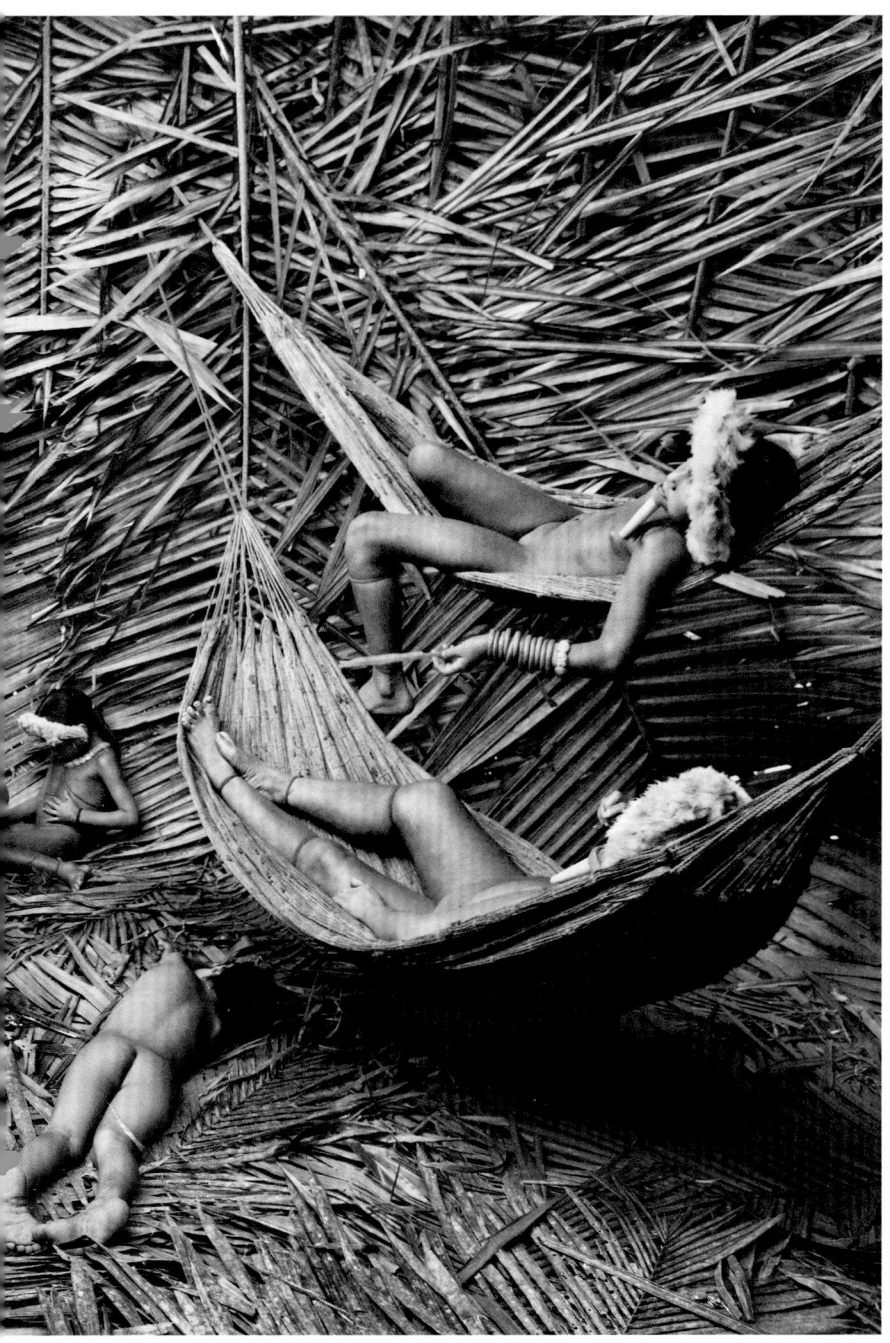

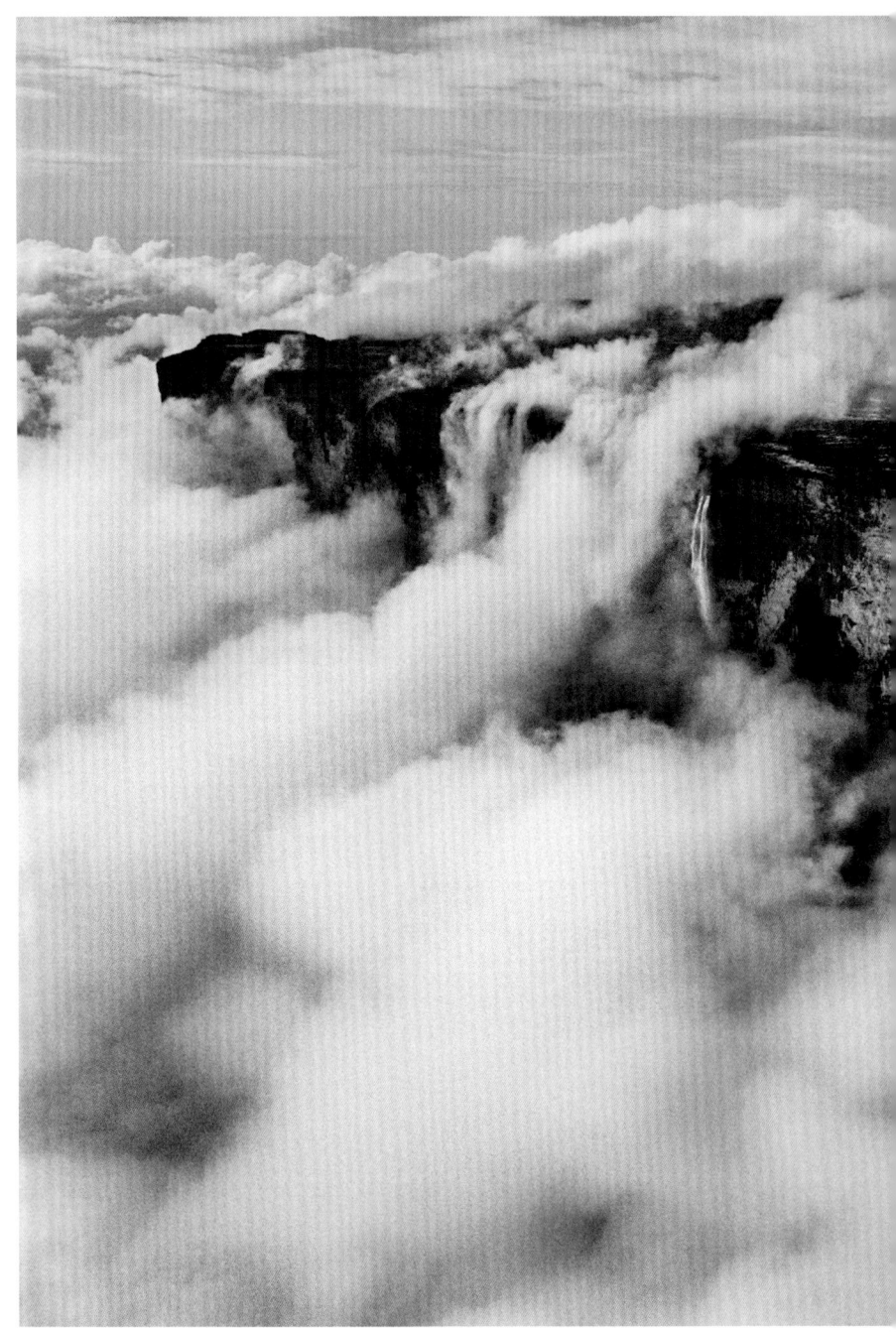

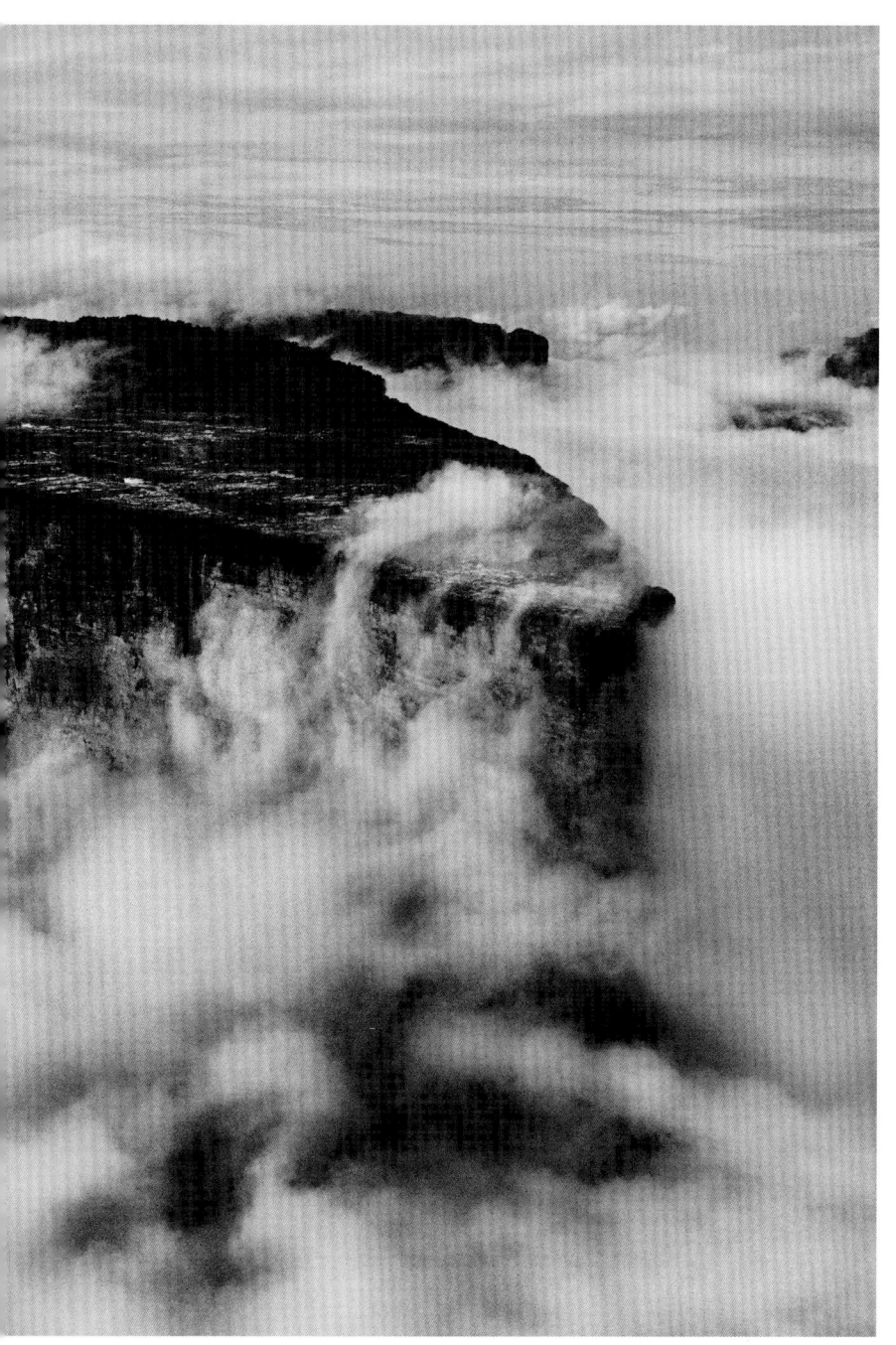

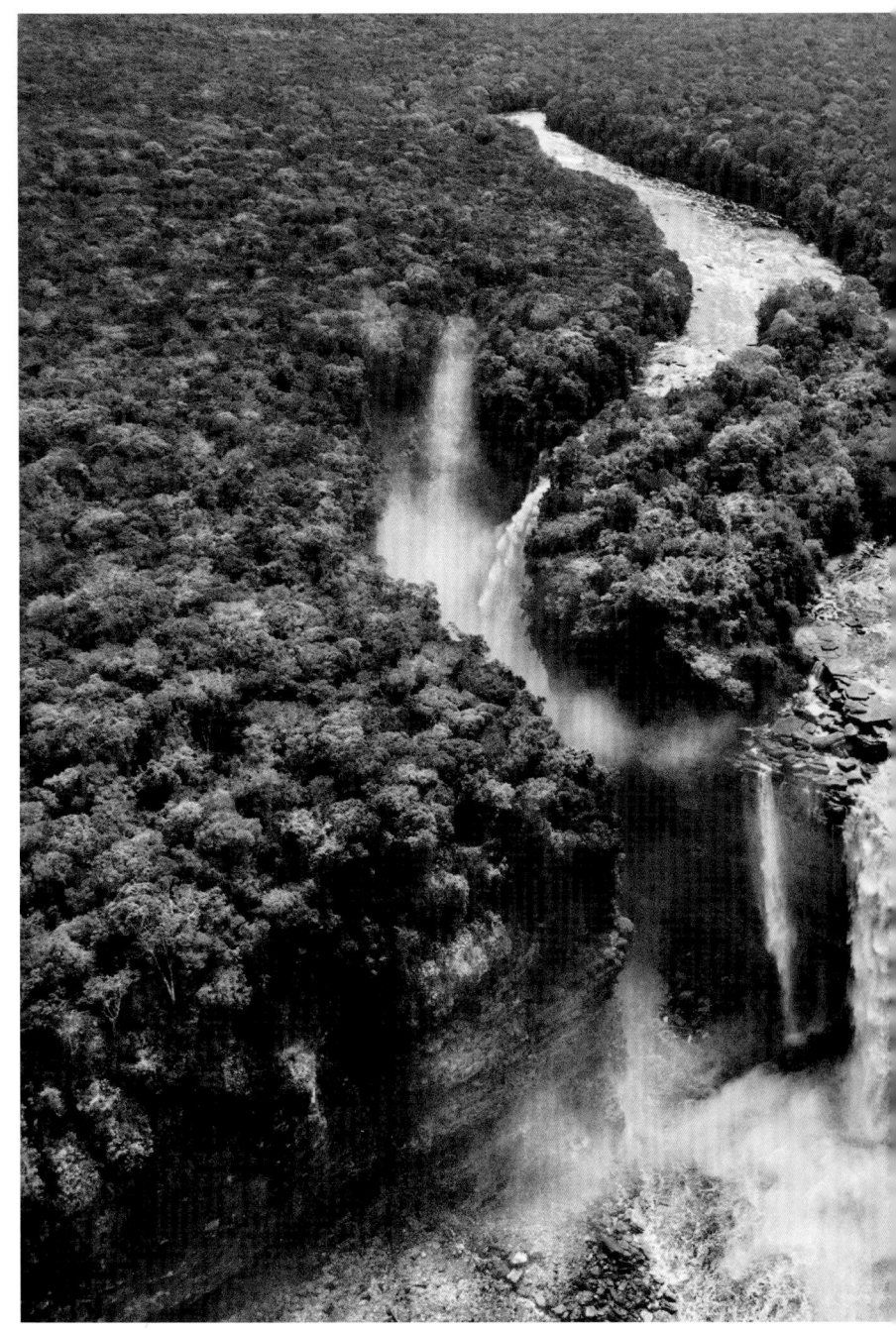

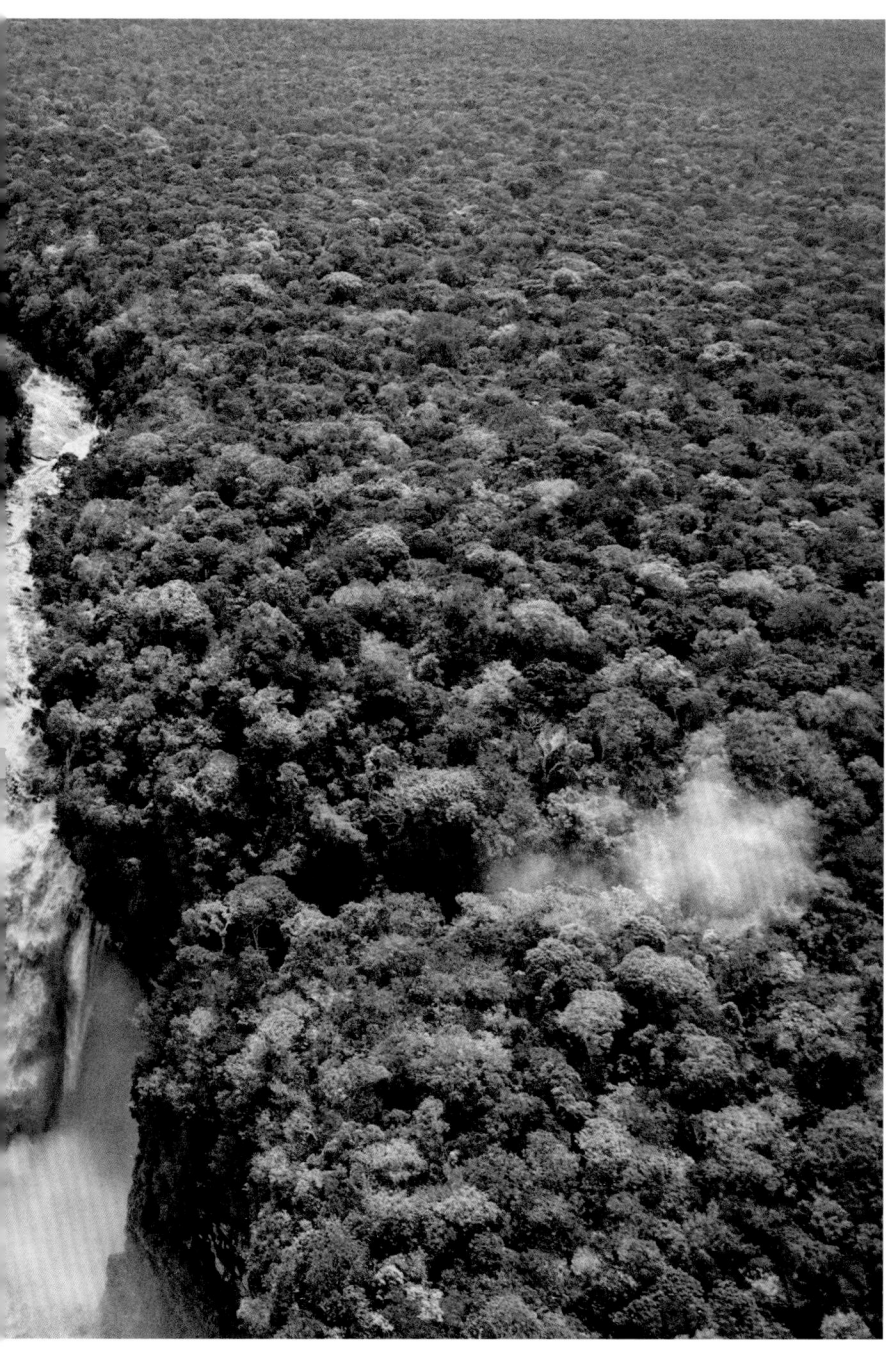

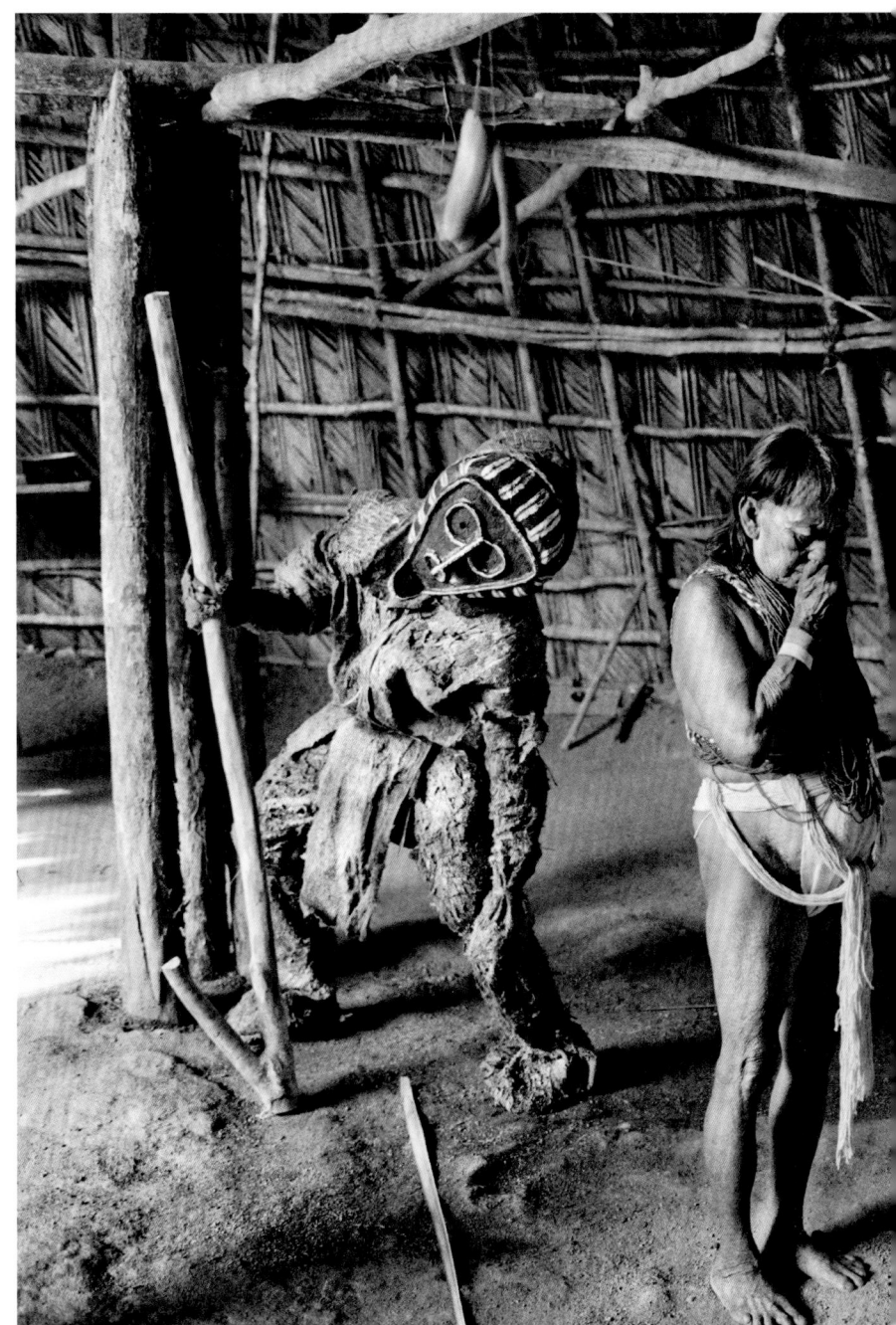

184

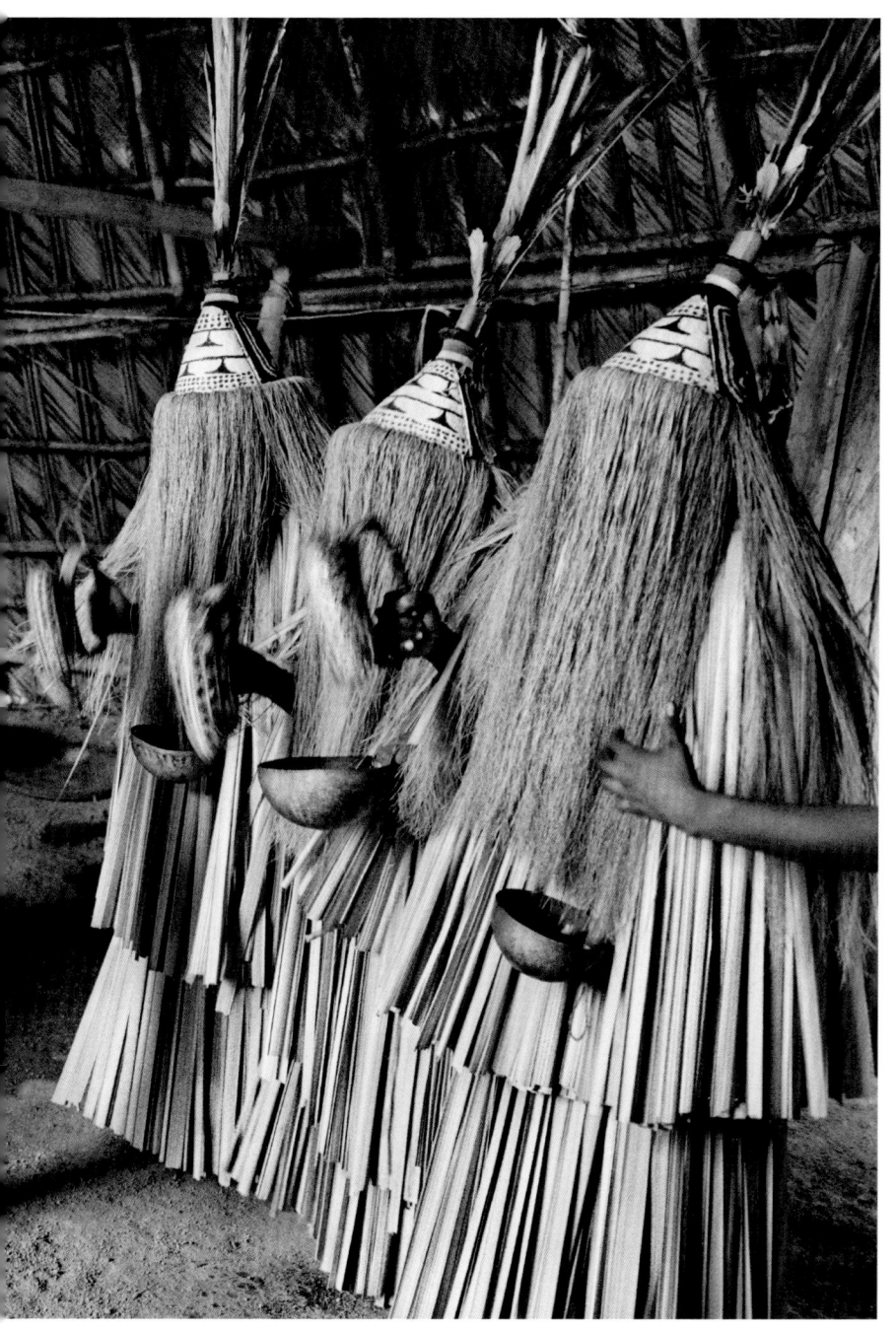

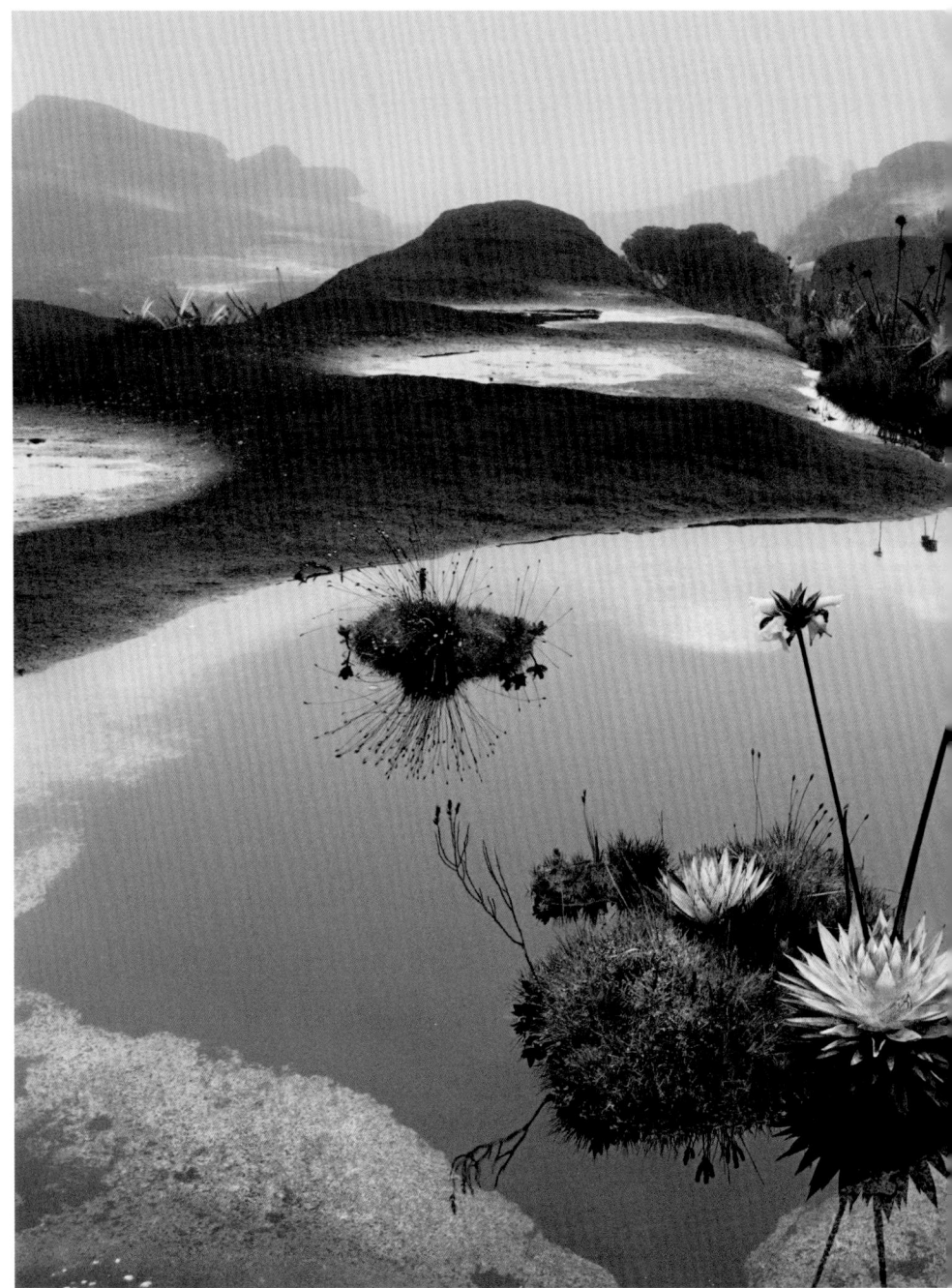

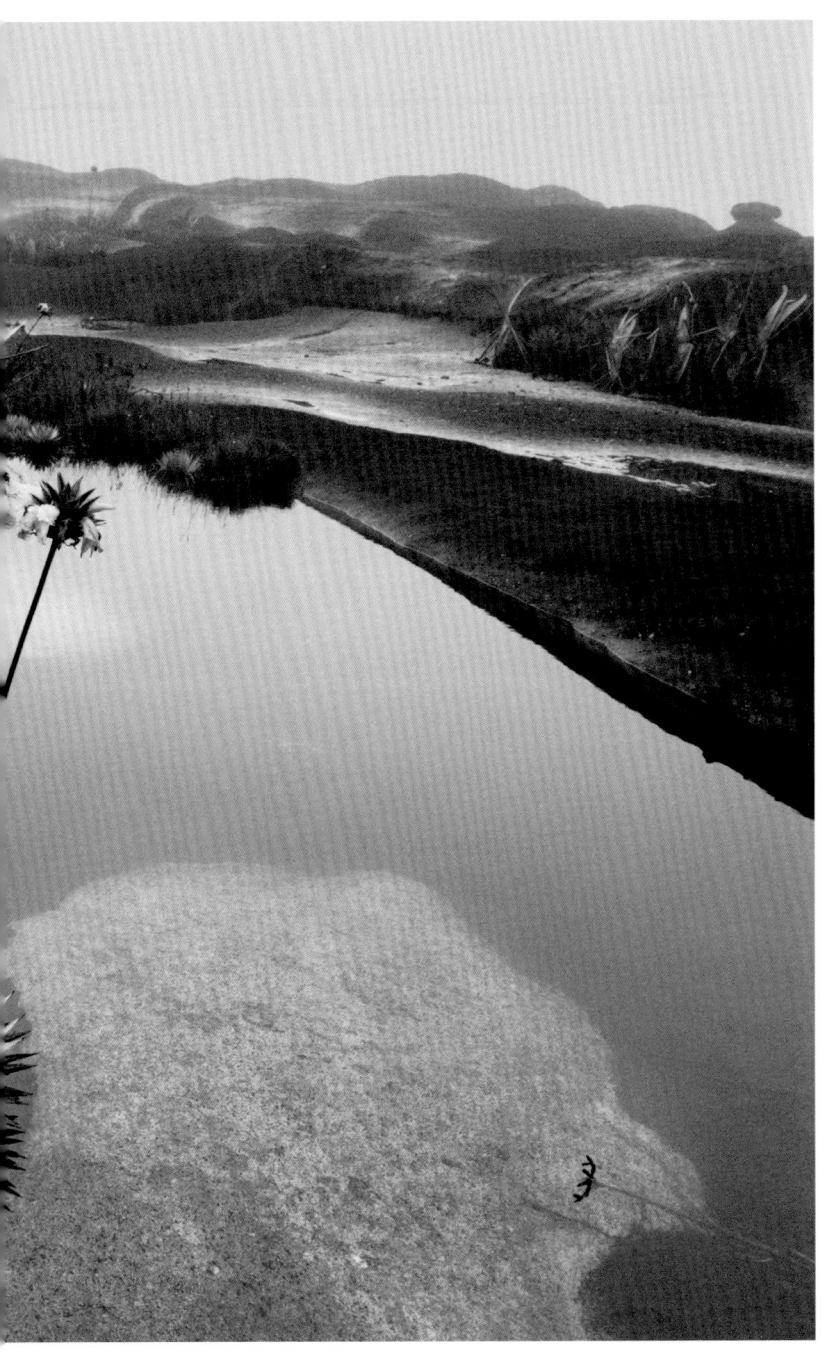

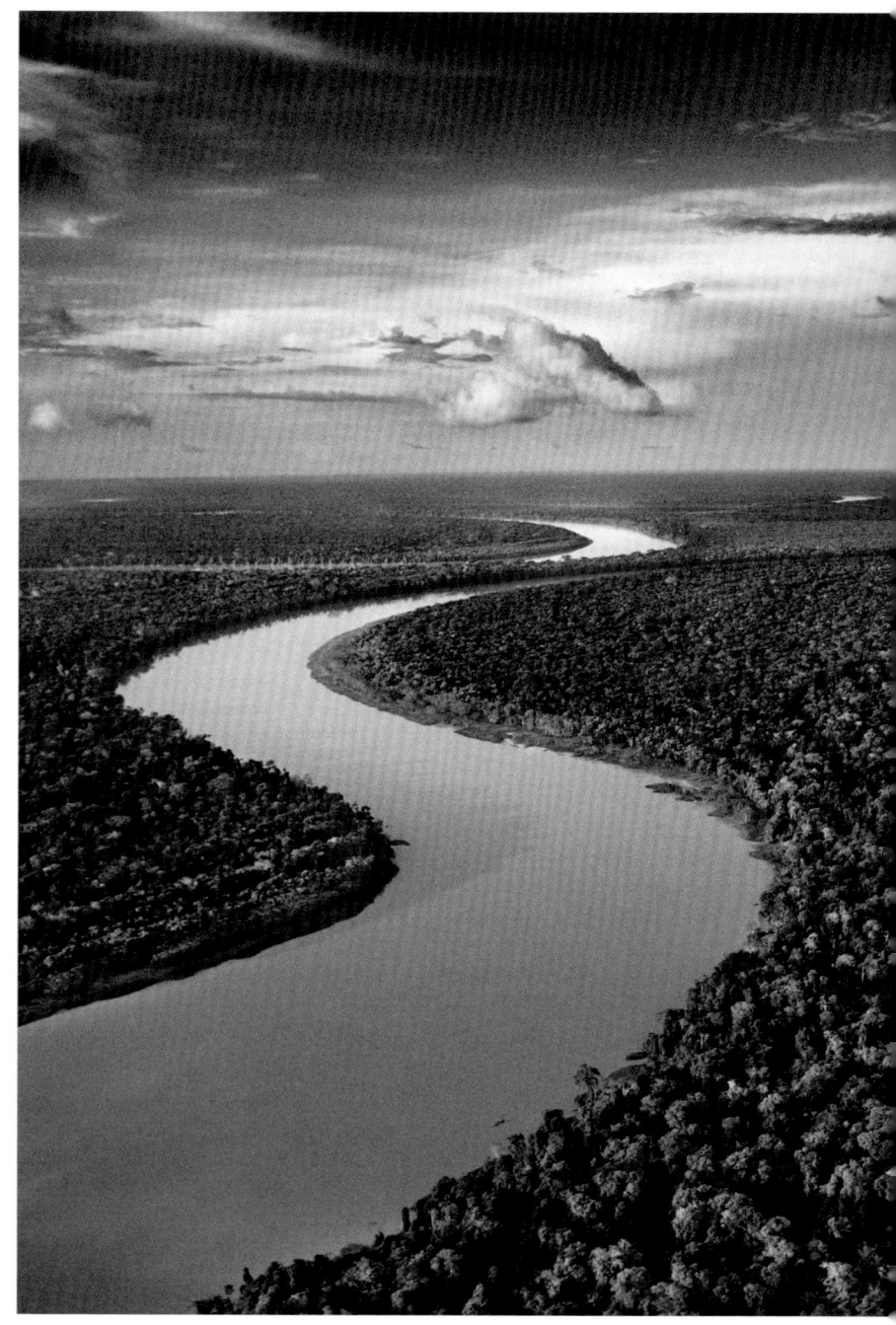

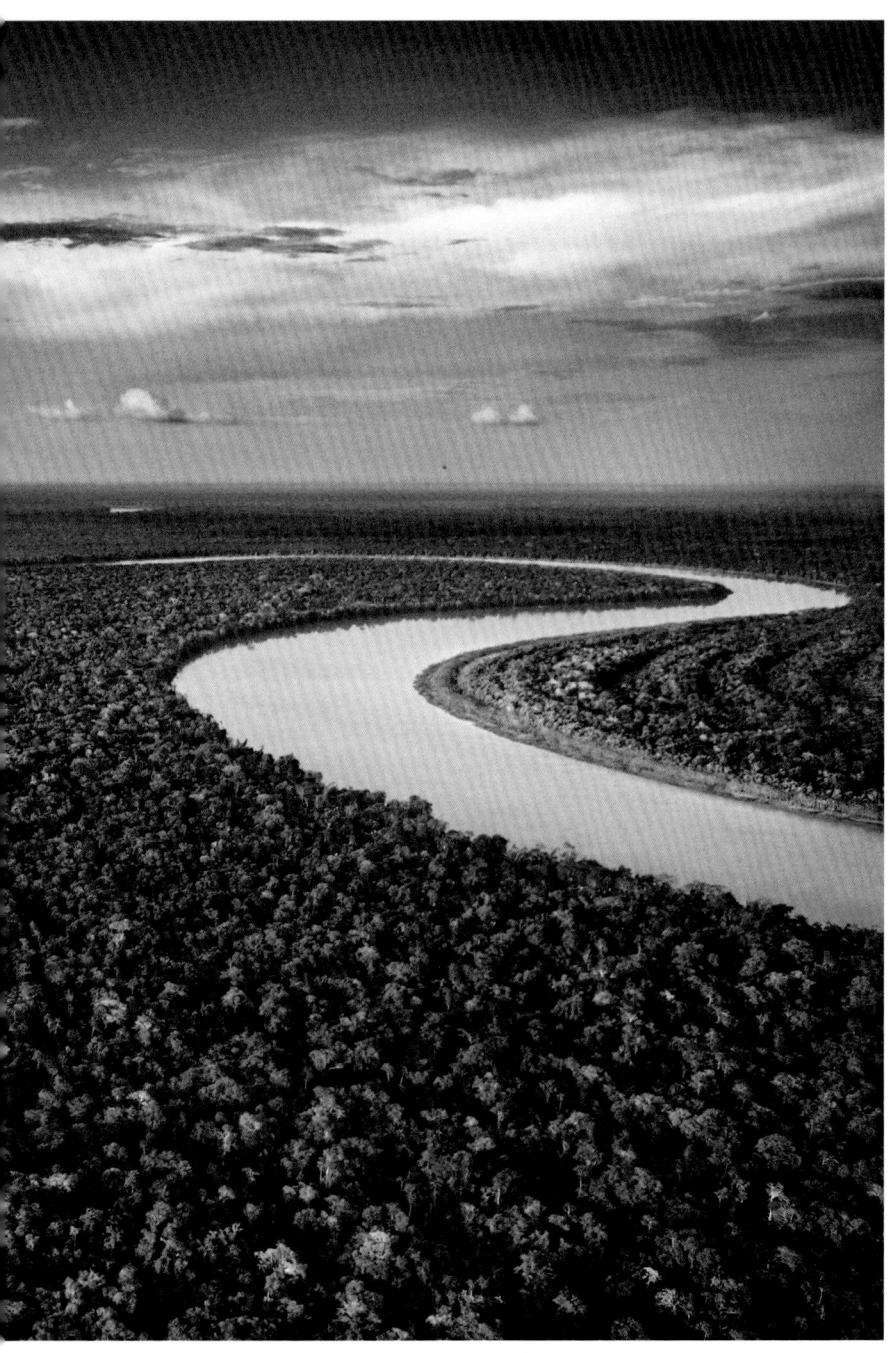

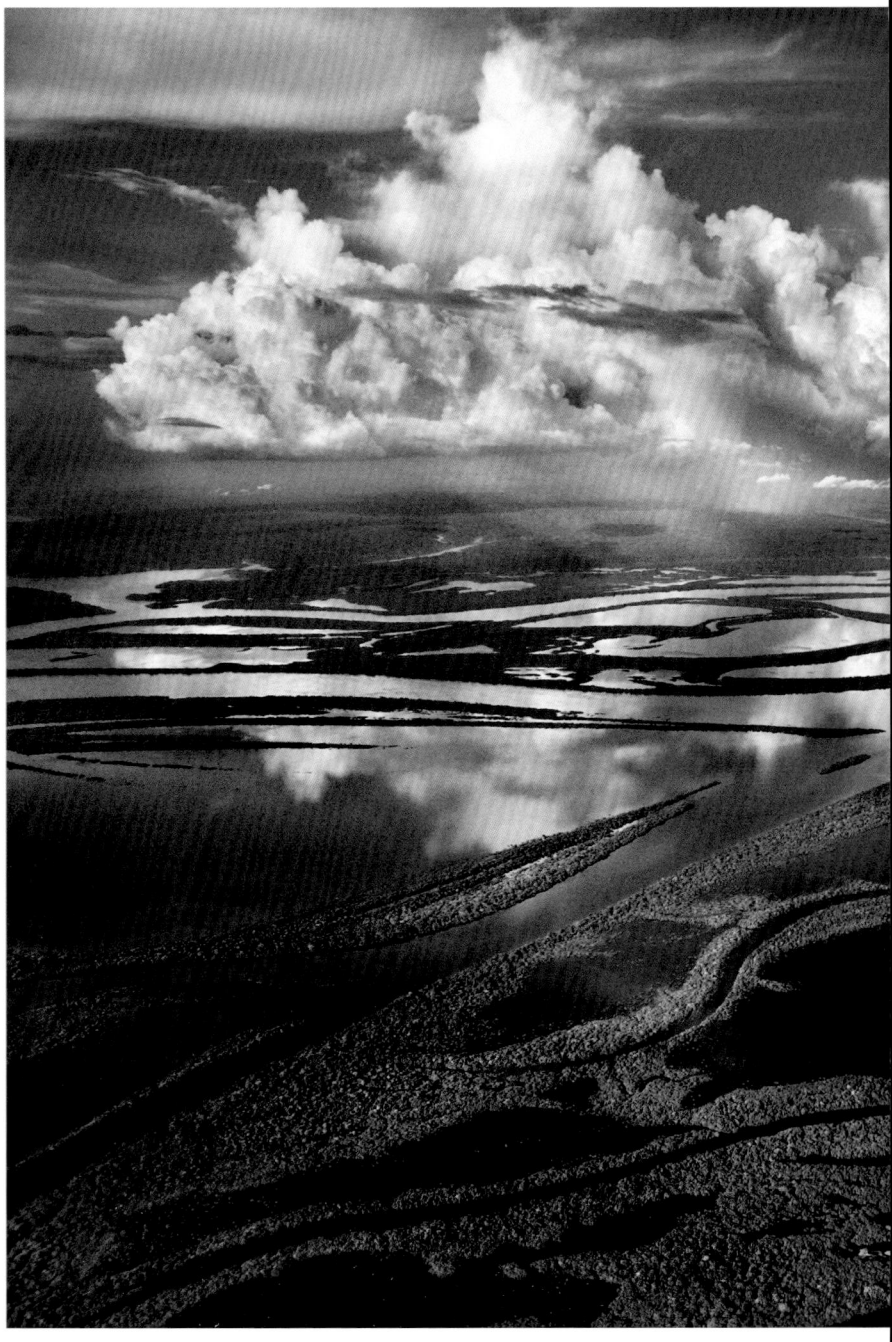

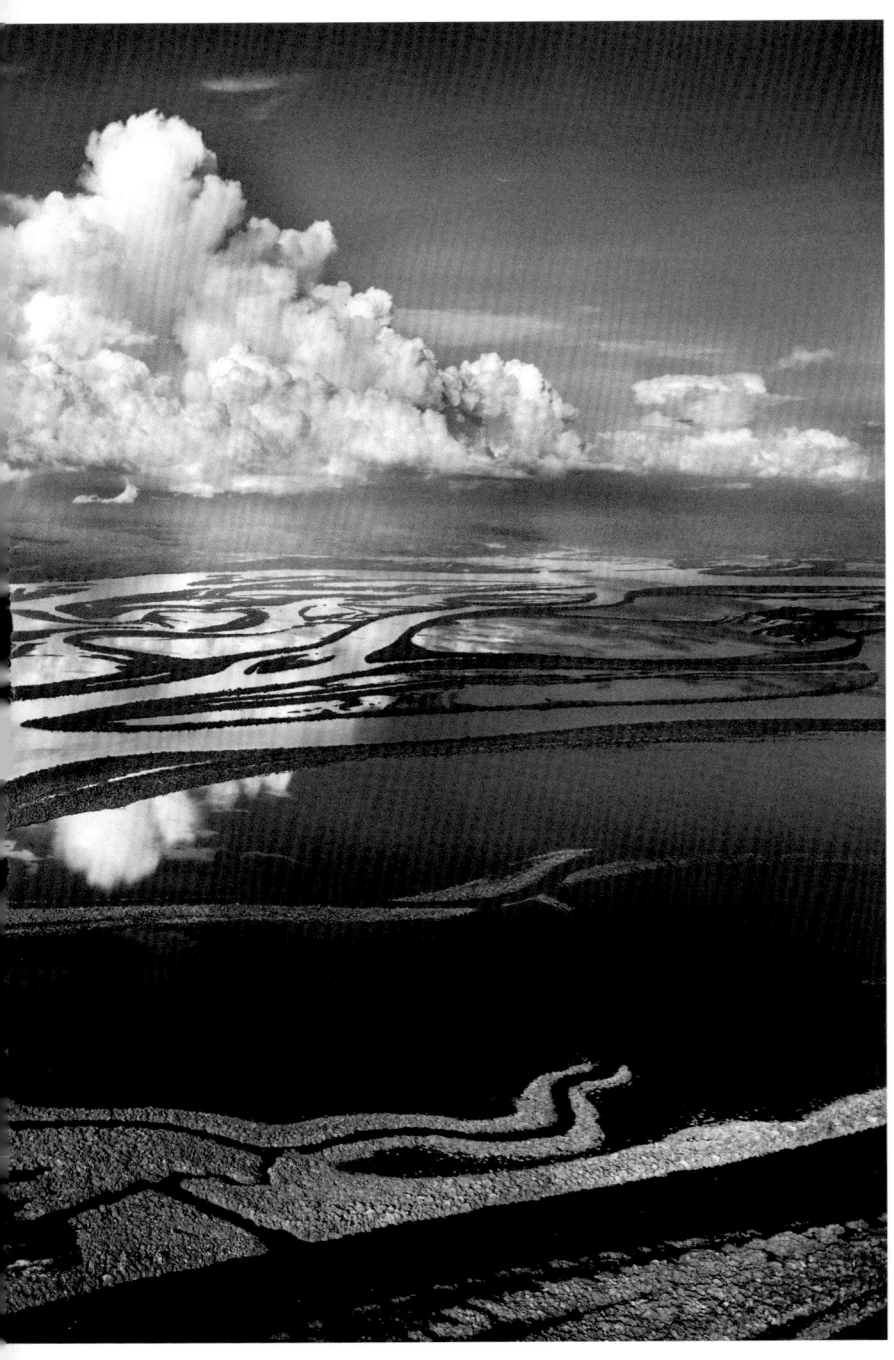

© 2025 TASCHEN GmbH
Hohenzollernring 53, D–50672 Köln
www.taschen.com

Photographs
© Sebastião Salgado

Texts
© Sebastião Salgado, Lélia Wanick Salgado

Editing, concept and design
Lélia Wanick Salgado

Staff
Françoise Piffard
Marcia Navarro Mariano
Olivier Jamin, *Digital printer*
Valérie Hue, *Digital printer*
Jacques Barthélemy, *Field assistant*

In cooperation with
Gérard Lamarche, Bernard Dumas, *Graphic assistants*
Adrien Bouillon, *Contact sheets, work prints*
Philippe Bachelier, *Consultant*
Dominique Granier, *Art prints*

Cover: The Arctic National Wildlife Refuge, Alaska, USA, 2009
Back cover: Marine iguana, Galápagos, Ecuador, 2004
Opposite: Sebastião Salgado with Indigenous girls, checking mosquito bites.
Zo'é Indigenous Territory, State of Pará, Brazil, 2009. Photo: Lélia Wanick Salgado

Printed in Italy
ISBN 978–3–8365–9401–1

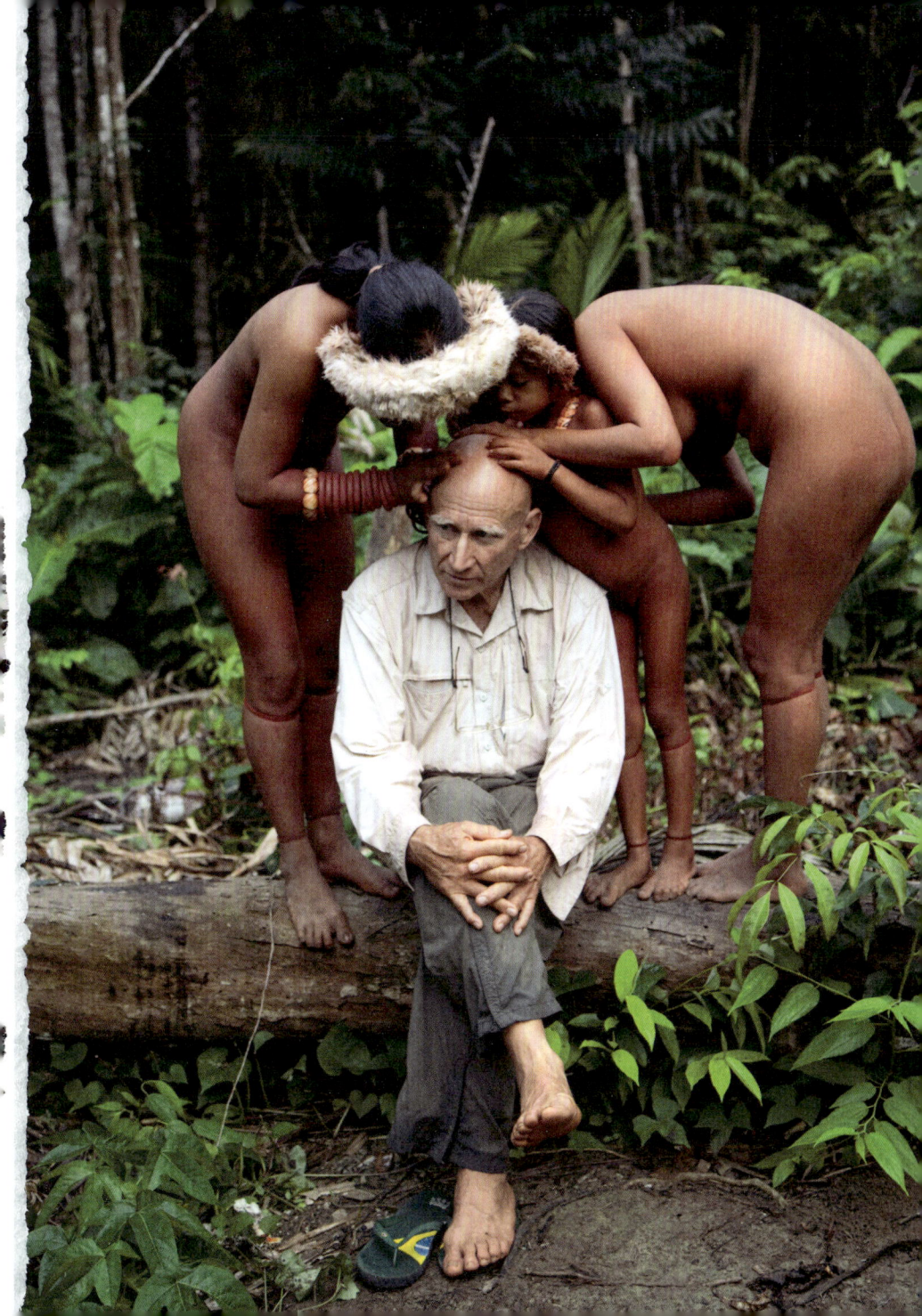